MW01007080

Praise for *My Russia*

"Jill Dougherty understands Russia—and Putin—better than anyone I know. Over many years as colleagues, I've witnessed her dedication, passion, and personal commitment to understanding the country and its people. This is the fascinating personal story of her Russia." —**Wolf Blitzer**, anchor of CNN's *The Situation Room with Wolf Blitzer*

"*My Russia* is the extraordinary memoir of a remarkable woman who has focused her professional life on Russia, from her high school days mastering the challenging Russian language through her years of service as CNN's Moscow bureau chief. Writing with the grace and passion of the Russian poets and authors she so admires, Dougherty applies her formidable skills as a foreign correspondent to narrate her decades of experience in the Soviet Union and Russia. She was a witness to many tumultuous moments in history, which she describes in rich, personal detail, including the Kremlin's brutal invasion of Ukraine in 2022. Her insights on Putin and the system that produced him could not be more timely or compelling." —**John J. Sullivan**, US ambassador to the Russian Federation, 2019–2022

"Jill Dougherty's memoir takes us through one stunning scene after another into those people and events that made the Russia we see today—and made Jill the acclaimed observer that she is. *My Russia: What I Saw Inside the Kremlin* is absorbing, compelling, personal, and insightful. Jill is clear-eyed about Vladimir Putin and other leaders she has seen close-up. But she is also filled with regard for so many of the Russian people she has gotten to know so well." —**Scott Simon**, host of NPR's *Weekend Edition Saturday* and one of the hosts of NPR's morning news podcast *Up First*

"In *My Russia*—a unique and deeply personal memoir—Jill Dougherty conveys a rare understanding of and feel for Russia and her people, drawn from exceptional experiences and vivid personal encounters over the five decades she has spent living and working in the country. With the eye of a skilled journalist and the ear of a gifted linguist, Jill is equally insightful and compelling in exposing the dark roots of Vladimir Putin's brutal war against Ukraine as she is in capturing the surprisingly hopeful spirit and essential humanity of the long-suffering Russian people. For Americans, few challenges in this century will rival the importance and complexity of managing our relationship with Moscow. *My Russia* is mandatory reading to better understand both the stakes and the opportunities inherent in that challenge." —**John R. Beyrle**, US ambassador to the Russian Federation, 2008–2012

"It is certainly not hyperbole for Jill Dougherty to title this book *My Russia*. She has done more than anyone else to illuminate Russia for the American public over the past forty years. As she is on the screen, Jill is a warm and wonderful companion leading us through her personal journey from studying in Soviet Leningrad to her final visit to Moscow to cover Russia's invasion of Ukraine. Jill's book brims with the kind of keen observation and deep personal reflection readers will expect from this veteran CNN Moscow correspondent." —**Fiona Hill**, CMG, senior fellow, Brookings Institution

"We know CNN reporter Jill Dougherty from her penetrating Russia reporting and astute analysis. In this great read, Dougherty takes us behind the camera, providing insights beyond the headlines on Russia, Putin, and the Russians themselves. In this highly personal memoir, we also learn a lot about the inspiring woman who broke the news. A must-read for anyone interested in contemporary Russia." —**Marie Yovanovitch**, former US ambassador to Ukraine, Armenia, and Kyrgyzstan

"Jill Dougherty has spent more than twenty years covering the rise of Vladimir Putin. Based in Moscow for CNN, she described herself as a Russophile, but her time covering the Kremlin exposed the barbaric underbelly of an authoritarian system that uses propaganda and violence to suppress dissent and crush the journalists and dissidents who stand in its way. *My Russia* is required reading for those who want to understand how a strongman can take complete control of a country as vast as Russia in less than a generation and the consequences of ignoring the danger the Kremlin still poses to the world today." —**Jennifer Griffin**, chief national security correspondent, Fox News

"Jill Dougherty's magnificent, evocative story of her turbulent years in Moscow for CNN reveals both her appreciation for the Russian people and their culture and her deep dismay at what Putin's Russia has become. Essential reading for anyone seeking to understand Russia today." —**Angela Stent**, author of *Putin's World: Russia Against the West and with the Rest*

"In *My Russia*, esteemed journalist Jill Dougherty takes readers on an intimate journey through the heart of a nation she has spent more than five decades studying and covering. Weaving together gripping stories of her experiences with deep insights and observations, Dougherty explores the complexities of Russia's rich culture, tumultuous history, and ever-evolving identity. A fantastic read." —**Clarissa Ward**, chief international correspondent, CNN

My
RUSSIA

My
RUSSIA

WHAT I SAW INSIDE THE KREMLIN

JILL DOUGHERTY

LYONS
PRESS

Essex, Connecticut

An imprint of The Globe Pequot Publishing Group, Inc.
64 South Main Street
Essex, CT 06426
www.globepequot.com

Distributed by NATIONAL BOOK NETWORK

British Library Cataloguing in Publication Information Available

Library of Congress Cataloging-in-Publication Data

Names: Dougherty, Jill, author.
Title: My Russia : what I saw inside the Kremlin / Jill Dougherty.
Description: Essex, Connecticut : Lyons Press, [2025] | Includes bibliographical
    references and index.
Identifiers: LCCN 2024037495 (print) | LCCN 2024037496 (ebook) | ISBN
    9781493087983 (cloth) | ISBN 9781493087990 (ebook)
Subjects: LCSH: Dougherty, Jill. | Dougherty, Jill—Travel—Russia (Federation) |
    Women journalists—United States—Biography. | Soviet Union—Politics and
    government. | Russia (Federation)—Politics and government.
Classification: LCC PN4874.D6975 A3 2025 (print) | LCC PN4874.D6975 (ebook) |
    DDC 070.92 [B]—dc23/eng/20241223
LC record available at https://lccn.loc.gov/2024037495
LC ebook record available at https://lccn.loc.gov/2024037496

♾️™ The paper used in this publication meets the minimum requirements of
American National Standard for Information Sciences—Permanence of Paper
for Printed Library Materials, ANSI/NISO Z39.48-1992.

To Valucha

And to Jill Eynon, for her support and love

Contents

Prologue   xi

1   The Education of a Russophile   1
2   To Russia   13
3   Kitchen Debate Redux   43
4   Smoking on the Job   63
5   A Tale of Two White Houses   79
6   Helping Boris   99
7   Yeltsin's Obit   117
8   Chechnya   133
9   Vodka   161
10 Putin's Kiss   185
11 9/11   197
12 Dubrovka   211
13 Ted Comes to Town   225
14 Stalin's Definition of Writers: "Engineers of the Human Soul"   235
15 Another Home   247
16 Kids on the Streets   261
17 A Headless Body   273
18 Fleeing Putin   287
19 Last Night in Moscow   293

Epilogue	299
A Note on Russian Names	307
Bibliography	309
Index	313

Prologue

Muscovy appeared strange to foreigners. Visitors from the West, such as Guy de Miege, secretary to the embassy sent to Alexis by Charles II of England, as well as many others, described it as something of a magical world: weird, sumptuous, colorful, unlike anything they had ever seen, and utterly barbarian.

—Nicholas V. Riasanovsky, *A History of Russia*
(Oxford University Press, 1963, page 217)

In early February 2022 I got a call from Atlanta. "Atlanta," for me, means CNN headquarters, and I felt that old shiver of excitement, along with a twinge of fear, when I heard the voice at the other end of the line asking "How soon can you get to Moscow?"

After three decades with CNN, I knew why they were calling. "How fast can you pack—do you have a visa [I always had an up-to-date Russian visa in my passport]—how soon can you join the team in Moscow?"

Although I had "retired" from CNN in 2014 after three decades as a correspondent, I still served as on-air analyst for the network on all things Russian. For months, there had been indications that Russia would invade Ukraine. The United States was saying it out loud. Almost a year earlier Moscow had started building up its forces in Belarus, massing them on Ukraine's northern border, but if there were plans to order the tanks to roll, it never happened.

I discussed the situation with my friends, all of them with deep experience in Russia, who were watching with concern and—for many, including myself—incredulity, as the number of Russian troops grew to over 100,000, along with tanks and artillery. The Biden administration dispatched US troops to beef up NATO forces in Poland and Romania. A red flag went up for me in November when CNN reported that CIA director William J. Burns flew to Moscow and met with senior Russian security officials, telling them directly that the United States was watching the buildup and there would be serious consequences if Putin gave the order to invade. The US ambassador to Moscow, John Sullivan, who was in those meetings with Burns, later told me the Russians insisted they had no plans to invade Ukraine, "and they said that right up until the day that the troops and tanks crossed, and the rockets crossed the border. . . . They lied to our faces! How could anybody accept that?"

Vladimir Putin certainly is capable of doing this, I thought. But would he? I had reported on Putin for more than two decades and knew that, despite his public image, the Russian president didn't always have a plan. Yes, he often operated on emotion, masked by expressions of sober rationality, but invading another country in the middle of Europe? It seemed more than irrational—it was crazy, and extraordinarily dangerous.

Then, the call from Atlanta. I packed, grabbed a taxi to Dulles airport, and left for Moscow. It was February 15, nine days before Russia invaded Ukraine.

Arriving in the Russian capital, I felt back home. In fact, it had been my home for nearly a decade. The familiar traffic-jammed drive into the city center, the hotel across from the CNN bureau, where I usually stayed—once a down-on-its-heels Soviet-era landmark, now a five-star luxury address, its parking lot crammed with Bentleys and Rolls-Royces.

I dropped my bags in my room and, on my way across the street to the bureau, I stopped at the Alphabet of Taste, an expensive but well-stocked supermarket, to pick up supplies. Salmon, yogurt, bread (gluten-free!), cheese, juice. There would be no time later, I was sure, to run out for food, but there would be plenty of coffee at the office.

As I walked into our compound, past the booth with security men who guarded the buildings where our office, along with those of other foreign news outlets, was located, I glanced across the parking lot at the top floor of the squat, nine-story, beige-brick apartment building where I had lived for almost a decade. The lights in the windows were on, and I felt a twinge of regret that I was no longer working in the Russian capital, a city I had grown to love.

I glanced over at the corner of the parking lot where a white armored personnel carrier had once stood for years. During the August 1991 hard-line coup against Soviet president Mikhail Gorbachev, CNN had transported it from Kosovo to Moscow. I laughed as I remembered the Russian colleagues who'd told me the rumor that if the personnel carrier ever left, it would mean Russia was finally stable. The APC was long gone, but Russia didn't feel any more stable.

The CNN bureau was crackling with the energy of journalists poised to cover major breaking news, correspondents, producers, and camera crews— CNN's own civilian army—all of them sure that, whatever happened, the team would be ready. Ted Turner's network knew better than almost any other media outlet how to cover breaking news. It threw everything it had at the story, and it showed in the wall-to-wall coverage.

As I walked back toward the live-shot studio I could feel it, that intoxicating brew of intense concentration, the tension broken by high-five banter in English and Russian, with plenty of jokes and dark humor. More producers and camera crews were arriving from other CNN bureaus in Europe, and CNN Moscow had hired young Russians to help out.

And yet, this time, I sensed something different . . . more menacing. The TV monitors in the bureau were tuned to state-controlled TV. Vladimir Putin was appearing, it seemed, on an almost hourly basis with lengthy, angry harangues about Ukraine. I listened in:

> The West is using Ukraine both as a battering ram against Russia and as a training ground. . . . The elites of the West make no secret of their goal: to inflict—as they say directly—"the strategic defeat of Russia" . . . we are talking about the existence of our country . . .
>
> Russia's clash with these forces is inevitable. It is only a matter of time: they are getting ready, they are waiting for the right time. Now, they also claim to acquire nuclear weapons. We will not allow this to happen. . . . We have been left no other option to protect Russia and our people but for the one that we will be forced to use today. The situation requires us to take decisive and immediate action.

Was it live? Recorded? I wasn't sure. Was I simply jetlagged? I was working the overnight Moscow shift so I would be available for primetime shows back in the United States. I came in to the bureau at about 9 p.m. local time and did live shots through the night until 8 or 9 a.m. I soon became confused. In two different TV addresses Putin seemed to be sitting in the same office, behind the same desk, wearing the same black suit, white shirt, and burgundy tie, with a bank of cream-colored Soviet-style phones, the Russian presidential flag and the national flag behind him. But the speeches supposedly were broadcast live on two different days. Was it all prerecorded at the same time? It felt like a giant kabuki theater, or, as the Russians would call it, "pokazukha," a Potemkin village of fakery.

Five days before Putin ordered his troops into Ukraine, President Joe Biden warned: "As of this moment, I am convinced he's made the decision" to invade. On Russian TV, commentators mocked Biden and other Western officials, calling them "stupid" and "mentally ill," claiming that the warnings about any invasion were simply "brainwashing" by the West. One comedian snickered: "They say there's going to be an invasion. I'm still looking at my watch. So, where's the invasion?"

And then it happened.

As I walked back to my hotel through the snow, Moscow's feeble winter sun tingeing the sky in the direction of the Kremlin, I felt I was being pulled back into the Soviet days, when Communist Party officials on the outs with General Secretary Leonid Brezhnev would be erased from official photographs, literally and figuratively. What was true? What was fake? How long had Putin been planning his "special military operation"?

I texted a friend, an opposition Russian journalist, to have some coffee and catch up on how he was doing. We set a date for a few days hence. Then, a new text from him: "Sorry, Jill, I can't make it. My family and I are going on vacation."

I knew there was no way a Russian political reporter was going on vacation as a war was being launched, but I immediately understood: He was fleeing Russia with his family. No explanation needed. Suddenly, I was back talking with friends in coded language, certain our conversations were bugged. Don't mention the war; don't explain how you are planning to flee the country. Many of them were, in fact, on their way out, buying tickets to Georgia, Armenia, Israel, Turkey—whatever they could find. They knew any invasion of Ukraine would be a turning point. They had no idea just how much it would upend their lives.

The propaganda show on television was getting weirder. Ten days after Putin ordered his troops to attack Ukraine, as Ukrainian and Russian forces were fighting and dying in Ukraine, he visited the Aeroflot aviation training center and sat down at a long oval table adorned with a centerpiece of delicate pink and white roses for a meeting with a bevy of well-coiffed female air crew members. In a few days it would be International Women's Day, a big holiday in Russia.

"Do you have any questions—or shall we just have some tea?" he asked politely.

One woman asked him the purpose of the "special military operation." Putin launched into a lengthy explanation similar to what he had said in his TV addresses. Then, as waiters poured the tea, his light conversation veered into a threat to use nuclear weapons. The women continued to ask him questions about what it all meant. He seemed a bit annoyed.

"We're starting to go around in circles a bit," he complained. "I basically already replied to this, but will say it again."

I was mesmerized. I grabbed another cup of coffee and sat down to watch the bizarre broadcast in detail.

A week and a half later, Putin wasn't so polite. In yet another TV address, Putin—this time wearing a dark blue tie—issued a chilling warning to Russians, like my friends, who opposed the war or were trying to leave the country: "Any people, and especially the Russian people, will always be able to distinguish the true patriots from the scum and the traitors, and just to spit them out like a midge that accidentally flew into their mouths," he snarled. "I am convinced that this natural and necessary self-cleansing of society will only strengthen our country, our solidarity, cohesion, and readiness to meet any challenge."

Like many of my friends, my CNN colleagues and I fled Moscow in early March, after the Russian parliament rubber-stamped a Kremlin-orchestrated law that made it a crime, punishable by fifteen years in prison, to call the war a "war." There was no way I could comment on Putin's attack against Ukraine without calling it a war.

My last night in Moscow, past midnight, after the other staff had left, I walked through the CNN Moscow bureau, now dark, with just the eerie glow of blinking red lights on the broadcast equipment. I had worked there, even slept there on the couch in my office, for almost a decade. I was set to leave the next morning, and I had the impossibly sad feeling I might never return. At least until Vladimir Putin is no longer Russia's president.

Russia will still be there when Putin is gone. But it will be a different Russia, irrevocably changed by his maniacal obsession with what he sees as his mission to rebuild the Russian empire. More than two decades ago, as he took the reins of power in Moscow, he vowed to protect "freedom of speech, freedom of conscience, freedom of the mass media" for his fellow citizens. In reality, he has methodically attempted to annihilate those rights.

As a twenty-year-old exchange student in Leningrad, I saw the crushing reality of Communism. Almost a quarter-century later, as a journalist, I watched Communist control crumble. I saw the hope in people's eyes as they chanted "Yeltsin! Yeltsin!"—the hope that Russia could change, that life would get better, that they would be able to choose their leaders freely and have a say in how they were governed. And I thought Russia *was* changing. The Cold War, I thought, was over.

Now, I'm fearful the changes that I saw, that I felt, that I lived through, were, in the end, ephemeral. Vladimir Putin is leading Russia back to those dark days. What will become of the country and the people to whom I have been so deeply bonded? I wrote this book to find that answer.

• 1 •

The Education of a Russophile

We were born in New York City in May 1949. I say "we" because there were two of us—my sister Pamela and myself. I am eleven minutes older. Four other siblings eventually would round out our family.

When Pam and I were three years old, our family moved from New York to Alexandria, Virginia, a suburb of Washington, DC, where my father Vincent, an FBI special agent, had been transferred. In a few years we moved again to Scranton, Pennsylvania, where my father was assigned as special agent in charge. My mother Ruth, a New Yorker, told me years later that, at first, she felt like she'd been exiled to Siberia, but she began volunteering for several women's organizations and soon made some good friends.

My earliest memories of Scranton do recall Siberia. Zipping up my one-piece nylon snowsuit, pulling on my red rubber boots, asking my mother to tie my scarf and help with my thick wool mittens, I'd trudge through mountains of snow, building igloos with ice "bricks" frozen in her baking tins. We had snowball wars, and sledded down the steep hills of our neighborhood, almost out of control, on our Flexible Flyers.

I'm pretty sure I never heard the word "Siberia" in those days. Twenty years later, I would find myself in actual Siberia, huddled in my shearling coat and fur hat, chatting with a group of Russians, my lungs burning as I caught my breath in the minus-30-degree air.

Pam and I grew up with the Cold War. The USSR and the United States, allies in World War II, turned on each other at war's end. A few months after we were born, Mao Zedong and the Communists defeated the Nationalists and took power in China. At the tender age of nine I began exploring my parents' collection of books and soon was engrossed in John

1

Hersey's *Hiroshima* and reports on Communist persecution of Catholics in Lithuania. "Godless Communism" became part of my vocabulary.

I was fascinated with the drama of Catholicism, so I set up a "chapel" in the attic of our late-nineteenth-century house, constructed an "altar" with two card tables, borrowed candles from my mother, improvised a "chalice" from a wineglass, memorized the Mass in Latin, and soon was hearing confessions from the neighborhood kids. Their sins weren't anything to write home about—the usual "I hit my brother three times"—but it felt good to give them a penance (one Hail Mary and no cookies for the day) and send them on their way, absolved, ready for another battle with their siblings. I guess I wasn't your average kid, but then, the Cold War did strange things to people.

When it came time for high school, we had to choose a major: either math or languages. I was horrified by arithmetic, but languages sounded intriguing. As language majors we had to study one classical language (Latin) and one modern language. French and Spanish, for me, seemed too commonplace, German too daunting. Then, there was Russian.

I had never studied a foreign language, but I had encountered the concept when I was about five years old. During World War II my father served as a US Marines intelligence officer in the Pacific and returned home to America with photographs he had taken in China and the Philippines. There were pictures of him in a flight jacket, braced against the cold, standing in front of reconnaissance planes; pictures of him in shorts, resting on a cot, in what looked like a jungle; and, most intriguingly for me, photos of him kneeling next to a very young Chinese boy, four or five years old, probably. He explained to me that the boy did not speak English. So, what did he speak? He spoke Chinese, my father explained. What was Chinese? I asked. It was his language, the way he and other people in China communicated, my father said.

I still remember that moment. In a very primitive way, I began to understand there was another way that little boy communicated, the way he talked with his parents and his friends, that was different from the way I spoke. He used other words that sounded different from English, but people he lived with understood them. The very idea was exciting, even revolutionary. Although I didn't know it, this was one of my first conceptual linguistic leaps.

HOW TO TALK WITH A COMRADE

The first word in Russian that I remember arrived with a splat: "Stol." Michael Peregrim, the high school teacher who taught us Russian, slapped the desk where we sat and almost yelled as he pronounced it. "Stol!"

"Shto eto?" he asked as we turned our blank faces to him. It was obviously a question. Then, with even more force, he slammed his hand down on the desk and shouted again, "Eto stol!" The synapses in my brain surged to life. "Desk? Table?" And that question of his—could it be, "What is this?" Mr. Peregrim never broke character in those first weeks, repeating and repeating questions and answers in Russian, pointing out concrete objects in our classroom at Scranton Central High School, leading us in tentative answers as we tried to mimic what he was saying. We were convinced he could not speak English.

I would try to form the words, but my tongue just wouldn't roll like that. I looked desperately for some meaning, for hints in the objects at which he pointed. But mostly I *felt* the words. "Stol" *felt* like what it was: a solid, physical object. Many years later, I would find out that it was, indeed, a very old word, thousands of years old, and its blunt, primitive force hit me like a rock.

In 1963, in Mr. Peregrim's Russian freshman language class, as he led us in pronouncing these still-strange sounds, I felt that I could actually see and feel the words as I pronounced them. Some, like "stol," were stolid, heavy. Others, like "slovo" ("word") were mysterious and evocative. Still others, like "lyublyu" ("I love") seductive as a kiss on the lips. I began to realize that speaking Russian meant I had to think differently. I could even change the order of words and—suddenly—make poetry. I awoke to the ancient, erotic power of words. I was seduced by the Russian language, by its voluptuous vowels, by its clashing consonants, hard and soft, the palatalized "l" a bosom on which I could lay my head in the middle of a sentence.

Once, many years later, Pam and I were back in St. Petersburg for the fiftieth anniversary of the exchange program in which we studied the Russian language at Leningrad State University. As we strolled through the Summer Garden, the early-eighteenth-century formal garden designed by czar Peter the Great, gazing at the white marble statues of Roman gods in stark relief against the dark green trees, we talked a bit about Latin, which we had studied for four years in high school, and then I waxed rhapsodic about the Russian language.

"I guess you feel the same way, right, Pam?"

Pam had gone on to get a PhD in Slavic linguistics and speaks six languages, so I presumed her facility in foreign tongues was the love child of an affair with Russian.

"Oh, no!" she shuddered. "I always wanted to study German, but *you* wanted to study Russian, so we asked Daddy and he said, 'If I were you, I'd choose Russian. You want to do something unique, to distinguish yourselves from others, so I would suggest you study Russian.'

"I still wanted to do German," Pam told me, "but when we went to sign up, the letter J comes before P in the alphabet, and you said Russian and I said 'Rats! Now I have to study Russian too!' But it was very fortuitous because of Mike Peregrim. He was incredible. If it were not for him, we wouldn't be here."

Pam readily admitted she initially was scared of Mr. Peregrim. "The whole class was scared to death of him!" she told me. "He had such a passion for the language and he drilled it, because Russian grammar is relatively complicated with all the declinations and conjugations, and you really have to know it. He had just been released from the army the year before—he was only ten years older than we were—and he drilled us as an army sergeant would drill his troops."

"It is a beautiful language," I said, wistfully.

"No, not really," she cut me off. "I don't think Russian's a very pretty language. I think it sounds pretty awful. Almost as bad as English. You know why there were so many Polish prisoners of war during the Second World War?"

"Is this a joke?" I asked her.

"No, it's true. 'Cause the Germans could tell they were out there—because you can't whisper in Polish!" she laughed. "Too many sibilants."

Michael Peregrim was indeed just a decade older than we were. He was short and powerful with a broad, square jaw and a blond buzz cut. He had that lovely combination of light hair, hazel eyes, and slightly tanned skin that I later would recognize as Slavic. With his long, thin nose and somewhat mournful eyes (although he was anything but), he reminded me of a saint on a Russian icon. Regardless of the weather he invariably wore a white, short-sleeved shirt with a pen or two in the breast pocket, black trousers, and white socks. He was coiled with the energy of a Red Army drill sergeant. For students who didn't behave (and there were some, which I never understood, since the Russian language is not for the fainthearted), he would suddenly bark, in northeast-Pennsylvania-accented English, "Shape up or ship out!"

Mike grew up in a neighboring town, Old Forge, speaking Russian. His parents were born in the United States, but his grandparents were from "somewhere in the area of Ukraine," as he told me many years later, when I sat down with him and his wife Pat at his kitchen table in Scranton a year before he died. I turned on my tape recorder. His grandmother, he told me, was one of ten children, and she "came to America with the idea of making a lot of money and then going back." Neither ever happened; her husband worked in the coal mines and was killed in a mining accident. With six children, she took in boarders to make ends meet and eventually married one of them.

The center of her life was St. Michael's Orthodox Church in Old Forge. She was illiterate, but she passed on her language and oral traditions to her grandson. Mr. Peregrim was four when his father died, and so he grew up in a household of Russian speakers—his mother, grandmother, and an uncle.

Since the late nineteenth century, Scranton's anthracite coal mines had drawn immigrants from Russia and Eastern Europe, from Ukraine, Poland, Czechoslovakia, Hungary, and each group, it seemed, had its own church. Most of St. Michael's parishioners came from eastern Poland and the Austro-Hungarian Empire. The congregation was formed in 1891 and it continues to this day, although the number of active members has steadily dwindled as the mines closed and succeeding generations moved away to find employment elsewhere.

It was the Cold War "Space Race" that launched Mr. Peregrim's teaching career. On October 4, 1957, the Soviet Union shocked the United States with *Sputnik* (the Russian word means "travel companion" or "co-traveler"), the first man-made satellite to orbit the Earth. It looked like a silvery basketball with four antennae trailing from its sides. It was tiny, only 22.8 inches in diameter, and it weighed just 184 pounds. It circled the Earth in 1 hour and 36 minutes. Down below, Americans watched in awe as the shiny sphere coursed across the sky, emitting a faint "beep . . . beep . . . beep"—a pulse to indicate its location, which could be picked up by radio.

The US government was alarmed. *Sputnik* was carried into orbit by the world's first intercontinental ballistic missile, the R-7. If the R-7 could launch a silver basketball into orbit, they worried, it could also hit the United States with a nuclear bomb.

Just a month later, the USSR launched *Sputnik II* on another ballistic missile carrying a heavier payload, and inside was a dog named Laika (in Russian—"a Husky"). Pam and I were just eight years old, but I remember the TV news reports. We both were fascinated that a dog—reportedly a stray female mongrel from the streets of Moscow—was flying over our heads. Sadly, we learned, Laika had circled the globe only nine times when a technical failure caused the satellite to overheat. Poor little Laika gave her life for her mission, and I remember my sadness mixed with amazement as I contemplated that fact.

But if Pam and I were concerned with the fate of Laika, the Eisenhower administration was seized with countering a grave national security threat. The United States had been developing an ICBM called the Redstone, but the decision to work on the missile and the satellite separately, plus bureaucratic infighting between the army and the navy, cost precious time. Now, the Soviets had succeeded, twice. It was a huge technological—and propaganda—victory. A confidential memo titled "Reaction to the Soviet Satellite—A

Preliminary Evaluation" by the White House Office of the Staff Research Group frankly listed the damage to American prestige:

1. *Soviet claims of scientific and technological superiority over the West and especially the U.S. have won greatly widened acceptance.*
2. *Public opinion in friendly countries shows decided concern over the possibility that the balance of military power has shifted or may soon shift in favor of the USSR.*
3. *The general credibility of Soviet propaganda has been greatly enhanced.*
4. *American prestige is viewed as having sustained a severe blow, and the American reaction, so sharply marked by concern, discomfiture and intense interest, has itself increased the disquiet of friendly countries and increased the impact of the satellite.*

The Soviet Union could now claim, the memo warned, that it had "opened a new era, marked by a spectacular overtaking of the U.S. in a vital field where we have been accustomed to count on superiority, and now compete with the U.S. as an equal."

Back in Scranton, Michael Peregrim began teaching high school Russian, but, as the Cold War grew frostier, he volunteered for the military and served two years—undoubtedly where he got his first buzz cut—then returned to Central High to teach French and Russian. To his horror, he found that the school had hired a Ukrainian to fill in for two years. "He taught them to say those round 'o's' and to use an 'h' instead of a 'g,'" he told me in our interview. "They were saying 'hovoryu po Russki'! They were speaking Ukrainian! I had to change them around!"

Mr. Peregrim began to proselytize for the Russian language, hunting for prospective students in their last year of grammar school. "I had to go out and recruit students," he told me. "I would go out to eighth-grade students, kids coming in, and I'd say, 'Do you want to take French, German, or Spanish? Or do you want to do something *different?*'"

Pam and I had no idea he was out there trying to sell teenagers on studying Russian. He never had to sell *us* on the idea, or tell us to "Shape up or ship out!" We were eager volunteers.

A YOUNG SECRET AGENT

With an FBI-agent father, I felt a special calling to study the language of the enemy. I knew my father's job wasn't like the work my friends' fathers did. He had a badge, and a gun, and he would often be called away on a moment's notice on assignments he couldn't talk about. I would later learn that shortly after World War II began, when he and my mother were living in New York, he had worked in counterintelligence, ferreting out foreign espionage agents.

I knew none of this in the early 1960s in Scranton, Pennsylvania, but I must have sensed it. Preparing for my first high school Russian class, I could see myself as a secret agent, uncovering the plans of America's wily enemies in the Kremlin. Taking a seat in Mr. Peregrim's class in September of 1963, I had no idea it would be one of the biggest decisions of my life.

Even as Mr. Peregrim was introducing Pam and me to the complexities of Russian grammar, he himself was enrolling in a new program the US government had quickly set up to train teachers of "critical" languages; with the Space Race at full throttle, Russian headed the list. *Sputnik* made it painfully clear that America was facing not only a technological challenge but an existential security threat. The United States lacked the experts in language and culture needed to speak Russian and to understand the history and structure of the Soviet Union. Only a handful of universities, let alone high schools, had Russian language programs.

The 1958 National Defense Education Act (NDEA) was a milestone, and in the summer after we joined his class, Mr. Peregrim applied for, and won, an NDEA fellowship at Northwestern University in Chicago. He had grown up speaking Russian, but it was a domestic version of the language, filled with words about cooking, food, church, and friends; plus, he needed training in how to teach the language. The following year, thanks to the fellowship, he spent five weeks in graduate language courses at Indiana University.

Mr. Peregrim was one of fifty-eight Russian teachers from big cities and small towns across America in the program, part of which included a trip to Russia, the first time Mr. Peregrim would visit the land of his ancestors.

"I went to Moscow, Tbilisi, Sochi, Sukhumi, Kyiv, and Leningrad," he recounted in my kitchen interview with him. "When I was in Russia, I went out by myself. I met these two girls. One wanted me to marry her. They hated the Communists. I remember standing on Red Square. They asked me where I lived, and I told them a little town outside of Scranton. 'How many rooms in your house?' 'Six.' 'How many people live there?' 'Three: my uncle, my grandmother, and my mother. Then my uncle died and there were two.' 'You should have six boarders!' they told me."

In Russia, Mike was surrounded by the living, breathing, changing Russian language. He learned the difference between the broad "o" of Moscow that sounded more like an "a," and the crisper, more articulated Leningrad (St. Petersburg) accent.

"I just got so enthralled with the language," he said. "I met this one guy and I asked him where the theater where Chekhov's plays are produced was located. He was a professor of literature at Moscow State University. He invited me to have wine and candy. I don't know if that goes together. We went to a hotel and spent two hours. He used words like 'discriminatsiya' [discrimination] which I had never heard. But I caught on real quick."

On the first of August, 1964, Mr. Peregrim bought a postcard at a Moscow kiosk. It was a black-and-white, nearly sepia-tone photograph of Red Square, with Russian "babushki" (grandmothers) in the foreground, strolling arm in arm toward Lenin's tomb; a father taking a snapshot of his two children and his wife, her hand on a baby stroller; and, over in the left-hand corner, toward the famous GUM department store, what looked like a naval officer and a woman with a briefcase. Soft, puffy clouds floated overhead, the scene framed by the branches of trees long since chopped down on Red Square.

When the card arrived in the mail, Pam and I studied every detail. On the address side was a bright red-and-orange stamp depicting a happy worker dressed in white, holding aloft a red banner with the hammer and sickle, a giant number "45" and the word "October," commemorating (two years earlier) the forty-fifth anniversary of Lenin's 1917 Great October Socialist Revolution.

"Dear Twins, Greetings from Moscow!" he wrote in Russian. "This is a very interesting city—beautiful buildings, wide streets, a lot of people. The weather here is wonderful. We arrived in Moscow on the 26th and we leave for Baku, in the south, the third of August." He signed it "Mikhail Mikhailovich," which, we already knew, was the polite way to address a man, using his patronymic, "son of Michael," since Mr. Peregrim's father's name was Michael, too.

Years later, I would get to know another Russian named after his father: Vladimir Vladimirovich Putin.

Mr. Peregrim returned to Scranton with a wealth of material: new, up-to-date vocabulary, for one. When we started learning Russian, we learned the word "pero" for pen. It turned out that was the word used back in the beginning of the twentieth century, when Mr. Peregrim's grandparents came to America, the equivalent of saying "quill pen." He taught us the new word: "roochka" (ballpoint pen). He also introduced us to new Soviet movies that cautiously opened up new, more liberal ideas that were percolating in society. One of them was *Beregis' Avtomobilya* (*Watch Out for the Car*), a satirical comedy-drama that subtly made fun of the Soviet system. It featured one of Russia's most famous actors, Innokenty Smoktunovsky, and it was my introduction to real Russians, scenes from real life. It began to transform my image of the USSR from a massive country of automatons to one of human beings with emotions and views that sometimes diverged from Communist ideology.

Pam and I were, I guess you'd say, serious students. We didn't drink or smoke or use drugs. We didn't even date. We hung out with other serious students in the Debate Society and the Russian Club, and that gave us all a certain sense of entitlement to show we weren't just kids. One day, when Mr. Peregrim was not in class because he was sick, a German teacher filled in and several of us Russian students hatched a plot.

Pam and I were to be the "Russian exchange students" from Moscow, and one of our fellow students, Leslie Nivert, volunteered to "introduce" us to the substitute teacher. We thought the teacher would undoubtedly catch on immediately once she saw our Irish names and get a good laugh out of it.

We entered the classroom a few minutes late with our escort, Leslie, who told the teacher we didn't speak English very well but were happy to meet her.

"How long have you been in America?" she asked us with a kindly smile. It quickly became clear she thought we were for real.

"It should have stopped right there," Leslie told me years later. "But it didn't."

I answered the teacher slowly, in Russian: "Nye ponimayu" ("I don't understand"). Leslie, who was a year behind us in Russian, didn't understand what we were saying. "I pretended to translate by making something up," she recalled years later. It was time to wrap this thing up, we could see. Leslie cut it short by saying we needed to see the principal, and we quickly exited the classroom.

The next day we were called into the principal's office and told sternly "that it was not a nice thing to do."

We later learned that back in the teachers' lounge, the German teacher had told her colleagues about her heartwarming introduction to the "Russian exchange students."

"But we don't have any Russian exchange students," the other teachers replied.

It was an embarrassing moment for her, and as our punishment the next day, Pam and I had to write over and over on the chalkboard some German words. With Pam, it rubbed off—years later, living in Austria, married to a German, she fulfilled her dream of speaking near-native German.

I stuck with Russian.

JFK

There were other subjects, of course, like English literature, Latin, history, and chemistry, but my life was soon consumed with Russian. I had one other interest in my young life, however: President John F. Kennedy. We were in sixth grade when he was elected, and I was inspired by the clever campaign song, sung by Frank Sinatra, which I had on a 45-rpm record and played over and over again.

> Everyone is voting for Jack
> 'Cause he's got what all the rest lack
> Everyone wants to back—Jack
> Jack is on the right track.
> 'Cause he's got high hopes
> He's got high hopes
> Nineteen-sixty's the year for his high hopes.
> Come on and vote for Kennedy
> Vote for Kennedy
> And we'll come out on top!
> Oops, there goes the opposition—ker—
> Oops, there goes the opposition—ker—
> Oops, there goes the opposition—KERPLOP!

Kennedy was Irish Catholic, as was I, and although I didn't fully comprehend the historic significance of his election, I was proud that such a young, vibrant, and intelligent man was now our president. That callowness, however, played a role in the 1962 Cuban Missile Crisis, which took place one year before we entered high school. I remember watching our black-and-white TV and seeing the reports about Soviet premier Nikita Khrushchev shipping nuclear missiles to Cuba, exploiting what he thought was Kennedy's youth and inexperience. I am sure my parents shielded us from the horror of that six-day standoff when Kennedy blockaded Cuba and the world was on the brink of nuclear war. But I also am sure that image of Khrushchev, by turns buffoonish and threatening, influenced my choice to continue to study the Russian language.

And so did John Kennedy's inauguration speech, challenging Americans to "ask not what your country can do for you, ask what you can do for your country." By studying Russian, by learning about the country that, in the depths of the Cold War, was America's existential enemy, I felt, just beginning my teens, there was something I could contribute. Within a few years, I would benefit from programs funded by the federal government that made it possible for me to pursue studies in Russian. I always felt I owed something to the country for that, and John F. Kennedy ignited that emotion within me.

In November of our first year in high school we were in biology class when a student burst in and yelled "Kennedy's been shot!" We all gasped—students and teacher alike. I went home in shock, walked upstairs to my bedroom, leaned up against a wall, and sobbed.

RUSSIAN MAJORS

Mr. Peregrim demanded a lot of his students, and the "mortality rate" for his Russian classes was high. In our first year there were twenty-seven students; the second year, eighteen. Then it went down to five. Finally, as our senior year began, Pam and I were the last ones left. The school wanted to cancel the class, but Mr. Peregrim volunteered to give up his free period to teach us, when he could have used that hour to have some coffee or just take a break. There was no classroom available, so we met in the auditorium. Years later, I asked him why he was willing to do that. "Because I didn't want to lose you two!" he said, laughing.

Our family moved from Scranton to Worcester, Massachusetts, when my father retired from the FBI and began another career as director of athletics at his undergraduate alma mater, Holy Cross. But Mr. Peregrim had offered Pam and me an entire senior year of personal tutoring in Russian, an offer we simply could not refuse. My parents asked our aunt Mildred if we could live with her for the year, and she agreed. She definitely earned her time in heaven.

We spent our senior year in high school studying from college textbooks that Mr. Peregrim bought with his own money, and our one-on-one classes paid off. We both aced the SAT test in Russian, and in September enrolled in Emmanuel College, a Catholic women's college in Boston's Back Bay, as Russian majors. We started with third-year Russian but soon ran out of courses to take. Luckily, we had met a fellow student a bit older than we were who suggested we look at the University of Michigan to continue our studies.

Ann Arbor had an intense atmosphere of study that attracted top scholars from the United States, Europe, and even the Soviet Union. When Iosif Brodsky, Russia's most famous contemporary poet—convicted and imprisoned on charges of being an "idler and a parasite"—was freed, he became university poet in residence at Ann Arbor. Professor Carl Proffer and his wife, professor Ellendea Proffer, founded the groundbreaking Ardis Publishing, which reprinted twentieth-century Russian literature almost lost in the avalanche of Soviet repression. Assya Humesky, one of our professors, wrote one of the best Russian textbooks I've ever used.

I was consumed with Russian—and Russia—by this point, but it was an odd juxtaposition. Outside, as I walked across central campus, students were protesting the Vietnam War and racial inequality. The campus felt ready to explode. As we watched the military draft lottery on TV, one student whose name had been chosen jumped to his feet and threw a chair at the TV. The Black Action Movement was marching and picketing, demanding the end of discrimination at the university. Angry students ripped library books off shelves.

I watched, but never felt a part of it. No one I knew was going to Vietnam. In my entire career I met only two Black students who were studying Russian. As I look back on that time from my perspective of fifty years, I seem incredibly disconnected from American reality and, in fact, I was. I already was living, emotionally and mentally, in Russia. My days were filled with reading Chekhov, puzzling over grammatical complexities of the language, and listening to Rimsky-Korsakov.

Pam and I lived on North Campus in what was called the "Russia House." We were required to speak only Russian, and we organized regular Russian cultural activities. There were, of course, concerts and films in Russian. Then, there were the Thursday-night parties which featured the closest thing to Russian black bread we could find in the local food store, along with the cheapest vodka we could buy.

I had my first drink in college, and I still remember feeling so much more at ease with my friends after a scotch on the rocks. Eventually, I felt the maudlin embrace of inebriation with vodka. At Michigan, during those Thursday-night parties in the Russia House, I loved everyone in the room, vodka loosening my tongue. I made speeches in Russian proclaiming how we were united in the bond of love for what the Russian writer Ivan Turgenev called the "veliky, moguchiy russkiy yazik"—the great, mighty Russian language.

> In days of doubt, in days of dreary musings on the fate of my country, you alone are my comfort and support, oh great, powerful, righteous, and free Russian language!

Most Friday mornings, I would wake up crumpled on the floor, surrounded by the snoring bodies of my fellow Russian students, all of us content in the knowledge that we were truly learning what made Russia tick.

Two years later, I would find myself in Russia, a young guide on a US Information Agency exhibit, answering questions from Russian citizens challenging me to explain why America was bombing Vietnam, and why Black Americans were being lynched. That experience would transform me and my understanding of what America was all about.

But first, we set sail, literally, crossing the Atlantic to begin studies at Leningrad State University as exchange students, living in a dorm with young Russian students, eating in the university cafeteria, all under the watchful eye of the KGB.

· 2 ·

To Russia

In mid-June of 1969 my twin sister Pam and I stood on the deck of the MS *Aurelia* in the New York sunshine, saying farewell to our mother Ruth. It was the ship with nine lives: starting out as a German freighter, seized after World War II, given to the Canadian government, sold to an Italian line, rebuilt as a liner, and chartered by the Council on Student Travel (the precursor to the Council on International Educational Exchange) as a kind of floating university to bring American exchange students to Europe. These days, of course, students would fly to Russia, but this, for me, just added to the romantic nature of the journey.

On board were approximately 1,400 American students. Among them were 3 professors and 48 students who had applied for and been accepted on an exchange program at Leningrad State University, now St. Petersburg State University. Six universities had joined in a consortium and, although we were enrolled at Michigan, we applied through the participating Universities of Kansas and Colorado.

In her purse, my mother was carrying an article that had appeared three months before in the Worcester, Massachusetts, *Evening Gazette*, announcing: "Twins to Study in Russia This Summer." Above the headline there is a photo of Pam and me sitting on the floor on either side of a portable record player, with the caption explaining that we were eager to add to our collection of Russian records. The article explained how we had won US government–sponsored fellowships to study at Leningrad State University. We would attend language classes, but there would be plenty of tours, movies, and theater productions to see, as well. Pam noted to the reporter: "One of the more interesting places scheduled is a tour of a vodka plant." I jumped in: "I think the idea behind all the activities is to keep us out of trouble. They

13

are very strict about what we can and can't do over there. Picture-taking is especially restricted. For example, we are not allowed to take pictures at airports, borders, shorelines, industrial centers, telephone and telegraph installations—or from airplanes." Pam added: "There are strong warnings about importing 'subversive literature,' and anyone caught doing this will be deported immediately."

I could see why my mother wanted to be there in New York to wave good-bye.

It took us nine days to cross the Atlantic, during which we gathered daily for classes and Russian language discussions. Our professors made it clear from the beginning that if we had any marijuana, we could not arrive with it (or any other drugs) at our first European stop—the French port of Le Havre. Most students took that as instruction to smoke it up as fast as possible. Marijuana held no attraction for me; crystal-clear vodka, preferably chilled in the freezer, was my drug of choice. But on the MS *Aurelia*, I wasn't drinking, I was studying. On that ship I met a young guy who would become one of my closest friends, Russ Burford. He had, as they say, a beautiful mind, quick, with big ideas and a constant stream of puns. He also was a lover of jazz and introduced me to Dave Brubeck and the Modern Jazz Quartet. I had found a companion for my explorations of Leningrad.

We spent the night in Paris, then flew Finnair to Leningrad. The choice of a Finnish airline was not accidental; they had regular flights to Russia. It was my first time in Europe, and I knew from that moment on I had to come back. There were three things I distinctly remember from the old hotel in Paris where we stayed: the minuscule elevator, wrapped by a metal cage, embraced by a winding staircase from which you could see the people inside; the smell of verbena soap; and the knock on the door in the morning as the maid brought fresh croissants, butter, and coffee with thick cream and white sugar. I was home.

I wanted to stay, but we were off the next morning to the airport and the flight to Russia. I was apprehensive. With my Cold War image of Russia, I expected to see soldiers on every street corner. In fact, the first thing I saw as I bent down to grab my backpack and exit the plane was a pair of tall, black, shiny leather military boots worn by a young but fiercely serious soldier. Exactly what I'd feared! There was no time to think. A surly female border guard checked our passports, and we collected our suitcases and boarded the Intourist bus to our dorm.

Pam and I came bearing gifts that we, and our parents, thought the young Russians we hoped to meet would like: for the girls, pantyhose (my mother's idea, obviously inspired by World War II nylon stockings), record albums by the Beatles, Kennedy silver half-dollars. The boys brought

American razor blades, which were eagerly accepted by young Russian men whose nicked faces were a painful testament to the hacksaw Soviet blades. At customs control we had to sign a document saying we were bringing no forbidden literature into the country. When we actually got to know some young Russians, we soon understood there were other things they were grateful to receive: decent-quality vodka, cigarettes, instant coffee—all of which we were able to buy with dollars at government-run "hard-currency" stores called Beryozka (Little Birch Tree) where only foreigners—not Soviet citizens—could shop.

For ourselves, we brought soap, which soon ran out, and Tampax, which was nonexistent in Russia. Most Russian women got by with "vata," or cotton wool. We soon found out that so many things we took for granted as women in America simply did not exist in Russia. Cosmetics from Eastern Europe occasionally would make their way into Soviet stores and were snatched up almost immediately. Decent or attractive underwear was impossible to find. Some women sewed their own bras. A top-down, centrally planned economy that measured production in terms of tons of iron and steel was simply incapable of making a soft, intimate garment that most government officials considered "bourgeois" anyway.

I felt a poignant mix of pity—and respect—for the fierce desire of Russian women to look beautiful and "feminine." To me, femininity was something from my mother's generation. I was never particularly interested in it, preferring to wear jeans and sporty clothes, but the Russian approach to beauty went far beyond my mother's sleek dresses. It was voluptuous, over the top, even if Russian women in the 1960s couldn't express it the way women in the West could.

To this day, I can recall the intense fragrance of the Soviet Union's most popular perfume, Krasnaya Moskva (Red Moscow). Introduced in 1925, it became the Soviet version of Chanel No. 5, a sophisticated fragrance in a nation that officially eschewed bourgeois pretension. But then, it didn't have much competition, since the czarist-era perfumer Brocard & Co., opened by Frenchman Henry Brocard in Moscow in 1864, had been nationalized after the 1917 Bolshevik Revolution and re-christened "Soap and Perfumery Factory No. 5."

Red Moscow was unmistakable, and it joined the concatenation of smells that defined my introduction to Russia. There was the fragrant blend of cigarette smoke and the fumes of too much vodka consumed in too short a time, baked-in sweat from clothes that needed washing (although there were no washing machines), with deep notes of an indefinable oily, metallic, almost three-dimensional smell that seemed to linger everywhere, especially in densely packed buses and on the metro.

Our dormitory, officially "Dormitory #6," stood on a corner on Myt-ninskaya Embankment, on the Petrograd side, just down the street from the oldest part of the city, the Peter and Paul Fortress. The narrow gold spire of its cathedral was a symbol of Leningrad, and it pierced the pale blue summer sky as we crossed the bridge over the Neva River.

THE DARKER SIDE OF THE CITY

Leningrad, a dank and forbidding swamp which czar Peter the Great chose as the strategic site of his new capital in 1703, has notoriously bad weather, but we were lucky that summer to enjoy a warm and sunny series of "White Nights." Russia's "Northern Capital" is, indeed, in Russia's north, and in June, when the sun never truly sets, the night sky is suffused with a delicate golden pink that blends with the pastels of the city's Italian Renaissance–style buildings, reflecting from the canals that crisscross the heart of the city.

That was one side of this exquisite city. But Leningrad also was the set-ting for a notorious murder that ignited Stalin's four years of bloody purges in the 1930s.

Sergei Kirov was the Leningrad Communist Party chief, a key member of the Politburo, and a popular, charismatic leader. In December 1934 he was murdered by an assassin. Stalin set out to revenge his death—or at least that is one theory. Thousands of Soviet citizens—members of the military, political leaders, members of the intelligentsia, and average citizens—were rounded up and executed. But another theory points to Stalin himself as the mastermind of the murder, an attempt to remove any political rivals. The mystery of Kirov's assassination has never been solved.

As exchange students in Leningrad, Pam and I would get to know the darker, Dostoyevskian side of Peter's masterpiece, the communal apartments carved up after the Bolshevik Revolution from once-elegant palaces and town houses of the elite, with their dark corridors, broken lights, and peeling paint. This was the Leningrad in which Vladimir Putin was growing up, even as we were unpacking our clothes in our university dormitory and gazing out through the oversize windows across the Neva, at the delicate greenish-blue Hermitage Museum, the Winter Palace of the czars.

Getting to know the seamier side of the city helped me, years later, to better understand Putin's view of Russia, and the world. In the summer of 1969, unbeknownst to Pam and me, Vladimir Putin was sixteen years old, living not far away from us with his family in a one-room flat in a communal apartment building in Baskov Lane. His building had no elevator or hot water, and the family shared a kitchen and toilet with other families. Years later Putin would tell the journalists who wrote his short biography, *First Person: An Astonishingly Frank Self-Portrait by Russia's President*, that he routinely had to beat off "hordes of rats" with a stick. The short book, just 207 pages in the English translation, remains the most detailed depiction of Putin's early life, a biography hastily concocted by the Kremlin to introduce the then relatively unknown Putin to voters just before his first election in 2000. Whether all of it is true is not clear, but it does provide intriguing insights into Vladimir Putin's early years, and some of it does ring true to me.

None of the details of his early life are particularly surprising. In immediate postwar Leningrad, and well into the 1970s and '80s, most people lived in similar conditions. In 2014, filming a short biography of Putin for CNN, my camera crew and I drove to Putin's childhood neighborhood, in the center of the city but far removed from the elegant St. Petersburg most tourists experience. Number 12 Baskov Lane turned out to be a prerevolutionary oxblood-colored building with peeling paint that once belonged to a baroness before being chopped up by the Bolsheviks into tiny flats. We walked from the street through a dark passageway into a courtyard and gazed up at the apartment where Putin and his family lived. It wasn't hard to imagine rats scurrying around.

As an exchange student in Leningrad, I visited several flats like this. Most families lived out their lives—eating, sleeping, having babies—in just one small room of their own, sharing a toilet and kitchen with other families. There was no shower; people had to visit the "banya"—public baths—to bathe.

Putin, in the book, talks a lot about his judo instructor, Anatoly Semyonovich Rakhlin, who died in 2013. During our CNN trip to St. Petersburg, we found his son Mikhail, then thirty-eight, a master in the sport of judo and trainer of the combined teams of that city. He told me his father began teaching young Putin when he was ten or eleven years old. In the beginning, his father told him, Putin didn't stand out. "He was very hardworking, but he didn't have a striking personality." But striking personalities can burn out early, he said. Putin achieved a lot because of his patience and hard work.

His father told Mikhail that Putin "had a reduced feeling of threat and a high pain threshold." He also had a unique skill: "In our sport, you're either a right-hander or a left-hander. He told me that Vladimir Vladimirovich was both; he had the same skills for his right- and left-hand strokes. "It was a unique trick and he efficiently used it. It's a rare skill. It means that your brain hemispheres are equally developed. Usually, one of them would dominate. I think this characteristic can predetermine many things."

In the book, Putin said he was hooked on books and movies about spies, like *The Shield and the Sword* (1968), and dreamed of becoming a KGB officer.

In fact, as he told his biographers, in ninth grade he went to the offices of the KGB directorate in Leningrad and asked for a job.

"That's terrific," one of the staff told young Vladimir, but the KGB didn't take people who approached them—*they* were the ones who did the approaching. Plus, he would need an education, most likely law school. So, in 1970, Putin applied to and was accepted at Leningrad State University's law department.

When Pam and I returned to the university for a full semester of study in February 1971, Putin was on the same campus we were, but as far as I know, none of us Americans ever met him.

DORM LIFE

In the summer of 1969, on our initial visit to Russia, we began by exploring our dormitory. Built in the early 1800s like Putin's family's apartment building, the structure had once been elegant, and the facade still told a tale of prerevolutionary St. Petersburg, with classical Greek figures supporting the balconies on the second floor. Any vestiges of czarist beauty, however, had been erased long ago.

At the entrance we encountered the "dezhurnaya," the on-duty key lady, as we called her. Room keys were attached to a small but heavy ball and chain that ensured no one would take it with them. This allowed the dezhurnaya to keep track of us, the cleaning staff to neaten up our rooms, and, crucially, the security staff to snoop on us and our belongings. From that moment on, I felt I was never really alone. Even the word "privacy" didn't seem to exist in Russian. Yes, you could say "uyedineniye," but that sounded more like "solitude," or even "loneliness." My Russian friends today use the word "privatnost," based on the English word, "privacy."

Our dorm rooms were enormous, with six metal beds and nightstands, one for each girl. My first night, I turned back the covers to sleep, grabbing hold of the starched, rough sheets that felt like fine-grade sandpaper, covered with heavy woolen blankets. Anticipating the certain abrasion to come, I felt somehow comforted by the spartan accommodations. On a plain wood table in the middle of the room, as in every dorm room, stood a narrow-necked glass carafe filled with water, yellowish even after being boiled. Leningrad's water supply was infected with *Giardia lamblia*, an intestinal parasite which caused severe diarrhea, and we were strongly urged to avoid any water straight from the tap.

The large common women's bathroom had toilets, sinks, and showers, but no hot water in the sinks, just one tap for cold. The showers, theoretically, had hot water twice a week. If we wanted to take showers at other times we would gather up our soap and shampoo and set off for the "banya," the traditional Russian baths, located a tramway ride away. Russians have been bathing in banyas for centuries, if not millennia, and we listened carefully as the attendant in the women's room explained how it worked. I immediately picked up at least ten new words in Russian.

We undressed, took a shower, then entered the sauna, kept a skin-peeling 200 or so degrees Fahrenheit. If you breathed in through your nostrils too fast, the sensation was like being singed with a wet iron. The sauna was lined with cedar and the scent was a woodsy mélange of cedar and astringent Soviet soap. We sat embarrassedly naked on benches constructed in three rows, hotter and more humid each level you climbed. The Russian women, babushki of an indeterminate over-sixty age, were unashamed, joyfully chatting with each other, following the rituals their ancestors in ancient Russia, no doubt, had celebrated.

We watched as they poured water from a slatted wood bucket on the coals, sending plumes of steam toward the ceiling, clucking happily as the temperature rose another few degrees. Since we were the only young women close by, they urged us with a contented sigh, "Byei menya, dochka!" ("Beat me, little daughter!"). I didn't understand, but soon realized that since they couldn't easily reach the middle of their backs, it was our job to use "venniki" (birch branches) to vigorously slap them on their backs. I was reluctant to do it in the beginning, but as I saw their obvious delight as the snap of the birch twigs turned their backs pink—a sign of good blood circulation—I thwacked away even harder.

When we all were a lobster-red we retreated to the showers again for a bracing cold deluge. Some of the braver members of our group followed the women into a small pool of icy water. I never liked cold water and I stuck with a tepid shower. But the ladies, after cooling down, promptly returned to the sauna for another round.

Seeing us, the babushki always exclaimed, "But you're too skinny!" In the beginning we found it very funny—almost all of them were portly—but I soon began to understand that these women, very likely, had lived through the infamous Nazi Germany Blockade of Leningrad twenty-nine years before. I imagined them, thirty or forty years old, huddled in unheated apartments, their daily ration reduced to a tiny cube of bread which, by the end of the Blockade, was made mainly of sawdust. I began to understand why they would eat with pleasure, and grow fat, and be grateful for the simple privilege of food.

When we emerged from the women's banya we met the male students outside, all of us giddy with our introduction to real Russians outside of the university. The boys gave us the man's version of sauna life, which featured numerous shots of vodka and lots of boisterous talk. On the way home, I tried to understand the emotions I felt in the banya—the sense that I had bonded with Russians in a primal way, even while realizing I would never really be a part of that clan. We were all women, with varying clothes and mannerisms, but they had been formed by the experience of being raised in the Soviet Union. No matter how well I spoke Russian, I would never fully comprehend how being "Soviet" shaped a person's mentality.

In Dormitory #6, we American students lived on the second floor and, above us, lived the students from the "brotherly countries" of Africa, or Asia. There were some Vietnamese who seemed to avoid us, and we did the same with them, except during the "toilet seat wars." Our ancient toilets down the hall were equipped with equally ancient wood toilet seats that would disappear periodically, stolen by the students who lived above. Whether it was motivated by pranking, or necessity, we never knew, but it became the mission of the boys in our American group to retrieve them, a job they usually carried out at night.

The African students were brought to Russia as part of the Soviet Union's efforts to influence future African leaders. In Moscow most of them studied at Patrice Lumumba University, named in honor of the former prime minister of the Republic of the Congo, Patrice Lumumba. He was executed in 1960 during an army revolt and, in the Soviet Union, was considered a hero of the anticolonial movement. African students at Leningrad State University, known for the high quality of its language training, underwent rigorous study of the Russian language, along with political/cultural indoctrination.

As Americans, we were considered part of the colonialist, imperialist West and rarely had the opportunity to talk or mingle with those more political students, although I did get to know a Nigerian student, Vincent, who was planning to marry a Russian girl. On the weekends, they often joined young Russians for parties and other "vecherinki" ("little evening parties"), but those get-togethers sometimes devolved into fights when an African boy asked a Russian girl to dance. This was my introduction to the official Soviet "brotherhood of nations," behind which lurked Russian xenophobia and wariness of outsiders.

To attend classes, we would head out the front door, walk across Most Stroitelyei (Builders' Bridge, now called Stock Market Bridge) toward Birzhevaya Ploshchad (Stock Market Square), with its classic Greek Revival, czarist-era stock exchange and the terra-cotta-colored rostral columns, designed to serve as beacons to light the way for ships on the Neva. Our classes were held in the pale green former Palace of Peter II, better known as the "Filfak" (Philological Faculty).

As a young girl, I was fascinated by the classic Greek columns that adorned many of the nineteenth-century houses in our Pennsylvania neighborhood, and I spent hours drawing their Doric, Ionic, and Corinthian capitals. Here, in Leningrad, before my eyes, I was stunned by what the American leader of our Kansas/Colorado group, professor Gerald Mikkelson, called "one of the world's most gorgeous displays of architectural virtuosity."

Across the Neva River we could see the dusky gold dome of St. Isaac's Cathedral; the magnificent "Bronze Horseman" equestrian statue of Peter the Great that had survived intact following the bombing during the Nazi Blockade; and the Admiralty, with its gilded spire. We were in the Soviet Union, in the depths of the Cold War, but there was no hiding the imperial czarist splendor of St. Petersburg. Although most signs of the czarist period had been removed after the Revolution, I found one spectacular double-headed eagle over a gate at the Fortress of Peter and Paul, a reminder that the Peter and Paul Cathedral was the traditional burial place for the imperial family. Years later, I would report on the burial of the remains of the last czar, Nicholas II, and his family, shot to death by the Bolsheviks.

Our teachers were dedicated experts who approached languages with scientific fervor. They plunged us into an intense program of grammar and phonetics, and their crystal-clear pronunciation felt to me like a work of art, a relic of the pre-Soviet days. More than almost any aspect of Russian culture, the language itself carries the deepest cultural—almost spiritual—significance. But the Russian language also is highly political; it had been revised, some would say "mauled," by the Bolsheviks, who not only changed the orthography, removing several obsolete letters, but introduced the mind-numbing mumbo jumbo of the verbose, empty bureaucratic language used by the Communist Party that still infuses the language today.

Our instructors also were very interested in how we, as young Americans, spoke English. Most of the English instruction at the university used British pronunciation, and our group offered a gold mine of contemporary American English. Some of us were chosen to be recorded in the language laboratory for future analysis. But when they began recording me, I was immediately rejected.

"You don't pronounce English correctly," one of the teachers told me. I was incredulous. They patiently explained to me, using charts of mouths and tongues, how the English "s" was supposed to be pronounced. It turned out I had a noisy, sibilant "s" and thus was unfit to use as an example of how to speak proper English. They even tried to correct my English pronunciation, but after twenty years of speaking that way, I found it impossible to put my tongue where they said it should be placed. I gave up and went back to my slightly lispy "s."

AMERICANS ON THE MOON

July 20, 1969, was a hot day in Leningrad, and it turned out to be historic. News reports announced the United States was about to land a man on the moon's surface. Actually, there were two men: Neil Armstrong and Buzz Aldrin, the crew of *Apollo 11*.

Our three American professors lived in the same room on the third floor of Dormitory #6, and they were the only ones who had a black-and-white Soviet TV.

"We heard about it early enough so that we could see it in real time," Professor Mikkelson told me many years later, when we met in St. Petersburg for the fiftieth anniversary of our program. "Just about all the students, American and Soviet, came into that room. We were jammed into it like sardines, about forty-five of us, watching this thing. I was happily surprised to see how genuinely the Soviet students were congratulating us, our nation, and our astronauts with this achievement," he told me. "Underneath, they probably felt some envy and disappointment that it wasn't their own who had done that."

It was the culmination of a mission announced by President John F. Kennedy in a speech to Congress in 1961, when Pam and I were in seventh grade. Here we were, in Leningrad, eight years later, our lives forever transformed by *Sputnik* and the Space Race.

Our academic study program at the university was demanding, with classes five days a week until the middle of the afternoon, followed by "cultural" excursions to various locations in the city, such as museums or historical sites. Since its founding by czar Peter the Great in 1703, the city has been renamed four times: its original name, St. Petersburg; its World War I name, Petrograd (adding a Russified "grad"—from the Russian word "gorod," or "city," instead of the Germanic-sounded "burg"); Leningrad, renamed in 1924 in honor of Bolshevik revolutionary Vladimir Lenin; and finally, St. Petersburg again, restored in 1991 after the collapse of the USSR.

When we arrived in 1969 it was proudly called Leningrad, the "hero" city that had survived the vicious nine-hundred-day Nazi Blockade from 1941 to 1943, during which an estimated 800,000 to 1 million inhabitants died from cold and starvation. One of them, I would learn years later, was a baby who would have grown up to be Vladimir Putin's older brother. He died of diphtheria in a children's home in Leningrad, set up to save the lives of children during the Blockade.

The hammer and sickle and other Communist insignia were everywhere in Leningrad, including a famous sign painted on the wall of a building on the main street, Nevsky Prospekt, during the Nazi Blockade, warning: "Citizens! During shelling this side of the street is the most dangerous." The sign is still there, repainted regularly. Every time I've passed it, it's been adorned with flowers and, every time, it brings tears to my eyes.

The 1917 Bolshevik Revolution started in Petrograd, as Leningrad/St. Petersburg was known at the time. One of our first outings as students was to the cruiser *Aurora*, the ship that had fired a blank shell to signal the assault on Czar Nicholas II's Winter Palace. The actual details of the warning shot are lost in the mists of history, but there was no doubt it was a site sacred to Soviet citizens. We dutifully listened to the guide announcing the size of the ship, its weight, and other minute details—a typical Soviet approach to most issues, I soon learned—citing facts and figures, but ignoring the overall meaning.

Some of us ate it up, but other students in our group who didn't speak Russian very well were bored, and began to rebel against the daily cultural and historical outings. Several of our fellow students planned to teach Russian or to work for the US government, but some—perhaps a quarter of our group, according to Professor Mikkelson—"were horrified by what they experienced." For some of them, it was the intensity of language instruction, the spartan conditions in the dormitory—especially the toilets—and the daily dose of Soviet propaganda. For others, it was knowing that their Soviet roommates were informing on them to the KGB.

"They were experiencing essentially the same things we were," Professor Mikkelson told me. "It's just that they had a completely different attitude toward it. It was fear and loathing." He laughed. "It's part of the question as to why any young American would be crazy enough to want to spend their life studying Russian!"

Pam and I, along with a couple of fellow students with whom we quickly became friends, found all of it exhilarating. Every day there was an adventure. Toilet paper was hard to find; most Russians got by using cut-up newspapers. We would make forays to the fancy hotels that catered to Western tourists—our favorites were the fabled Astoria and the still-elegant Yevropeyskaya Gostinnitsa (European Hotel). The key to getting in was to look like you belonged there, that you were from the West. Soviet citizens, except for the occasional "shishka," or big-shot Soviet bureaucrat, were not allowed in, and to make sure they never did get in, every hotel had a doorman who would stick out his arm firmly and block their way.

It wasn't just our clothes, it was our bearing, the way we walked, an almost imperceptible something that defined us as "not Soviet." The doormen had that sixth sense. Most of the time they let us pass by. Once in, we would linger for a few minutes in the foyer, then make our way to the ladies' room ("Zhensky tualyet"). Invariably, inside the door, there was an older woman, seated, holding in one hand a roll of imported Polish toilet paper—pink, gray, or bluish, with the consistency of crepe paper—and a pair of large scissors in the other hand. She would methodically cut the paper in tiny quarters, then stack those triangles into piles. The piles would be carefully placed in cream-colored plastic holders inside each stall—a graphic illustration of why the Soviet Union had "no unemployment."

As our teammate kept the woman chatting, the other teammate would grab several handfuls of toilet paper and stuff them in a plastic shopping bag. It was theft, a serious crime against the people, but we were desperate.

In all our outings we learned new vocabulary as well as nuggets of truth about how the Soviet system functioned on a human level. We began carrying an "avozka" with us at all times, a cotton string bag that could fold neatly into a pocket or purse, ready to be deployed in case you came upon a queue at a store where they were unexpectedly selling a lot of, say, bananas from Ecuador, or shoes from Yugoslavia. "Avozka" roughly translated into "that little just-in-case thing," and that, to me, was a charming example of what made the Russian language so endearing.

Many of us also encountered a word they didn't teach us at the university: "fartsovchiki," the earliest form of independent "businessmen" in the Soviet Union, although you also could call them "black marketeers." All stores were owned and run by the government. The fartsovchiki (almost invariably young men) would haunt streets like Nevsky Prospekt, looking for tourists and foreigners, asking, usually in English, whether they had anything to sell. They also exchanged rubles for dollars, paying far more than the official rate. Most often, they were interested in buying Western blue jeans. The black marketeers would then sell those jeans to others and pocket the difference in price, something that was completely illegal and could get them arrested. But jeans, T-shirts, cigarettes, and other Western goods simply were not obtainable in the USSR, at least to the average Russian.

As for the Communist Party "nomenklatura" (the Soviet Union's "Deep State," composed of members of the Communist Party who held ruling positions in government or industry), they had their own stores with no signs outside, usually hidden behind windows shielded with blinds, where "apparatchiki" (Party members) who had worked abroad and had foreign currency could buy things like washing machines—unimaginable for their fellow citizens.

In the book *First Person*, Vladimir Putin's wife Lyudmila recounts that the family had no savings when they were preparing to return to Russia after Putin's tour as a KGB officer in East Germany. Their German neighbors gave them a twenty-year-old washing machine which they transported back home to Russia and used for five more years.

Shortly after we arrived in Leningrad, two of our fellow students, apparently skipping class that day, ended up in the Astoria Hotel. There they ran into Hubert Humphrey, President Lyndon Johnson's vice president, who was in town visiting the US Information Agency's "Education-69" exhibit that was touring the Soviet Union as part of a government exchange program. Just half a year before, Humphrey had lost the election to Richard Nixon.

The students invited him to visit our dorm, and he took them up on it. All the Americans showed up, along with a few Russian students. With no access to American news, we were happy for some updates, but, as Professor Mikkelson later recalled, there was a serious moment.

"One of the things I remember most clearly is there was an African American student in our group," he told me, "and here Hubert Humphrey was talking about baseball, and this student got really irritated and interrupted him and said, 'Senator Humphrey, how can you come and talk to us about things like that when our cities are burning?'"

What we did not know at the time was that, during the 1968 election, the Soviet government had offered to help Humphrey in his race against Richard Nixon, a fierce anti-Communist. The longtime Soviet ambassador to the United States, Anatoly Dobrynin, wrote in his memoir, *In Confidence*, that the Soviet leadership had secretly offered Humphrey assistance—including financial—for his campaign.

Dobrynin thought it was a dangerous idea that could backfire, but Soviet foreign minister Andrey Gromyko ordered him to approach Humphrey anyway. Dobrynin says he followed through during a breakfast at Humphrey's home. "Humphrey, I must say," Dobrynin wrote, "was not only a very intelligent but also a very clever man. He knew at once what was going on." Humphrey diplomatically refused, thanking the ambassador for Moscow's "good wishes."

The American students who got the most out of their experience in Leningrad that summer managed to make friends with young Russians—not an easy thing to do, since befriending a foreigner could create problems with the authorities for any Russian who dared to do it. Our Soviet roommates, two strong-armed gals from Ukraine, were undoubtedly informing on us to the security services, and we knew our dorm rooms were bugged. We even had proof, of a sort: One night, sitting around, chatting in our room, one girl pointed out a loose board in the parquet floor. We jokingly said it would be a great place to hide something. The next day, a repairman showed up to fix it.

TANYA AND SERGEY

Pam and I, along with our fellow student Russ Burford, had been urged by a previous American student in Leningrad, Joe, to look up his friends, Tanya and Sergey. He told us where they lived, but in those days, they had no phone, and neither did we, so we used the traditional method Russians employed to find each other: Pam and I, with Russ as our backup, set out one afternoon on the tram to Prospekt Gaza, in the Admiralteisky section of the city, on the left bank of the Neva River, one of the oldest sections of Leningrad.

The tram itself was a *Dr. Zhivago* experience. It was made of wood, probably decades old, and it clanged along tracks through the historic center of Leningrad, slowing to cross the eighteenth-century Lomonosov Bridge, with its four stone towers linked by heavy nautical chains. As I gazed out through the window at the passing buildings, their formerly pastel colors obscured by soot, I remembered the scene in the film *Dr. Zhivago*, released just four years earlier, in which Lara sits, just as I did, at the window and unexpectedly sees Yuri Zhivago, her lover, as he walks, completely unaware of her, down the street.

The movie was based on the 1957 novel *Dr. Zhivago*, by Boris Pasternak, which had been banned in the Soviet Union but won the Nobel Prize for Literature in 1958. The manuscript was smuggled out of the USSR and published in Russian in Italy, and later, in the United States. Set during the 1917 Bolshevik Revolution, Soviet officials were furious at the positive, even romantic, depiction of the czarist elite, and what they perceived as the degrading view of workers and peasants. And so, in their relentlessly vindictive way, they set about to erase the author from society. Pasternak was forbidden to accept the Nobel Prize and banned from the Soviet Writers Union, which was the only way writers or poets could be published or make their living. He died of lung cancer in 1960, nine years before we began our studies in Russia.

I had seen the movie version of *Dr. Zhivago* several times before arriving in Leningrad, and the tragic love of Yuri and Lara, the drama of the Revolution, which had played out just across the river from our dormitory, plus the repressive atmosphere of Communist control, colored my every experience. But nothing quite prepared me for my introduction to a communal Russian apartment, or for my introduction to Tanya and Sergey, with whom I remain friends to this day.

We left the tram and walked a couple of blocks, approaching their apartment building, as usual in Leningrad, through a dark passageway that felt like a mineshaft and opened into an inner courtyard. The wood door at the entrance was a battered brown, and the lock had been bashed in. The acrid odor of cigarettes and dried urine hung in the air.

We headed for the elevator, enclosed in a metal cage painted a sickly green, but it was broken. Along the wall hung a phalanx of narrow mailboxes of the same color, smashed in as if someone had taken a hammer to them. We trooped up the concrete stairs silently, trying not to bump into the spaghetti-like tangle of exposed electrical wires that snaked up the walls.

We found what we thought was Tanya and Sergey's apartment. I should say "the door to the communal apartment in which they lived," since, as we would soon learn, other people shared the flat with them. The door was metal, padded on the outside with dingy brown Naugahyde-like quilted material. A young man about our age, brown-haired, not very tall, with long hair, a mustache, and a devilish laugh, opened the door. It was Sergey. We said hello. He greeted us, but motioned for us to come inside quietly. He later explained that our accents in Russian might give us away as foreigners, and he wasn't eager to have his neighbors know he was consorting with people from capitalist countries.

We found ourselves in a cramped hallway, just beyond which was a disheveled kitchen where a neighbor was cooking something sour and pungent. Beyond that was a tiny toilet cubicle (there was no shower). Down the short hallway was another door, which was the actual entrance to the single room in which he and Tanya lived. Tanya—blonde, smiling, with a round face and an expression of wry amusement—greeted us and quickly ushered us in.

It could not have been more than about fifteen or sixteen feet long and perhaps twelve feet wide. It was living room, dining room, and bedroom combined, with a bed that served as a sofa by day, a narrow bed for both Tanya and Sergey at night. Nine months later three of them would live there when their son Anton was born, the room becoming a little smaller when they moved a crib into the corner.

To the right was a cabinet with glass doors, inside of which Tanya had arranged plates, bowls, cups, saucers, and glasses. In the corner was a record player. In the middle of the room, under an oddly elaborate antique brass chandelier, stood their dining room table, which, when they were not eating, was used for writing and other work. The walls were papered in a pinkish-beige paper with an imperceptible geometric pattern. Icons, several of them, hung on the walls, their "oklad" covers gleaming gold and silver, cut out to reveal the faces of the saints beneath them. Sergey, it turned out, was buying icons, along with samovars and other decorative items from the nineteenth century, from small churches in the countryside.

We brought a record album from the States with us that day as a gift, Jim Morrison and The Doors, along with a carton of Marlboro cigarettes, Stolichnaya vodka, and instant coffee, all of which we had purchased at the hard-currency Beryozka store. Sergey immediately put the record on the record player, laughing hysterically when I called it a "patephon." He explained that the word, the equivalent of "gramophone," had gone out of use half a century before. Young Russians used the word "proigrivatel" ("player"), and I soon realized I had a lot of vocabulary updating to do. Still, the album was a major hit with Sergey, simply unobtainable for average Russians. Morrison's mesmerizing voice, his teasingly erotic urgency, needed no translation.

Tanya, almost magically it seemed, brought out plate after plate of "zakuski": sausage, boiled eggs, chicken, beet salad, "selyodka pod shuboi" ("herring in a fur coat"), "stolichniy" salad with that wonderful combination of potatoes, peas, carrots, and tiny chunks of pickle, stalks of dill and parsley, black bread, white bread, butter. I now could see what the word "gostepriimnost" really meant; the English "hospitality" didn't seem to really capture it. For me, it began to define what made Russians "Russian": an all-enveloping warmth, abundant, exuberant, almost overbearing, like being hugged to the bosom of a deliciously zaftig woman. As soon as we finished a dish, Tanya was urging us to have more. Sergey cracked open the vodka, pouring it into shot glasses, and for the first time, we began to drink like Russians. It would not be the last.

Sergey talked, Tanya listened and smoked and, from time to time, interjected a bemused "Nu Sergey!" ("But Sergey!") as if he were a little boy misbehaving. "Vipeem!" ("Let's drink!") Sergey would announce, pouring more vodka in our glasses as soon as they were empty. We drank to us, we drank to them, we drank to Jim Morrison, we drank to America, we drank to "Piter" (the nickname for the prerevolutionary name of Leningrad, St. Petersburg). Drinking with Russian friends felt like complete, exuberant debauchery and, at the same time, like a sacrament.

Fueled by alcohol, we would sing along and, from time to time, try to walk without stumbling to the toilet, which was surprisingly clean, bearing in mind how many neighbors (it appeared to be at least two other families) used it. There was no toilet paper; cut-up newspapers had to suffice.

Tanya would offer us cigarettes—the Marlboros we had brought, not the "papirosi" they often smoked, which were long cardboard tubes containing a plug of bitter tobacco in a thin paper wrapper—strong, and cheap. I never smoked, but sitting at the table with Tanya and Sergey, surrounded by the Dostoyevskian voices of communal flat neighbors, I felt an urge to hunker down, drink until I could drink no more, to be one with my friends in their inner exile, to speak the language I'd spent so much time trying to master, to talk about music and art and a free life, and to feel that, in this moment, in this tiny communal apartment, we were safe from all the menacing "Sovki" ("Soviet jerks") that Sergey hated so much. I felt such an odd combination of emotions: excited to the point of euphoria, depressed to the point of tears.

I never really knew what Sergey did for a living. But then, a lot of Soviet citizens toiled away at meaningless jobs in anonymous offices, arriving at work in the morning, hanging their jacket on the back of their chair so it would look as if they had just stepped away for a minute, and then disappearing for hours. My sister Pam thought Sergey was either working for, or cooperating with, the KGB. It was entirely possible. I never asked him in those days, and I still haven't, but I am quite sure he never worked with the security services. He and Tanya were the first Russian friends we ever had. They had let foreigners, even Americans, into their apartment and into their lives. I cherished those evenings when I felt like "rodnaya" ("close family"), and I never wanted to break that spell. Besides, I was probably too naive to entertain any doubts about Sergey's reliability or honesty.

There was a lot left unsaid in the Soviet Union. I sensed, almost physically, that there were questions you simply didn't ask, things you didn't say, because everyone lived in that tenuous balance between the inner and the outer life. At home, with close friends, you could be your authentic self. You were emotionally safe but, at the same time, extremely vulnerable. In Stalin's time, you could be executed for telling a joke. Preserving the sanctity of "kitchen conversations" was paramount. Russians have so many expressions that convey this: "This is not a telephone conversation" means "We can't discuss this on the phone" (it's bugged).

Even the powers that be, the security services, the "militzioneri" ("policemen"), had their own tacit way of expressing this: "You know what we want you to do; we know what we are supposed to pretend to do." It all was based on lies, and people knew they were lying. Sometimes, it was to save a life, or a career. But it was still a lie. And lying eats away at the inside of a person, and a society.

I can write this now, half a century later, and I can see it more clearly for what it was, how ultimately warped it all was. As it was happening, I felt it, viscerally; no one explained it to me. It began to form some of my deepest feelings about Russia: passionate attraction mixed with revulsion. Years later, I came upon a quote by Sergei Vinogradov, a Russian Impressionist artist of the late nineteenth and early twentieth centuries: "But Russian life is impossible to understand: strange and frightening. Such a combination: cruelty and kindness, brutality and sentimentality, collapse and liveliness."

In his fascinating book, *Everything Was Forever, Until It Was No More: The Last Soviet Generation*, anthropologist Alexei Yurchak describes what he calls the "internal paradoxes of life under socialism":

> What tends to get lost in the binary accounts is the crucial, and seemingly paradoxical fact that, for great numbers of Soviet citizens, many of the fundamental values, ideals and realities of socialist life (such as equality, community, selflessness, altruism, friendship, ethical relations, safety, education, work, creativity, and concern for the future) were of genuine importance,

despite the fact that many of their everyday practices routinely transgressed, reinterpreted, or refused certain norms and rules represented in the official ideology of the socialist state.

After a long evening with Tanya and Sergey, we would realize we had to get home to be ready for classes the next day, and to make it back to the dorm before Leningrad's drawbridges went up to allow ships to pass. As Tanya hugged us good-bye, Sergey invariably would throw on his jacket and accompany us down the dark staircase to the dimly lit street and flag down a passing private car, which was the usual way to catch a ride in those days, to take us back to our dorm. He would pay in advance, chivalrously never allowing us to spend our rubles. One night I complimented him on his steel-rimmed eyeglasses. A few weeks later, as we saw Tanya and Sergey for the last time before returning to the United States, he gave me his glasses as a gift. I learned to be careful complimenting a Russian on a scarf or a hat or a piece of jewelry; they might literally give you the shirt off their back.

There would be many times I, too, would be overcome by emotion as I said good-bye to my Russian friends. It felt like a giant metal gate was slamming shut, leaving Tanya, Sergey, and other friends I would make over the years locked behind, unable to leave. And yet, in my guilty heart, at those moments, I was happy to leave, relieved to be able to board a plane and go home to freedom. Invariably, though, I would soon be longing to return to Russia.

WINTER IN LENINGRAD

After our summer of language study in 1969, Pam and I returned to the University of Michigan, then spent the summer in Worcester, Massachusetts, with our family. We both got summer jobs taking ID photos of people for MasterCard. In my free time, sitting in the sun, I read novels, filled with the kind of excitement tinged with naive hubris that only a twenty-year-old with a bad case of intellectual pretentiousness can have.

"I just finished good ole Flaubert's *Madame Bovary*," I wrote to an Irish friend from Ann Arbor, Dónall ÓBaoill, with whom I became close friends. "I really did like it and had basically the same feeling about Emma as I had about Anna Karenina. She is just a bit too old for me to really understand, but I can still see why she did a lot of what she did." (Anna, in Tolstoy's novel, was in her late twenties.)

That summer Pam and I also received a gift box, more like a crate, from Tanya and Sergey. I had sent them a small anniversary gift that, miraculously, made it through the Soviet mail without being stolen. In return, they sent us a bottle of Soviet champagne, perfume, slides of Leningrad, two small books, one wooden "matryoshka" nesting doll that opened to reveal six ever-smaller replicas of the original doll, and a packet of picture postcards depicting Russian samovars.

At summer's end we returned to Ann Arbor and, with all our extra courses in Russian, plus high school Advanced Placement courses, we graduated a semester early with BAs in Slavic languages and literature. And, once again, thanks to more US government funding, we returned in February 1971 to Leningrad State University for a semester of advanced Russian.

We were back in Dormitory #6, with its view of the Hermitage, but this time, there were no blue skies or sun glinting off the spire of the Peter and Paul Fortress. The Neva River was frozen over in white slabs of ice that looked like shattered glass, the temperature was a bone-cracking minus-20 degrees Fahrenheit, and the cold damp pierced our coats as we braced against the wind, trying not to be blown off the bridge we crossed on our way to classes. The feeble sun didn't rise until 9 a.m. It took actual physical strength to make it to the Filfak, but getting places in Leningrad was like that. I loved walking because I could experience the city and capture in my mind's eye snapshots of the real life Russians were living: Women queuing up at stores with what seemed to me comically utilitarian Soviet names, like Khleb (Bread), Moloko (Milk), Riba (Fish), Myaso (Meat), but I could see they were on a serious mission to buy whatever the store had lucked into supplying that day. I watched men approaching other men for a cigarette, or a light from a match that flared bright, that first drag gleaming like a coal fire.

In February, the flimsy floral dresses the Russian women wore so gleefully in the summer of 1969 were hidden away in closets. Now, they hurried down the streets in formless woolen coats with fur collars or occasionally a "shuba," a long fur coat—the best way to keep warm, I soon learned; gloves, boots, and fur hats were de rigueur. If you had the temerity to break the rules about wearing a hat, a grandmother on the street was sure to dress you down in a loud voice, insisting you should be ashamed of yourself. Men had their uniform, too: a wool coat, wool scarf, fur hat, gloves, and, almost invariably, a leather "portfel" (briefcase), brown or black, with a strap, that might contain anything from important papers to a sausage lunch.

As I walked, I thought of a game I'd invented when I was about nine years old. I called it "exploring." I played it alone; that was the whole idea. This was a solitary quest, the harder the better. It was best played in the winter when it was cold, and where, in our northeast Pennsylvania town, we would usually get several feet of snow.

I would set off, lifting my legs high to push the wet, white mounds out of the way, shocked by the icy clumps that would inevitably slide their way down the insides of my boots. It was hard, but the physical effort warmed my muscles. Besides, this had to be a challenge. That was the point. My nine-year-old brain raced with the intoxicating thought: Could I make it to my goal? It was me against Nature.

And that is how I made my way through the streets of Leningrad. Would I be able to find my way? Would I feel overwhelmed by the cold and wet? Would I finally arrive at a store I struggled to find, only to see a big sign saying CLOSED—SANITARY DAY? Would I never be able to find a bathroom? Along with the catastrophizing, however, each sortie was an adventure. I returned with new words and more photographs. Just before Pam and I left for Russia, my uncle, a professional photographer, gave me a Leicaflex SL camera with three lenses. It weighed more than I did, but the lenses were so finely honed and created such beautiful images that I lugged it everywhere. I shot Koda-chrome slide film, which provided intense depth and saturation, even in the low-light conditions of wintertime Leningrad.

Our trek from Dormitory #6 across the bridge was worth the torture. My sister Pam and I were some of the most linguistically advanced students, and so were assigned to two of the best professors at the university: Inna Sergeevna and Robert Eduardovich. I knew how lucky we were to have had Michael Peregrim as our high school teacher, and these two Russian teachers were superb, with the same selfless dedication that Mr. Peregrim had.

The Semester Russian Language program was sixteen weeks long, from February through the end of May. It was run according to a protocol signed jointly by the Council on International Educational Exchange on the American side and, somewhat incongruously, by Sputnik, the Soviet Youth Travel Bureau (allied with the Soviet travel agency Intourist) on the Russian side. Our resident American director and assistant director had to coordinate both with Sputnik and with Leningrad University's Foreign Study Office and the Department of Russian for Foreigners.

Our classes covered more complex aspects of the language, including phonetics, "the practice of oral speech," grammar, reading, and translation. We studied Russian and Soviet literature as well as the geography of the Soviet Union. The university also provided lectures on subjects like "Lenin as the Founder of the Soviet State," and "The USSR: A Multi-National State," presented by true-blue (or should I say red?) members of the Obshchestvo Znanii (Knowledge Society), professional propagandists who specialized in Marxist/ Leninist cultural and political enlightenment for the masses. Motivated by these lectures to delve more deeply into art, I wrote a paper for one of my classes on Picasso, but I was reprimanded for praising such a "decadent" artist.

As the weeks went by, I felt more confident in my ability to speak Russian, but the intensity of study, the monotonous food with starches and almost no vegetables, the cold, and the dark took their toll. Our Soviet roommates rarely talked with us and seemed to spend most of their time frying doughy things in oil. I made the mistake of accepting a plate of something—I believe it was deep-fried "oladi" (thick pancakes), prepared by one of them—and was violently ill for several days. One of our American students became more and more depressed, unable to sleep, and soon her eyes were rimmed with black circles. More serious depression set in, and she eventually had to be sent home to the States.

THE KGB LAW STUDENT

Meanwhile, in another building on the campus of Leningrad State University, Vladimir Putin was studying law. In his pre-election biography, he told the journalist authors that it was hard to get into the prestigious university, that there were 100 slots, and only 10 were reserved for high school graduates. Putin, who described himself as a troublemaker in grammar school, said he turned himself around and doubled down on the subjects that would help him gain entrance to the university. Once accepted, he studied hard, he explained. His parents supported him, but he took a job chopping trees in the lumber industry to make some money.

Law school in the Soviet Union was a five-year course of undergraduate and graduate study anchored in subjects like History of the Communist Party and Marxism/Leninism, but it also covered criminal law, civil and family law, and comparisons of law in socialist vs. "bourgeois" countries. Ultimately, it was a training institution for the KGB and the Communist Party bureaucracy.

As Putin tells the tale, at university he eventually concluded that the KGB had forgotten about him and his youthful interest in joining the agency. But in his fourth year, he was approached by a man who did not reveal whom he represented, instead telling Putin about a "future job assignment." That's how Putin learned he was being groomed by the KGB. In *First Person* he admits that he never even thought about the murderous Stalin-era activities of the security services. "My notion of the KGB came from romantic spy stories." As he put it: "I was a pure and utterly successful product of Soviet patriotic education."

Many years later, when I learned more about Putin's time at Leningrad State University, I thought of my father Vincent, who, before he joined the FBI, graduated from Georgetown University Law School and was admitted to the bar. Could there be any similarity between Putin and my father?

The very thought seemed sacrilegious. My father, although much older than Putin, was on the opposite side in the Cold War, an ardent foe of

Communism. Vince joined the FBI in 1941 and could have been exempt from serving in the military during World War II. But he resigned from the FBI and joined the US Marine Corps, serving as an intelligence officer for Marine Air Group #12 in the Pacific and China. I still have a copy of his typed letter of resignation, dated March 6, 1944, which he sent to "John Edgar Hoover, Director, Federal Bureau of Investigation, US Department of Justice, Washington, DC."

"During the past several months," he wrote, "I have carefully considered my work as a Special Agent with the Federal Bureau of Investigation in relation to the war effort. Obviously, such consideration, of necessity, was weighty and pregnant with meritorious arguments for and against my continued affiliation with the Bureau."

He explained that he considered his work with the FBI part of the war effort. He went on to outline how the local draft board had classified him draftable, and that the FBI was appealing that classification, making the case that he should be deferred.

My father called that "debatable," and continued: "And this, coupled with the fact that I am willing to serve my country in any capacity makes me believe that my case should not at any time become the subject of an appeal. I have therefore decided," he wrote, "to voluntarily enter military service and seek combat duty." Although the FBI warned him he would not have a job when he returned, the Bureau changed its mind when he came home after serving two years in the Pacific Theater.

Was there any similarity in my father's and Putin's values—their beliefs about their countries? My father died in 1989, and sadly, I never had a chance to ask him about any of this. He was an outgoing man, but a quiet patriot who didn't talk about his love of country; instead, he acted on it, as I later learned from documents I retrieved from my mother.

Vince was born in 1914 in a town close to Scranton and went to the same high school my sister and I attended. In college he majored in philosophy. He graduated from Holy Cross College, where he was a quarterback and half back on the 1937 undefeated football team. With the FBI he served in Seattle, Salt Lake City, and Washington, DC. He was assigned to the New York City office in March 1941. I know all of this because of a curriculum vitae my father compiled in 1946. In it he wrote that his job in New York "was at first concerned with the investigation of criminal matters and counterespionage."

He provided intriguing details: "Shortly after the outbreak of World War II, I was selected to organize and establish a special contact service for the New York City office of the Federal Bureau of Investigation. This service was, in brief, based on the selection of completely trustworthy, patriotic, and effective individuals strategically placed in spheres, both social and business, in which foreign espionage agents sought information. The service expedited the investigation of and more firmly welded the patterns for the successful prosecution of such espionage agents. The extreme confidential aspect of the service necessitated careful sifting and selection of the individuals to be used."

As I read this, I am smiling. That is pretty much how my father talked. His legal and FBI lexicon affected even how he yelled at us kids. "You little prevaricator!" he would cry in desperation, discovering a half-eaten hot dog in one of the toy chests below our benches in the breakfast nook.

The parallels with Vladimir Putin, as far as intelligence work goes, are obvious. Although it's impossible to delve into the mind of Putin, I see some similarity in his early desire to serve his country, although he seemed more attracted to the glamour of being a spy. But my father and he grew up in very different countries, Vince in a nation of laws, although an imperfect democracy. They also were very different men. My father was not interested in money, except as the means to pay for the needs of our family, especially education—not an easy task, with six children to put through school. And he was a man of principle who also was kind. Putin, as I observed him, always retained a thuggish core which would erupt at times, betraying his "cool" exterior.

Vince returned from the war to an indisputable superpower. Putin grew up in a nation ravaged by World War II and served in the KGB as the Soviet Union was unraveling. Many in the West considered Russia the Cold War "loser" during this period, and they reveled in it. I can understand how, having seen the suffering that his city, and his family, endured during the Nazi Blockade of Leningrad, Putin would vow that, on his watch, nothing like that would ever happen again. And I can see how Putin emerged from the Cold War with a chip on his shoulder—a visceral anger toward the countries he thought had tried to bring Russia to its knees. The initial salary of a KGB officer was meager, but over the years, as he climbed the ladder of Russian officialdom, Putin was able to amass immense wealth and enforce a system based on corruption. That said, I have never believed that personal enrichment alone has defined Putin's worldview, even if it is the key factor in how Putin's Russia works. Power and control, I believe, are his main motivations.

In the early 2000s, Russia was hit by a wave of terrorism. As CNN's Moscow bureau chief, I talked with the KGB many times, interviewing senior officers about bombings and other attacks carried out by Chechen militants. Putin was trying to make common cause with the United States, to convince President George W. Bush that Chechens and Al-Qaeda presented the same threat.

On one occasion, we were invited to Lubyanka, the unofficial name for the late-nineteenth-century building that has served over the years as headquarters for the first Soviet secret police agency, the Cheka; for the KGB; and for its successor agency, the FSB. It stands in the center of Moscow, facing Lubyanka Square, after which it got its nickname, a massive yellow-red brick edifice that also contains a prison and a museum. The person we were to interview was delayed, and we were shown into the former office of Yuri Andropov, KGB head from 1967 to 1982, and general secretary of the Communist Party's Central Committee from 1982 to 1984. Putin joined the KGB under Andropov and frequently expressed his respect for him. Ten years after a plaque honoring Andropov was torn down from the walls of Lubyanka, Putin, then prime minister, reinstalled it.

Andropov's office at Lubyanka was kept as it was during his leadership, a kind of museum, with his dark wood desk at one end of the large room, a huge conference table in the middle, and a screen at the other end that could light up to show maps and other presentations Andropov used in briefings with other senior officials.

Our visit had been planned a few days earlier. Knowing I would be visiting the famous headquarters, I had brought along a small gold FBI pendant given to my father in 1952, to mark ten years of service. My mother had given it to me after he died. On the front, in the middle, a sword stood vertically, supporting balancing scales of justice on either side; over the top, the inscription "Fidelity, Bravery, Integrity." On the bottom was inscribed the year 1908, when the FBI was founded, and on the back, "Federal Bureau of Investigation, V. G. Dougherty, in recognition of 10 years of faithful and loyal service, 1952."

As I took it out of my purse, I noted with some irony a similarity: the KGB insignia featured a sword, standing vertically on a shield, overlaid with the Soviet hammer and sickle. No scales of justice. I quietly took the pendant, held it tight, placed it gently but briefly on Yuri Andropov's desk, and said to myself, silently, "Well, Vinnie, you finally made it here."

DO SVIDANIYA, LENINGRAD!

As a student in Leningrad, during that winter-to-spring semester in 1971, I was experiencing firsthand the control the Communist Party exerted on every aspect of life in the Soviet Union. I knew the government read every letter we sent home or to friends in the West. Two letters and a birthday card that I planned to send to my Irish friend Dónall back in Ann Arbor went missing.

But the ideological control went even deeper. For my term paper, due at the end of the semester, I had chosen what turned out to be the heretical subject of what I thought were similarities between the Russian writer Anton Chekhov, to whom I felt a deep attraction, and the Impressionist painters. My Russian professor thought it was an odd, almost ridiculous subject. To his credit, however, he judged me on my Russian language skills and not on the content of the paper.

The cultural life of Leningrad, although heavily controlled by the Party, was extraordinarily rich. Even if the subject might be held firmly in line by the censors, the talent and creativity of Russian actors and musicians could not be. There, in Leningrad, I had my own creative birth, exposed for the first time to world-class opera, concerts, art, and literary lectures. I found it intoxicating, and it never stopped being that for me; even the smell of books—cheap Soviet editions with their brittle paper and pungent odor of paper glue—was alluring. Twenty years later, as CNN's bureau chief, my favorite thing to do, just by myself, was to buy a ticket to the Moscow Conservatory, where Pyotr Ilyich Tchaikovsky had been a professor, settle into the deep wood chairs with their velvet seats, and abandon myself to the emotions the music conjured within me.

My letters to Dónall became a way of collecting my thoughts and impressions of Russia, of the people I met, the experiences I had, and of the physical landscape. "Right now, I'm sitting on the rocky beach at the Peter and Paul Fortress," I wrote in mid-April, halfway through the semester.

The weather ever since we got back has been excellent, although a bit cold. In the 50s but with the most fabulous sun and cloudless skies. The city really grows on you. Looking out from here I can see a whole panorama of the city—St. Isaac's Cathedral, the Stock Exchange, the Admiralty. And now that winter is over (we hope), the buildings are being painted. They're uncovering bushes and trees from the protective pine branches they cover them with, and people already wear bathing suits at the beach near the Fortress. Even when it's in the 30s (Fahrenheit)! But what's really amazing are the people who go swimming already. They literally have to push the ice out of the way. The ice here has almost entirely melted, but now the ice from Lake Ladoga is coming down the Neva and actual icebergs stick near the shoreline. I suppose those people are nothing compared to the "Walruses" who, in the middle of December, cut out a small swimming pool in the ice on the Neva (which you can walk across, the ice is so thick) and go swimming.

By early May, we American students were tired, physically, emotionally, and psychologically. I was still trying to gain back the weight I had lost after eating my Soviet roommate's cooking-oil-soaked pancakes. We had our final exams: composition (my paper on Chekhov and the Impressionists), translation, phonetics, and grammar. Although challenging, as I told Dónall, I was still able to "spend my time in pleasant debauchery" with Russian friends, in bars and theaters.

On May 29, 1971, after four months at the university, our course had come to an end. We packed up, thanked our professors, and I took one more long look across the Neva at the Hermitage. At the airport, going through customs, the guards ordered my sister Pam to give them her handbag. In it was her address book. She waited, nervously, for about an hour while they, undoubtedly, copied all the names and numbers of Russian friends, then handed it back. It was a valuable lesson I never forgot. I silently said "Do svidaniya" ("Good-bye") to Leningrad and to Russia, not knowing if that literal translation of "until we meet" would ever come true.

As it turned out, it would—many times over, for the next half-century.

A PARALLEL EXISTENCE

I would see Tanya and Sergey, too, many times over the years. They moved from their communal apartment into a faceless, Soviet-style block apartment farther out from the city center. They had more room, but the brutal blankness of the buildings was depressing. These were brief trips, usually connected with work, where we talked, and ate. (No smoking and no drinking, at least on my part; I had stopped drinking in 1978.)

I thought about them frequently, and as time passed, the feeling grew that I had to talk with them, and see them, again. My memories were still vivid, but I needed to understand, from the perspective of five decades, what *they* thought about our time together, what they understood about their country, so utterly transformed from the time that Pam, Russ, and I climbed aboard that tram and headed for their tiny apartment across the Lomonosov Bridge.

In 2017 I visited Tanya and Sergey in their house on the outskirts of St. Petersburg, where they had long since moved from their Soviet apartment. I found them waiting for me on the sidewalk leading to a rambling one-story "dacha" (cottage), surrounded by fruit trees and a vegetable garden tended by Tanya. As I entered, I braced for the acrid smell of papirosi cigarettes, but found instead the enveloping aroma of borsch, and, on the table, a spread of fresh tomatoes, black bread, pickles, and an assortment of sausage and other meat, served with traditional black Ceylon tea, not vodka.

I should add a note on the word "borsch." The pronunciation in Russian—or Ukrainian—is the same, but in English, it is spelled at least three different ways: borsch, borshch, borscht. I prefer "borshch," which is closer to the correct Russian pronunciation, but I have bowed to the general consensus on "borsch." However you spell it, I adore it.

Tanya, looking ruddy and amused as always, let Sergey talk, as he loved to do, but humorously interjected exasperated comments from time to time.

"What did we talk about in those days?" I asked them.

For once, Tanya beat Sergey to the punch. "About everything! Music and politics and new films, books, records, and we drank . . . How many years have gone by!"

Sergey, too, measured time in drinks. He recalled our first encounter in 1969. "In July, the twelfth of July, Tanya and I got married, and we met you just before that, and we drank with you for the first time." He laughed. "Well, we had our health, and we were in the mood!" He laughed even more, remembering our introductions at their communal apartment. "You came in and asked, 'Hello, is this where Tanya and Sergey live?' He pronounced it with a rough approximation of the accent we had in Russian—I hope banished by now—not a typical American accent, but with a touch of what Russians usually thought was the Baltics. "And I said 'Come in! Come in!' It was a completely different life."

As Sergey often did, he immediately launched into a joke:

> A Westerner, I don't know if it's a German or an American or an Englishman, gets into a taxi in Moscow and says to the driver, "Let's go!" "Where to?" the driver asks. "Turn right." "And now where?" "Now straight." And they go on for the whole day, and the Westerner looks out the window and keeps repeating: "How lucky you are! How lucky you are!" And at the end of the day, he pays the driver, and the driver says, "Can I ask you a question? Why did you keep saying 'How lucky you are?'"
>
> The Westerner's reply: "Because what I was saying was 'How lucky you are that you don't know how badly you live.'"

Sergey interrupted our conversation to take me to a back room, a bedroom with walls draped in football scarves from famous European, Russian, and even American teams. He described each one in detail, what team it was, where he'd obtained it. There was even one from the Seattle Sounders. Although I wanted to talk about Russia, he wanted to talk about America, which he had visited, unbeknownst to me, in 1990, just one year before the Soviet Union collapsed.

"So, when you're young," he eagerly explained, "you read about America, Jack London, America as a free country. I'll never forget when, in 1990, when I came down the stairs from the plane at Kennedy airport, it was the air of freedom! A friend, Yura, was supposed to pick me up but he was in Boston. And a girl came up to me in the airport and said, 'Are you Sergey?'

and I said yes, and she said, 'Yura told me to find you, and you are supposed to take me to Boston.'"

Sergey said he knew nothing about the plan and ended up spending the whole day and night at Kennedy airport because he didn't know how to call Yura. He finally found out how to get to Boston by bus and ended up at the main bus terminal at 4 a.m. "I saw a lot of interesting things there!" he marveled. "So, on my very first day in America I saw crazy people—they were drunk! They were pissing right there—so I really had to see all of that."

I suddenly had the distinct feeling I was in the middle of *Odnoetazhnaya Amerika* (*One-Storied America*), a 1935 satire by Soviet writers Ilf and Petrov. Based on their road trip across America, it was hugely popular in the Soviet Union.

"And there was a policeman standing there in a black shining uniform," Sergey went on. "He looked great with all the pockets and things, and he's standing there peacefully while around him are all these people. They knew if they were drinking out of a bottle in a paper bag, the police couldn't come up to them. And Central Park, it was amazing! But from five p.m. to seven p.m., all these people come out—"

Just like in 1969, Tanya interrupted Sergey to exclaim, "Why are you telling Jill about America?"

"Because those are my impressions, and she's interested in that!" he said, brushing her off. "So, after five p.m., these cars come up and they open their trunks and they set up these speakers and they're playing this music, and they're Black men and they have these gold chains. And at night, even if you're in a taxi, you really had to convince the driver to take that road through Central Park—they'd say, 'I'm not going!'"

With that, Sergey began pulling out old pictures he'd taken in New York, and Philadelphia, and Boston. Tanya grabbed me by the hand and led me out to the garden. Sergey followed us out, continuing his stream-of-consciousness travelogue.

"This was the best time in life, ever! Because there was such energy, such optimism. There was fresh air and hope for something. But what's happening now?!"

There, in the garden, I felt like I was back in their communal apartment, sitting at the table, smoking and drinking and talking, talking. Sergey's soliloquy confirmed my conviction that Russians, at heart, are obsessed with America. In the Soviet days, their leaders would rail against the United States and its rapacious capitalism, but even then, I would meet Russians, prevented by their own government from traveling, who dreamed of visiting America, with its skyscrapers and cowboys, an image conjured up by the adventure writings of the early-twentieth-century American writer Jack London, who became wildly popular in Russia. This fascination has dimmed over the years, and today Vladimir Putin rails against the United States, calling it "satanic." For Putin, the biggest sin of all is that America is not obsessed with Russia. "No one listened to us then," he once chastised Americans, "So, listen to us now!" He was boasting about Russia's nuclear weapons, but the complaint, to me, was more visceral.

Even now, with Putin's "war against the West," with all the Kremlin's cries of "Russophobia" and American "imperialism," Russians still dream of coming to America. An April 2024 poll by the Russian polling company, the Levada Center, showed that, among Russians considering emigrating abroad, the top country was the United States, followed by Germany, Italy, and Turkey.

Tanya, Sergey, and I went back into the kitchen, Tanya brewing more tea, Sergey and I settling in again at the table, just as we had in their tiny communal apartment decades ago.

"When we met," I reminded him, "you didn't have any hope. We all thought the Soviet Union would just go on forever."

For the first time, he told me about his family, and I began to understand his anger.

"I was born the eighteenth of July, the feast day of St. Sergey of Radonezh. And that's why I'm named Sergey. My grandfather was a real believer, a deeply religious man, and he was quite well off. When the Bolsheviks came, they took everything he had earned and saved with his hard work all his life. He wasn't a bureaucrat, a deputy or anything, simply a worker, and he and my grandmother had seven or eight children. And the Bolsheviks took everything. They put him in jail. He was in the camps [the Gulag] for eight years. My grandmother was left without a home. It was a miracle with the children. She found a little work so they could eat. Then, when my grandfather returned, he built a house with his own hands. He did that with each of his children. When one was born, he would build a house so they could eventually live there. This was in Donetsk, Mariupul, and Yuzovka [a former name of Donetsk, all cities in Ukraine]."

Sergey said he was very sorry he had never asked many questions of his grandparents. "And now they are gone! If they came back even for one hour, I would have a mass of questions!"

When Sergey was twelve, he said, his grandfather died, but before his death he managed to tell Sergey, "When you grow up, those Bolsheviks won't be here anymore. They will go away because they are anti-human, they can't exist very long." There were some who were honestly convinced of the righteousness of their cause and led the revolution, Sergey told me. "But, on the other hand, how can you have an honest Trotsky? They thought there would be a general revolution with all their slogans. They didn't care about the country or the people. They wanted to ignite a revolution. But there are no historical documents that say Russia was in a revolutionary state at that time. There aren't! And Lenin didn't know that there would be a revolution in February, a democratic revolution, that the Bolsheviks overturned."

As I sat there, in 2017, looking at friends from half a century ago, I realized that while I knew some of their pain, I could never fully comprehend it. A whole lifetime for Sergey's grandfather, stolen. Sergey himself, raised in a country that never allowed him to fully express his thoughts or deepest feelings. Instead of expanding his life, as he reached his twenties, when we met, the Soviet system narrowed his life, forcing him into internal exile within the four walls of the communal apartment he shared with Tanya and their son, Anton.

"You know, even then, internally, we had changed our lives," he said, almost to himself. "We were living a kind of parallel existence, alongside the official one. There were official things—like we knew there were marches and demonstrations—but we'd come home, turn on the music we liked, read the books we wanted to read, hang out with people we liked. And we had just this little, tiny apartment—just a little room! But all the same, inside, we were free! That's the most important thing. And maybe that's why we drank a lot of alcohol!" He laughed, ruefully. "Maybe."

• *3* •

Kitchen Debate Redux

On July 24, 1959, Richard M. Nixon, then vice president of the United States, wearing a dark suit and tie, visited the first American exhibition in Moscow. In black-and-white pictures from that time, you can see him leaning against a railing, behind which is a model American kitchen. There's a washing machine with its square glass window nearby, on top of which sits a box of SOS scouring pads. Nixon is gesturing at the shorter, stouter Soviet premier, Nikita Khrushchev, who stands next to him, wearing a loose-fitting, light-colored suit and tie, his left hand clutching a white fedora, his index finger jabbing toward the washer.

You can see they don't agree about something, and their verbal duel mushrooms into a vigorous debate about capitalism and Communism, becoming one of the memorable moments of the Cold War. The kitchen was part of a model house built for the American National Exhibition at Moscow's Trade Fair at Sokolniki Park. The house was outfitted with the latest labor-saving devices that had revolutionized American women's lives and about which Soviet women could only dream, which was, of course, the underlying message of the exhibit: Capitalism provided a better life for its citizens than Communism did. But that didn't deter Premier Khrushchev.

"How many years has America existed already? Three hundred? One hundred fifty years of independence. Well, then, we will say one hundred fifty years, and this is the level of her achievement. We have existed not quite forty-two years. And seven years from now we will be on the same level of achievement as America. And the following years, we'll continue to surge ahead! And when we overtake you at the crossroads, we'll wave back at you, very friendly!" Khrushchev smiled broadly, and this brought a wave of laughter from staff and journalists crowded round. The discussion was recorded in

43

the cutting-edge format of color TV and was shown on American networks. An edited version was broadcast on Soviet TV and thus entered the annals of Cold War propaganda as the Kitchen Debate.

The US exhibit was part of the US–Soviet Cultural Agreement, signed by both countries in 1958. The Soviet exhibit had opened in New York just a month before. In the late 1950s competition between the Soviet Union and the United States was playing out not only in terms of how advanced each side's missiles were (a subject that also came up in the Kitchen Debate) but also in regard to the quality of life for individual Russians and Americans. World War II was over, the American economy was booming, and American women, especially, were seeing the benefits of a consumer society, with washing machines, dryers, ranges, and other devices designed to make their lives easier. The Soviet Union, on the other hand, was still rebuilding from the massive destruction of the war.

The Moscow exhibit had the best that a consumer society could offer, even a fashion show and modern art exhibition, and it was a major success: 2.7 million Soviets visited it that summer and, as part of that cultural agreement, the US Information Agency (USIA) launched a series of exhibits in Russia that continued until the Soviet Union ended in 1991. The themes of those exhibits—eighteen in all—which traveled to cities across the USSR, were varied: Plastics, Transportation, Graphic Arts, Hand Tools, Education, Agriculture, Information. A large measure of their success was due to the fact that young, Russian-speaking Americans served as guides, explaining the equipment on display but, more importantly, answering questions, often personal ones, from Soviet visitors.

And so it was that Pam and I, once again, found ourselves back in the USSR, this time for six months as guides on the 1972 "Research and Development USA" exhibit. Pam had already started graduate school, enrolling in a PhD program in Slavic linguistics at the University of Chicago, moving beyond Russian to study Polish, Serbo-Croatian, and Old Church Slavonic.

I, on the other hand, after graduating from the University of Michigan, went home to my parents' house in Massachusetts, volunteered as a docent at the Worcester Art Museum, and began to read. I kept a long and growing list, written out in longhand, of all the books I devoured. I had always been interested in American history, and I dove into Bernard Bailyn's *The Ideological Origins of the American Revolution*; *Santayana on America*, edited by Richard Colton Lyon; and Richard Hofstadter's *Anti-Intellectualism in American Life*, all of which have stood the test of time in making sense of America.

I had applied to graduate school at the University of Michigan, Columbia, and Georgetown, but, in contrast to Pam, who succeeded in getting financial assistance, I did not. My parents gently encouraged me to get a job;

it had somehow escaped me that I had to make a living. My plan was to work for a year or two, get rid of some of my student debt, and finance my way through graduate school. After a conversation with my parents, I realized that, with my knowledge of Russian, the best place to look for a job would be in Washington, DC, where we had lived as toddlers. My father was happy to drive me down to start looking.

The CIA seemed like a natural place to start, but I began to change my mind when, during an interview at CIA headquarters, I asked if I could go to the ladies' room. The agent with whom I was speaking summoned a person to accompany me, who waited outside the restroom and then escorted me back.

I did not see myself as a spy. With dark hair, freckles, and blue eyes, I looked like a map of Ireland, not like a blonde-haired, green-eyed Slav, and although I spoke very decent Russian, I had an accent. After that initial interview, I concluded that I would probably end up in the basement of Langley headquarters reading Soviet agricultural magazines and filing reports that no one would ever read.

The next interview was with Voice of America, USSR Division, and that, happily, is where I eventually landed as a Russian-language broadcaster. Pam had finished her master's degree work in one year and was able to sign up for the exhibit. I was eager for another adventure in Russia.

TRANSLATING AMERICA

Both for Pam and for me, the USIA exhibit, although a challenging assignment, was a dream come true—a chance to spend half a year directly interacting with Soviet citizens, explaining America to them, traveling to cities we had never seen before. The "Research and Development USA" exhibit was designed to illustrate technological cooperation between the US federal government and private companies. Twenty-six of America's top corporations, many of which were connected to the US space program—Kodak, American Cyanamid (maker of Formica), Westinghouse, GM, and others—provided equipment, products, and artifacts. They included a mechanical arm from *Apollo 10*'s Command Module 106 (dubbed "Charlie Brown"), launched on May 18, 1969, as part of the dress rehearsal for *Apollo 11*'s landing on the moon two months later—the same landing we had watched from our dormitory in Leningrad on July 24, 1969.

The exhibit lasted a year and traveled to six cities: Tbilisi, Moscow, Volgograd, Kazan, Donetsk, and Leningrad. Pam and I were on the second half, beginning our stint as guides in July in Kazan and ending in December in Leningrad. During that year more than 2 million Soviets came through the doors of the exhibit, spoke with young Americans, picked up souvenir lapel buttons ("znachki") which promptly became collectors' items, and experienced a little bit of America, a "soft power" presentation of America's achievements in R&D.

In June of 1972 we began our three-week training in Washington, which included learning about the history of US–Soviet cultural relations as well as the technical side of the exhibit. We had to memorize, in Russian, what each part of the exhibit was about since we would be assigned to different stands where we would go through our prepared talk, then answer questions from our Soviet visitors. As we were told, and soon would learn in person, many of those questions had nothing to do with R&D. The Russians, inundated with propaganda and cut off from almost all independent sources of information, were eager to hear directly from Americans about life in the United States, including its racial inequality, the Vietnam War, and the independence of American media. We would have to explain those hot-button issues in Russian, without being defensive or combative—a challenge for most of us, in our early twenties.

In July our guide group flew from Washington to Moscow, arriving just in time for the Fourth of July party at the US embassy. It was a short visit to Moscow, but both Pam and I noticed that people on the streets seemed better dressed than two years before. There were more fruits and vegetables available, and service in stores had improved.

The next day we departed for Kazan, capital of the Republic of Tatarstan, approximately 500 miles east of Moscow. Up to now, my experience in the Soviet Union had been in Leningrad, which at times felt a bit exotic, thanks to the peculiarities of life under Communism, but in every other aspect was thoroughly European.

Kazan is an ancient city on the Volga River, at the crossroads of medieval trade routes that once stretched from Scandinavia to Iran. In the thirteenth century it was part of the "Golden Horde" Mongol Khanate, and, after the Golden Horde's destruction by Timur the Lame (Tamerlane), it became the ruling center of the Khanate of Kazan. Russia tried to conquer the Khanate numerous times. Finally, in 1552, Czar Ivan the Terrible succeeded, razing the Khan's castle and constructing on its ruins the magnificent, white-walled Kazan Kremlin (in Russian, "kreml" means "fortress") that stands to this day.

Kazan's residents were mostly Tatars, a Turkic ethnic group, Sunni Muslims who spoke both Russian and the Tatar language. We had two fellow exhibit guides, a mother and daughter, who were Tatar-Americans, and they quickly became the center of attraction. I was mesmerized by the brew of East and West, Islam and Christianity. Russian culture has been shaped by the cultures of many peoples who have been brought, willingly or unwillingly, into its empire's embrace; after all, it is not uncommon for enemies to end up adopting the mores of the people they abhor. I've always tended to romanticize things, and on the plane, strains of Russian composer Alexander Borodin's music echoed in my head, the sensuous "Polovtsian Dances" from his opera *Prince Igor*.

THE SOVIET "MELTING POT"

Kazan was my first real introduction to the question of "nationality" in the Soviet Union, an issue that remains a thorny one, even in Vladimir Putin's Russia. In Russia, "nationality" does not mean the country you live in. It signifies a distinct ethnic group, with its own culture, language, religion, and traditions. The czarist empire, and the Soviet one that succeeded it, included approximately 100 "nationalities." Melding them into a unified nation was an enormous challenge which the Soviet leaders solved in a way that was radically different from America's "melting pot."

In the United States, at least in theory, each successive wave of immigrants defines itself as "American" virtually from the moment they step off the boat. They might be Italian-American, Irish-American, or Slovak-American, but overriding that is the legal definition of every person as an "American" first, a member of an ethnic group second.

The Soviet Union had fifteen national "republics," the largest of which was the Russian Republic. But smaller ethnic groups—the Bashkirs, the Buryats, the Komi People, the Crimean Tatars—also were given their own territory, legally defined as autonomous republics and oblasts. Each did have a certain amount of autonomy, with its own language, schools, and cultural institutions like theaters and dance troupes, and, theoretically, each had the right to self-determination and even secession from the USSR. Significantly, each Soviet citizen had his or her "nationality" written in an "internal" passport (identification papers), including Jews, who were considered a nationality and had their own territory (the Jewish Autonomous Oblast, with its capital, Birobidzhan, close to Russia's border with China).

The legal basis for listing a nationality was, in theory, to protect the right of self-determination for each one, although the practical implication of this could be harsh. It often meant that the individual—for example, a Jew who was required to list "Yevrei" as his nationality—could find it hard, or even impossible, to be admitted to a top university.

The nationality issue did not die when the Soviet Union collapsed. Ethnic Russians comprised about 55 percent of the population of the USSR, and today's Russian Federation, one of fifteen independent nations that emerged in 1991 from its ashes, is approximately 80 percent ethnic Russian. To denote an ethnic Russian, the Russian state uses the word "Russkiy." A non-ethnic-Russian is "Rossiiskiy." But it's not always an easy fit, and especially in the southern Caucasus region, there is always the danger of ethnic tension.

As we would soon learn, our visitors at the exhibit in Kazan were extremely interested in knowing what our nationality was. When I told them I was American, they would try to correct me, saying, yes, they knew I was American, but what was my *nationality*? I explained that my "ethnic background" was Irish and English, using the word "proizkhozhdeniye" (meaning extraction, or ethnic background), which was technically correct, but hard for the Soviets with whom I interacted to truly comprehend.

WELCOME TO THE HOTEL VOLGA

Kazan might have had an impressive image nine hundred years previously, but what Pam and I saw in July of 1972 was a dusty Soviet city that had been officially "restricted"—closed to foreigners—until just before we arrived. The Soviet Union had dozens of "closed" cities, off limits to outsiders and foreigners, most of them military sites or nuclear facilities. Entrance was allowed only with a special visa. The residents often were forbidden to even discuss what went on in their town.

There was no "first-class" hotel in Kazan; not a good sign. The term, of course, had a different meaning in the USSR than in the United States: "Bedbugs and no services," as I put it in the first of many letters to our parents. Our "home" for a month was the Hotel Volga, a stone's throw from the Volga River, close by the train station, but this was one instance in which "location, location, location" had no significance. The lobby was hot and dirty, our room even worse. Pam and I borrowed brooms and swept up the spiders and dust from the floor to make it habitable. The curtain material covering the windows was almost transparent. I imagined the panes had last been washed around the time of the Russian Revolution. We went off to the market to buy some food and found a few tomatoes, cucumbers, and bread.

As I was writing this, I decided to see whether the Hotel Volga still exists, and, indeed, it does. I found it on Tripadvisor, at a budget-friendly $28 per night. One customer review convinced me that, even after renovations, the soul of the Soviet version of the Hotel Volga lives on: "The best thing I can say about this hotel is its location. It's not far from the train station, sporting facilities and an easy walk to the Kremlin. If your [*sic*] only looking for a bed for the night the hotel will be fine, but more than that be careful if coming here that you know what your [*sic*] getting." We guides stayed there for a month, and we certainly had no idea what was in store.

Within days of arriving, I wrote to my parents again, describing the Hotel Volga in detail:

> Normal by Soviet standards, complete with such strange things as an elevator which "only goes up"—I swear on a stack of Bibles that the desk woman told me this! Also, our floor, where all of us are staying, was closed off from the rest of the hotel. The elevator, when it was finally fixed, would not stop at the third floor, the door leading from the main staircase was locked and nailed shut on our floor, and we were forced to walk down a long, narrow passage to gain access to the back stairs! All for our "protection." We were finally able to arrange a refrigerator for our offices, but they turn it down every night to conserve electricity. It took us almost a week to get ice! This place really does have elements of surrealism from time to time.

Pam, too, was not impressed. "Kazan, as a city, although it has nearly one million inhabitants, is quite provincial," she wrote in a letter dated July 7, 1972. "It's really like something out of the 19th century, maybe the 16th, plus electricity. In the space of two blocks last night I saw women washing clothes at a pump, horse-drawn carts, and hordes of gypsies. Really, the outside world has passed Kazan by."

I soon had my fortune told by one of the gypsies at the open-air market. "You must be less naive and your prince, who is not far away, will come. A great change is coming in your life. There has been a family unhappiness recently, but all will turn out well. You will live to be 89." All that for 25 kopeks.

If Moscow and Leningrad were information deserts, devoid of Western newspapers and magazines, Kazan was even more arid. We were able to get *Newsweek* magazine flown in from the embassy in Moscow, along with embassy news bulletins. We also managed to get our weekly movie, brought back by guides who flew to Moscow weekly for food and other supplies, but the films (*The Astro-Zombies* from 1968 was one) weren't always up to my exacting standards. I did buy a decent-quality Soviet shortwave radio to listen to Voice of America and the BBC ($25 in the foreign currency store). "I consider it an investment," I wrote. "It will be invaluable."

The site in which the exhibit was housed was a spectacular feat of American engineering know-how, a geodesic dome 250 feet in diameter, designed by famous architect R. Buckminster Fuller. It was shipped to Kazan from the previous exhibit venue, Volgograd, where it had been carefully dismantled. Construction crews using cranes and heavy equipment pieced it together again, and we began assembling the stands on which we would work. It was real physical labor, using hammers and screwdrivers and other tools. We also laid the carpet: gray indoor-outdoor carpet squares that had been cleaned as thoroughly as possible but still held dust from the shoes of roughly 1 million Russians who had visited the exhibit in the previous three cities. I enjoyed the work; as a girl, I'd loved building things, and the physicality helped calm my nerves for the upcoming interaction with a daily stream of thousands of Soviet citizens.

The sun rose at 3:30 a.m., and temperatures in the dome during the day were in the 90s. Somehow we still completed the physical labor of setting up the exhibit ahead of schedule, so we set off for the beach on the Volga River. This grimy patch of brown sand would become our respite from the eight-hours-a-day, six-days-a-week work schedule. Invariably, however, we would lie there in the sun for just a few minutes before a local person or two would approach, apologize for disturbing us, and then launch into a series of questions they hadn't been able to ask at the exhibit.

AMERICAN "HOOLIGANS"

On opening day visitors were standing in line for hours before the doors opened, even though the local authorities seemed to have shut down any publicity. As usual in the Soviet Union, however, people were ingenious at communicating by word of mouth.

"So far, there has been no advertisement of our show by the Soviets," I explained to my parents. "They have advertised a Venezuelan dance troupe, a few movies, the weather, etc., but we just don't rate, I guess. This is rather typical of Soviet attempts to keep their people as removed as possible from contamination by Americans. (They referred to the guides on the first half of the exhibit as 'hooligans' in the Moscow press. Ah well!)"

I was working on three different stands: first, one outside the dome, where I demonstrated a Lincoln Continental (more on that later); second, inside, under the dome, where I explained how a Kodak Instamatic camera worked; and third—by far the most interesting for me, and one that attracted enormous attention—the one with the "Boston Arm," an artificial arm developed by Liberty Mutual that was advertised as obeying thought commands. Although definitely advanced for its time, in reality, it worked by picking up tiny electrical charges in the wearer's arm.

The Boston Arm had been developed for the US space program, but the Soviet visitors were more intrigued by its potential as a prosthetic device.

We already had noticed a seemingly significant number of people in town who were missing limbs. In a shockingly pathetic indication of the inability of the centrally planned Communist economy to provide for the needs of its people, we saw no wheelchairs. Men who had lost both legs propelled themselves about low on the sidewalks on what looked like skateboards, pushing with their hands which they bound in protective gloves. We soon learned that many of them were veterans of World War II who had been severely wounded and shipped off to Kazan to live out their days. There apparently was little or no rehabilitation and certainly no rights for the disabled.

From the very first day, the exhibit was packed. We averaged 12,000 visitors a day and, one evening, in just a half-hour, 1,500 people swarmed through the doors. Once inside they saw, literally, another world of inventions and spin-offs from the US space program used for civilian life back on Earth.

Sadly, I would later learn that a year before our exhibit opened, in spite of the Soviet Union's record of achievements in space, beginning with *Sputnik*, the nation had lost three cosmonauts in a terrible accident. For our visitors, the memory was still painfully fresh.

That doomed Soviet space mission, dubbed *Soyuz 11*, started auspiciously. Two months previously, in April 1971, the USSR had set yet another milestone: to place in orbit the world's first space station, *Salyut 1*. Cosmonauts Georgy Dobrovolsky, Vladislav Volkov, and Viktor Patsayev were the first crew to serve on the station, spending twenty-three days there. On June 30, they began the return to Earth, but when they tried to separate their reentry capsule from the station, a valve was jerked open and the capsule, with the three men in it, quickly depressurized. They died within minutes.

Our two nations were the only ones in space in those early days, and although we were enemies on the ground and competitors in space, in that human thirst to explore, we were the same. I remembered how, back in our Leningrad dorm, when an American walked on the moon, our fellow Soviet students were genuinely happy for the United States' achievement. One of my personal heroes was Soviet cosmonaut Yuri Gagarin, the first man in space, with his infectious smile, his bravery, and his trademark cheer—"Poyekhali!" ("Let's go!"). As I studied the faces of the visitors to our exhibit in Kazan that opening day in 1972, I felt a closeness, a camaraderie, simply as fellow human beings.

There were moments, however, when we seemed so different. In the first few days of the exhibit one person asked me if the US government had given us all new teeth. At first, I thought I hadn't understood the question and asked him to repeat it. He told me that all the guides' teeth looked so good; surely the government had given us all special dental treatment so we would be able to impress our Soviet visitors? I didn't know whether to laugh or cry.

Soviet dental care was abysmal, and it was painfully obvious. I assured him that these were our own teeth, and the government hadn't paid for anything.

Our time on the stands invariably began with an explanation of the display but soon developed into a discussion of life in America. Our visitors wanted to know every personal detail: How old were we? Where were we from? Was it true that it was warm in the United States year-round? What kind of education did we have?

There were many serious questions too: Could Black people go to school? Why were Black men lynched? Were all the newspapers owned by capitalists who dictated what could be written? Why was the United States bombing innocent people in Cambodia?

Questions like these required complex answers. I believed my mission was to tell the truth, and to try to explain the context of these issues as best I could. I tried to find ways to make comparisons with life in the Soviet Union, but I soon realized the gap was immense. Soviet citizens were cut off from outside information, able to watch only state TV and listen to government-controlled radio. All newspapers and magazines were owned by the government, controlled by the Communist Party. Russians described their dilemma with a famous joke: The two central newspapers were *Pravda* ("The Truth") and *Izvestia* ("The News"). As the joke put it: "There is no 'Truth' in the 'News' and no 'News' in the 'Truth.'"

Although impacted by Russia's full-scale war against Ukraine in 2022, today's Russians can travel abroad relatively freely if they have the money. Young people are on the Internet, posting Instagram pictures, watching video blogs and YouTube videos, the majority living in decent apartments and drinking cappuccinos in sidewalk cafés—at least in the bigger cities. Sadly, the Putin government increasingly is trying to control Russian citizens' access to outside information, but, comparatively speaking, it's mind-boggling to think how cut off from the world the vast majority of Soviet citizens were in the early 1970s.

Most of the questions the exhibit visitors asked were sincere, and I spent hours on the stand, engaged in fascinating and often vigorous discussions. In my spare time I had to research some things I knew little about, like trade unions and retirement benefits, although our training had touched on some of these aspects of life in America. There were, invariably, KGB "agitatori" (agitators, provocateurs) who would mill about in the crowd, ready to pounce if the visitors pressing close to the stand seemed to react positively to something we said. Eventually, I could pick them out on sight—men and women, always alone, always with their rough surliness, each question designed to challenge or humiliate. The other Soviets knew better than we guides did who these provocateurs were, and an uncomfortable pall would fall over the crowd when they started their barrage of questions.

One day, a rotund, pugilistic woman in jacket and blouse of an indeterminate dark color pushed her way to the front of the crowd and almost yelled her questions at me. "Where are you from? Who are your parents? How many children in your family?" She rattled them off like a machine gun, and with every answer I gave her, she looked more and more triumphant. Finally, she puffed herself up and hurled a loud "Vryosh!" ("You're lying!") at me. I noticed in passing that she was using the impolite form of the verb instead of the polite form, similar to the "tu/vous" forms in French, which, in Russian, is an insult to a stranger.

"Another young woman guide on this exhibit—over there on the other side—said the very same thing! She said she lives in Massachusetts, her father is an FBI agent, her mother is a homemaker, and there are six children!" Obviously, she said, we were prepped by our bosses to spout these made-up stories.

I have never been as grateful for an insult as I was at that moment. The crowd almost held its breath, shocked by her ferocity. I waited a beat and answered: "I'm not lying. That other guide is my twin sister who's working on the stand over there."

The crowd exhaled and almost, or perhaps it only seemed that way to me, applauded. They were as relieved as I was that our KGB agitator had been put in her place.

More unpleasantness was to come. We were informed by our Soviet minders that no Americans could travel outside of specific stops on buses and tramways within Kazan, an even stricter travel restriction than the usual 40-kilometer-from-the-city rule for foreigners. Twice, I was approached by people asking me to smuggle letters out of the Soviet Union, a guaranteed way to be arrested.

But there were light moments, too, like Pam's experience working on the stand displaying three cars: a Pinto, a Javelin AMX, and a Lincoln Continental. One man in the audience asked her whether Americans could buy the cars on credit. The Soviet car-buying system required paying the full amount in cash. Pam replied, "Of course." One proud Soviet piped up: "We also have a system of credit!" Another Russian turned and cracked: "Sure we do—the only difference is they buy cars on credit, we buy shirts!"

Our guide work was simultaneously exhilarating and exhausting, and it sometimes felt surreal. Right in front of us, slightly lower than our platforms, Russians would gather, attracted by the display, hesitant at first to ask questions. I would break the ice, beginning my spiel, but wishing we could just jump into the questions about everyday life. It invariably happened, as one curious person would ask where I lived in the United States. Answering that would lead to more questions, like, How big was our apartment? When I told them I lived in a house with my parents, they were astounded by the fact that we had so much space to ourselves.

Housing was a painful subject. I already knew the conditions in the communal apartment where my friends Tanya and Sergey lived. In other Soviet cities, many people lived in dilapidated buildings dubbed "Khrushchyovki," named after Soviet leader Nikita Khrushchev, who had ordered the prefab buildings to be constructed quickly in the aftermath of World War II. They were squat—usually five stories high, the maximum height according to required government "sanitary norms," built without an expensive elevator—and ugly. But they were a necessary evil. According to some Soviet estimates, 40 to 50 percent of the housing stock was destroyed in the war. The new, replacement buildings, poorly constructed from the start, quickly deteriorated, and the word Khrushchyovki was transformed into a pun, "Khrushchyobi," by combining Khrushchev's name with the word for "slum."

If the official requirements for apartment sizes and amenities like plumbing were publicized, the real state of Soviet housing was a state secret. People waited for years to get apartments. And even now, sixty years later, some of the last Khrushchyovki are being torn down to make way for better-constructed buildings.

Russians these days are not as desperate for housing as they were in the 1960s and '70s, however, and a proposal by Moscow's mayor in 2017 to demolish many of the remaining Khrushchyovki raised a howl of protest from some Muscovites, who had renovated their apartments, spending significant sums on adding European-style energy-efficient windows and other amenities. Others complained that the new buildings the mayor promised to build would be located far from downtown, raising suspicions that the whole program was a plot to give members of the elite access to valuable downtown sites for future luxury apartment buildings.

But in 1972 it was still the Soviet Union, and as I talked with our exhibit visitors, I could see that housing issues went far beyond a mere recitation of statistics. Even though my family was not rich, I often felt uncomfortable describing my parents' house, with its several bedrooms, its washer and dryer, its spacious yard and trees. I wanted to be honest and tell them what it was like, but I knew as I watched their faces that they were probably going to go home to a cramped flat in a nondescript concrete apartment building, where the hot water might not work, where all of these labor-saving devices— ironically, some of them spin-offs from the R&D programs for which our exhibit was named—were an impossible dream.

In a letter to my parents I described the sadness that sometimes would overtake me as I spoke with the visitors:

The really exhausting part is the emotional and psychological side. As I told you, Kazan was just opened this year to tourists. It's quite old and run-down, people have really been cut off and are quite poorly off, even by Soviet standards. Poor medical care is quite obvious. We've noticed many cases of uncorrected crossed-eyes, broken glasses, no dental care, skin diseases, and many amputees. So, when the Americans, in their perma-press shirts and perfume arrived, the town was taken! We get very good service in all the restaurants, we are mobbed for autographs, people stand in the hot sun for 2–3 hours to get in, young kids come back and linger at certain stands every day, etc.

But this is only one side. The heartbreaking side appears when these people, especially the young kids, ask you how your life differs from theirs, what your house is like, etc. And you have to explain a life they'll *never* have a chance to see. Just yesterday, an acquaintance of mine was led off before my eyes by a uniformed cop and a plainclothesman for giving me his address and asking some questions about the US educational system.

So, you see, it all is a bit frustrating . . . a very good experience, of course, but you almost learn more about the U.S. here in Kazan than you do about the USSR. People can rightly criticize the richness of American society, which can be accused of satiety with worldly goods. But this doesn't mean that everyone in the U.S. *has* to have two TVs or three cars. But at least the possibility of living relatively well *exists*. Here, your heart goes out to the intellectual who must waste two hours standing in line for a scrawny chicken when he could be composing music or writing a book. Often, people ask us, "Why do you need a Lincoln Continental?" I think this question *really* reveals a lot about the Soviet mentality. The point is— no one *needs* it, but it's there if you want it. You may call it disenchant- ment, or realization of the truth or whatever, but the Soviet Union is not exactly the place I would want to spend the rest of my life—I've learned an awful lot just in almost two months.

NO SEX IN THE SOVIET UNION

Kazan also turned out to be my introduction to sex in the Soviet Union. I should clarify: I did not engage in sex in the Soviet Union. In fact, I had the impression that Soviet citizens were a puritanical bunch, a presumption that turned out—as did so many of my preconceived notions about the USSR—to be utterly mistaken.

There is a humorous expression: "There is no sex in the Soviet Union." It came from the 1986 first-ever TV "tele-bridge" hosted by Soviet journalist Vladimir Pozner and American media personality Phil Donahue, a pioneer of journalism who died in August 2024. For the tele-bridge, two studios, one in Leningrad and one in Boston, were linked by satellite, with studio audiences of Russians and American citizens talking with each other. It was a revolutionary moment in television history, with participants discussing real-life issues. One American woman complained that so much of American advertising is based on sex, and asked whether Russians had the same problem. A Russian woman proudly proclaimed, "We don't have any sex, and we are categorically against that!" which, predictably, was followed by hilarious laughter. She later explained that what she was trying to say was "We don't have sex, we make love."

My adventure observing the mating habits of Soviet people began on an excursion, arranged by Sputnik Travel, to a youth summer camp on the Volga River run by the Komsomol, the All-Union Leninist Young Communist League. At the camp our young Russian friends showed us their cabins, spare but serviceable. One of them was locked and the campers explained that their buddies inside needed some "time alone," but I could eventually be allowed in. I was living a monastic existence at the time, by choice, but I soon realized they were having sex in the cabin, and that this particular afternoon pastime apparently was quite common. In another cabin a few of us girls changed into our bathing suits for a swim, and when I returned, I found one of the Russian girls holding my bra and making a pattern out of it with paper. She told me she intended to sew a bra just like mine—another "defitsit" ("shortage") product in the Soviet Union. Comfortable or attractive Western-style brassieres simply did not exist.

That was Soviet reality, but, studying Russian, I'd also learned an expression that so perfectly describes Soviet *unreality* that it made its way into English: "Potemkin village"—a fake structure, a fake experience, that's created to impress others, usually in order to hide the reality of something. Historically, it comes from the family name of Grigory Potemkin, Empress Catherine the Great's favorite lover, who ordered the construction of a fake village to impress her during her visit to Crimea in 1787.

On another trip to the countryside near Kazan, I learned that Potemkin villages had not died out in the eighteenth century but were alive and well, just a short bus ride from our exhibit site. One sunny afternoon we guides set out in good spirits, free from work in the hot exhibit hall and happy to see a bit of nature. The bus had no air-conditioning, of course, but I was charmed, looking out the windows at the small wood houses we passed along the way, painted in bright colors, some with picket fences in front.

When the bus stopped for an hour's break and a picnic lunch, some of us more intrepid guides decided we would walk as far as we could in the time allotted to see what we could see. Our Russian escorts wanted us to see only what they had planned, just the pretty dachas, not what might have been lurking in a poor village with no indoor plumbing. They tried to dissuade us from our hike, but we set out at a gallop.

It was a bright, hot day, and the fragrance of the wildflowers and tall grass baking in the sun was sweet and pungent. When we got to what we figured was the point at which we should turn back, we came upon a little cluster of simpler wood houses, with some old women, short and squat, sitting on benches, and a young girl, very pretty, with whom we struck up a conversation.

I noticed, to my surprise, that she seemed a bit dressed up, more than necessary for a hot day in the country. She also, or was it my imagination, seemed to have on a bit of makeup. I complimented her on her dress and she thanked us. "They told us you were coming," she explained.

Suddenly, it was clear: This was a Potemkin village. A real village, yes, with real people, but on our way back to the bus, we analyzed what we had just experienced and came to the inevitable conclusion that our Soviet minders had gone to the trouble of calculating how far physically fit young Americans could walk in a half-hour and warned everyone in that little hamlet that the Americans might be coming, and to put their best foot forward.

Pam always was more down-to-earth about Russia than I was, and, as is her way, painfully honest. In my heart, I was always conflicted: deeply attracted by the Russian language and culture, repulsed by the brutishness of the Soviet Union.

Writing to our parents that summer, Pam told them the work was physically taxing and emotionally draining. "In evaluating our impact on Kazan, I think that we made a lot of people (25,000 on the last day alone!) a little more aware of what the U.S. is all about," she wrote. "We've also shown them that, although their government does print a lot of information about America, it presents far from a complete picture. For example, every Russian knows about unemployment in the U.S.; now they know from us about unemployment compensation. At the very least, we've shown these people that there is more than one way of thinking and working. Everyone in the city knows that we did not particularly like Kazan, and during the last week, they were trying to pinpoint exactly why. I really felt bad, because most of the people are extremely warm and hospitable and would give you the shirt off their back. You don't want to insult people by telling them that they live in a prison, which is a slum (also, you don't want to be kicked out of the Soviet Union), so what can you do?"

DONETSK

Working as guides on US Information Agency exhibits, answering questions for hours from Soviet citizens, living for a month at a time in the cities the exhibit toured, buying food at the local market—all of it gave my sister Pam and me a unique insight into life in the USSR. And now, we would see another side of Soviet life—in Ukraine.

Our next city was Donetsk, in what was then called the "Ukrainian Soviet Socialist Republic." We were now in the Donbas coal-mining region, the center of the Soviet Union's heavy industry manufacturing, producing iron and steel.

"Our hotel is quite nice, immaculately clean and well located," I wrote home. "We even have our own private dining room! Although most people had billed Donetsk as the Gary, Indiana, of the USSR it's not at all like it. The city has a population of roughly one million and, although the central city is surrounded by mines, it is untouched by their grime—everywhere there are parks, flowers, quite well-stocked stores, and a nice atmosphere generally. It's a relatively young city, founded in 1869 by an Englishman named Hughes who carried the first patent on iron smelting to the Ukraine. It was first called Youzifka, then Stalino, when it was Khrushchev's base of power. It's obviously quite wealthy and industrialized. People are much better dressed than in Kazan!"

As I reread this letter, half a century later, my heart sinks. Donetsk—a key city in what since 1991 has been the independent nation of Ukraine—is now occupied by Russia, illegally declared the capital of the so-called "Donetsk People's Republic." Russia is waging a vicious war against Ukraine, something inconceivable when we guides arrived there in September of 1972.

As soon as the exhibit opened, I could see it would be a different experience from Kazan. I was beginning to comprehend the vast differences among the fifteen Soviet republics that stretched from Europe to Asia. "It's becoming harder to answer our visitors' questions," I wrote, "because they ask much more sophisticated questions, and also phrase them more intricately. The youth, especially young boys, are sometimes quite outspokenly liberal and pro-Western. Almost all of them listen to Voice of America, and some even listen to Radio Liberty."

Even Pam, who had more of a jaundiced eye toward our Soviet experience, was warming up: "More people in Donetsk are unbelievably friendly—they actually smile—and they know a lot more about the U.S. It's much easier talking with them because we can eliminate the very basic facts and start on a higher plane. For example, in Kazan, it took us two weeks to convince people that unemployed people in the U.S. do not starve; here in Donetsk, people want to know, "What is the average unemployed compensation?" These people are a lot more relaxed with Americans. They'll tell you if they like a product that they see at the exhibit, and they'll criticize (carefully!) their own way of life."

The KGB provocateurs, however, were more organized than in Kazan. "It's usually a rather sleazy 30-year-old man," I explained to my parents, "who comes up (this happened yesterday) say, to a computer stand and asks the guide what the computer can do. When the guide explains, the provocateur comes out with a question like 'Oh, so could it calculate how many innocent children American troops have killed in Vietnam?'"

In between cities we were able to travel on our own for two weeks, while the engineers moved the exhibit's geodesic dome by rail to the next city. For our first journey, Pam and I chose the Baltic republics of Estonia, Latvia, and Lithuania. For the second, we headed for Central Asia. I was astounded by the vastness of the Soviet Union, with more than 8.5 million square miles, the largest country in the world. Unlike the United States where you can find regional differences—for instance, between Texas and Vermont—the USSR joined together more than 100 distinct ethnic groups. Traveling through the Baltics, and then Central Asia, felt not only like moving through different countries but like moving through different centuries.

From Turkmenistan, we sent a postcard home: "We are now in Ashkhabad, capital of Turkmenistan, just east of the Caspian Sea. Ashkhabad is a young city, founded in 1881 as a frontier town on the Iranian border. We are very close to the border; just out our windows rise very high mountains that form the border with Iran. Ashkhabad is smack in the middle of the Kara-Kum desert, the largest in Central Asia, and survives only thanks to the longest canal in the world. Half an hour out the main street from our hotel the city ends, and the camel herds begin."

As we explored the city we noticed four radio towers. "What is this?" I wrote. "No industry to speak of (except rug weaving), physically a dust bowl out in the middle of a desert and kept alive by the Kara-Kum canal . . . what for? Well, it's a real military city. One night we were awakened by the sound of tanks, soldiers marching, and orders barked . . . all in preparation for the Nov. 7 celebration of the Great October Socialist Revolution (but at 2 a.m. and down the main street?). Sometimes it's a bit tense taking pictures because you never know when a soldier or army vehicle will step into the picture (forbidden!) or whether someone will be there telling you to stop taking pictures of the slums."

On our next trip, we headed for Lithuania, more than 2,000 miles away. In Vilnius, a British friend introduced us to young Catholics active in the

Lithuanian liberation movement. I recalled from my childhood reading about the repression of Catholics. In a letter home I described the people we met: "One guy and his wife frequently travel, ostensibly on museum business (he is an artist), but actually are meeting with national minorities in the USSR, urging them to retain their traditions and resist Russification.

"Our new Lithuanian friends were so kind, sincere and dedicated," I wrote, "that it was sad to think of what I would do in their place, seeing my country being taken over by the Russians, but not being powerful enough to take any decisive counter measures. Lithuania and Estonia are definitely the least Russified of the Baltic states!"

Held fast in the iron grip of Communist repression, some republics still managed to preserve some of what made them unique. The Baltics, despite the repressive internal security, still felt like Western Europe. Central Asia, with its Turkic languages and Muslim religion, was filled with color, aromas, and spicy food. And yet, one of the deepest sources of pride for some Soviet citizens was their belief that they were part of something big and powerful and important, a united Soviet people. The lyrics to a pop hit from 1972 captured the emotion: "My address is not a house or street; my address is the Soviet Union."

Two decades later, when the Soviet Union was no more, the lyrics became an ironic postscript. More recently, in an era of increasingly popular post-Soviet nostalgia, inculcated by the Kremlin's propaganda, they express for some Russians a deep longing for that camaraderie, and the swagger of a former superpower.

A JOB AT "THE VOICE"

Throughout the six months of the exhibit, I was waiting to hear about a job I had applied for as a Russian-language broadcaster at Voice of America. The long process of language testing, interviews, and background security clearance were over. My first in-person challenge was presented by the man who eventually hired me and became my mentor, Vladimir Mansvetov, chief of the features branch of VOA's Russian Service.

A true intellectual in the Russian tradition, Mr. Mansvetov and his family fled Russia for Prague after the Bolshevik Revolution. His father was a writer, a political leader of the Russian émigré community, and, still in his teens, Vladimir became a poet. Literature was his lifelong pursuit. In 1940 he fled Nazi-occupied Prague and settled in the United States. He joined Voice of America the year it was founded, in 1947.

He was an elegant man, tall and thin, who seemed to always have a cigarette in hand. (In those days you could smoke in the office.) "What kind of work are you doing now?" he asked me. At that point, I was still at home with my parents, volunteering in the art museum.

"Go back and write a radio script about that job," he told me.

I had no idea how to write a radio script, but I cobbled together some thoughts. It apparently did the trick, as I soon found out.

The closest I had come to real journalists was while working on the USIA exhibit in Donetsk, where CBS had taped a short report for the evening news. The correspondent was Murray Fromson. I was one of three guides he interviewed. Fromson kindly invited Pam and me, along with a few other guides, for dinner at his apartment when we got back to Moscow. On our next trip to the capital, we took him up on it. His wife Dodi made spaghetti, and we were lucky enough to share an evening of conversation with them, along with two giants in the world of foreign correspondence currently working in Russia: Hedrick Smith of the *New York Times*, and Robert Kaiser of the *Washington Post*.

Kaiser was posted to Moscow in 1971, so he had just a year under his belt in the capital when we met him, but in 1976 he wrote his perceptive explanation of the truth behind the myths about Russia, *Russia: The People and the Power*. Hedrick Smith's masterpiece of reporting that reads more like a novel, *The Russians*, was published the same year. I already was a fan of both journalists, who approached Russia—so vast and complex—from a human perspective. I had never studied journalism, except for one course I took at Michigan and promptly forgot, but I did love literature and reading.

Working as a guide on the exhibit, I was beginning to develop tools that are useful, even necessary, for journalists, although I didn't think of it in those terms. I enjoyed striking up conversations with strangers, engaging them in dialogues about themselves. I also, by nature, loved to explain things to people. Even as a kid, I would run home to my mother and tell her what had happened on the way to school, what I'd observed, and why it was important. If I hadn't become a journalist, I probably would have become a teacher. Years later, I would do both.

And there, right at the end of the exhibit, in the last city, Leningrad, I received a sign from the heavens that I, myself, was headed toward a career in journalism. I received official notice that I was hired at Voice of America as a Russian-language broadcaster. My first day at work would be February 1, 1973. My salary: $9,053 per year. We packed up the exhibit, carefully cleaned the *Apollo 10* command module, and headed back to Washington.

• *4* •

Smoking on the Job

VOA job offer in hand, I needed to find a place to live in Washington, DC. I found a studio apartment in Dupont Circle, bought a white, three-speed Raleigh bicycle, and mapped out my route to Voice of America, located in the HEW (Department of Health, Education, and Welfare) building across from the National Mall at 330 Independence Avenue SW.

Walking through the newsroom on my first day at work, I noticed that many staff members were smoking cigarettes, including Mr. Mansvetov, who had hired me. It was legal in those days, and it created, I felt, a very Russian atmosphere. I didn't smoke, but I thought it could improve my writing style. I bought a pipe and some expensive tobacco and lit up. This, of course, was not what an average twenty-four-year-old American woman did in those days, but then, being an average twenty-four-year-old American woman was the last thing I wanted. I saw myself as a woman of the world, polished by her sojourns to the capital of exoticism, the Soviet Union. Soon, some of my male colleagues at VOA were stopping by my desk, giving me hints on how to fill the bowl, tamp down the tobacco, and keep the pipe lit. It all felt very Tolstoyan.

My Russian language skills were good, but I had never sat in front of a radio microphone, broadcasting live to listeners in the Soviet Union. I was petrified. The Russian service provided a tutor, a man who formerly was involved with the theater, who drilled me in proper pronunciation and more fluid reading, but I was afflicted with a bad case of "mic fright," as I later learned it was called.

I began having a dream that recurred regularly for years. I am in a massive gymnasium at the University of Michigan. I am standing in a line with hundreds of other students. We are snaking our way around the perimeter of

63

the gym and, every few yards or so, a teacher hands us a piece of paper with something printed on it. Everyone gets a paper but me. The teachers assure me: "You'll get yours farther on . . . just keep walking." But as I get farther and farther around the gym, I am the only one left empty-handed.

Finally, I am at the head of the line. A professor hustles me forward, directing me to sit at a small wood table in front of a gigantic microphone. "But I don't have anything to read!" I protest. On the wall ahead of me is a clock, its hands counting off the seconds. As the hands strike 12, another instructor raises his index finger and points at me: "You're on!" I open my mouth and—nothing comes out.

It was a nightmare, but it actually happened to me during my first month at VOA. It was my turn to read the news bulletin. I collected my stack of news headlines, opened the door to the studio, took my place at the microphone, and steadied myself to begin reading at the top of the hour.

The engineer pointed at me and . . . I was speechless. My heart was racing, and I felt as if I couldn't breathe. He looked at me, confused, then realized I was panicking. He cut the mic, began broadcasting some music, and I stood up, mortified. Walking down the corridor to my office, I felt like a failure. I wanted to run home and hide in a closet. Or quit my job.

I loved the process of writing, but no matter how many wonderful scripts I wrote, broadcasting live was a terrifying experience for me. And yet, there was no alternative. It was what I'd been hired to do. So, I kept at it, steeling myself, praying I wouldn't freeze up again. I never shared my fear with anyone. Eventually, the terror subsided—at least, enough to do my work—but it plagued me for decades, and almost derailed my career in journalism.

I was one of a handful of Americans working in the Russian service. We bonded over the uniqueness of working in a microcosm of the Soviet Union, which included bearing witness to the internal divisions in Soviet society that lived on, even in capitalist America.

I would arrive at work, invigorated by my bike ride, and greet Olga (the names have been changed to protect the innocent), who sat near the entrance to the office. "How are you?" I would ask. "Oh," she replied, "I'm furious at that Boris—what an idiot! He understands nothing about literature. And I am convinced he has sympathy for the Communists!"

I soon understood that the Russians who had left Russia before World War II or were the children of émigrés who had fled the Bolshevik Revolution considered themselves superior to more recent newcomers. The fact that some of them were Jewish, while the earlier émigrés were Russian Orthodox, added another dimension. Some were dissidents in their native country, with their own ideas about "fighting Communism." They had come from various republics in the Soviet Union, and some carried with them ethnic prejudices and grievances. Many years later, this would help me understand the adage that if you have two Russians, you'll end up with three political parties. The biggest threat facing liberal opposition political groups that emerged at the end of the Soviet Union often was not from the Kremlin, but from their internecine fighting with other opposition groups.

At VOA, perhaps because as an American I had no emotional stake in those "family feuds," I was more fascinated than repulsed by the battles. Everyone I came to know had a complex personal history. All were born and raised in the USSR. Many fled via circuitous paths, taking refuge in France, in Turkey, in Harbin, China. Almost all had surmounted poverty, political repression, or physical danger. Everyone seemed to have a story more intricate than the plot of any thriller.

They had an ironic and, for some, a cynical sense of how the world functions, how life can turn out in unimaginable ways, but even if some were difficult to deal with, outspoken or impolite, I grew to respect them for the sheer willpower they had to have to survive. They seemed more emotionally complex than my American friends, and my social life soon revolved around friends from the Russian service. Dinners were transformed into literary debates. Romantic affairs simmered beneath the surface. The guests might include a poet, a writer, a Georgian prince strumming a guitar.

During the day, I was getting an education in broadcast journalism, specifically radio. VOA was broadcast on shortwave radio, included with most Soviet-made radios, in order to cover large distances in the USSR. Many Soviet citizens, however, used shortwave to get banned news of the outside world—or about their own country—by surreptitiously listening to foreign broadcasts, primarily the British Broadcasting Corporation (BBC), West Germany's Deutsche Welle, VOA, Radio Free Europe, and Radio Liberty. The last three were funded by the US government, and the Soviet government spent millions of dollars on "jamming" the signal.

In his "insider's account" of that information war, Alvin Snyder, former director of the US Information Agency's satellite TV service, Worldnet, traced how the Soviets, under Stalin in 1948, began jamming VOA and the BBC broadcasts. Jamming was done by emitting electronic noise—high shrieks and low-pitched growls—on the same radio frequencies that Soviet citizens were trying to tune in to, making it impossible to hear what was being said, or played. An astounding 10,000 Soviets were employed in the effort.

In his book, *Warriors of Disinformation: America's Propaganda, Soviet Lies, and the Winning of the Cold War*, Snyder described how "almost every Soviet town with a population of more than 200,000 had a 'jamming center' where noise was brewed, then transmitted from another location. By the mid-1950s there were 2,000 jamming stations in operation."

It was only in 1987, during Soviet leader Mikhail Gorbachev's policy of *glasnost*, that the USSR stopped jamming VOA broadcasts.

Listening to shortwave radio broadcasts on VOA at home was permitted, but playing broadcasts outside, where others could hear them, was against the law, and those who did risked arrest. But some Russians, even in the worst of the old Soviet days, managed to create their own internal freedom. In the mid-1980s, during a trip to the Soviet Union, I met a man who was a jazz lover, although this label doesn't even begin to capture his fascination with that quintessentially free American musical form. When I visited him in his Leningrad apartment, he immediately led me over to a tall, narrow card-file cabinet, like the ones you used to find in libraries, made of wood, well-worn.

"Coleman Hawkins, I love his music!" he exclaimed. He pulled out a drawer and flipped through the dog-eared oblong white cards on which he had written in small Cyrillic letters his own liner notes about recordings by Hawkins, and still more for other artists—Louis Armstrong, Count Basie, Ella Fitzgerald—each listing their name, songs they had recorded, the titles of albums and labels, dates recorded. It was this man's own personal library of the history of jazz.

When I asked him where he had gotten all that information, he told me he listened to Willis Conover's *Jazz Hour* on Voice of America. Conover, a deep-voiced host with an encyclopedic knowledge and love of jazz, was a mega-star in the Soviet Union. His daily broadcasts on shortwave radio were jammed by the Soviet authorities, so my Russian friend often could catch only a snippet of the music, along with fragments of information about the recordings. The time and effort it must have taken for him to collect and organize that information astounded me.

Over the years, I met other Soviet citizens who, in that same single-minded, almost obsessive way, sought out the information they needed, or simply wanted, sometimes at their own peril. An estimated 28 million Soviet citizens tuned in to VOA at least once a week, according to a Harvard University study conducted in the 1970s. They were thirsty for information, such a valuable and dangerous commodity to the Communist authorities that they kept it literally under lock and key. Printing presses were owned by the government. Radio and television stations were government-run. Typewriters and photocopiers were accessible only to certain trusted Party members. I once was detained at passport control in Moscow when they discovered that I had a "samizdat" copy of lyrics by the singer-songwriter Vladimir Vysotsky, a typed carbon copy. The border control officers forced me to sign a document attesting to the fact that I was trying to take illegal copies out of the Soviet Union before they allowed me to board my flight.

The United States waged its propaganda war against the Soviet Union with what Snyder described as a "full-service public relations organization, the largest in the world, about the size of the twenty biggest US commercial PR firms combined." It included the US Information Agency, Voice of America, and Radio Free Europe / Radio Liberty (RFE/RL). "Its full-time professional staff of more than 10,000, spread out among some 150 countries, burnished America's image and trashed the Soviet Union 2,500 hours a week with a tower of babble comprised of more than 70 languages, to the tune of over $2 billion per year." (Al Snyder was clever, as I learned after I met him, so this is a pun on the biblical Tower of Babel, the ancient myth and parable meant to explain why the world's people speak different languages.)

US government–sponsored international broadcasting ignited debate right from the start. As Mark G. Pomar explains in his book, *Cold War Radio*, there were those who believed that Russian-language broadcasting was a tool of "unconventional warfare" aimed at communicating directly with Soviet audiences, to help them think independently and, thus, undermine Communism. But how to do that?

"Did VOA and RFE/RL need to target Soviet crimes, economic failures, and aggressive foreign policy? Should the two radios focus on life in the West, thereby exposing the shortcomings of the Soviet Union only indirectly, or should the broadcasts dwell on Soviet history and domestic problems?" Pomar writes. "And should the radios accept the label of propaganda or resist it?"

THE *NIGHT OWL* SHOW

Sitting at my desk, twenty-four years old, writing scripts and choosing records to spin, I was blissfully unaware of the magnitude of that debate, and my listeners didn't seem to mind it either. I personally received letters from Soviet citizens who said they enjoyed my book reviews and music broadcasts. One of the most popular VOA programs was the *Night Owl* show, broadcast at midnight, Moscow (4 p.m., Washington, DC, time). It was a mix of music, news, and discussions about culture and life in America, much like the kind of discussions I'd engaged in while a guide on USIA exhibits in the Soviet Union. In spite of my mic fright, I almost enjoyed hosting it when it was my turn, opening the show with the phrase "Good evening! At the microphone is Jill Dougherty"—an impossible name to pronounce in Russian—"Welcome to the *Night Owl* show!"

I learned how to do interviews, recording them on a Nagra portable tape recorder. I learned to splice tape and add music with the help of the studio engineers. My first trip was to the Grand Ole Opry in Nashville, where I did a report on country music. Country music was as foreign to me as it was to Russians (I was listening to jazz and R&B), so I explored the genre along with my Soviet listeners.

Reading the news, I noticed we had a significant amount of coverage focused on Africa. I soon realized it was in response to the Soviet Union's involvement, including military, in countries like Angola, Ethiopia, and Uganda. The objective was to spread worldwide Communism, project Soviet influence throughout the developing world, and counter the West's political and economic interests.

Postcolonial Africa became another venue for Cold War proxy fights. The Soviets trained guerrilla fighters and supported an attempted countercoup in Ghana. In 1960 the United States and Belgium helped depose the left-wing head of Zaire, Patrice Lumumba. I now understood better why I met several Russian officials who spoke perfect Portuguese, why Moscow created Patrice Lumumba University to train promising young African leaders in Marxism–Leninism, and why other African students were living in my dormitory at Leningrad State University.

As the USSR collapsed, that influence waned, only to be restored by Vladimir Putin, who attempted to strengthen ties with the so-called "Global South." The purpose was similar: to counter Western influence, exploit Africa's natural resources, and revive the Soviet Union's claim to make common cause with "anticolonialism." Putin used many of the same tools the Soviets employed: disinformation, interfering in elections, and the services of mercenaries from private military contractors like Yevgeny Prigozhin's Wagner Group.

Al Snyder was a frequent visitor to the Russian service. He would talk with the staff, and I began chiming in with my views of Soviet propaganda and how VOA was trying to counter it, citing my own experience on USIA exhibits in the USSR.

A few years later, Snyder left government service and became the executive news producer of the NBC-owned-and-operated TV station in Chicago, WMAQ-TV. One day, out of the blue, he telephoned me and asked whether I had ever considered working in television. I was happy at VOA, but, after four years, it had become routine—except for minor panic attacks as I prepared for going live on air. I told him I would be interested and soon flew to Chicago to be interviewed for a job. While I now had radio skills, TV was on another technical level. They sent me out with one of the most experienced cameramen, Charlie Boyle (nicknamed "CB"), and he patiently rolled tape, over and over, as I tried to record a "stand-up" for a trial report on skyrocketing coffee prices.

I was shocked when I got the news that I was hired. I gave my supervisors at VOA notice, packed my bags, and moved to Chicago in early May 1977. I was used to the relatively mild climate in DC, but I did take along a raincoat and a sweater, just in case. I would need them.

DISCOVERING AMERICA

Arriving in Chicago was like rediscovering America. Up to this point, whether I was in college, on the exhibits in the USSR, or at Voice of America, I had been living in a Russian cocoon. Washington was its own kind of silo, where my friends were fixated on international events, especially ones focused on the Soviet Union.

The "Windy City" did have some similarity to Russia, with its bitter winters and scorching summers, and it even had ethnic neighborhoods, like Ukrainian Village, where I could buy dark rye bread. But the world of local television was, for me, a foreign country. WMAQ had several top-notch journalists like Carol Marin and Ron Magers, but its focus was on local news.

I started out as a producer, learning how TV worked, going on shoots with camera crews, writing scripts and news reports for the reporters under whom I worked. One year later I, myself, became a reporter and began covering fires, plane crashes, and local politics, as well as numerous human-interest stories. I spent hours on the streets in the dead of winter, occasionally sprayed with water from fire department hoses that quickly turned to ice. One St. Patrick's Day—a big holiday in Chicago—I ended up in an Irish bar, doing a live shot. As the anchor introduced me, one of the bar patrons gleefully poured beer over the right sleeve of my plaid wool blazer.

I had no interest in local news, but I learned a lot about television, especially the technical innovations that were transforming broadcast journalism. WMAQ, one of the largest and most successful stations in the country, led the way. When I arrived, they were still recording feature stories on film. We would go on shoots with what we call a "three-man band": a cameraman (they were almost all men), a lighting technician, and a sound tech. We edited those features in a film-editing suite, where an experienced editor, just as in the movies, would screen long reels of film, cut it into spaghetti-like segments, and splice them together, careful to avoid "jump cuts"—an edit that breaks the sequence of an action—something that, in those days, was considered a faux pas in film editing. The crews were old-school perfectionists, always wearing sports jackets and ties. I soon realized they were artists, and I spent as much time with them as I could, quizzing them about the entire process.

Within just a few years, however, the station had switched entirely to videotape, and the three-man crews were down to two-man crews. Gone was the lighting expert, and soon, the sound tech would be eliminated too. The videographer was on his own. In time, it changed the entire look of television news. Jump cuts were done deliberately in order to create the feeling of kinetic action. Cameramen stopped using tripods; handheld, wobbly video felt more real. And then, there were live shots, live broadcasts from the field, made possible by the miniaturization of TV equipment and the use of microwave trucks, which would set up at the location of the news event and feed live video, via satellite, back to the news bureau.

Sometimes, the new live technology was used simply to make a report more dramatic. One of my first live shots was from a platform at a downtown station on the subway, which Chicagoans call the "L." A man had been shot, and my job the next morning was to stand on that platform where he met his demise and report "live" from the scene. The entire thing, to me, seemed ludicrous.

But there was more cognitive dissonance to come. The station had introduced a "beat" system of reporting, where each reporter specialized in a subject. My beat was called "Beat the System." The concept was that I would scope out bargains for consumers, to save them money or time—for instance, where to buy shoes for your kids on sale. I had absolutely no interest in the subject, but that was my job, so I dutifully searched for show ideas. I found what I thought was a fabulous idea at a ritzy bar in Chicago's most expensive neighborhood, the Gold Coast. To my amazed pleasure, I discovered you could get unlimited hors d'oeuvres if you bought a drink. Now, that was news I could use! I was still nervous about doing stand-ups, so I did my research for the report by quickly downing two gin and tonics. It helped to calm my mic fright, at least temporarily.

In time, however, the mini panic attacks I suffered doing live shots, plus my total lack of interest in local news, took their toll. I felt derailed, investing enormous amounts of time and energy in work that held no meaning for me. There was no one I felt I could talk with, not even Al Snyder, the man who had hired me. I felt like I was letting him down.

One afternoon, he invited me into his office and asked why I wasn't including in my reports the usual "stand-up bridge"—the short on-camera appearance by the reporter to explain something, or "bridge" to another part of the story. I told him I thought the story should tell itself through the people interviewed or the pictures from the scene. While that was true, a large part of it was the fact I was simply scared to be on camera. Somehow, I just knew I couldn't admit that to anyone. What could have been done about it anyway? Al probably would have suggested talking to one of the more experienced journalists who might have gone through the same thing. But I thought I was the only one suffering from mic fright, so I kept it to myself.

One morning, about two years after I'd started working at WMAQ, the editor assigned me a story: take a camera crew downtown to Marshall Field's department store, set up outside in front of the windows, and do live shots, telling our audience how shocking it was that the windows were decorated for Christmas when it wasn't even Thanksgiving yet. I asked whether she was serious. She was.

I had been working on a story about domestic violence, a new subject the media was beginning to cover at the time. That would be shelved so I could report on the commercialization of Christmas. Something inside of me rebelled. I just couldn't do it, and I told the editor that.

She looked confused and said I would have to talk with the supervising editor. I told him the same thing. Finally, within an hour or so, I found myself back in Al Snyder's office. I think he understood my dilemma; after all, he knew me when I was at VOA, and understood how Russia and international news were my passion. But this was how local news worked.

Nonetheless, I couldn't do it, and I told him so. And then, I heard myself say: "And I think I can't do this job. I quit."

Al looked at me, shocked. Refusing to do a story was one thing. Leaving major-market television, a job that so many budding reporters would sell their souls for, seemed crazy. And it was. After all, Al was the man who had believed in me and given me an unbelievable chance at a career. Still, I saw no alternative. I signed a letter of resignation, not knowing what I was going to do next, but convinced I would not be standing in front of Marshall Field's that afternoon.

Chicago was the beginning and the end—or so I thought—of my TV broadcasting career. But it also was the beginning of something else. I had become good friends with Norma Quarles, an NBC correspondent with a storied career in broadcasting as the first Black woman to file reports for network TV. She also had a scintillating personality, and one September night she invited a large crowd from the network and WMAQ to her apartment for a party.

I arrived after a day at work, intending to stay for a while and then go home. I was in a career that typically attracts type A personalities, and I definitely was type A, but I also was shy. I noticed a woman on the other side of the room who looked different from all my TV buddies. She was glamorous and had an infectious laugh. I said hello. Her name was Valucha, and everyone called her just that, Valucha. Her full name was Vera Lucia Murgel de Castro. She was born in Brazil and was a well-known singer in town. We spoke in French, I'm still not quite sure why. I was enchanted, fascinated, smitten. I waited a week before calling to invite her for lunch, which she accepted. From that day on, we would be together for almost thirty years.

MY WOODSTOCK DAYS

While the mic fright panic attacks may have subsided, as I was no longer in front of a camera, they were soon replaced by a low-grade panic over how I would pay the bills. I set about becoming a freelance journalist. I submitted a radio story to National Public Radio, which had a lively Chicago bureau with three unique and talented journalists: Scott Simon, Jacki Lyden, and audio producer Jonathan "Smokey" Baer. NPR began using me as a stringer.

I had been an ardent fan of NPR since 1973, when I discovered it two years after it first went on the air. I had just moved back to Washington from Russia, and one afternoon, sitting on the floor of my studio apartment, setting up my elaborate home sound system complete with amplifier, mixer, turntable, speakers, and a TEAC reel-to-reel tape player, I tuned in to a radio station. It sounded like nothing I had ever heard on American radio, the reporters telling their stories with humor and intimacy. Then I heard the utterly unique voice of Susan Stamberg, who was co-hosting NPR's newsmagazine *All Things Considered*. I've been a fan ever since that day.

I found more freelance work as a Midwest stringer for *Time* magazine, and began writing travel stories and other features for the *Chicago Tribune* and other publications. It was financially precarious but personally satisfying.

I did not abandon my interest in Russia. I found part-time work with an educational travel provider called Academic Travel Abroad, accompanying tours to the USSR. It was the ideal freelance job: I was able to return to the Soviet Union, learn from the academic experts who lectured on the tours, meet more Russians, experience world-class cultural activities—and get paid well to do it.

I also was hired by the US State Department to accompany groups from the Soviet Union on official trips to the United States. Most of the visitors were legislators from the various republics, and their agendas included meeting with local and state legislators across America. The tours were designed to give the Soviet visitors an understanding of America's diversity. We traveled to Minneapolis; to Las Vegas, where one female Soviet lawmaker won several dollars in a slot machine—a thrilling experience in any case, but especially for a Communist exploring the dark heart of capitalism; and to Texas, where they met author and newspaper columnist Molly Ivins, famous for her salty humor, her irony, and her unique talent for skewering political personalities.

Our Soviet visitors were dumbfounded. Driving down long, dusty roads in Texas and visiting Ivins at her home was, I am sure, beyond anything they had ever experienced. She was, as the Russians described her, "expansivnaya," which didn't totally capture her larger-than-life persona. As we gathered in her living room, she invited them to help themselves to the large collection of alcoholic beverages she had on hand. Within minutes, everyone seemed at ease, and they soon were laughing at her hilarious banter.

I was not, by trade, a translator, but I had to do some of it on this trip, so I decided not to join in the libations. But as we were preparing to leave, I heard her bid farewell by using a phrase I had never heard in English and had no idea how to translate into Russian: "I hope you had a fuckingly good time!"

She said it with a big smile and then a huge laugh, which gave me a second to think how I could handle this. I knew only one Russian equivalent for the F-word, and I quickly noted she was using a unique adverbial version. So, I took my one obscene Russian word and quickly slapped on the linguistically correct adverbial ending. I heard a gasp and then stunned chortling from the group. One of the men, who had inhaled several vodkas, actually fell on the floor holding his stomach, laughing hysterically. I had passed my test, and the group began to treat me (almost) like one of their own.

The trips took place in the 1980s, and I began to see, more than a decade before the Soviet Union collapsed, that the underpinnings of Communist political control were weakening. On one flight I sat next to one member of the group, in his thirties, who struck me as an up-and-coming leader: charming, smart, sophisticated in a very un-Soviet way. As we chatted, he finished off several drinks and began to speak quietly but determinedly. "The whole system is screwed up," he said, in Russian. "No one believes in it anymore."

I felt he was being honest, and yet, what did that mean? I knew from my time in the Soviet Union how suffocatingly complete the government's control was, how many people lived in fear, how dissidents were sentenced to decades in labor camps or confined to mental hospitals. When I was in high school, I read Alexander Solzhenitsyn's *One Day in the Life of Ivan Denisovich* (in English). Soviet premier Nikita Khrushchev had allowed this to be published during his more open period, dubbed "The Thaw," while most of his other books were banned in the Soviet Union. In 1968, *Cancer Ward* and *In the First Circle* were published in the West. In 1973 perhaps his most famous book, *The Gulag Archipelago*, which detailed the torturous conditions in the country's labor camps, was smuggled out of the USSR to Paris and New York on microfilm.

And yet, here I was, talking with what I thought was a committed young Communist leader who told me that he no longer believed in the Communist system. My Leningrad friends had shared with me their hatred of the system.

I always thought they were a lonely minority, but my seatmate on this flight claimed that many Soviet citizens felt the same way. It was my first inkling that the Communist Party's grip was weakening, but it would take until 1991 for all of it to come crashing down.

CHICKEN NOODLE NEWS

Back in Chicago, I expanded my freelance career to include some news writing at a local TV station. The job was way below my capabilities, but it helped pay the bills. Then, in the spring of 1983, my career took a radically different direction. I received a call from the Chicago bureau of Cable News Network. "Fledgling" does not adequately describe CNN in its early days. Some dubbed it "Chicken Noodle News." Its founder, Ted Turner, was better known at that time as the brash owner of his father's Atlanta billboard business. In 1970 he created the Turner Broadcasting System, after purchasing a UHF TV station. Ten years later, with CNN, he invented twenty-four-hour cable news. Nothing like it had existed before.

With today's plethora of cable news channels, it's hard to imagine a time when American families sat down together to watch the evening news, broadcast at the same time every evening, and anchored by star journalists like Walter Cronkite. CNN set out to fill twenty-four hours a day with news—initially, quite a challenge, editorially, technically, and financially. But Ted attracted mavericks who believed in his concept of news. Many of his early employees worked without a salary for the first year.

The Chicago bureau chief, Jeff Flock, apparently had seen some of my reports for WMAQ. He contacted me and asked whether I was interested in joining the network. He later told a reporter who was doing a story on me: "We're all plagued by people who want to work in television news because they want to work in television news. But Jill wanted to report on news she cares about. In my view, she wasn't well suited for local news. She was wasted in local news."

I was intrigued by the idea of twenty-four-hour news, and had reached the point in my freelance career where I'd begun to miss the camaraderie of working with other journalists. I agreed to meet a CNN camera crew downtown where I would record a two-minute stand-up about the local founder of a civil rights group called the Rainbow Coalition. It was, of course, Reverend Jesse Jackson, who later that decade would twice run for president.

I rehearsed the stand-up over and over, met the crew in a park, recorded it, and, about a week later, was told I had the job. I was back in TV.

I was now CNN's Midwest correspondent. I was still doing some local news, since many events in Chicago—politics, business, international trade, even weather—had national significance. I also got to report on some breaking Soviet news. Premier Leonid Brezhnev had died the previous year, and Yuri Andropov, head of the KGB, took his place, only to die fifteen months later. Konstantin Chernenko filled the slot but lasted only a year before he fell victim to emphysema. It was just a quick report, putting the string of deaths in context, but I was happy the supervising editors in Atlanta had turned to me to explain Russia on air.

Ted Turner visited our Chicago bureau several times, and I soon saw that he was far more than just an adventurous entrepreneur. He was an environmentalist before people knew the word. The first time I saw him, he came through the door, passing by our coffee station with its Styrofoam cups, and hit the ceiling. "Get rid of these things!" he yelled. "Don't you know they pollute the environment?"

He considered CNN more than a domestic US network; it was an international network, and we were not just American citizens, we were citizens of the world. Referring to the United States, correspondents didn't say "we" or "our country"; we called it "the United States," "the "U.S.," or, occasionally, "America."

When I finally visited CNN headquarters in Atlanta, I saw what an international team we had, with correspondents like Christiane Amanpour (who at that time was just starting out as a lowly desk assistant in Atlanta), a British citizen whose father was from Iran. I met former Soviet citizens working for the network; reporters, editors, producers, and videographers from Beijing, Australia, Central Asia, Eastern Europe. I was inspired by our mini United Nations, which worked toward one common purpose: to give our viewers the most accurate view of the world that we could. In 1997 Ted Turner donated one billion dollars to the UN, calling it "humanity's greatest hope for a better planet for my grandchildren and for people everywhere."

My job with CNN provided another benefit: getting to know Ed Turner, the network's executive vice president (no relation to Ted), a brilliant television executive and one of the first people Ted Turner hired when he started the network. Ed took a personal interest in his staff, and I enjoyed the energy he injected into our coverage, as well as his outsize sense of humor. He was my image of a newsman, born with a "nose for news" and an uncanny ability to predict where it might break out next. CNN would be there to cover it, be it desert, mountaintop, or presidential palace. This meant dispatching news crews could present monumental challenges.

Fortunately, our equipment was changing fast. Video cameras were shrinking in size, and the twelve large anvil cases of satellite dishes and other equipment we had to ship to the scene of breaking news were being replaced with smaller handheld equipment. I loved being a part of the team, flying off to cover breaking news, even if, for me—so far—all of it had been in the United States. I longed to travel to international locations, including to Russia, places where CNN was sometimes the only news crew on the ground.

I felt increasingly that I needed more education on issues I was hoping to cover, and found what I thought was a way to do that. A friend told me about a new program at the University of Chicago called the William F. Benton fellowships in broadcast journalism, the purpose of which was, as the university put it, to enable mid-career journalists to "bring greater depth and understanding to their work." For half a year I would be able to take courses in Russian, arms control, and, for fun, Shakespeare.

I wanted to apply, but decided to check with Ed Turner first.

"A fellowship? At a university?" he bellowed. "You should be in the trenches, doing reporting, not in some academic program," he told me.

"But the program is fantastic," I protested. "I'll learn so much! With Russian and arms control, it's right up my alley!"

"If you take that fellowship, don't bother coming back to CNN," he warned.

It was a real dilemma. I sincerely thought the studies would make me a better correspondent, as well as prepare me for possible reporting on the USSR, and yet I knew Ed had a point: I needed more experience in the company beyond what I could get in the American Midwest. He was giving me an ultimatum, and that, for some reason, infuriated me. I told Ed I was taking the fellowship. He told me he meant what he said. I was out of TV again.

The fellowship program, under the direction of its founding director, John Callaway, one of Chicago's leading journalists, raised my reporting to a new level. Not only was I at one of the top universities in the country, I also was learning about the arcane subject of arms control, taught by leading experts in the field. I had a personal tutor in Russian, and in my Shakespeare course, my love of language and literature was reborn, even though the professor commented that the sentences in the papers I wrote for class were remarkably short—a trait I chalked up to writing pithy TV news reports.

When the fellowship ended, I felt ready for another step in my journalism career. I was sure it would not be at CNN, as long as Ed Turner had his way, so I returned to my freelance writing. Valucha and I had bought a small 1920s-vintage Sears Roebuck cottage in New Buffalo, Michigan, a resort community on the shores of Lake Michigan that was experiencing a rebirth due to an influx of Chicagoans looking for summer homes. Many of them were journalists, and Valucha and I began writing amusing *New Yorker*–style articles for the local paper, the *New Buffalo Times*. In our "Red Pencil Patrol" column, named in honor of the local "Red Arrow" highway, we corrected the grammar of local officials and misspellings on local signs. The paper's owner soon made us managing editors, and we delved more seriously into local politics and the mushrooming development that was transforming the community.

We began buying and renovating houses. We were good at it and made some money, but as five or six years passed, I felt more and more that I was headed down the wrong path. I enjoyed living in the country, working at the paper, and spending time with good friends, but something was missing.

We had kept a small apartment in Chicago, a relatively short ninety-minute drive away. I went back and forth once a week or so, and on the way there, I would think of Chekhov's *Three Sisters*—how Olga would cry: "Yes! Quickly to Moscow!" and Irina would chime in: "Sell the house and finish with everything here and—to Moscow!"

Chicago became my Moscow.

POSTCARD TO MY BOSS

One afternoon in the spring of 1990 I was taking my usual run in Michigan along Lakeshore Road, a beautiful jog amid giant oaks and towering pine trees. My father had died the year before and I was still feeling unmoored by the loss. As I picked up speed, I suddenly had the strongest physical sensation that he was there with me. The road was empty; I was totally alone. But I felt his presence, and a message that seemed to grow clearer as I ran: "It's time to get back to your career."

I am not superstitious or particularly religious, but I sensed deeply that he was right. Part of me almost didn't want to hear it. Michigan was a necessary experience, a refuge after years of intense study and work that had begun in high school. And yes, it was an escape from the fear I had about live shots and the pressure of a full-time job in television. But I knew that living in a small town, working at a local newspaper, and renovating houses was not my "mission" in life.

I turned around and ran even faster down the road toward home. I told Valucha what had happened, as strange as it sounded. She listened to me intently and then said: "Let's get you back to CNN."

I thought I had burned the bridge to the network and was sure Ed Turner would never talk to me again, but Valucha, always creative, had a suggestion.

"Let's write to him." She grabbed a pen and a small index card. "Okay, so you can start by saying that you made a mistake and want to come back to CNN."

That seemed a bit too direct for me, but Valucha then sketched out three boxes for Ed to choose from. "So, you can give him three options. One: No way; don't bother coming back. Two: I'll think about it. And three: Come back."

It was pretty gutsy, but at this point, I had no better idea, so I agreed. I wrote out what Valucha had suggested, put the card in an envelope, and stuck it in the mailbox.

A few weeks later I got a call. "Can you come to Washington?"

It was an auspicious time to rejoin the network. The Gulf War was igniting, and CNN made broadcasting history with its live reporting from Baghdad, correspondent Bernard Shaw announcing: "The skies over Baghdad have been illuminated." CNN was the only twenty-four-hour news network, and when the Iraqi government warned journalists to leave, the CNN team—Shaw, John Holliman, Peter Arnett, and producer Robert Weiner, along with one of the network's most experienced combat-zone producers, Ingrid Formanek—decided to stay. Their riveting live reports solidified CNN's reputation as the go-to network for breaking news, a reputation based on talented and dedicated personnel in the field, support and direction from CNN executives, and technical staff who transformed newsgathering with innovative technology.

I became a "firefighter," dispatched by supervisors in Atlanta to fill in at CNN bureaus around the world for reporters called in to cover the war. I ended up in Miami, Moscow, and Washington, DC.

And then, thanks to Charles Bierbauer, a fellow correspondent who noticed my work, I was offered a job covering the White House. Charles had covered Moscow and the Pentagon, and now was CNN's senior White House correspondent. Valucha loved Chicago, had made her own career there over many years, and yet, she said yes. Yes, she would move to Washington. It was the first of several relocations because of my career, but she never stopped me. And I never stopped being grateful.

• 5 •

A Tale of Two White Houses

In the spring of 1991 I began to report on the presidency of George H. W. Bush. I got back in TV just in time: By the end of the year, the Soviet Union would be gone.

After a months-long, in-depth background security check, I finally had the "hard pass" that would allow me to work as a credentialed member of the media at the White House. Arriving for my first day of work, pass in hand, I presented it to the Secret Service officer, then moved to the turnstile, put my briefcase and handbag on the conveyor belt, stepped through the "mag"—the magnetometer that screens for metal objects—and pushed open the small door leading to the White House driveway.

Today, as you walk down the drive, there is a mini city of booths for television crews on your right. These are semipermanent structures, sturdy tent-like enclosures that shelter the cameras, sound equipment, crews, and correspondents from rain and snow. Each enclosure has an opening behind it with a picture-perfect view of the White House.

There were no booths when I first started working at the White House. We simply stood on the front lawn, the videographer set up the camera, and we did our live shots, closer to the White House but more exposed to the elements. Once, in the middle of a live shot, I was dive-bombed by a bee that I had to swat away with a microphone.

As you walk farther down the drive, you pass the entrance to the West Wing where the president's Oval Office is located, the door protected by two Marine Corps sentries who are on duty when the president is at work. Turn left and you quickly find the door to the press briefing room and the offices of media organizations that are accredited to cover the White House. The briefing room was constructed under President Richard Nixon, who had it installed over the original White House swimming pool, built in 1933 for President Franklin D. Roosevelt, who swam as therapy for polio. By Nixon's time, the number of television networks was growing, and the decision was made—extraordinary, when you think about it—to have the media work just a stone's throw from the Oval Office. Walk through the briefing room and, at the back, you will find some media booths, which usually have just enough room for two correspondents to work, sometimes elbow to elbow.

CNN, as the newcomer back in the 1980s, was given a booth down a flight of stairs in the basement, where most of the radio correspondents and news agencies have their offices. Our booth was approximately twelve feet deep and nine feet wide, but into that space were crammed desks, office chairs, and a soundproof recording booth in the corner. There was a tiny refrigerator, to hold our lunches; however, I quickly learned we had to eat our sandwiches at the computer. Once you arrived at the White House for your shift (morning or evening), you were there until the White House press office announced a "lid," meaning no more official announcements would be issued. That, of course, did not necessarily mean there would be no more breaking news. The lid could be broken by unexpected developments, and our days and nights were long.

Valucha and I found an apartment located just a fifteen-minute walk from the north gate of the White House. Living this close came in handy when I had to get to the White House quickly. For instance, on September 13, 1994, when a man stole a two-seat Cessna 150 and flew it to the White House, crashing on the South Lawn and skidding up to the house right under the president's bedroom.

Luckily, President Bill Clinton, First Lady Hillary Clinton, and their daughter Chelsea were sleeping at Blair House across Pennsylvania Avenue as repairs were being made to the White House ventilation system.

When the news broke at about 2 a.m., I was fast asleep. The phone rang, and our producer, Sol Levine, a man with an advanced sense of humor and irony, told me matter-of-factly: "A plane just crashed into the White House." I told him it was not funny to wake me up in the middle of the night to tell me a joke.

"This is not a joke," he said.

I threw on some clothes, grabbed my running shoes, and jogged the eight blocks to the White House.

During the first few months of covering President George H. W. Bush, the stories I reported on were mostly domestic issues, especially the weak economy. Wolf Blitzer had joined the team as senior White House correspondent, and he was an excellent booth-mate: always in a good mood, ready to help whenever I asked for advice, and never bringing any pungent lunches into the almost airless space.

Breaking news from Russia soon intervened. I had not been following news from Moscow very carefully—I was overwhelmed with learning the ropes of domestic issues—but I was aware of the political ferment swirling around Soviet president Mikhail Gorbachev as he planned for a New Union Treaty that would have replaced the Soviet Union with a new entity, a voluntary federation.

THE COUP

On August 4, 1991, I noticed a report that Gorbachev had gone on vacation. As I would learn in an interview many years later, the US ambassador to Moscow, Jack Matlock, had been privately informed by Moscow mayor Gavriil Popov that senior members of the KGB, the Defense Ministry, and other officials were planning a coup. Matlock warned Gorbachev, but, he told me, the Soviet president did not consider it a serious threat.

"I had been given a warning that there was a conspiracy developing against Gorbachev," Matlock recounted. "I was asked to warn Gorbachev. And I tried to do so without naming the people involved. He didn't take it seriously. But it turned out that the people we had identified a month before the coup were, in fact, the leaders of the coup."

There was an ironic twist, he explained: "When we made that report, President Bush talked to Gorbachev on a telephone line that was maintained by the KGB and actually named my source, the mayor of Moscow. And later, the mayor of Moscow told me that he thought that that leak was one of the reasons that a full coup failed." The head of the KGB, who was organizing the coup, suddenly realized he had a leak, and he had to stop planning. "It was so poorly planned," Matlock told me. "Many of the people who were expected to do certain things, like arrest Yeltsin, simply refused to do it when the coup came."

In that 2020 interview, one of a series I conducted with former American ambassadors to Moscow as part of the Monterey Initiative in Russian Studies' Ambassadorial Series, Jack Matlock told me he had sent his first message back to Washington that the Soviet Union might break up in July 1990, eight months before it happened.

"I didn't predict it then precisely," he explained. "But I said it was possible, which I think came as a very great surprise to Washington. And I know later, now that these things have been declassified, I was told President Bush asked for an evaluation from the NSC [National Security Council]. And the NSC evaluation said that, well, the embassy had been unnecessarily alarmist."

Matlock believed that if the most progressive Russians no longer wanted to preserve the union, then the Russian republic would be better off independent of the other Soviet republics. And if Russia felt that way, the USSR was doomed, "because it was very clear that the predominant opinion in many of the other republics [was that they] wanted to leave the Soviet Union, wanted to leave the system."

Back in Washington in the CNN White House booth, I, along with everyone else in the world, including people in Russia, it seemed, was glued to reports from CNN Moscow, led by bureau chief Steve Hurst. The moment was dire; the coup was deadly real, and its leaders were bumbling. They cut the phone lines to the dacha where Gorbachev and his wife were vacationing. Back in Moscow, the leader of the coup, Soviet vice president Gennadiy Yanayev, couldn't keep his hands from trembling as he addressed a news conference.

From our Washington vantage point, events were confusing and changing fast. With a CNN Washington news crew, I headed for the Russian embassy to see what diplomats there might know about the coup, but, as I explained at the beginning of my report: "They may have a forest of antennas on the roof, but when it comes to breaking development in Moscow, the Soviet embassy is saying it's in the dark as much as anyone else."

One thing was clear, however: As Gorbachev languished in Crimea, Russian president Boris Yeltsin had seized the moment, setting up headquarters in Russia's "White House," the parliament building facing the Moscow River, just down the street from the American embassy and across the river from our CNN Moscow bureau. The coup organizers had ordered troops onto the streets of Moscow, and tanks rumbled down the wide Kutuzovsky Prospekt past our bureau offices. CNN had a ringside seat to history, able to aim its cameras on the phalanx of forces moving right under our windows straight toward the parliament building.

Ambassador Matlock was back in Washington, having served his term as ambassador to Moscow, and the incoming ambassador, Robert Strauss, had not yet arrived in Russia. The deputy chief of mission, James F. Collins, was in charge of the embassy. The coup, Collins told me, was a "surprise and a shock. It wasn't that we hadn't heard rumors of coup plotting and this kind of thing for months," he said. "We had, but you kept hearing them to the point when it was the 'boy who cried wolf' story. Nobody really had a sense that this was real."

TANKS IN THE STREETS

In that interview, Ambassador Collins relayed to me one of the most riveting accounts I've heard from an American describing what happened on the ground in Moscow, along with a clear explanation of the stakes for the United States.

The embassy, literally and figuratively, was right in the middle of the coup. The coup leaders, proclaiming they were in charge of the country, said Gorbachev was "indisposed" in Crimea; *they* were running the Soviet Union now. They promptly declared a state of emergency and ordered troops and tanks to surround the Russian White House. The nickname sounds like the official name of the US president's residence in Washington, DC, but it refers to the building's color. At the time, it was called the "House of the Soviets of Russia" and was the primary location of the Soviet government. After the Soviet Union collapsed, it was renamed the "House of the Government of the Russian Federation."

Now, with the coup-plotters holding Gorbachev and his wife hostage at his official dacha in Crimea, opponents of the coup set up their headquarters at the Russian White House. Boris Yeltsin, president of the Russian republic, led the resistance, announcing that he was defending the constitutional order as well as Mikhail Gorbachev, and refusing to obey any directives from the coup leaders.

The coup unfolded early in the morning in Moscow, Collins told me, which meant that everyone in Washington was asleep, and so, for several hours, he and the staff at the embassy, just a block away from where events were unfolding, were basically alone. "We had called our watch officers in Washington and let them know what was happening, but we didn't have any guidance."

Collins, for now, was in charge of the embassy. "That was one of the very few times that, as a Foreign Service officer . . . I actually made a decision without anybody telling me how the guidance should be implemented," he recalled. "We didn't see it as appropriate for the official representation of the United States to have anything to do with the people who had simply proclaimed themselves new rulers. We had not heard from President Gorbachev. We had not heard anything that suggested that what was being done in the name of constitutional order in the Soviet Union had any legal basis."

At about two o'clock in the afternoon, Yeltsin's staff asked Collins to come to the Russian White House and receive a message from President Yeltsin. "We were inside the barricades," he told me. "There were crowds of people, and when I went in the car to the White House with the [American] flag, I didn't know whether they were going to throw rocks or cheer. Well, they cheered. In essence, the message was asking Washington not to recognize these self-proclaimed authorities, and to stay with the constitutional order and support the rule of law and President Gorbachev."

When Collins returned to the embassy, he had a call from President Bush, who said he hoped the embassy staff was safe. "I think what I most remember telling him, was that there are many reasons it's not at all clear this coup is going to succeed, and we should be very careful and not jump to any conclusions or recognition. And we didn't, and I think . . . we were on the side of history, but also we were on the right side."

For three days Russia's fate was unclear. At the Russian White House, the tanks took up their positions, ordered by the coup-plotters to aim at the building. But the tank commander, in an act of great heroism, refused that order and directed his men to turn their tank's guns around, pointing out, away from the building. Yeltsin, in an image seared into history, climbed atop one of the tanks, pulled several sheets of paper from the breast pocket of his dark suit, and addressed his fellow Russians. He called for a "universal, unlimited strike" throughout the country. "The peoples of Russia are becoming masters of their destiny!" he proclaimed.

THREE DEATHS

As much as the White House in Washington was a crucial vantage point from which to watch the standoff in Moscow, I was eager to jump on a plane and join the CNN team in the Russian capital. Within a week, I was finally there on the streets, covering the failed coup's aftermath. Three young men had been killed, crushed by tanks, or possibly shot in a tunnel near the Russian White House. A camera crew and I set out to file a report.

"For days," I began, "parents have been leading their children on a sort of stations of the cross, placing flowers and icons, things they hold dear, even food and drink—an ancient Russian way of speeding the soul to eternal rest."

I spoke with several young people, bleary-eyed, who were still guarding a bus used as a barricade the night the boys died. If, as I noted, "some older Russians feared their young people were more interested in blue jeans than in government, the deaths of the three men seem to have sparked just the opposite."

"It's very sad for the fellows, very sad," one of the young men on the street told me. "They died defending us. The life we used to have, thanks to them, I hope, will be over, and a time of freedom will begin."

Details of what had transpired during the house arrest of Mikhail Gorbachev were still murky, but we were able to secure an interview with Russian prime minister Ivan Silayev, who described how he and five members of parliament flew to the Crimea to rescue Gorbachev.

Silayev knew the coup would not succeed, he said, but "history tells us people in that situation can do anything. They could have physically eliminated the president. That was the main danger. We wanted to save the president, save his life." The men took with them forty armed guards, but, the prime minister said, they were not prepared for combat operations. "We knew if shooting broke out the president could have been physically eliminated on the pretext that we started it. We anticipated all sorts of events, but we did not open fire."

The plane carrying the delegation landed at the airport located one hour from Gorbachev's dacha in Crimea. They piled into two cars, leaving their guards behind, and drove at breakneck speed. The president's bodyguards had been alerted.

"We walked in, the president walked in . . . We embraced, and we saw that Gorbachev was in good health."

Gorbachev wanted to tell them what had happened to him, but there was no time. "We said, 'Mikhail Sergeyevich, we can talk later, but tell Raisa Maximovna and your family to pack up. We've come to take you back to Moscow." When Gorbachev mentioned his own presidential plane, the lawmakers told him it might not be safe, that they had a large plane, a Tu–134, and it was time to go.

The president's wife walked down the stairs and said hello. "I kissed her hand," Silayev told us, "but she looked under stress. But there was only one hour left; in two hours we would be back in Moscow.

"She said 'Thank you,'" he continued, "but her condition was very depressed. Many people in the group had seen Mrs. Gorbachev before. She is a very balanced, cultured person. But she did not recognize us. She was overwhelmed. She found it difficult to understand what we were saying. It was only on the plane that she came back to normal.

"I am very glad I had a chance to participate in that operation," Silayev said. "We understood that, if something should happen to us, or the president, the people would sweep away all the leaders of the coup. We were risking our lives, but Russia was behind us."

With Moscow bureau chief Steve Hurst and other correspondents who had arrived before me covering the breaking news, I focused on the political aftermath of the failed coup. One of the first shake-ups hit the KGB, the vanguard police force of the Soviet state, and one of the key organizers of the coup. The day after the coup ended, a giant crane was wheeled onto Lubyanka

Square, the KGB headquarters. Crews attached a metal cable to the neck of the massive statue of secret police founder Felix Dzerzhinsky and lifted it from its pedestal, as 10,000 people on the street cheered and cried "Down with the KGB!"

Vladimir Kryuchkov, KGB chief during the coup, was arrested, along with three KGB generals, and they were charged with treason. The entire ruling board of the KGB was fired, I reported, on orders of President Boris Yeltsin. Yeltsin created a commission tasked with planning how to reorganize the security service, the largest in the world, and create guarantees that it would never again act illegally. This never fully happened. The KGB was renamed the FSB (Federalnaya Sluzhba Bezopasnosti; Federal Security Service), but it continued to carry out some of the same repression as its Soviet counterpart.

There were calls for opening the archives on KGB crimes. According to most estimates, it was responsible for the deaths of some 10 million Russians—executed, starved, or sent to camps in the Gulag. Some archives were opened, but files on individual KGB officers and secret informers would not be. Russian society was too agitated, officials explained, and releasing informers' names could lead to tragedy.

There were shake-ups in the media as well, and I stayed on in Moscow for several weeks to report on it. For twenty-three years, *Vremya* ("Time") was *the* evening news, the mouthpiece of official government policy, but one week after the coup, *Vremya* was yanked off the air and quickly replaced with *TV-Inform*. In the anchor chairs were Tatyana Mitkova and Dmitry Kiselev, who had been fired several months previously for their on-air criticism of censorship. (Ironically, less than a decade later, Kiselev would become propagandist-in-chief for President Vladimir Putin.)

During the coup, the only independent radio source in Moscow was Echo Moscow radio station. The KGB shut it down for twenty minutes, but it was quickly back on the air, reporting live from the barricades, using radio frequencies illegally. (Echo Moscow would survive for three decades more, a beacon of independent journalism in Russia, only to be shut down after Putin launched his full-scale invasion of Ukraine in February 2022.)

In the wake of the coup, government-controlled print media, too, was in turmoil; Tass, the official government news agency, had dutifully reported on the coup and published the plotters' pronouncements. Now, the old head of the agency was cleaning out his desk, and a new head—Gorbachev's former spokesman—was in his place. Even *Pravda*, the official newspaper of the Communist Party, which Gorbachev shut down for supporting the coup, was reborn as an independent paper.

Yet, even in those heady days of what looked like a victory for a freer media, there were misgivings from some seasoned journalists: A liberal television journalist told me he was "greatly worried" by Boris Yeltsin's ban on *Pravda* and some other Communist newspapers. "I think this is very wrong," he said, "because it's a new kind of suppression of freedom of opinion."

Centrifugal forces were pulling the Soviet Union apart, and even after almost seventy years in the grip of the Communist Party, disintegration suddenly seemed inexorable. What's more, two men who hated each other—Mikhail Gorbachev and Boris Yeltsin—were accelerating that process.

Gorbachev was trying to preserve the USSR, but transform it into a new, less centralized kind of union that gave more power to the fifteen constituent republics and to regional and local governments. Yeltsin, in a far more radical way, was intent on dismantling Communist control and, with it, not only the Communist Party but the Soviet Union. Russia, in his view, should be the first-among-equals heir to the USSR.

Time was running out. The new head of the KGB told CNN the Soviet Union was facing serious economic and political instability. "There's a worst-case scenario," he said. "We will not be able to deal with the problems facing us, particularly the economic ones, and people will be fed up. They won't care about democrats, or conservatives, or communists."

I witnessed that fear and frustration when a CNN camera crew and I drove to Moscow's "Red Guard" neighborhood and found Raisa and Ivan Kosachev, two of the millions of ordinary Russians who were fearfully watching the confusing events, gathering the last potatoes from their small garden plot behind their apartment building. "Everyone's saying they're frightened, there's going to be hunger," Raisa told me. "It's going to be hard. We don't have much here, but it will help."

Raisa was still employed, but Ivan, her husband, was retired and on a tiny pension. Food prices in the stores had gone up three times, he told me. They had enough money to get by, "but if you have children or a large family, it's going to be hard," they said. "We don't have any order at all, and we don't have any leader."

On September 6, 1991, half a century after the Baltic States had been forcefully annexed by the Soviet Union, President Gorbachev recognized the independence of Lithuania, Latvia, and Estonia. Other republics, too, were preparing to abandon the USSR.

In early September, I covered a memorial procession for the three young men—Dmitrii Komar, Ilya Krichevski, and Vladimir Usov—who died defending the Russian White House during the coup. According to the Russian Orthodox faith, the souls of the deceased remain among the living for forty days.

The marchers followed in the footsteps of the men that cold autumn night, moving slowly from the Russian White House where Boris Yeltsin had stood fast against the coup, then on to the street where they were killed. A woman I spoke with told me: "There are no words. One would hope it would never happen again, that there would be peace and happiness for our children and our grandchildren. I'm so sorry for those fellows."

At the cemetery, young marchers were lighting candles. One girl said quietly, "We don't have freedom yet. This was just the first step."

That evening at the Bolshoi Theater, there was a requiem for the three, with Russian Orthodox hymns and the Jewish Kaddish being sung together for the first time in the historic theater. There was a final farewell to them from a young veteran who, like the three men, had fought for the Soviet Union in Afghanistan. A tribute from poet Andrei Voznesensky captured the nation's grief, and gratitude. They were, he said, the "Trinity of a New Russia," children of a new culture, no longer afraid. "If our life is comparatively free," he said, "it will be thanks to their memory."

CHICKEN KIEV

My focus was on Moscow and on the rush of events unfolding on the streets, but I wondered how the Bush administration was making sense of what was happening. Covering the American White House was still my day job, and I would need to understand the president's policy when I returned to the United States.

On August 1, less than three weeks before the coup, President George H. W. Bush had flown to Kiev, the capital of what was then still the Soviet Republic of Ukraine, and delivered what would later be known derisively as the "Chicken Kiev" speech to the Supreme Soviet of Ukraine. Although Communists still dominated the legislature, Ukrainians already were pushing for independence from the USSR. The American president told them to slow down:

> We support the struggle in this great country for democracy and economic reform, [but] . . . freedom is not the same as independence.
>
> Some people have urged the United States to choose between supporting President Gorbachev and supporting independence-minded leaders throughout the USSR. I consider this a false choice. In fairness, President Gorbachev has achieved astonishing things, and his policies of glasnost, perestroika, and democratization point toward the goals of freedom, democracy, and economic liberty. We will maintain the strongest possible relationship with the Soviet Government of President Gorbachev. But we also appreciate the new realities of life in the USSR.

Gorbachev, in his *Memoirs*, described President Bush's visit to the Soviet Union in late July 1991 to sign the Strategic Arms Reduction Treaty, just three weeks before the coup. Bush's willingness to work with Gorbachev helped create a partnership, even loyalty, between the two leaders, Gorbachev wrote. "Two qualities were characteristic of all of [our meetings]: a high degree of mutual trust, despite divergent opinions on some issues; and a high degree of agreement not only on current but also new, emerging problems."

For the Bush administration, those "divergent opinions" focused on the fear that the collapsing Soviet Union would be swamped by the kind of chaos that was unfolding in Yugoslavia. America's priority was managing the reduction of nuclear arms as well as the sociopolitical economic order.

"They had a stake in Gorbachev," Ambassador James Collins told me, "and in what he stood for and what he was trying to do. . . . We thought, I think quite simply, that it was moving in the right direction, and that Gorbachev had demonstrated that he was prepared to see an orderly devolution of the system . . . into something new, in which the Soviet Union could be a constructive player, or at least a partner on whom we could count, and, in that sense, the U.S. felt the stake in the Soviet Union surviving."

Bush, essentially, was saying to the nationalist movements, "Be careful. Take your time." For them, it wasn't a popular message.

In Moscow, seeing these events unfold in front of me, talking with Russians, trying to comprehend how they understood the seismic changes they and their society were undergoing, I had no desire to return to Washington. Moscow was where my heart—and my mind—were. It was impossible to see where all this ferment was leading, but at night, in my hotel room, I was close to tears—grateful for the chance to experience it all, and inspired by the hope that I saw in the eyes of Muscovites who poured into the streets, chanting "Yeltsin! Yeltsin!"—yet so fearful that things could suddenly lurch into chaos. Could the Communists reassert control? Would there be civil war? Who would regulate the nuclear weapons, scattered as they were, throughout the Soviet republics? Would the windows, now so open to the winds of change, be slammed shut again?

My temporary assignment in Moscow ended and I returned to Washington. By mid-October, I was covering Anita Hill's accusations of sexual harassment against Supreme Court nominee Clarence Thomas and the despicable administration attempt to paint her as "delusional." President Bush was conferring with friends and advisers on how to organize his reelection campaign. The economy was in trouble, and I followed the president, in a poorly conceived, even ridiculous photo op, as he went on a shopping trip with First Lady Barbara Bush to a J. C. Penney department store in suburban Maryland where he bought a pair of socks for $28.

I tried to stay motivated, but none of it seemed to matter anymore. Events in Moscow were accelerating, and I knew that White House officials were fixated on the dangerous implications of that instability. What I did not know at the time was the drama tied to Russia unfolding just a few offices away from our CNN booth at the White House.

It was obvious that Bush administration officials, as well as the president himself, remained focused on Gorbachev, even as control over the Soviet Union was slipping rapidly from his grip. But in a September 5 memorandum to the president, marked "Secret," later declassified, National Security Adviser Brent Scowcroft described what he called a "revolution triggered by last month's coup." A new union treaty and constitution were in the works, he said, that would create a "voluntary union of probably ten republics." The role of Russia, he said, would be key. "Whether or not a strong center can be maintained," he noted, "particularly in defense and foreign policy, will have a key effect on our ability to carry out a normal bilateral relationship."

In stark terms, Scowcroft described the struggle between Gorbachev and Yeltsin for control over the new union. Yeltsin, he said, already was carrying out a "second coup," placing ethnic Russians in key roles. "If Yeltsin should lose his taste for the union," Scowcroft warned, "he could decide to give up on Gorbachev. Gorbachev will then lose much of his constituency, since his main value is to keep Yeltsin in check. Such a scenario would lead to uncontrolled disintegration."

The situation was, indeed, fluid. The National Security Archive at The George Washington University contains the record of a four-hour conversation at a dinner hosted by King Juan Carlos of Spain the evening before the October 1991 Madrid Peace Conference. The purpose of the conference, chaired by Bush and Gorbachev, was to find a solution to the Arab–Israeli conflict. But it evolved into a fascinating discussion of the internal dynamics of the Soviet Union as it was sliding toward collapse. After the Soviet leader presented his detailed vision for the new union and described the scale of the challenges facing him, Bush summed up Gorbachev's predicament as a "stunning, breathtaking drama." "We are holding our breath as we watch it unfold," he said to Gorbachev, "and we wish you luck."

Less than four months later, that drama took another, even more cataclysmic turn. By then, I was back at the White House and, in our daily briefings with Press Secretary Marlin Fitzwater, we quizzed him: Was another coup under way, a political one, with Boris Yeltsin daily amassing more and more power, as Mikhail Gorbachev's power weakened? Fitzwater denied it was a coup; he called it a "transformation."

The administration began planning for an international conference in January to discuss coordination of humanitarian aid to the Soviet Union.

But looming over everything was the fate of the Soviet Union's vast arsenal of 27,000 nuclear weapons, along with weapons-grade plutonium and uranium.

The Soviet republics were spinning out of Moscow's control, asserting their right to manage their own affairs. On December 8, Yeltsin placed an extraordinary telephone call to Bush. "Today, a very important event took place in our country," Yeltsin announced, "and I wanted to inform you myself before you learned about it from the press."

Russia was not going to sign a new union treaty. It was too late for that. Instead, Yeltsin explained, Russia, Byelorussia, and Ukraine had signed an accord creating a commonwealth of independent states that would assume all international obligations of the Soviet Union, as well as provide for "unitary control of nuclear weapons and non-proliferation."

Bush tried to interject. "Boris, are you—"

Yeltsin broke in: "This is extremely, extremely important. Because of the tradition between us, I couldn't even wait ten minutes to call you . . . This is really, really hot off the press. To be frank, even Gorbachev doesn't know, although we shall inform him right away."

Three days later, Secretary of State James Baker inspected a cargo plane loaded with 150,000 pounds of army cots, blankets, and clothing that he would take with him on a trip to Russia, Ukraine, Byelorussia, Kyrgyzstan, and Kazakhstan. He would meet with their presidents and with Gorbachev— a reconnaissance mission and a final farewell to a nation, he said, that "as we know it, no longer exists." The comment infuriated Gorbachev: "While we're still trying to figure things out, the U.S. seems to know everything already. I don't think that's loyalty."

Publicly, Bush took a back seat, allowing Baker and his ambassador to the Soviet Union, Robert Strauss, to prepare the American public for what could be a major commitment of US taxpayer dollars. Making that case with severe economic trouble at home was a dangerous move, politically, for President Bush.

But Ambassador Strauss told CNN: "I would rather run the risk of wasting two billion and having this thing blow up in our face than look back ten years or five years from now and say, 'My goodness, if we had spent two billion more, the forces of anarchy, the forces of fascism, or whatever force could take over there in troubled time. We could have, maybe, held it all off."

Reporting from the White House, I tried to sum it up: "So the president finds himself being criticized for doing too much internationally and, at the same time, not enough, as domestic politics complicates how President Bush responds to the Soviet crisis."

THE LAST SOVIET PRESIDENT

Just a few months previously, I had personally witnessed the aftermath of the coup against Gorbachev. I now was witnessing the probable end of the USSR. I grappled emotionally with what seemed to be this inconceivable truth.

As an exchange student in Leningrad, I saw Communism's iron grip on the life of every Soviet citizen. Deprived of the right to emigrate abroad, some of my friends, like Tanya and Sergey in Leningrad, became internal émigrés, structuring a private, parallel existence to the harsh reality of Soviet life. It was horrid, but to think that all of this would suddenly come tumbling down seemed impossible.

As a new White House correspondent, I often ended up working holidays, and that included Christmas Day, 1991. I arrived early as usual and settled in for what I expected would be a boring news day. President Bush was at Camp David. As I was turning on the computer and television monitors, unbeknownst to me, President Bush was receiving a telephone call from Mikhail Gorbachev.

It came at 10:03 in the morning, Washington time. The transcript once marked "Secret" was declassified, thanks to the work of the National Security Archive. Gorbachev began by wishing George Bush, his wife, and his family a Merry Christmas. "Well, let me say that in two hours, I will speak on Moscow TV, and will make a short statement about my decision." That decision was to resign as president of the USSR.

In our CNN booth in the basement of the White House, I made some coffee and checked some news wires. In just a few hours, I would be running to the front lawn of the White House to report the administration's reaction to what Gorbachev was about to announce to the world.

"I have sent a letter to you, George," the declassified transcript shows Gorbachev told Bush. "I hope you will receive it shortly. I said in the letter a most important thing. And I would like to reaffirm to you that I greatly value what we did working together, with you, first as Vice President and then President of the United States." Although what he is saying is momentous, history-making, the tone of the conversation is respectful and warm, even intimate, like two old friends chatting about their lives.

"As for me, I do not intend to hide in the taiga, in the woods," he assured his American friend. "I will be active politically, in political life. My main intention is to help all the processes, here begun by 'Perestroika' and 'New Thinking' [the title of Gorbachev's 1987 book is *Perestroika: New Thinking in Our Country and the World*] in world affairs. Your people, the press here, have been asking about my personal relationship with you. I want you to know at this historic time that I value greatly our cooperation together, our partnership and friendship. Our roles may change, but I want to assure you that what we have developed will not change. Raisa and I send to you and Barbara our very best wishes."

Gorbachev had two crucial things he urged Bush to do: "I would like you to bear in mind the importance for the future of the commonwealth that the process of disintegration and destruction does not grow worse. Our common duty is to help the process of cooperation among the republics."

The other matter had to do with nuclear weapons. "I am resigning my duties as Commander-in-Chief and will transfer the authority to use the nuclear weapons to the president of the Russian Federation . . . I can assure you that everything is under strict control. As soon as I announce my resignation, I will put these decrees into effect. There will be no disconnection. You can have a very quiet Christmas evening."

Bush told Gorbachev he had sent him a letter. "In it, I express the conviction that what you have done will live in history and be fully appreciated by historians." And then, this touching reminder of happier times: "That horseshoe pit where you threw that ringer is still in good shape. That reminds me that in my letter to you, I say I hope our paths will cross soon again. You are most welcome in the U.S. Perhaps we could even meet here at Camp David when you have straightened out your affairs."

It was the final conversation between two presidents of two superpowers. In just a few hours, one superpower would be no more, replaced by fifteen independent nations, each a former Soviet republic. The Cold War was over, sealed by a virtual handshake.

"At this special time of year, and at this historic time," George Bush told Mikhail Gorbachev, "we salute you and we thank you for what you have done for world peace. Thank you very much."

"Thank you, George. I was glad to hear all of this today," Gorbachev said. "I am saying good-bye and shaking your hand. You have said to me many important things and I appreciate it."

"All the best to you, Mikhail," Bush said.

"Good-bye," the last president of the Soviet Union replied.

Now, the news was breaking in Moscow, and I grabbed my live-shot script and raced to meet the camera crew on the front lawn. President Bush was cutting short his Christmas Day at Camp David, I reported, and was preparing to deliver a speech to the nation on the historic significance of events in the Soviet Union. With my pen, I underlined the phrase "historic significance" and quickly added the word "former"—it was now, and would be for all history going forward, the "former" Soviet Union.

The collapse of the Soviet Union was swift, and from August 1991 until December 25, 1991, unstoppable. As I stood on the White House lawn, I thought of the conversation I'd had with that inebriated Russian parliamentarian on a plane over the Midwest back in the late 1980s. I remembered his words: "No one believes any of this anymore!"

That Christmas night, from Washington, I watched Mikhail Gorbachev address the Russian people, announcing he was stepping down as president of the USSR. It was clear he was unsettled. "I have firmly stood for independence, self-rule of nations, for the sovereignty of the republics, but at the same time, for preservation of the union state, the unity of the country," he said. "Events went a different way. The policy prevailed of dismembering this country and disuniting the state, with which I cannot agree."

And then, in brutally honest terms, he described the nation he had tried to reform and, at the same time, preserve.

"The society was suffocating in the vise of the command-bureaucratic system, doomed to serve ideology and bear the terrible burden of the arms race. It had reached the limit of its possibilities. All attempts at partial reform, and there [have] been many, had suffered defeat, one after another. The country was losing perspective. We could not go on living like that. Everything had to be changed radically."

Gorbachev's reforms, ultimately, were not radical enough, but he pointed to one enormous victory: The totalitarian system had been destroyed.

"This society acquired freedom, liberated itself politically and spiritually, and this is the foremost achievement which we have not yet understood completely, because we have not learned to use freedom."

The profound truth that Gorbachev spoke touched me deeply. Images of my Soviet friends, of what I had experienced in Russia, limited as it was compared to theirs, flooded my mind, and my heart.

"We live in a new world," he continued. "The Cold War has ended; the arms race has stopped, as has the insane militarization which mutilated our economy, public psyche, and morals. The threat of a world war has been removed." And yet, he admitted, "The old system collapsed before the new one had time to begin working.

"I am leaving my post with apprehension," he said, "but also with hope, with faith in you, your wisdom and force of spirit. We are the heirs of a great civilization and its rebirth into a new, modern, and dignified life now depends on us, one and all."

It was, I felt, a sacred moment, a turning point that Gorbachev had met with honesty and bravery. I stored those thoughts and emotions for a time, later, when I could examine and try to comprehend more fully what was happening.

But here in Washington, President Bush was addressing the nation from the Oval Office.

"During these last few months, you and I have witnessed one of the greatest dramas of the twentieth century," Bush said, "the historic and revolutionary transformation of a totalitarian dictatorship, the Soviet Union, and the liberation of its peoples."

Bush thanked Gorbachev "for years of sustained commitment to world peace, and for his intellect, vision and courage." Bush continued:

> Mikhail Gorbachev's revolutionary policies transformed the Soviet Union. His policies permitted the peoples of Russia and the other republics to cast aside decades of oppression and establish the foundations of freedom. His legacy guarantees him an honored place in history and provides a solid basis for the United States to work in equally constructive ways with his successors.

George H. W. Bush gave Boris Yeltsin what he wanted: recognition of Russia as the heir to the Soviet Union. The United States would quickly grant formal diplomatic recognition to only six of the new nations: Ukraine, Armenia, Kazakhstan, Belarus, and Kyrgyzstan—states that had made specific commitments to the United States on human rights, market reform, and control over nuclear weapons. The United States would establish diplomatic relations with the remaining republics—Moldova, Turkmenistan, Azerbaijan, Tajikistan, Georgia, and Uzbekistan—only when they made the same commitments. The Baltic nations had already won their freedom.

I watched the live video from Moscow as the red Soviet flag, with its gold hammer and sickle and one star, was slowly lowered over the Kremlin, and the white, blue, and red tricolor of the Russian Federation was raised in its place.

I ended my Christmas Day at the White House with a long, slow walk home in the dark. In the rush of live shots, the need to report quickly and accurately, there was no time to feel the moment. Now, I felt stunned. The country I had studied since I was a teenager was no more, splintering into fifteen new nations. But something even more momentous was happening in the minds of the people who would now define their own future.

I thought of President Bush's speech: "This is a day of great hope for all Americans. Our enemies have become our partners, committed to building democratic and civil societies. They ask for our support, and we will give it to them. We will do it because as Americans we can do no less. For our children, we must offer them the guarantee of a peaceful and prosperous future—a future grounded in a world built on strong democratic principles, free from the specter of global conflict."

But I also thought of one of the last live shots I did that night from the White House lawn. Russian president Boris Yeltsin had taken the reins and, as I reported, "At least some in the Bush administration have viewed Boris Yeltsin's impatience with some concern. But now, he is the man they must deal with."

Most of my career in Moscow with CNN has coincided with the presidencies of Boris Yeltsin and Vladimir Putin, but at the White House, in my temporary postings to Moscow during the early 1990s and after I became bureau chief, I also reported on and interviewed and followed Mikhail Gorbachev. Over the years, my respect for him has only grown. Thanks to him, the official end of the Cold War was relatively peaceful. Thanks to him—ironically, because this was not his intention—the Soviet Union collapsed in 1991.

On August 30, 2022, Mikhail Gorbachev died. He had been ill for a long time and it was clear there was no hope of recovery, but news of his death still was shocking. He was a monumental figure, and when he was suddenly gone, it seemed to me both inevitable and impossible. I was in Washington, on my way home on my bicycle, when CNN called, asking me if I could quickly give my thoughts on air. There was no time to find a camera or a laptop to do a live shot. I spoke on air by phone, a throwback to the many breaking news events in Moscow when the network was in "rolling coverage," and the intimacy of the moment, with only words, no video, helped me to concentrate on the significance of his life.

RAISA

As I talked with the anchor, I flashed back to September 1999, when I stood on a Moscow street in front of the Russian Cultural Center, reporting on the death of Gorbachev's beloved wife, Raisa. She had died of cancer just a few days short of what would have been their forty-sixth wedding anniversary.

I had always respected Gorbachev and his relationship with Raisa. I was amazed by their un-Soviet deep attraction for each other. I had never seen a Soviet leader and his wife behave like that. She was an intellect in her own right, a professor of philosophy, a lecturer at the prestigious Moscow State University, a woman with a sense of style who was not afraid to show it. Raisa Gorbachev touched a nerve in Russian society, infuriating some, inspiring others.

I stood for hours doing live shots for CNN on the street in front of the Russian Cultural Center where her memorial was held, feeling intensely sad.

One woman I interviewed expressed my thoughts. "I feel very sad, of course, for our former president," Irina Vladimirovna told me. "And, for the most human of reasons, I feel sad for them."

And so, on the day Mikhail Gorbachev died, I sat down to write a story for CNN's website on the Gorbachevs' life together for forty-six years. It was not the Soviet president's political career I was trying to capture, or his role in world history. It was his simple, human side that, in the end, is one of the greatest gifts he left to Russia.

> His funeral took place in Moscow's famous Hall of Columns, where Russians have said farewell to other Soviet leaders, some revered, some reviled, like Vladimir Lenin, Joseph Stalin, and Leonid Brezhnev. But Gorbachev, the first—and last—to bear the title of Soviet president, was unlike any of these other men. After him, the Cold War, and the Soviet Union, were no more. And, unlike those hard men, buried in their own tomb or in the Kremlin Wall necropolis, Gorbachev will be laid to rest in Novodevichy Cemetery next to his wife, Raisa Gorbacheva, the woman with whom he shared an unending love affair.
>
> Just as Gorbachev, with his "glasnost" and "perestroika," flung open the windows of the Soviet Union to "new thinking" that brought freedom and hope to his fellow citizens, Raisa Gorbacheva transformed the image of Soviet womanhood with her intellect, engagement in society, beauty and style. But most revolutionary of all, in the twilight of the gray, oppressive Soviet Union, was their enduring love affair.

Who knew a Soviet leader could be passionately in love? And he didn't hide it. In a 2012 documentary, Gorbachev reminisced about Raisa: "We walked through our whole life holding hands, she had something magnificent about her . . . she was like a princess."

Gorbachev inspired his fellow Soviet citizens "to break free from the shackles of Soviet uniformity," I wrote, "to be individuals who live their lives based on personal freedom—freedom to make their own choices, read what they wanted to read, discuss what they wanted to discuss."

And he was able to do that because he, himself, was a real person, a "chelovek," as the Russians say, and so was his partner in life, Raisa.

When I finished writing that article, I sat at my computer and cried. For the beauty of that time, with all its pain, for the tragedy that would befall society in the Russia of Vladimir Putin.

· 6 ·

Helping Boris

In those early January days of 1992, as I walked to the White House each morning from my apartment in Foggy Bottom, I felt the earth had shifted. Almost overnight, the Soviet Union was gone, at least legally, and Boris Yeltsin was president of a new Russia.

Russia, the biggest and richest of the fifteen Soviet republics, got most of the attention, but fourteen other former republics were redefining their sovereignty in a transformed world. Reporting on the dismantling of the USSR from Washington, not Moscow or the region, was a challenge. Russia, Ukraine, and Belarus were now members of what they called the "Commonwealth of Independent States." The five Central Asian republics—Kazakhstan, Kyrgyzstan, Tajikistan, Turkmenistan, and Uzbekistan—soon joined them, followed by Armenia, Azerbaijan, Georgia, and Moldova. The three Baltic states—Estonia, Latvia, and Lithuania—wanted no part of any new union.

It helped to have my high-school map of the Soviet Union in my head when I was doing live shots from the White House lawn. I had traveled to a number of those republics, and my basic understanding of Soviet economics and, even more important, conditions in those republics, helped me understand why breaking up, as the song goes, is so hard to do.

The rulers in the Kremlin, famous for their "Five-Year Plans" measured in tons of steel or giant dams built, were the ones who decided what each republic would produce. The result was something like a giant assembly line stretching across eleven time zones. Uzbekistan grew cotton, Georgia produced fruit and wine, Ukraine manufactured missiles and heavy machinery, leaving most republics with a kind of monoculture. They might provide an individual component, but they lacked the rest of the required ingredients. The republics traded with each other, shipping their products across huge distances to other republics, but there was very little trade with the non-socialist world. After the 1991 collapse they were no longer part of that massive assembly line, and most of them had no means of producing the wide range of products, let alone consumer products, that a modern country needs. The result was severe economic dislocation and even starvation. In the West, people cheered the end of Communism; in many former Soviet republics, the people felt set adrift.

Many years later, in Tbilisi, Georgia, I spoke with a colleague who explained that, even though most Georgians wanted economic freedom and democracy, some felt that, for them, democracy had not paid off. The USSR was gone, Georgia was an independent country, but life still was tough. "If they don't feel that the price they paid, all of that economic pain they went through after the breakup, was worth it," she explained, "then they begin to wonder whether 'democracy' is worth it, whether it means anything. They're more willing to think it would be better to go back to the old system." Politicians who benefited from the old system were more than happy to keep that old system in place, thus undermining attempts by these newly independent countries to join Western political and economic alliances like the European Union.

Even in those early post–Soviet days, the Bush administration understood the potential dangers if Yeltsin's economic reforms failed to improve Russians' lives. The White House was trying to play midwife, easing the pain of this difficult rebirth. I soon was reporting on Operation Provide Hope, an economic aid program that was up and running a month after the collapse of the USSR. The US Air Force was loading transport planes with food and desperately needed medical equipment, airlifting it to Russia, Ukraine, Belarus, Moldova, and the poorer former Central Asia republics.

The president's spokesman, Marlin Fitzwater, denied the shipments were merely symbolic, and the Kremlin was happy to agree. Yeltsin, faced with growing public anger over empty store shelves, was eager to show he had won something from his budding friendship with George H. W. Bush. In public, the Bush administration played the role of cheerleader for the Russian president, but behind the scenes, White House officials were concerned about his unpredictability. They trusted Soviet president Mikhail Gorbachev, but Yeltsin was a different leader with a different personality. He would thank the United States for its help and, in the same breath, place the burden for his success, or failure, on the shoulders of the Americans. Bush's challenge was to help guarantee Yeltsin's economic reforms, without appearing to let Yeltsin dictate the terms.

I was glad to be reporting on Russia, even from Washington, but I was concerned that Yeltsin's wins on his trip to the United States were not translating to success at home. He was racing against the clock, and the economic situation was deteriorating—fast.

One of the biggest dangers was what would happen to the thousands of nuclear and rocket scientists in the former Soviet Union. Weapons cutbacks meant unemployment, and the White House feared a nuclear "brain drain" from Russia if those scientists decided to sell their knowledge to renegade countries. Secretary of State James Baker was planning to discuss the possibility of hiring some of those scientists during an upcoming trip to Moscow. There was even talk of developing a "Star Wars" missile defense system that would be given the green light to purchase Russian technology.

But I was soon yanked back to what I thought of as my day job, reporting on the myriad other issues on the administration's plate—immigration at the US Southern border; Mideast peace talks; the continuing specter of Saddam Hussein in Baghdad; but, most of all, the 1992 presidential election, just ten months away. President Bush's approval rating was at an all-time low, and much of that was due to the economic recession at home in the United States. Things were so bad that he had to admit at one campaign stop, "This economy is in free fall." Talking about any plans to help Russia and its economic woes seemed like political suicide. The White House organized an international conference to drum up assistance to Russia and announced a $24 billion aid package, but it ended up being mostly broken promises.

I was on the campaign trail for the first time in my life, and I expected the Bush–Clinton battle to be a real "The Boys on the Bus" experience, as *Rolling Stone* reporter Timothy Crouse described it in his book on the 1972 McGovern campaign. There were antics, of course, like rolling oranges or apples up the center aisle as our press plane took off, fighting the thrust of the engines. But I was pleasantly surprised to find myself on press buses racing at night from town to town, with reporters (male and female) singing lullabies and whispering good night over the phone to their children and spouses back home. I learned a lot about America, but my fixation with Russia and Yeltsin's survival overshadowed much of that.

The Bush campaign's mood on the campaign trail was growing darker. As we climbed the steps to the press "risers" where we would stand in the middle of the crowd with our camera crews and producers, we were sometimes pelted with cans of soda, or paper cups filled with ice. Republican rally-goers were now sporting caps with the slogan "Blame it on the Media," and slapping bumper stickers on their cars, urging: "Annoy the Media: Re-elect Bush!" The crowds took it literally.

Election night I was in the small group of pool reporters who followed Bush to the Westin Galleria Hotel in Houston where his most fervent supporters were gathered to celebrate what they were hoping would be a victory.

Behind the stage, Bush's deputy campaign manager, Mary Matalin, was foul-mouthed and furious. By the end of the night, Bush had lost to Clinton 43 percent to 37.4 percent. We were led through a back entrance into the ballroom for Bush's concession speech, and I could see the men in tuxedos, the women in long dresses and even gowns, clutching small American flags on miniature gold-painted sticks. As we passed one group, a few of them began poking us in the shoulder with the sticks. I could see the fury on their faces.

BILL AND BORIS

Bill Clinton was now the president, and it was his turn to deal with Russia. He had a personal interest in the country, as he had spent a week in the USSR as part of a student winter tour when he was a Rhodes Scholar at Oxford. During the 1992 election campaign he criticized George Bush for not doing enough to help the newly independent country during the harsh Russian winter of 1992. As Russia scholar Angela Stent explains in her seminal book, *The Limits of Partnership: US–Russia Relations in the Twenty-First Century*, the Bush administration "rejected the idea of a [post–World War II style] Marshall Plan for Russia and limited its involvement in assistance programs." That caution also affected the Bush administration's policies on democracy promotion, she added. The Clinton administration would be different; building a new US–Russia relationship was paramount.

As president, Clinton reached out for guidance on Russia policy to a friend from his university days, Strobe Talbott, his Rhodes Scholar roommate. Talbott had gone on to become a highly respected journalist, working with *Time* magazine for more than two decades before joining the government. He reported from Eastern Europe, the State Department, and the White House, and served as *Time*'s Washington bureau chief, editor at large, and foreign affairs columnist. He was a true Russia expert; in the 1970s he translated and edited two thick volumes of former Soviet premier Nikita Khrushchev's memoirs. In the Clinton administration he served as ambassador at large and special adviser to Secretary of State Warren Christopher on the New Independent States.

Covering Bill Clinton as a CNN White House correspondent, I was excited by the energy as the new team took over. I reported for pool duty at 1600 Pennsylvania Avenue as the new president started out on his morning jog, fueled by a cup of coffee. His Russia policy seemed energized as well. In their first seven years in office, Bill Clinton and Boris Yeltsin met eighteen times. In front of the cameras, every time Clinton and Yeltsin got together it seemed to turn into, as Angela Stent described it, "The Bill and Boris Show." They appeared to have developed a real personal rapport. Both men were six-foot-two, and both had the shoulders of NFL linebackers. Standing just a few yards away from them at news conferences, I often tried to estimate who wore the bigger suit jacket.

At a news conference during their summit meeting in Hyde Park, New York, in October 1995, for example, Yeltsin opened his remarks by saying he was leaving the United States more optimistic than when he'd arrived. Then he switched gears and laid into the media standing before him. "You were writing that today's meeting with President Bill Clinton was going to be a disaster!" he thundered. Clinton looked a bit confused, but turned it into a joke, throwing back his head and guffawing.

But Yeltsin wasn't finished. "Well, now, for the first time," Yeltsin paused for effect, "I can tell you that—*you're* a disaster!" Clinton cracked up, bent over, and laughed his head off, then grabbed Yeltsin by the shoulder and laughed uproariously again. Yeltsin gleefully turned to him with a Cheshire cat grin.

Behind the scenes, things were not as jovial. Clinton, indeed, wanted to show Yeltsin his strong personal support, especially when it came to the Russian president's economic reforms. The devil's dilemma was that those reforms, so important to Russia as a whole, were harsh, perhaps even too harsh, for many individual Russians. On the eve of the Moscow Summit, Clinton's national security adviser Anthony Lake wrote a secret briefing memo to the president, declassified in 2024. In it, Lake called Yeltsin "arguably your most important foreign counterpart," adding that "support for reform in Russia remains at the top of your foreign policy priorities.

"Yeltsin will greet you in Moscow as a man dedicated to reform but burdened by Russia's many problems at the start of its third year of independence," Lake told the president. "He and the reform movement he leads have just emerged from a bitter and turbulent two-year power struggle with the dying institutions of the old Soviet Union."

"The press and elsewhere charge that we bet too heavily on Yeltsin and reform," he told Clinton. "They point to aggressive Russian behavior toward its neighbors and to the electoral success of [Vladimir] Zhirinovsky [a right-wing nationalist politician] and the communists to support their thesis that the Russians will now revert to a more traditional authoritarian and aggressive posture at home and abroad."

Reading that memo decades later, I could see how prescient Lake was: "Specifically, many believe Yeltsin may have to slow the economic reforms in the wake of the elections," he said, "and maintain the edge on the nationalists by pursuing a tougher policy in the Baltics, Moldova, and with Ukraine—as well as at the Security Council. Your top priority in Moscow will thus be to reaffirm with Yeltsin the Vancouver framework [the summit in April 1993] for a close US–Russia partnership built on a Russian commitment to democratic political and market reform."

Angela Stent was my academic adviser for the master's thesis I wrote at Georgetown University, and we frequently discussed the Clinton administration's Russia policy, which she helped to formulate at the State Department's Office of Policy Planning. In her book, she said Clinton "initially raised high expectations about re-creating the US–Russia relationship in what became the second—and more ambitious—reset since the Soviet collapse.

"By the end of Clinton's two terms, however," she explained, "these expectations had not been met. They probably could never have been." It was, she said, a "selective partnership, where cooperation and competition coexisted, albeit in fluctuating proportions." Whatever happened, she predicted, "Russia would not evolve as a Western-style democracy, and American influence on Russia's internal evolution would be circumscribed."

That, to me, was the core of the problem. Too many in the United States believed that just because the Communists no longer ruled Russia, Russia would see things the way the Western democracies saw them. It was a naive and false hope.

"HILLARY TRIPS"

Bill Clinton was the public face of US policy toward the new Russia, but First Lady Hillary Clinton was playing her own role, traveling to several former Soviet republics, highlighting the effect that the jarring transition from Communism to a free-market economy had had, especially on women, and how the United States was trying to help. As the female correspondent on CNN's White House team, I was the natural choice to accompany Mrs. Clinton on what we referred to as "Hillary trips."

One of the most memorable was to Central Asia, which had some of the poorest republics in the Soviet Union. At her first stop in Almaty, Kazakhstan, she told a conference on women in politics: "Too many women are the first to lose their jobs and the last to get new ones. Too many women are barred by law, by tradition, or by ignorance from exercising their rights. Too many women are trapped in an endless cycle of poverty, unable to get access to education and credit."

In Bishkek, Kyrgyzstan, we followed her to a local market where she spoke with women who had received "micro loans" from the US Agency for International Development (USAID) to finance small businesses or build homes. In Tashkent, Uzbekistan, she attended the opening of a Women's Center at the Tashkent Medical Institute. I had visited all three countries twenty years previously and I could see the poverty which, it seemed obvious, would only increase, as those now-independent countries tried to build their economies anew.

On the way back to Washington, Mrs. Clinton stopped in Russia and, finally, in Lviv, Ukraine. The highlight was a speech to more than a thousand people at the magnificent neoclassical opera house where she explained the major themes of her trip. She was introduced by her chief of staff, Melanne Verveer, whom I had gotten to know on the trip and who, I soon learned, grew up not far from where I was raised in Scranton, Pennsylvania. Melanne, a Ukrainian-American whose grandparents had come to America from western Ukraine, made a moving speech in Ukrainian. The audience was mesmerized by a person so full of empathy for the difficulties they were going through. A quarter-century later, I would watch with horror as Russian troops launched a massive aerial bombing attack on Ukraine, striking Lviv and other cities.

Hillary Clinton's press entourage was small, mostly women correspondents, and it provided a unique opportunity to see Hillary up close, to ask about her impressions of the countries she was visiting, and the stakes for those countries. In March 1996, we boarded a US Air Force plane in Washington and took off for Bosnia and Herzegovina, and the town of Tuzla. The Bosnian War had just ended three months previously, after a cease-fire was negotiated in Dayton, Ohio, and US troops were stationed at Tuzla Air Base as part of the NATO Implementation Force. Clinton's comments about that trip became a point of controversy in her 2008 run for the US presidency.

In one campaign speech she claimed she remembered "landing under sniper fire." She said there was supposed to be a greeting ceremony at the airport, "but instead we just ran with our heads down to get into the vehicles to get to our base."

I took careful notes on that trip. It began, I wrote, with Mrs. Clinton coming to the back of the plane to talk with us: "Black raincoat, blue denim work shirt, absolutely no makeup, hair brushed back in a recent cut. Looked a little tired but her photographer said she's psyched for the trip."

We were on a huge C-17 transport plane with shrink-wrapped pallets of M&Ms and other candy, #2 pencils, and toys. I had a chance to talk with her speechwriter, Lissa Muscatine, who told me Mrs. Clinton did not do much speech preparation. She's very intelligent and lawyerly in her presentations, she said, but there's a downside: She tends to make an argument logically, buttressing it with specifics; while this makes her point irrefutable, sometimes there are too many details and facts. Hillary was easier to write speeches for than Bill Clinton, she told me. Our conversation was interrupted as Mrs. Clinton came back and shook hands with everyone, talking about the camps she would visit, and the cards and letters she was taking in for the troops from their families.

As we descended for our landing, I took quick notes: "We all don flak jackets, camouflage, as we arrive plane lands very quickly, just a few seconds, with enormous thrust." There was no gunfire. We did not "run with our heads down." On the tarmac to greet her were US officials and the acting Bosnian president, Ejup Ganić. In a 2016 *Washington Post* "Fact Checker" article by Glenn Kessler, Lissa Muscatine said we were put on a C-17 because "it was a plane capable of steep ascents and descents precisely because we were flying into what was considered a combat zone. We were issued flak jackets for the final leg because of possible sniper fire near Tuzla."

I personally cannot vouch for her explanation of the C-17, but it seems logical; it is known as a flexible and powerful cargo plane, thanks to its four engines, each of which is rated at 40,440 pounds of thrust, and both our descent and departure were extremely fast and steep. I was told we would wear flak jackets in case there was any "threat," which could have included sniper fire, but once we landed, it appeared the US military had things well in hand. Later, as we helicoptered to military outposts, we looked down on villages below, their houses with the roofs blown off. At Camp Alicia we peered out over newly discovered minefields, then flew on to Camp Bedrock with its MASH hospital.

Throughout, I found Mrs. Clinton extremely composed, but not stiff and formal as she sometimes was depicted. She had a wicked sense of humor, a very effective repertoire of impersonations of politicians, and, as the trip wore on, she would tease us in the press corps by turning the tables, taking photos of us, and barraging us with questions: "What is the significance of this theater? Make your answer less than twenty-five words, eight seconds long! Will it stand the test of time, Ms. D?" She sometimes joined us for dinner, and I had some stimulating conversations with her about the media, and about the Islamic movement in the Middle East.

As I watched, and listened, and talked with her, it confirmed my initial impression that Hillary was one of the most linear, logical thinkers I have ever encountered. Bill Clinton, with his enormous charisma and great personal warmth, as well as high intellect, felt somehow circular, a broad thinker who would expand his speeches with personal asides and emotional appeals. Although they both are lawyers by training, Hillary felt more like the barrister, as Lissa Muscatine told me on the Bosnia trip. Quite a combination, I thought, to have those two brains united in one married couple.

But the Clintons ignited more than ideas, as I could see as soon as I started covering the Clinton White House. The public reaction to the change of administrations from George H. W. Bush to Bill Clinton shocked me when I read some of the faxes that began flooding into our CNN booth in the basement of the White House press section.

This was the pre–social media era, so if someone wanted to send us a message, they sent it by fax. I would check the fax machine regularly to make sure we weren't missing any important official announcements, but also to see what the public mood was. During the Bush administration, we would receive missives with criticism of the president expressed in what nowadays would seem like genteel terms: "George Bush doesn't know the first thing about the economy!" one person would write. "Get him out of there! He doesn't care about working people!" another would complain.

As soon as the Clintons hit town, the gloves came off. "Spawn of the devil!" "They should be stabbed in the heart and disemboweled!" Some of the faxes were pages-long rants, scrawled in tiny handwriting, with odd little drawings. Some were so threatening and frightening, I turned them over to the Secret Service.

This was not just political antipathy, it was actual hate, and much of it seemed based on strange interpretations of biblical prophecy. When Hillary Clinton described a "vast right-wing conspiracy," it began, to me, to make sense.

This was my introduction to "Hillary World," and there would be more to come nearly two decades later, when CNN assigned me as foreign affairs correspondent covering Hillary Clinton as US secretary of state.

MOVING TO MOSCOW

On a spring morning in 1997, sitting at the computer in our cramped CNN news booth at the White House, I got a message from Eileen O'Connor, CNN's Moscow bureau chief. She said she wanted to talk privately, so I moved into our even tinier soundproof recording booth.

Eileen, a colleague and personal friend, told me she was planning to leave Moscow. Would I be interested in becoming bureau chief?

I was stunned. It was sudden, unexpected, and yet, at that moment, it seemed to me somehow preordained, the way it was meant to be. My whole life with Russia—my high school and college days, my months in Leningrad as an exchange student, my temporary reporting trips to Moscow—it all came together in that moment of *yes*. Of course, I wanted to be Moscow bureau chief; of course I wanted to return to Russia, to live and work in Moscow.

I took a deep breath. "Yes, I would be interested in the job," I told Eileen. She had cleared the call with her supervisors. The next steps would come quickly.

I walked out the White House drive that evening and headed for home. I was elated, but worried. Six years before, when CNN had appointed me White House correspondent, my partner Valucha had pulled up stakes and moved with me from her beloved Chicago to DC, leaving behind her home of more than two decades, a flourishing singing career, and a ton of friends. Now, I realized, I would have to ask her to follow me again, this time to Russia. There was no way to bring it up gently. It was either yes or no. I knew it was the right decision for me, the culmination not only of my career, but my entire life of dedication—addiction?—to understanding Russia.

I considered putting off the discussion until evening, but I knew it was impossible.

"Meu bem [Portuguese for "my darling"]," I said, "I've been offered a job in Moscow as the bureau chief."

Valucha was incredulous. Moscow? Russia? The former Soviet Union? Snow? Cold? Siberia? Her fiery personality was on full display.

"How could you even think of this? How can a Brazilian possibly survive there? It's freezing! You moved me here to Washington. I had to leave Chicago! Now we have a home here and you want me to pull up stakes again? No!"

There was nothing I could say. The storm was raging, and I had to shelter in place until it passed. Valucha was furious.

I was frozen in grief, knowing how painful this must be for her. I tried to describe it as an adventure, but as I heard myself say it, it seemed ludicrous. Valucha did not need any new adventures. She wanted a home, security, a chance to restart her own career. This, I knew, would be one of the most difficult things I would do in my life, but I had to do it. I knew it would be a life-changing experience for us both.

Miraculously, after a day of turmoil, she said yes. Yes, I will go to Moscow with you. Yes, I'll pull up my life here. She said it with some resignation. But she said it with love.

I now had to talk with my supervisors about Moscow. They were, as I expected, very happy I had agreed to take the job, but they had one concern. I had never hidden the fact that I was gay, but I had never advertised it before, either. Now, I had to be clear that I planned to move to Moscow with my partner, who was a woman, a fact that presented several challenges. Valucha and I were not married because, at the time, legally, there was no marriage equality. To allow Valucha to move to Moscow legally, we would need a Russian work visa, and that meant CNN would have to define her as an employee of the bureau. And that is how Valucha, an artist for whom using a pair of pliers was a challenge, became a "technician." We both found it hysterical, but necessary. She would go on to contribute to the bureau in many different ways, none of them, however, technical.

My bosses also had another concern which they tried, gently, to raise with me. In Moscow we would have to be "discreet." I assured them that we were not going to discos every night. In typical CNN style, as soon as the ink was dry on the contract, we were packing our apartment and heading for Moscow.

In all my trips over the years to Russia, one of the first considerations was not necessarily what I was setting out to do there, but what supplies I should bring with me to survive. The USSR of the 1960s, for example, had almost no Western medicines, so I had to pack enough to last for several months, just in case. It had no decent shampoo, or contact lens solution, toothpaste or soap. Things were much improved by 1997 when I took up the post of bureau chief, but old habits die hard. My first thoughts were about where we would live, what our apartment would be like, what clothes and personal items we should take, and where we would buy food.

The apartment we inherited from Eileen O'Connor was located in a "diplomatic ghetto" of sorts, a complex of several tannish-colored, nine-story brick buildings owned and managed by GUPDK, a commercial arm of the Russian Foreign Ministry that provided housing for diplomats, journalists, and other foreign officials and representatives. In Soviet times, foreigners were not allowed to live anywhere else but in this official housing, which was monitored—bugged—by security services.

CNN rented both our bureau offices and several other staff apartments in the complex. It faced Kutuzovsky Prospekt, a main thoroughfare that leads out in a westerly direction from the Kremlin, named in honor of the famous Russian army commander who led his country's defense against the invasion of Napoleon. Anchored on the banks of the Moscow River by the Ukraina Hotel, one of Moscow's neoclassical, Stalin-era "Seven Sisters" buildings, it was considered a swank address even in Soviet times, and several Soviet leaders—including Leonid Brezhnev and Yuri Andropov—had apartments at Kutuzovsky Number 26.

Our apartment buildings were not swank, but they were relatively well-built by Soviet standards, well maintained, and had the added advantage of being located along the route that the Russian president, to this day, traverses almost daily in his motorcade from his suburban residence to the Kremlin. Our studio had a bird's-eye view directly down Kutuzovsky toward the center of the capital, an invaluable camera location during Yeltsin's 1993 military assault on the Russian White House.

Like all the CNN non-Russian staff, we lived just across the parking lot from the CNN office and studios. There were some commercial rentals on the ground floor of the office building, including a beauty salon and, in 1997 when we arrived, a small convenience store for basic commodities and snacks. In those days it had a painfully limited food repertoire, but as time went on, it became a bellwether for the Russian economy. By the time we left, almost a decade later, the Russian version of 7-Eleven had been transformed into a luxury car salon selling Porsches.

There was another, larger, grocery store across the street, and that's where we did most of our food shopping. Within a few weeks of arriving, Valucha, who had just started Russian-language lessons with a tutor, asked me: "How do you say 'The customer is always right' in Russian?" I laughed and asked what she was planning to do with that phrase. "The salespeople at the food store across the street are so surly and impolite," she explained, "and there's a security guy who glares at everyone when they enter and monitors everywhere they go," she said.

For me, this was standard Soviet behavior. I resolved to wait a bit before I warned her of other Soviet traditions that still hadn't died out: the "Sanitary Day" sign that would unexpectedly appear on a store's door, alleging that the staff was cleaning the premises; the "Zakrit" ("Closed") signs that suddenly appeared on the front door of the store where you sorely needed something; the occasional "Remont" ("Renovation") signs that could mean anything from the store's plumbing had burst, the manager had more important things to do than open the store, or the store was closing indefinitely for "repairs."

For now, Valucha needed some American-style consumer encouragement, and so I taught her the phrase "Pokupatel' fsegda prav!" ("The customer is always right!"), which I knew would make no sense in Russian. But she bravely tried it out on a regular basis, especially when she was leaving the store under the glaring eye of the security man. I realized that the very concept was so foreign, just six years after the end of the Soviet Union, that it was useless to even try. But I also understood that, just as with my experiences as an exchange student in Leningrad, or as a Russian-speaking guide on USIA exhibits, I would learn more about modern Russia from daily life experiences like this than from any briefing by some faceless official.

Some of my biggest lessons in Russian reality came in a little park located just down the street from our office. "Park," actually, is not a precise definition. It was a cut-through from Kutuzovsky Prospekt to the other major road running roughly parallel to our street, Bol'shaya Dorogomilovskaya Ulitsa. Two one-lane driveways ran parallel alongside a dirt yard, delineated with the broken remains of what once was a short iron fence. Drivers would streak down the roads, cut across the dirt, weaving in and out of the parade of dogs, pedestrians, and children in strollers pushed by their mothers or grandmothers. In those days, anyone who had a car ruled the road with an infuriating sense of entitlement. They stopped for no one.

In time, the Moscow city government provided funds to turn the area into a park. I was pleasantly surprised to see they did a good job, installing attractive iron borders, building sidewalks, constructing fountains and statues, seeding the area with grass, planting flowers and bushes, yet preserving two roads for drivers to make it through from one major thoroughfare to the other. Before the project was complete, however, the drivers were back, rolling over the borders, zigzagging across the turf, leaving gashes in the earth, laying waste to the city's attempt to create a pleasant respite for the neighborhood.

One day, as Valucha and I walked through the park to check on progress, a black Mercedes charged toward us, intent on taking the shortest route to Dorogomilovskaya Street. Valucha was using trekking poles, making her walks more invigorating. As the car bore down on us, obviously expecting us to jump out of the way, Valucha decided to make a stand. She spread her feet apart, planted herself in a cruciform position, trekking poles crossed over her head, and refused to move. The driver slammed on the brakes, rolled down the window, and yelled "Get out of my way!" but Valucha stood her ground. The standoff lasted seconds, but it felt like hours. Then, to my post-Soviet amazement, the man in the black Mercedes backed away and took the other small road over to Dorogomilovskaya, I am sure wondering who the insane woman in the park was.

Russia was changing, I could feel it. But, to this day, I never dare to walk across an intersection as a pedestrian, assured that traffic will stop for me, even if I have the crossing light and the roadway is striped, unless I establish eye contact with the drivers. Old Soviet habits were still alive, vestiges of a time when only a few cars were on the streets of Moscow. What cars there were belonged to Communist Party bosses and other bureaucrats who sat in the backs of shiny black Chaika limousines, protected from proletarian view by crisp white curtains.

I sensed, within this obnoxious behavior, a deeper lesson in Russian reality, a disturbing undercurrent of entitlement, the belief that, in almost any situation, someone must be on top, more powerful than the other guy. It was always a zero-sum game; if someone wins, someone has to lose. There was no such thing as win-win.

I had seen that dynamic play out many years before, when I was an exchange student in Leningrad, when men with burly arms blocked average Russians from entering foreign currency stores where only foreigners like us could shop. I will never forget the humiliating disdain with which those burly men treated their fellow citizens.

As I settled into my office at the CNN bureau, insights into post-Soviet Russia came not only from the people I interviewed but often, unexpectedly, from daily encounters with our Russian staff. I already spoke Russian quite well and almost too grammatically, although I never shook a slight accent that most Russians couldn't place. "Are you from the Baltics?" they would ask.

Then, there was the issue of my name. Even for English speakers, "Dougherty" was a challenge to pronounce, and for Russians it was incomprehensible. Plus, the "gher" (which, in Irish, should have a breathy "h" pronunciation) was dangerously close to the pronunciation for an off-color word for a part of the male anatomy. Lena, the office manager, quickly Russified my first name by adding the "ochka" ending: "Jillochka." I had ended up with the Russian version of "Jillykins."

But it was not only my name, and my accent—it was what I said and how I said it that marked me as a foreigner.

In English, if I want someone to do something for me, I usually phrase it as: "Would you mind handing me those papers?" You can say that in Russian, but no Russian (at least one who grew up in the Soviet Union) would ever say it that way. Our office manager, Lena Berezovskaya, a woman of my age who had worked for CNN for many years and knew every Soviet and post-Soviet bureaucratic trick (she described herself as an "old cadre crow") immediately stopped me in my tracks.

"You simply can't say that!" she shouted. "No one will take you seriously!"

"But why?" I asked.

"Because it sounds quaint, stilted, and stupid! In Russia you have to order people to do things and then, maybe, add 'please.'"

I never stopped saying "please," but I did change my phrasing, ending up with "Hand me those papers—please."

"NORMAL" LIFE IN MOSCOW

During my first few years as bureau chief, most of my life was taken up with work. It was a steep learning curve, not only in terms of covering breaking news, but also trying to understand how the Russian capital worked, who the power players were, and how to gain access to them. Moscow is a huge city with a population of at least 12 million, but the people who run it—and, by extension, the entire country—actually are part of a relatively small and, one could say, incestuous group.

Many of the top Russian officials and business leaders, I found, had grown up together. The Soviet Union was just six years in the past, and at that point, everyone in a position of power had grown up in the USSR. They had gone to the same Young Pioneer summer youth camps. They had attended the same schools—for diplomats, Moscow State Institute of International Relations (MGIMO); for journalists, Moscow State University. Most of them came from big cities (e.g., Putin and his St. Petersburg clan). They married each other, divorced each other, had affairs with each other. If, in Washington, there were "six degrees of separation," in Moscow, it felt like two.

I started making friends (speaking Russian helped) and began socializing. Moscow has always been a party city, captured in perfect detail by Lev Tolstoy, and I found myself at soirees that might have been described in a chapter of *War and Peace*, except that the nobility were replaced by oligarchs, superrich Russians, the country's "captains of industry." Most of them started out as young Communist Party members and, as the USSR disintegrated, bought up state assets on the cheap, eventually controlling industry, finance, mining, media—almost the entire economy. From the outset of his presidency, however, Putin set about taming them. He set one basic rule: Make as much money as you want, but stay out of politics.

Moscow, with all of its government ministries and ways to bribe your way into riches, was quickly being populated by millionaires—and billionaires. They shopped in luxury stores and ate in expensive restaurants. I remained emotionally faithful to the first Russian city I knew from my twenties, St. Petersburg, but, in spite of the excessive displays of wealth, Moscow soon worked its way into my heart. St. Petersburg was the European face of Russia, the cultural capital. Moscow was Russian through and through, and I soon found it had a deep and rich cultural life, with an inexhaustible number of concerts, art exhibits, and plays.

In the city center, near the Kremlin, every block was like a history book, and I made it a point to walk places I could have driven to. Our bureau was just a couple of blocks from the Moscow River, about an hour's walk to Red Square, and my peregrinations took me through some of the oldest neighborhoods in the city, like Zaryadie or Kitai-Gorod (literally, it could be translated as "China Town," but the origin of the name was far older, referring to wooden stakes), and some of its loveliest, like Patriarch's Ponds. I've always felt that cities have a soul, especially ones that are thousands of years old, and I learned that people have lived in the area of what is now Moscow for about 10,000 years.

St. Petersburg appealed to my love of baroque and neoclassical architecture, with its rational, European nature. But I was quickly seduced by Moscow's stunning unpredictability and its winding streets. I turned a corner and suddenly encountered the orange-tinged wood house where Lev Tolstoy lived. I smiled as I found myself on Molochny Pereulok (Milk Lane). I gasped on the day I unexpectedly discovered the apartment building where the poet Marina Tsvetayeva lived, on Borisoglebsky Lane, a stone's throw from the bustling New Arbat Street.

There were, of course, things that could happen only in the Moscow of the early 2000s, like the time a friend and I were walking down Kutuzovsky Prospekt near the CNN bureau, just a few hundred feet from the sushi restaurant that had opened at the edge of our small neighborhood park. I never ate there, although I am a lover of sushi. It might have been the clientele that put me off; they parked on the sidewalk, blocking pedestrians, and today, as usual, it was a sea of Mercedes-Benzes and Bentleys. As we got closer to the entrance, two bodyguards emerged from a Bentley, one toting a machine gun. They were guarding a bald guy who quickly headed inside. A year or so later, one of the restaurant's clients was gunned down at his table, perhaps as he reached for more sashimi.

I lived in a much more traditional Russian world. On winter weekends I would rise early, make a quick cup of coffee, dress in warm pants, a jacket, hat, scarf, and mittens and head out in the car for Sparrow Hills near the hilltop campus of Moscow State University. In the back of the station wagon I had my cross-country skis. The pros invariably were already there in the forest of birch and aspen trees, older Russians swooshing by on wood skis. Someone, I never knew who, already had packed down the snow with a wide, flat board, creating a winding path to follow up and down the hillocks and valleys. After an hour or two of skiing, I would brush the snow off my skis, and myself, and head back down the hill to Kutuzovsky Prospekt. A breakfast of dark, intoxicating Borodinsky bread, toasted, with some Georgian cheese on top awaited me.

In Soviet times, I always drank tea. Coffee was a revolting brew of hot water with a whiff of coffee, but a decade after the Soviet Union disappeared, the coffee craze hit Moscow like a jolt of caffeine. Starbucks had not yet opened a shop, but several Russian companies jumped into the market: Coffee Mania, Coffee Bean, Zen Coffee—the menu would fit right in on the streets of any American city: "Espresso, cappuccino, latte . . ."

By March of 2002 there were roughly forty coffee shops in the capital serving an estimated 10,000 customers a day, many of them young professionals who could afford the equivalent of $1 to $5 a cup. But that $5 also offered a cheap way to get together with friends in a pleasant, European-style atmosphere. Russian coffee drinkers liked to linger over their java, and they also liked to drink it at night. The peak hours in the coffee shop near Moscow's Conservatory, in fact, were between 5 and 8 p.m. One thing that didn't become popular, at least initially, was take-out coffee. As one barista at Coffee Mania told me: "The expression 'Let's have a cup of coffee' doesn't mean 'Let's drink coffee.' People don't come here just to drink coffee; they come for the atmosphere, to be with other people."

I made the Conservatory's Coffee Mania my home away from home, and sitting there, sipping a latte, I felt calm and happy. Six years had passed since the collapse of the USSR. Politicians in Europe and the United States began talking about the "peace dividend." Now that the USSR no longer threatened the world, and Russian leaders like Gorbachev and Yeltsin were opening the country, talking about "democracy" and "free markets," they thought, why did the West need to defend itself? The threat was over.

That theory, however, turned out to be very wrong.

· 7 ·

Yeltsin's Obit

R_elaxation of tensions._ The phrase seemed to appear in almost every news report from Moscow. Russia was turning into a "normal" country.

Many American media slashed their Moscow staff, leaving behind a local Russian producer. If major news broke, TV networks would fly in correspondents and videographers from London and other European capitals. I thought this was a bad idea. Russia might not have tanks rolling down the streets, but roiling political changes were under way. In order to understand it all, you had to be there to see it.

When I arrived in Moscow, the CNN bureau had twenty-five employees, which is large for a foreign bureau. Russia was never completely "at peace," and as a result, we kept our staffing high until the late 1990s, when it was my unenviable job to "downsize" the bureau. In Russia, "staff" had a different meaning than it did in other bureaus. It included the news personnel: correspondents (we had two Americans); producers (two Russian producers and usually two American or British Russian-speaking producers); two cameramen; a sound technician; associate producers or interns; an office manager; a cook; a cleaning woman. We had a fleet of several cars that had to be maintained amid the challenging conditions of bad roads and subzero weather. That meant having three drivers able to carry out those functions, and who were skilled in the inscrutable art of tracking down street addresses in Moscow's byzantine system.

When the Bolsheviks came to power, they obliterated czarist, and even some traditional Russian street names. In post-Communist Russia, many streets were renamed, restored to their previous titles. The continuation of our broad six-lane avenue, Kutuzovsky Prospekt, as it crossed over the Moscow River on its way toward the Kremlin, had been named Kalininsky Prospekt in the early 1960s in honor of Mikhail Kalinin, the Bolshevik revolutionary. The avenue was widened at that time, slashing through one of Moscow's most beautiful old neighborhoods, the Arbat, parts of which survived, still nestled behind the Russian Foreign Ministry. Skyscrapers were hastily constructed to emulate the New York City skyscrapers that so impressed Nikita Khrushchev during his US visit in 1959. Muscovites quickly nicknamed them "Moscow's dentures."

For the uninitiated, trying to find an address in Moscow, with its arcane numbering system, was a mind-bending challenge, and having experienced bureau drivers was critical. Uber and professional taxi companies were still a decade or more in the future. The number of cars on the roads was exploding, leading to huge traffic jams.

Even after the Soviet Union was gone, bureaucratic demands lived on. At the CNN bureau, a slew of documents had to be notarized; applications for visas had to be filled in with no misspellings or incorrect digits; requests for interviews often had to be formally written and faxed in advance. Every bit of technical equipment—every videotape, every cable, every lightbulb, not to mention camera and microphone—had to be imported and listed on lengthy and detailed written declarations called "carnets." Each time we left Russia for a shoot in another former Soviet republic—for example, Georgia or Ukraine, now independent countries—we had to produce our lists for the Russian customs officials at the airport. If one digit was off, they might not allow us to take our camera with us, or bring it back in. All of this required trained and experienced Russia staff that could troubleshoot our encounters with customs.

At the bureau we had other staff required by the peculiarities of Soviet traditions that survived the political end of the Communist system. One was our cook. Explaining to our Atlanta accountants why she was necessary was both a financial and diplomatic challenge.

On the face of it, a cook sounded like a luxury. She served up a full meal for lunch, as is the Russia custom, the main meal of the day: steaming purplish-red borsch made from beets, with a dollop of sour cream on top; or "ukha"—fisherman's soup with a chunk of fish and plenty of onions and carrots; or, my favorite, "solyanka," another fish soup but with the added zest of salted cucumbers and green olives.

At our office, soup was just the first course for lunch. It was followed by the main course, beef or chicken or fish; white or (my other favorite) black bread, preferably Borodinsky; and finished off with desserts and tea and coffee. To Americans, used to grabbing a sandwich for lunch, it seemed excessive, but there were several good reasons to have a cook in the Moscow bureau, as I explained to my supervisors in Atlanta.

In Soviet times, providing meals to employees was an expected part of an employer's responsibility. Our workdays were extremely long, lasting into the wee hours of the morning, thanks to the eight-hour time difference with East Coast United States. A live shot for an evening US primetime news program would mean keeping news crews in the bureau until 3 or 4 a.m. The couch in my office, many nights, became my bed. Cooked meals were a necessity also because fast food in Russia was still a few years away. Yes, there was the famous McDonald's in downtown Moscow, and a new Pizza Hut not far away from our office, but no one could survive on burgers and pizza night after night. According to our Russian labor contracts, we had to provide meals if staff worked overtime. Having a cook and buying our own groceries, in the end, was cheaper, healthier, and more convenient.

Nevertheless, my task was to downsize, and I did. Saying farewell to members of our team who had worked so hard and so well for so many years was emotionally wrenching, but we managed to find ways to compensate them fairly. In some cases, technological advancements dictated the changes. New and smaller digital camera equipment was easier to carry, for example, and we no longer needed a recording engineer on every shoot.

Yet, even as we reduced personnel, the CNN bureau remained one of the largest—and busiest—international news operations in Moscow. The ongoing Chechen conflict, political upheaval, presidential summits, elections, terrorism, and, finally, the 9/11 attacks in the United States kept our bureau in a constant state of readiness, to be expanded quickly if teams from London or other bureaus had to be deployed to Moscow. Early on, I packed a "run bag" and left it by my front door, filled with medicine, personal supplies, underwear, cash, prepackaged food, boots, and other gear that could get me through a week or two of breaking news. And there was plenty of breaking news to come.

YELTSIN'S MANY DEATHS

Soon after I began my job as bureau chief in the spring of 1997 I got my first in-person encounter with Boris Yeltsin at a short "press availability." I wanted to ask a question that went beyond breaking news—that would capture the essence of the Russian leader.

"What will be your legacy?" I asked.

Yeltsin looked at me furiously. "I'm not dead yet!" he bellowed.

I was taken aback, but quickly realized what Russians meant when they described Yeltsin's "expansivny kharakter" (literally, "expansive character," but more accurately, "unrestrained emotional largesse").

In my previous post as White House correspondent I had some opportunities to observe Yeltsin as I reported on the Bush administration's attempts to stabilize relations with a newly independent Russia. On the morning of February 2, 1992, I joined the small group of press pool reporters gathered for the short drive by government van to Maryland to cover Yeltsin's visit to Camp David. To emphasize the importance the administration attached to Yeltsin's success, President Bush had invited the Russian leader to his presidential retreat, with its rustic, clubby atmosphere reserved for an exclusive group of world leaders. As Robert Strauss, the US ambassador to Moscow, put it: "We've got a lot riding on him here. We have a big stake in the success of Boris Yeltsin. Because Yeltsin's success hopefully means democracy's success."

Our group of journalists stood behind a rope line as Yeltsin, in a gray-striped sweater, and Bush, in a windbreaker with presidential seal, approached the microphones. Bush expressed hopes for a "true partnership," Yeltsin thanked his "friend George." "Going forward," Yeltsin said, "we don't consider each other potential opponents, as it was up to now in our military doctrines." The relationship would now be marked by "full openness and full honesty."

I asked a question in Russian: "Boris Nikolayevich, do you think you are getting sufficient economic assistance from the United States?"

"What's important is not just aid," he began. "We're looking for support for our reforms, cooperation in a lot of different areas . . . I didn't come here just to stretch out my hand for help. No! We're calling for cooperation, cooperation for the whole world, because if reform in Russia goes under, that means there will be a Cold War, and the Cold War's going to turn into a hot war. This is again going to be an arms race. Again, this will be the same regime we just recently rid ourselves of. We can't allow that to happen!"

On the eve of that visit, Ambassador Strauss sent a cable back to the State Department with his assessment of Yeltsin. "The Russian leader is firmly in the domestic political saddle," he wrote, "but he continues to struggle with the results of the imperial breakup he helped bring about and with the garrison state he inherited." The ambassador, however, saw "no credible substitutes waiting in the wings."

Strauss described Yeltsin as "dominating . . . and domineering," but also noted he had a "uniquely charismatic link" with his fellow Russians. "Russians appreciate Yeltsin's force of personality, his down-to-earth approach to issues and his determination to effect basic change.

"Resentment of soaring prices was growing," but the Russian president, Strauss said, "retains the support of the great mass of the Russian people and will use that support to steer his economic reform programs through the difficult months ahead." Toward the end of the cable, however, he added this warning: "There is a great deal more political and economic ferment in this country than television viewers in the West imagine."

That cable was declassified by the State Department in 2015. I wish I'd seen it when I began writing Boris Yeltsin's obituary.

Almost all media outlets prepare obituaries of famous people in advance, to be ready to publish or air immediately when they die. Over my years as bureau chief, I was forced to revise my Yeltsin obit on a regular basis. Despite five heart attacks, pneumonia, hospitalizations, regular unexplained disappearances from public view, odd behavior, slurred speech, and other indications of serious medical problems, he continued not to die. His press secretaries invented the excuse that the president was "working with documents," a phrase that soon entered the modern Russian lexicon, along with a wink and a nod.

Every four months or so I would try to schedule a short break from work with a trip to nearby European countries but, invariably, CNN editors in Atlanta or London would call me on my mobile phone, frantically ordering me to cut short my vacation and return immediately to Russia because Mr. Yeltsin was "dying." He did not die until almost a decade later, on April 23, 2007, after I had left my Moscow post and returned to Washington.

Most of my Yeltsin obit remained the same, and at the time of his death, I was still torn, trying to evaluate his role in modern Russia's history. I began with video and sound of the iconic image of Yeltsin on a tank: "This is the Boris Yeltsin the world will long remember: August 1991, astride a tank . . . the president of Russia facing down a coup against Mikhail Gorbachev, president of the Soviet Union."

Then, a quote from Yeltsin himself: "At that time, I had only one thought—to save Russia, to save this country, to save democracy and the whole world. Anything else would have led to chaos."

But the image I chose next expressed the duality I felt: video and audio of tanks firing on the Russian White House, the large white government building facing the Moscow River, a short walk from our bureau: "But this, too, is Boris Yeltsin . . . October 1993 . . . Troops, on orders of Yeltsin, open fire on the Parliament House, the very building where he had made his stand two years before."

Mikhail Gorbachev—whom Yeltsin and his aides had rescued during the dark hours he was held hostage by the 1991 coup-plotters—was, nevertheless, a severe critic of Yeltsin, and the 1993 attack Yeltsin ordered on the Russian White House, where rebellious lawmakers were holed up, infuriated him. In his 1995 *Memoirs* Gorbachev wrote: "When I turned on the television on the morning of 4 October I was shocked by what I saw. Not even in my most terrible nightmares could I imagine that in the center of Moscow Russian tanks . . . would methodically, and in cold blood, be firing at Parliament! . . . This was madness . . . It was unforgivable!"

Gorbachev later described Yeltsin as "dominated by ambition and love of praise and position . . . he was prepared to take the most extreme steps in order to show he could do everything, that anything was in his power . . . he has trampled on democracy!"

I found it maddeningly difficult to see where the upheaval in Russia was headed. So much of our reporting was personality-driven: the "Bill and Boris Show" during the Clinton years, the drama of "rescuing" the nascent Russian democracy, still at risk from a Communist resurgence. It remains so today, although the plot has shifted from Boris Yeltsin "building democracy" to Vladimir Putin destroying it.

But the broader stakes in those early days were, indeed, high. True, Communists no longer ruled Russia; shortly after Gorbachev was freed from captivity during the attempted coup in August 1991, he banned the Communist Party of the Soviet Union. Three months later, Yeltsin had nationalized the Party's property. But he never banned Communism itself, and its adherents—its true believers and its careerists—already were regrouping, carving out new political parties from the carcass of the party of Lenin and Stalin.

Any attempt to resurrect Communism was seen, not only by Yeltsin's Russian supporters but by US administration officials, as a mortal danger. Misgivings and concerns about Yeltsin's democratic failings—including engineering his 1996 reelection, thanks to funding from Russia's oligarchs and advice from American PR agencies and election consultants—were set aside. Post-Soviet Russia had to pass the existential test of simply surviving, and that meant keeping the Communists from regaining power. Kremlin-allied oligarchs who now controlled the media created a terrifying image of what would happen if Communism once more ruled Russia.

The 1996 election was, at its heart, a referendum on whether the wrenching changes of the past five years—dismantling the Communists' centrally planned economic system and purging it with the "shock therapy" of Western-style economic reform—was worth it. Many Russians concluded it was not. Pensions, for example, went unpaid for years, and millions of retired Russians, for whom minuscule pensions were their only income, were living hand to mouth. At one point, the government owed retired Russians the equivalent of more than two and a half billion dollars. During the election campaign, Yeltsin promised to repay the retirees, but he never fully did. Elderly Russians watched helplessly as prices that, under Communism, had been controlled by law, were liberalized, rising uncontrollably. Exasperated, some hit the streets in protest.

One of the earliest stories I covered in Moscow was the series of protests by coal miners. They were working in exceedingly dangerous conditions but were not being paid—in some cases for half a year or more. Millions of rubles that the government set aside for the miners disappeared or were misspent. I had a personal interest in the miners; some of my own Irish ancestors had worked in the coal mines near Scranton, Pennsylvania.

The plight of the Russian miner went back to the waning days of the Soviet Union. At the end of the 1980s, as the Soviet economy ground to a halt, President Mikhail Gorbachev introduced his economic reform program, but the miners went unpaid. Then populist leader Boris Yeltsin seized the moment, putting himself squarely on their side, demanding Gorbachev's resignation. Gorbachev was forced to curtail his reforms.

But in February 1996, the tables turned. Now it was Yeltsin, president of the Russian Federation, who could not manage to restore the miners' wages. One million of them walked off their jobs across Russia. The miners took their protest to Moscow. Yeltsin managed to find a temporary solution for the back wages, but the structural problems of the mining industry remained. In 1998, the miners were back protesting in Moscow.

To this day, I can hear the clatter of miners' helmets as the men, most still wearing their sooty work clothes, banged them on the cobblestones of Gorbaty Most (Hunchbacked Bridge) near the Russian White House. They waved banners threatening to push Yeltsin from office.

To see the plight of the miners up close, we flew to Siberia, to the city of Kemerovo. The first thing I noticed was the snow. It fell from the sky in a flurry of white, but within minutes it was covered with a fine, black, sooty ash. The sky was gray, the buildings, too.

We headed for a meeting where strike organizers were planning their next steps. There we met a young miner's wife, Inna, who bore a striking resemblance to Julie Christie in the film *Dr. Zhivago*. She and her husband were in their early thirties. She told me that he, like most of his fellow miners, already was suffering from black lung disease. Many miners died in their early forties. Inna said she dreamed of moving to Moscow, but she ruefully admitted it would never happen. I felt intensely sad as I boarded our plane back to the Russian capital, something Inna would never be able to do.

Yeltsin did manage to find money for old-age pensioners, but the government still owed millions in back wages to Russians working in state enterprises and the military. The anger and frustration of voters who once looked to Yeltsin as their protector festered. So many had counted on him simply to make life better, but so far, it just seemed to get harder. I would go for long walks through Moscow and stop in food stores along the way. Often, all I saw was bare shelves. On the street, old women were selling their meager belongings—shoes, socks, a small teapot, a tiny bunch of flowers—anything that could bring them a few kopeks, enough to survive for another month.

Once again living in Russia, I began to understand a truth about the end of the Soviet Union that ran counter to the way so many Americans understood it. Like many Westerners, I considered the demise of Communist control as a victory of democracy and free markets. I approached it from the abstract ideal of Jeffersonian democracy. But most average Russian citizens did not see it that way. After seventy years of Communist ideology, the old slogans were empty, the butt of bitter jokes—like the old Soviet "anecdote" about Communism: "They always say Communism is on the horizon, but what's a horizon? A horizon is an imaginary line that gets farther away the closer you get to it." Or, one of my favorites: "Under capitalism, man exploits man; under Communism, it's the reverse."

Russians were no longer attracted by ideology, and very few had any understanding of Jeffersonian democracy. The institutions of Western-style democracy, like an independent judicial system, still needed to be built. The Russians I interviewed on the streets of Moscow and other cities in the summer of 1997 were pragmatic: Was there enough food in the stores? Could they afford it? Would their factory be shut down? That was the ultimate test of "democracy."

THE BODY ON RED SQUARE

There was one political standoff I reported on that was based not on economic woes but on ideology and symbolism: whether to remove Vladimir Lenin's embalmed corpse from its red granite tomb on Red Square. He had died more than seventy years before but had never found eternal rest. After his death in 1924, his waxen body was embalmed, dressed in a black suit, and publicly displayed, first in a wood sarcophagus, then, in a massive granite tomb.

Over my years in Russia, I had visited Lenin's tomb several times and was eerily drawn to it. Long lines of visitors, Russians and foreigners alike, would wait for hours in the snow and cold on Red Square. They were eventually ushered into the mausoleum as if they were in church, sternly directed by guards to keep quiet, and keep moving. Lenin's body, looking pale yet airlessly alive, lay in a coffin under a bulletproof glass enclosure. The experience felt somehow religious, although Soviet Communism banned the practice of religion. Throughout the former USSR, statues and monuments to Lenin were being toppled, but to Communists, Lenin's tomb would be sacred for eternity.

Yeltsin, always the crafty politician, knew his proposal to move Lenin's body would strike a nerve and seemed pleased not only with goading the Communists, but also with putting an end to their political movement. Red Square, he scoffed, "should not look like a cemetery," and he proposed holding a national referendum. "Let the people decide whether to bury him in a Christian way or leave him as he is."

In early June I took a camera crew with me and headed for Red Square. Muscovites we spoke with seemed divided on the issue, but public opinion polls showed more and more Russians thought Lenin deserved a proper burial, preferably in St. Petersburg. "I read that Lenin wanted to be buried together with his family," one man told me. "So why not?" Another complained, "We've already destroyed our values in this country—nothing's sacred anymore. Let Lenin stay where he is!"

The referendum was never held and, to this day, the literal embodiment of the Soviet Union lies on Red Square. A few years later, the next president, Vladimir Putin, would not only keep Lenin's tomb on Red Square but also leave a number of Soviet symbols in place, renewing them, molding them into his own version of Russian national identity.

In 2024, more than three decades after the Soviet Union ended, most Russians believed that Lenin's body should remain in the mausoleum. A poll by the Levada Center showed the majority of Russians still thought Lenin had played a positive role in the history of Russia. In fact, the share of Russians who believed that had actually increased. In 2006, for example, 40 percent of the poll's respondents thought that way. By 2024, 67 percent agreed.

Shockingly, when asked how they thought Lenin would be remembered in forty or fifty years, only 5 percent thought people would remember him as a "cruel dictator, prepared to sacrifice the lives of millions." It was another example of the growing trend of "Soviet nostalgia," one that Vladimir Putin would foster and exploit.

BURYING THE CZAR

Other bones with deep historical, political, and religious significance lay, still unburied, a thousand miles away in the Ural Mountains, in Yekaterinburg. It was the city where Russia's last czar, Nicholas II, his wife, Alexandra, their four daughters and one son, along with four members of their staff, were brutally murdered by the Bolsheviks in 1918. Their bones were finally discovered in 1979 in a forest where the executioners hid them, then exhumed in 1991. The remains of two of his children—Maria and Alexei—were missing and later found and identified, but they have not been buried, the result of political infighting and the opposition of the Russian Orthodox Church.

A year after I began working in Moscow, I traveled to St. Petersburg to report on the final interment of the czar and his family in the Romanov family crypt inside the golden-spired St. Peter and Paul Cathedral within the Peter and Paul Fortress—just a stone's throw from the dormitory where I had lived as an exchange student in 1969 and 1970.

The solemnity of the moment was profound. President Yeltsin, along with his country, had been grappling with the concept of "repentance" for the Soviet terror. Some wanted Russia to admit the horror, give restitution to its victims, and rebuild the nation, cleansing it of the stain of Communism. Communists, of course, rejected this out of hand. Still others wanted to move on, to bury the painful past without atoning for it. That is the path the next Russian president, Vladimir Putin, would take two years later.

On that July day in 1998, on St. Isaac's Square in St. Petersburg, I watched the faces of Russians, their eyes focused on the funeral cortege of the last Romanov czar as it passed slowly by, silent, respectful, but betraying little emotion. Is this what it would have been like eighty years ago, I asked myself, if Nicholas II had been publicly buried soon after he was shot? At that time, many probably would have cheered that "Bloody Nicholas" was dead at last, that the man whose reign was marked by war and revolution was finally gone.

For many of those people on the square that day, Nicholas was an afterthought, not someone a worker who hasn't been paid in weeks or months thinks much about. But politicians, religious leaders, and members of the Romanov family were fixated on this burial, and they were divided. Taking their cue from the Church, many Russian politicians declined to attend the ceremony and, for months, President Yeltsin had said he would not take part. Behind the scenes, his aides said he was caught in a difficult position, not wanting to alienate the Church.

Suddenly, the day before the burial, Yeltsin announced he would go. The president known for abrupt, unexpected—and populist—decisions acted true to form. But members of the extended Romanov family, now living abroad, were split as well, one branch boycotting the burial, calling its modest scale a travesty. The main branch of the family—some fifty members from Europe and the United States—traveled to St. Petersburg to bid a final farewell to their relative, Russia's last czar.

Just before the caskets of the czar and his family were to arrive Thursday in St. Petersburg, members of the Romanov family gathered in the foyer of the Astoria Hotel, most of them elegantly dressed in black. The head of this branch of the family, Nikolai Romanovich Romanov—a tall, distinguished man with gray hair and an aquiline nose—told me that perhaps this burial, which recalls the mistakes of Russia's past, would help it to avoid more mistakes in the future.

Most Russians I talked with that day said, regardless of the dispute, it was time to give Nicholas and his family a Christian burial. Others claimed Russia should pay less attention to a czar from the past and more to its own suffering citizens of today. The debate would smolder for years, but Russia has never managed either to fully deal with its past—czarist or Communist—or to alleviate the suffering of its poorest citizens.

In his speech that day, Boris Yeltsin tried to heal what he called the "uncompromising split in Russian society" into "us" and "them," which he said still divided Russians. "We have long been silent about this monstrous crime," he said. "We must tell the truth: The Yekaterinburg massacre has become one of the most shameful episodes in our history. By burying the remains of innocent victims, we want to atone for the sins of our ancestors. Those who committed this crime are as guilty as are those who approved of it for decades. We are all guilty."

The political divide, however, did not heal, and Yeltsin, despite his political charisma, failed to improve most Russians' lives. Reporting from his early rallies, I heard him speak to his fellow Russians with a shocking, un-Soviet honesty. In the early days, I saw the excitement and hope in the eyes of his supporters. In contrast to the turgid speeches of leaders like Leonid Brezhnev, here was a man who sounded like a real, and sometimes fallible, human being. In the spring of 1997, just a few months before I arrived, he delivered his state of the nation address, admitting, "We are stuck halfway, having left the old shore; we keep floundering in a stream of problems which engulf us and prevent us from reaching a new shore."

By this time, however, Yeltsin was running out of excuses. Stage-managed by PR advisers, including his daughter and "image adviser" Tatyana Dyachenko, and his literary aide, Valentin Yumashev, who would later become Tatyana's husband, Yeltsin went to sometimes ridiculous ends to prove he was still running the country. A few weeks after I started my Moscow job, Yeltsin went on vacation, nine months after he had survived a quintuple heart bypass operation.

In the old Communist days, Russian leaders who went on vacation virtually disappeared. All of that changed with Boris Yeltsin's summer holiday. In a photo op straight out of an American president's book, Yeltsin started his monthlong retreat in the bucolic setting of northern Russia, but it didn't take long before he was speaking out on NATO expansion: "We're going to categorically oppose that!"

His wife, Naina, told reporters he'd never change: "The first two days he slept in, but then it was meetings, it was work, it was papers, it was telephone. You can't do anything about it! It's in his blood!"

He fished, he visited a farm, he captained a ship, he vetoed a controversial law on religion, he ordered the army restructured, and negotiated with the Finnish president in a sauna, saying, "It felt so good to beat the Finnish president with Russian birch twigs!"

Yeltsin, even a sick Yeltsin, seemed to have nine lives, but in the summer of 1997, the Russian president was facing a series of public relations disasters. His justice minister, Valentin Kovalev, was embroiled in Russia's first sex scandal. The story broke when the tabloid *Sovershenno Sekretno* ("Top Secret") published nude photographs in an article entitled "The Minister Has No Clothes: Secret Frolics of the Department Boss." The pictures came from a videotape, broadcast on Russian television, that appeared to show the justice minister in a sauna allegedly frequented by the mafia, engaging in group sex with naked women. The minister's lawyer dismissed it as a fake.

Russia, indeed, was becoming like the West in more ways than one. Just a few months later, news broke of Bill Clinton's affair back in Washington with Monica Lewinsky. The symmetry was oddly jarring. But, as I found out when I visited a factory to ask Russian women what they thought of Clinton's behavior, one of them said it was fine with her; it just made Clinton more attractive.

It didn't take long before Yeltsin was facing another scandal: a tell-all account by his former bodyguard and confidant, Alexander Korzhakov, recounting his decade with Russia's president, describing him as a chronic alcoholic, paralyzed by indecision.

THE TYCOONS

Russian politicians had been attacking each other for much of the post-Soviet period with charges of corruption and embezzlement. Now, sex and personal misconduct had become another weapon in the never-ending Kremlin political wars. My posting in Moscow began at the height of those wars, fought by men who, just a year previously, had saved Boris Yeltsin's political life: industrial and media tycoons, the so-called "clan leaders." Men like Boris Berezovsky, who began his working life in Soviet times as an engineer and head of a department at the USSR Academy of Sciences, then turned his high intellect to more lucrative post-Soviet ventures in the burgeoning automobile market.

When I met Berezovsky, he had transitioned into the media market, gaining control over ORT television, the heir to the Soviet-era Channel 1, and building it into a mass-media empire with two TV channels, the newspaper *Nezavisimaya Gazeta*, and a major magazine, *Ogonyok*. Zelig-like, with dark, piercing eyes, he seemed to be everywhere at once, sharing control of the Russian oil company Sibneft, serving as CFO of Aeroflot, the Russian airline, and, finally, becoming a member of Yeltsin's Security Council. He was, in effect, Russia's first oligarch, and he played a key role as part of the rich and powerful coterie of Yeltsin's advisers who exploited their media outlets to ensure that Yeltsin beat the Communist candidate, Gennady Zyuganov, in the 1996 presidential election.

A compact man with a coiled energy about him, Berezovsky seemed to have his hand in everything, even freeing hostages held for ransom in Chechnya, and I struggled to follow the skeins of his connections and influence. Since the end of Communist rule, the national resources of Russia had been quietly sold off to businessmen with close ties to the Yeltsin government, who bought them up at bargain-basement prices. In July of 1997, Russia's biggest privatization yet—an auction for one-quarter of the giant state-owned telecommunications holding company, Svyazinvest—sparked an all-out financial and media war.

Just beginning my reporting in Moscow, I tried to boil down the story to simple-enough terms for TV, but it was complex even for an in-depth newspaper article. And yet I sensed where it was leading: Yeltsin himself would pay the political price for the battle rocking the already shaky foundations of his government. And Russia itself would pay the price for the so-called "media wars."

On the surface, the media seemed free. Echo of Moscow, the news radio station I listened to throughout the day, was doing real journalism, and I eagerly listened to the ferocious debates over Yeltsin's policies. On Saturday nights, I watched *Kukly* ("Puppets"), a political satire show that used puppets representing Russian politicians and celebrities, including the Russian president.

Behind the scenes, however, media outlets had become prime targets for investment by Russia's biggest companies. Gazprom, for example, Russia's natural gas monopoly, had stakes in or supported more than two dozen newspapers and television stations. Media mogul Vladimir Gusinsky owned newspapers, magazines, and radio and television stations. Some of those holdings overlapped, creating a complex web of financial power—and politics—and sometimes those interests clashed.

INVENTING THE "MAN OF ACTION"

Russia's media wars were about money, no doubt, but they also were the product of the 1996 presidential election, in which some of Russia's best-known journalists had abandoned the principles of journalism for what they claimed was a higher cause: saving Russia from falling back into the hands of the Communists. As a result, almost all mentions of the Communist Party boss, Gennady Zyuganov, were shut down, any gaffes by Yeltsin covered up.

My first summer in Moscow as bureau chief, Boris Yeltsin, a sick man with a heart problem, was transformed by his PR staff, the "analytical group" who rescued Yeltsin's faltering 1996 campaign, into a "man of action." They even showed the ailing Yeltsin climbing into the cockpit of a new Russian fighter jet to prove it. The group polled the Russian public on a weekly basis, asking whom they would vote for and how they thought Yeltsin was doing. At one point, Yeltsin's approval rating stood at a shocking 8 percent.

I admit I initially was swayed by the argument that, if the Communists returned to power, Russia's nascent independent media would be quickly snuffed out. But, as would become clearer when Yeltsin's heir, Vladimir Putin, took the reins, despite some individual journalists who adhered to high standards, most of Russia's mass media found it extremely challenging to evade the influence of their owners.

Yeltsin's government became a revolving door, as he fired one prime minister after another. One day, in my CNN office, as I was unpacking books and supplies that I had brought from Washington, news broke that Yeltsin had dismissed Viktor Chernomyrdin, along with his entire cabinet. In a minute the phone rang. It was the news desk in Atlanta, asking me to go on the air immediately and explain it all. New to the intricacies of Yeltsin's politically chaotic governing style, I stumbled my way through an impromptu "beeper"—a report by phone. There was no time to set up the camera for a live shot.

In August 1999, Yeltsin fired yet another prime minister and replaced him with the relatively unknown Vladimir Putin. The revolving door finally stopped. Yeltsin named Putin as his successor and, at the end of his New Year's Eve address to the nation, shocked the world. He began slowly, turgidly.

"I want to ask for your forgiveness. For the fact that many of the dreams we shared did not come true. And for the fact that what seemed simple to us turned out to be tormentingly difficult. I ask forgiveness for not justifying some hopes of those people who believed that at one stroke, in one spurt, we could leap from the gray, stagnant, totalitarian past into the light, rich, civilized future. I, myself, believed in this, that we could overcome everything in one spurt."

His face was swollen. He looked tired, and ill.

"I turned out to be too naive in something. In some places, problems seemed to be too complicated. We forced our way forward through mistakes, through failures. Many people in this hard time experienced shock. But I want you to know. I have never said this. Today it's important for me to tell you.

The pain of each of you has called forth pain in me, in my heart. Sleepless nights, tormenting worries—about what needed to be done, so that people could live more easily and better. I did not have any more important task."

And then, the bombshell: "I am leaving. I did all I could. . . . A new generation is relieving me, a generation of those who can do more, and better."

Yeltsin announced he was stepping down, putting the duties of the president of Russia in the hands of Vladimir Putin. For three months Putin would be head of state. In March, presidential elections would take place.

My first two years in Moscow—the Yeltsin years—were a welter of dizzying events: war, economic dislocation, protests, political instability. Understanding it all, let alone explaining it to our viewers, was tough. Part of that was the newness of it, diving into the crosscurrents of historic change. Part of it was Yeltsin himself and the chaotic nature of his presidency. Part of it was simply Russia itself.

Then, suddenly, there was Vladimir Putin, the man some called the "Accidental President." Quiet, disciplined, nose to the grindstone, refusing even to campaign publicly for the presidency, Putin seemed the one who could calm the waters roiled by Yeltsin.

Boris Yeltsin handed the presidency to Vladimir Putin and, with it, a ticking time bomb of a problem: Chechnya.

· 8 ·

Chechnya

In 2002 my colleague and friend, journalist Anna Politkovskaya, published a book, *The Second Chechen*. She didn't need to finish the phrase with the word "War." Any Russian who lived through that period knew exactly who she was and what she had experienced. A well-known and highly respected journalist for the independent newspaper *Novaya Gazeta* ("New Gazette"), she had witnessed the war from the beginning and had chronicled it in searing human detail.

Boris Yeltsin launched the First Chechen War. It lasted from December 1994 until the end of August 1996. It began as a war of independence by the predominantly Muslim region. Moscow waged a brutal campaign to keep it as part of Russia, but it ended in a stalemate: Chechnya had de facto independence. It was an ignominious defeat for the Russian army, and for President Boris Yeltsin.

Three years later, in August 1999, Islamic fighters from Chechnya, led by the terrorist guerrilla warlord Shamil Basayev, swarmed over the border with the neighboring republic of Dagestan, seizing several villages, and declaring the "Chechen-Dagestan Islamic Republic" independent of Russia. Increasingly influenced by Islamic extremists, Chechnya's war for independence was turning into a jihad.

"RUB THEM OUT EVEN IN THE OUTHOUSE"

Just three days after the militants attacked, Yeltsin named forty-six-year-old Vladimir Putin his new prime minister. Putin, a relatively unknown member

133

of his administration, was secretary of his Security Council and, briefly, head of the FSB intelligence service. Now, Chechnya was Putin's problem. Putin quickly vowed that, this time, Russia's hands would not be tied.

Russian warplanes roared into Chechnya, striking targets across the breakaway republic, the first time in three years Moscow had launched such raids. The Kremlin claimed it was waging a NATO-style "pinpoint" air campaign to wipe out terrorist training camps—part of what it called an "international" terrorist network. Shamil Basayev, the rebel leader, threw the charge right back at Russia, calling its air strikes "terrorism" directed against civilians. His brother Shirvani warned their Islamic fighters were ready to launch "phase two" of their campaign. "The assault on Dagestan was just a rehearsal," Shirvani declared. "It has nothing to do with oil or territory. This is a jihad."

As she wrote in the introduction to her book, Anna Politkovskaya had covered that first war and now was reporting on this new conflict. "Why?" she asked. "Because I am a journalist, and because my paper sent me to Chechnya . . . not because I am a war correspondent and know the subject well. Quite the opposite: because I am a deeply civilian person."

The idea, she explained, was simple: "For me, a deeply civilian person, the sufferings of other deeply civilian people—the residents of Chechen villages and cities upon whose heads the war had collapsed—were much more understandable." Anna traveled from her home in Moscow to Chechnya every month, beginning in July of 1999, when the Basayev raid on Dagestan unleashed a flood of refugees to neighboring republics, especially Ingushetia, where at least 160,000 people had fled the fighting.

"I saw a lot of grief," she wrote. "The most important part was that many of my heroes, about whom I have written these past two and a half years, are dead. Such a frightening thing has happened. It's medieval." Carpet-bombing, flattening towns and villages, murders, rapes—this was the merciless pattern Vladimir Putin would later employ in Syria and against Ukraine.

On the title page of her book, Anna Politkovskaya once wrote to me, "Dear Jill! Thank you for your great interest in this, our most difficult tragedy." Chechnya, and the death and suffering it created, was a "difficult" tragedy.

Lilia Shevtsova, one of the most perceptive analysts of Russia, defined that difficulty more precisely in her 2007 book, *Russia—Lost in Translation*: "Yeltsin's war accelerated the demise of Russia's reforms. Putin's war in Chechnya not only squeezed him into the presidency but also continues to legitimize his personalized power."

Ominously, she added: "Moreover, this was a new kind of war—against the internal and external enemy—which has implications for Russia's development that at the moment are difficult to grasp."

Anna Politkovskaya was a fierce critic of Vladimir Putin and even in the early days of his presidency described herself as "obsessive in my opposition to Putin," who, she believed, was leading Russia back to Soviet enslavement. In her 2004 book, *Putin's Russia*, Anna wrote: "The social apathy shown by society is immense. And it serves as an indulgence to Putin for the next four years. We reacted to his actions and speeches not just sluggishly but with fear. We showed this fear of ours to the Chekists [an early Soviet word for the KGB] rooted in power. And this only ginned up their desire to treat us like scum. The KGB respects only the strong—it devours the weak . . . there is no better gift for him than to feel the crowd, which must be subjugated to their will, to have its heart at its heels."

On October 7, 2006, the birthday of Vladimir Putin, Anna Politkovskaya was assassinated, shot dead in the elevator of her Moscow apartment building. She was forty-eight. Predictably, some suspects were arrested. Authorities named the "killer": a thirty-year-old Chechen. After a trial, and a retrial, five men were sentenced to prison for her murder. The organizer of the assassination, the person who ordered the murder, was never identified.

Vladimir Putin, reacting to Anna Politkovskaya's assassination, called it an "appalling crime," but demeaned her even in death: "Her capacity to influence political life in Russia was extremely insignificant."

FLEEING THE KILLING

September 1999 began with a car bombing outside a five-story apartment building in the Dagestani city of Buynaksk. The victims were mostly women and children, some the families of Russian military personnel. As rescuers pulled the dead and injured from the rubble, news reports said a bomb was found—and defused—in another part of town. Investigators immediately suspected Islamic militants. Russian forces had succeeded in driving the rebels out of Dagestan, back across the border into Chechnya, but hundreds returned, seizing more villages. The Russian air attacks resumed, but one rebel commander was defiant: "There will be much blood" in store for Russia, he vowed.

The Russian military unleashed its heavy weapons—warplanes, helicopter gunships, and tanks—and Yeltsin brushed aside his new prime minister to personally chair an emergency session of his Security Council. "These bandits aren't Muslims!" he bellowed. "They have no nationality, no faith, no God, no Allah. They're killers!"

He berated his generals: "How is it possible for us to lose a whole village? A whole region! How did it happen? Why are there more terrorist acts on military compounds than any other place? It's because of the sloppiness of the military!"

The escalating battle in Dagestan was a problem for the Kremlin, which continued to insist it did not want another war: "This is not a war . . . this is an antiterrorist operation," insisted the Interior Ministry spokesman (an eerie foreshadowing of the definition Putin would use in 2022 to describe his full-scale invasion and war against Ukraine).

But Yeltsin's press secretary, Dmitry Yakushkin, finally had to admit: "It looks like it's a war. I would agree that it's extremely dangerous. You know, for years, we talked about the danger of separatism in Russia. Well, here we have that real danger."

Dagestan was exploding. It was Vladimir Putin's job to stop it.

By September Putin had been Russia's prime minister for less than two months. He now was consumed by Chechnya, the open wound that had never healed. Russia's stability, and Putin's own political future, depended on how he dealt with it.

September 9, 1999, marked a personal anniversary for me—twenty-two years since Valucha and I had met in Chicago—but we didn't get the chance to celebrate. At midnight the night before, in Moscow, I was awakened by news that there had been an explosion at a nine-story apartment building on Guryanova Street in the working-class Pechatniky neighborhood on Moscow's southeast side. My cameraman, producer, and I quickly loaded up the car and raced to the location where rescue workers were digging through what was left of the building.

The explosion had sheared off the entire middle section, exposing the apartment interiors, leaving behind shattered window frames, curtains blowing in the breeze, furniture dangling precariously from what once were floors. I could see a coat still hanging by a hook, the rest of the apartment blown away. The building was illuminated with giant lights, creating a ghoulish bluish glow over the scene. Sixty-four apartments had collapsed, one on top of the other.

As we filmed from the street, held back by police cordons, the rescue crews would suddenly go silent, straining to hear any sounds of survivors trapped in the wreckage. Residents of the building, still in their pajamas, were being led to ambulances. Some were crying; others were too shocked to make a sound.

In that Moscow night, the dead were buried beneath tons of smoking wreckage. As rescuers pulled more bodies from the rubble, neighbors stood by, shocked by the magnitude of the explosion. I spoke with a woman named Vera, who told me she had friends in the building. She stood by holding a lighted candle in her hands. She said she was praying for God to help the living and take the souls of the dead to heaven.

There were four deadly bombings at apartment buildings in Russia in less than two weeks. Prime Minister Putin announced that if these were terrorist acts, "it means we are confronted with a cunning, impudent, insidious and bloodthirsty adversary." In a meeting with President Yeltsin, he said he was "certain that we will surmount the problem, but only if we recognize the seriousness of the threat to our country . . . and, having faced this danger, mobilize the forces and resources to meet the challenge." In public comments Putin used rougher language: "We'll pursue the terrorists everywhere . . . we'll rub them out even in the outhouse."

Putin's tough talk was winning hearts and minds. A poll showed that nearly half of all Russians thought his government was doing a good job. Putin's own positive ratings, while still numerically minuscule, as were the ratings for most Russian politicians at the time, jumped from 2 percent to 7 percent in just one week. After Yeltsin's drinking and disorganization, here was a decisive man who might, some Russians thought, be able to protect them from the terrifying onslaught of terrorism. Alexei Pushkov, a Russian defense analyst, said Putin had shown himself to be a "very tough and resolved man—a kind of civilian, but with military reflexes."

We returned to the shattered apartment building on Guryanova Street several times over the next few weeks. It was clear that residents of the capital were convinced they knew who was to blame for the wave of terrorism. "This bears the mark of the Chechens," one man told us. "We should kick them all out of Moscow."

OPERATION WHIRLWIND

It began in a fury. Federal and Moscow police carried out what they called a massive "antiterrorist campaign" against, most often, people from the Caucasus, especially Chechens, people many Russians referred to as "Blacks." In addition to carrying out random checks in Moscow's streets and in private apartments, "Operation Whirlwind" security forces swept through outdoor markets where many of them worked. Police searched for explosives, arresting anyone without a registration permit that allowed residence in the capital, or anyone they thought looked suspicious.

Human rights groups estimated that 20,000 people had been arrested so far, and the authorities did not dispute that number. Some people didn't wait for the knock on the door; they fled the capital, petrified of the expanding raids, now tormenting citizens of other, poorer, former Soviet republics who had come to Russia in search of work. At the Kursky train station I spoke with one man from Azerbaijan who told me, "If they catch you—to hell with you if you've got a face from the Caucasus! There's fighting in Chechnya and we're suffering for it. What do we have to do with that?"

The raids assured some Muscovites, but others were furious at another target. We found Raisa, a woman who appeared to be in her fifties, standing outside a still-smoldering bombed-out apartment building on Moscow's south side. She told me she had lost a sister and a brother-in-law, and pointed to what once was her flat. "Show this to Yeltsin! I'd shoot him dead if somebody gave me a machine gun! He took an oath to protect us! Where is he?!"

Other Russians told us they had lost any faith in law enforcement. "The state, the people who are supposed to do something about that, they are busy getting rich," Pavel told me.

Just eight years before, a repressive Communist system kept average citizens in line, but terrorism was unheard of. "Maybe it was better in terms of security," Svetlana told me, "but it was worse in terms of freedom. We had to choose. Of course, freedom is better, but now, everything depends on us."

Yeltsin was flailing. Russians were looking for someone who could defend them, a tough leader. Vladimir Putin was positioning himself as that man. The political stakes were high. "Defeat in Chechnya," I reported, "would mean the end of Vladimir Putin's presidential ambitions."

I was right, but I was wrong in my conclusion in a report I filed later that month: "Ironically," I said, "Putin's growing strength could have a downside. As with previous prime ministers, the more powerful he becomes, the greater the danger President Yeltsin, sensing a rival, will fire him." In reality, Yeltsin had chosen Putin as his political heir.

I had no idea that in just three months' time, Yeltsin—in a surprise move—would step down from the presidency, with Vladimir Putin taking his place.

But that autumn, everywhere Yeltsin looked, there was trouble. In Russia's volatile south, a war against Islamic militants. In the media, a barrage of reports on alleged money laundering and Kremlin kickbacks. In the political arena, enemies of the Kremlin were uniting.

Yeltsin's supporters—what was left of them—were in disarray. The economy was in crisis. Until Putin, prime ministers had come and gone in a dizzying spin, fired—one after the other—by the president. Yeltsin's health remained in doubt as the reins slipped from his hands.

"Here in Moscow there are many versions of what's next," I reported on air. "Many rumors in a city that thrives on rumors. But never before have those predictions been so openly discussed."

Rumors were rife that Yeltsin might resign voluntarily, perhaps in September, but his spokesman shot that down: "I don't think that will happen, because President Yeltsin, one of his main goals . . . is to ensure a normal, civilized, change of power, probably for the first time in Russian history."

Yeltsin's wife, Naina, was confident. "If his health allows—and we all depend on God's will—he will never move to the sidelines," she said. As one Russian newspaper put it: "Anyone who thinks Yeltsin will step down in September doesn't know our president."

PUTIN'S WAR

Prime Minister Putin, meanwhile, was authorizing talks with the president of the Chechen republic, Aslan Maskhadov, as a kind of "listening session," but he cautioned he was dubious of any concrete results. Chechnya's leader, he demanded, had to condemn international terrorism, declare his readiness to expel armed bands, and agree to extradite "criminals." It was the same negotiating strategy Putin would employ years later in Syria and in Ukraine: Insist you're open to peace talks—and then start bombing.

Now, in Chechnya, the Russian air force was hitting bridges in the capital, Grozny, and other sites in the north of the republic. By the end of the year, Grozny was decimated, leveled by relentless aerial attacks that killed thousands, many of them Russian pensioners. The defense minister vowed his air force would complete its mission of "ripping this infection out by its roots."

We soon were visiting troops wounded in Dagestan and Chechnya who were being treated in Moscow. At the Reutova military hospital we met Slava, shot in the kidney and the lung. After some rehabilitation he was able to sit up. He told us that he and his fellow soldiers weren't sure how much they were being paid to fight. About 25 to 50 rubles per day, they estimated, the equivalent at the time of about $1 to $2. They were underequipped, too, even as Moscow's military leaders spent millions of dollars developing the new Topol-M nuclear missile. And now, in the midst of the Chechen conflict, the military was unveiling the draft of a new doctrine. Oddly, it seemed to me at the time, it did not name guerrillas or armed militants as Russia's main enemy.

On the streets of the Chechen capital, meanwhile, Chechen men were performing a war dance, following in the steps of the "Zikar," a centuries-old mystical Sufi dance. A woman at a podium shouted "The treachery and cruelty of the enemy knows no limits! Allahu Akbar!" People in the crowd held signs saying: "Stop the genocide of the Chechen people!" The Chechen people, along with the ethnically related Ingush, already had experienced severe repression during World War II, forcibly relocated by Stalin from their homeland to Central Asia, a process in which it's estimated that a quarter of them died. They were not allowed to return until 1957.

But video like that hardly ever appeared on Russian TV, and there were almost no Russian journalists reporting from the Chechen side of the conflict. A Russian journalist colleague told me that if a TV crew went to work in Chechnya, it would be extremely dangerous. "Only local journalists work there," he said, "and it's a problem because their image isn't entirely objective."

Chechnya's lawlessness spawned widespread kidnapping and torture, a thriving business that drove all but the most intrepid away. Even reporters and news crews visiting refugee camps mostly came with their own bodyguards, toting automatic weapons. That complicated the Chechens' attempts to get their story out. Chechen president Aslan Maskhadov brought several groups of international journalists into the republic—under guard.

Time magazine's Paul Quinn-Judge explained: "They are extremely nervous about the danger of people being kidnapped. They will admit this privately, though they won't go into it in public. At the moment, our movements are very circumscribed by their concerns about safety."

As a result, most Russians had a one-sided view of the war: Russian guns bombarding what were described as "terrorist" camps, with almost no reports on casualties, either military or civilian. Only selected Russian media—and no international media—were allowed to report from behind the Russian lines.

"If we publicize the announcements of bandits and terrorists, then they'll make these statements every day," said a spokesman for the FSB, "and that creates fear, so we, unfortunately, would be letting that happen."

Western leaders were watching worriedly as Moscow continued its Chechen offensive. Moscow's endgame wasn't clear. Would Russian troops stop with one-third of Chechnya under their control? Or could it mean a replay of the first Chechen war, which killed more than 80,000 people?

Boris Yeltsin had tried to convince America and Europe to support his campaign to subdue the breakaway republic. But when he sent Russian tanks rolling into Grozny, unleashing a bloodbath, with massive civilian casualties, it gave Washington and its European allies second thoughts. Weakened politically and under siege from corruption scandals, Yeltsin was trying to redefine the conflict—not as a war over Chechen independence, but as a war against international terrorism. At the same time, the Kremlin was rejecting any Western mediation of the conflict, calling it an "internal problem."

By the end of September 1999, Prime Minister Putin indicated that Moscow might resort to commando raids in Chechnya, but a full-scale ground operation would be highly controversial. Meanwhile, the constant airstrikes on Chechnya were forcing thousands of Chechen civilians to flee for neighboring republics.

THE WOMAN IN THE BUS

In early October I flew with a camera crew and producer to Ingushetia to report on the wave of refugees fleeing Moscow's carpet-bombing of Chechnya. On the ground in the city of Nazran we connected with a local "fixer," with whom CNN had previously worked, and trusted, who drove us to Ingushetia's border with Chechnya. The road west from the Chechen capital of Grozny was now a major escape route for a refugee exodus that already had topped 125,000. At the Sunda refugee camp 4,000 people were registered, with more arriving every hour. The tide was overwhelming the camps that officials had hastily set up.

We found a large field rapidly filling with families, some sleeping on the ground, others using whatever they could find—plastic sheeting, tarpaulins, sheets—to construct improvised tents to protect themselves from the elements. The camp had tents only for half the people there. Men used axes to chop firewood for campfires; women were pulling out pots and pans they had managed to grab as they fled; children raced about between the tents. Many had left everything and set out on foot for safety. "They want to move us to railroad cars," an older woman named Amanat told me. "I don't want to be moved around like cattle. I want to go home."

A young man named Shirvani said he had lost sixteen relatives in the last war. The previous week he'd packed up his family and fled Grozny. "The last straw was when, literally, 1,200 meters away, two whole families, neighbors, perished in a bombing. After that, the kids wouldn't stop crying, everybody was crying. I just couldn't do it anymore."

The refugees told us they had no idea how long they would be there—where, or how they would survive the approaching winter. They couldn't decide whom to blame for their plight: the invading Russians determined to knuckle under never-quite-independent Chechnya, or die-hard warlord rebels. One woman told me: "We don't trust anybody—not the Russians, not our own government. All we can see is the bombers and the destruction."

On the edge of the field, I noticed what looked like an abandoned bus. I could see a few people inside, including an elderly woman holding her leg as if in pain. We walked over and I climbed in, asking the woman about her leg. She told me that she had cancer, and I could see what looked like an unhealed wound on her calf. The scene shocked me; I could see the woman was in bad shape, with no medicines, no doctor, forced to sit on a hard seat on a cold bus.

As I spoke with the woman, I felt grateful, yet guilty, that I had good health care back in Moscow. But the sight of her wound triggered a nagging worry about my own health. I silently promised myself that, when I got home, I would check with a doctor about something I never seemed to find the time to deal with.

THE LUMP

In the summer of 1999, my partner Valucha and I flew back from Moscow to Florida to visit my mother in West Palm Beach. Moscow could be hot in the summer, but arriving in Florida, I felt an intoxicating sensual overload, smelling the tropical air and basking in the warm sun. One of my greatest pleasures was taking a daily jog on Flagler Drive, along Intracoastal Waterway. I usually did it in the morning, before it got too hot. That day, I started slowly, then picked up speed as I headed south. For that hour, at least, Yeltsin, the political battles, Russia's economic troubles, were forgotten.

When I got back from my run I jumped in the shower. Drying myself off I noticed in the mirror what looked like an indentation in my right breast. I vaguely recalled a pamphlet from the American Cancer Society listing that as a possible sign of cancer. My mother had survived two bouts of breast cancer, so I quickly made an appointment with her physician. But, instead of ordering a mammogram, her doctor advised me to simply "watch it" for a while. I flew back to Moscow thinking it was no big deal, but as a few weeks went by, the dent did not go away. I felt a bit more tired than usual, but I always found something more important to do than to go to a doctor in Moscow.

The tsunami of events in Moscow seemed, at times, almost overwhelming. In early October Yeltsin had, once again, disappeared from public view. He had the "flu," his aides explained, and from time to time they would release a few seconds of video, often with no sound, showing him at home or meeting with his prime minister.

"There's no president in Russia. That's the reality in which we live," said Pavel Voshchanov, Yeltsin's former press secretary. "The people running the country are Prime Minister Putin and the president's daughter, Tatyana," opined a political observer. Tatyana Dyachenko was Yeltsin's official image-maker, and the expert explained that she was making all the decisions. If there's a need to sign a president's decree, it's Tatyana who delivers the signature, he said. "There is no way to get access to the president, other than through her."

The Kremlin "family," as it was called, was now fixated on guaranteeing its "post-Yeltsin" survival. In public, Prime Minister Putin was winning public praise for his handling of the conflict in Chechnya, as well as for his ability to stay clear of any political infighting; behind the scenes he was arranging for Yeltsin to leave office—without being prosecuted for any alleged corruption.

This all meant hours of live shots late into the night, but my mind kept returning to the image of that woman in the refugee camp with cancer. I promised myself to check out the indentation I had noticed on my breast, despite my mother's doctor's recommendation to "keep our eye on it." I telephoned the international medical clinic where we, and most foreign journalists in Moscow, were treated and made an appointment with a French doctor. After a quick physical examination, he promptly ordered a mammogram. The results were ready within an hour or so, and as I sat in his office, the technician came in and told him it was negative. He smiled wryly and said, with a slight French accent: "I do not think so." He ordered a sonogram.

Quite clearly, I could see a lump that looked like a black mass in a sea of grayish-white. "I'd advise you to return to the United States and find a surgeon who can remove this," he told me. Within two weeks I was back in West Palm Beach, where a surgeon excised the lump. Valucha came with me to the follow-up appointment. I brought a pad and pen to take notes.

"We biopsied it," the surgeon explained. "It's what's called 'invasive ductal carcinoma." My hand began shaking slightly. "So, that is cancer?" I asked. "Yes," he replied. "I couldn't get clean margins, so you'll have to have another operation to do that."

I had a second operation in New York and then began six months of chemotherapy followed by weeks of radiation. The French doctor in Moscow was right: There was no way I would have any treatment in Moscow. The old Soviet free-health-care system was in tatters. If you could find a good physician, you usually had to pay him or her on the side, with money or something else; in small towns and villages people sometimes paid with a chicken.

A few years later, a friend in Moscow was diagnosed with breast cancer and I went to the hospital to visit her. It was a shocking confirmation of what the French doctor was alluding to. Her mother was there to help her out during the first day after surgery. She brought her own bedsheets from home; in the hospital they were either nonexistent or dirty. They had to clean the bathroom themselves. The walls were painted a sickly green and, near the toilet, they were spattered with something brown. Over the years I had seen hospitals in many Russian towns and cities, hospitals with no running water, no heating, not enough anesthetic, but here we were in the richest city in Russia, at a major urban hospital. My friend's mother said their surgeon was excellent and I had no doubt he was, but there she was, sweeping the floor so her daughter wouldn't have to step on dirt.

THE RED DEVIL

From a hotel room in New York City, and then from West Palm Beach, I tried to follow the news from Moscow. At 4:15 a.m. on New Year's Eve I got a call from the CNN news desk in Atlanta, alerting me that Boris Yeltsin had just announced he was stepping down and turning over the powers of the presidency to Vladimir Putin.

I raced to the computer and saw Eileen O'Connor reporting, the correspondent to whom I owed my job in Moscow. She was back in Moscow, filling in. Valucha urged me to do some radio, and I filed a piece for CNN, still trying to make sense of what was happening in Russia. I should have paid better attention a few months previously when rumors were swirling in Moscow about Yeltsin stepping down. Now, a presidential election was scheduled for March, and I wanted to be there to see it.

Mostly, however, my days were consumed with recovering from the surgery, and then undergoing chemo. I decided to take the most aggressive course I could, and that meant intravenous infusions with Adriamycin, nicknamed "The Red Devil," quite appropriate, I thought, for my Russia fixation. But it's not a funny drug: It can damage your heart, you lose your hair, and after my first treatment, I vomited.

I started a diary to keep track of my progress: "My second cancer chemo treatment," I wrote on January 4. "I sit in a big, blue, comfortable chair, my left arm hooked up to an IV. Annie the nurse goes through the chemicals I'll be getting: Ativan, Zofran, Adriamycin, Cytoxan . . . things to calm me down, steroids so I don't react to things too strongly, one name after the other, a Tower of Babel of medications."

What kept me sane was the love and support of Valucha and my mother, as well as a close friend who was going through the same thing. Valucha said that, with my bald head, I looked like the political adviser James Carville. Humor helped, and so did continuing to run. I ran every morning, even chalking up a decent pace in the Race for the Cure. I knew that, by summer, six months of chemo and six weeks of radiation would be over, and I would be back in Moscow, strong again and ready to meet any challenge. At least that's what I hoped. I used a mental trick as I went through that road to recovery: I thought of myself not as a sick person, but as a healthy person temporarily going through a challenge. I was glad I liked wearing baseball caps.

"Giving up control, turning it over, letting go completely—these are the things I want to do, but I cling to the thought that all my substance is tied to being strong, energetic," I wrote in my diary. "I think if I begin to reverse that, I will have to replace it with something strong but not aggressive . . ."

Twins to Study in Russia

The Misses Jill M. and Pamela J. Dougherty will leave for graduate study in Russian at Leningrad State University, Leningrad, U.S.S.R.

The twin daughters of Mr. and Mrs. Vincent G. Dougherty of 10 Lenox St., the girls were awarded grants from the Ford Foundation. They are December graduates of the University of Michigan, Ann Arbor, where they received bachelor degrees in Russian. In 1969 the girls each received a $1,000 grant for undergraduate study at Leningrad State University under the National Defense Education Act.

After an orientation in Paris, the girls will spend four months in the Soviet Union. During their spring vacation, they will tour Moscow, Tbilisi in the Georgian Province, Kiev in the Ukraine and Yalta on the coast of the Black Sea.

Pamela J. Dougherty

Jill M. Dougherty

Breaking news! But then, in 1969, being an exchange student in the USSR was pretty rare. (*Evening Gazette*, Worcester, Massachusetts, February 1, 1971)

Kitchen interview, more than fifty years later, with my high school
Russian teacher, Michael Peregrim. (Author's collection)

Off to Russia! Pam and I say farewell to our mother, Ruth,
and sister Joan, July 1969. (Author's collection)

Our class at Leningrad State University, winter 1970. (Author's collection)

One of the first photos I took with my uncle's Leicaflex in Leningrad, appropriately, with a huge poster of Lenin, circa 1970. (Author's collection)

My oldest friend from Russia, Sergey, circa 1969. (Author's collection)

"Social media" in the USSR: Russians leave notes for
each other, circa 1972. (Author's collection)

Soviet hipsters, circa 1972. (Author's collection)

Talking with Soviet visitors to the USIA exhibit, Kazan, 1972. (USIA photo)

Pam welcomes visitors to the *Apollo 10* command module,
USIA exhibit in Kazan, 1972. (Author's collection)

From one of your listener.

Moscow '76.

Photo sent to me by a Soviet listener to VOA, 1976. (Author's collection)

Soviet president Mikhail Gorbachev signs his book
for me, circa 1992. (Author's collection)

Boarding the press plane for a trip with Secretary of State
Hillary Clinton, 2010. (Author's collection)

Moscow protests against government corruption, 2017. (Author's collection)

One of the oddest photos I ever took of Putin, as he smiles wistfully
(at me?) at Valdai Discussion Club, 2014. (Author's collection)

Opposition TV channel TV Rain broadcasts from a private
apartment in Moscow, 2014. (Author's collection)

Reporting from Tuzla, Bosnia, March 1996. (Author's collection)

Pam and I in the Summer Garden, St. Petersburg, attending the fiftieth anniversary of our Leningrad State University exchange program, 2017. (Author's collection)

ПРЕЗИДЕНТ РОССИЙСКОЙ ФЕДЕРАЦИИ

Руководителю Московского бюро телекомпании CNN
госпоже Дж. Доугерти

Уважаемая Джилл,

Выражаю Вам признательность за многолетнюю плодотворную работу в Москве, за объективное освещение событий, происходящих в нашей стране.

Уверен, что большой профессиональный и жизненный опыт позволят Вам успешно продолжить деятельность на новом посту. Надеюсь, что Вы и впредь сохраните добрые чувства к России и ее народу.

От души желаю Вам творческих успехов и всего самого наилучшего.

В.Путин

« II » июня 2005 г.
Пр-987

Putin's farewell letter to me as I left my CNN bureau chief post, June 2005, asking me to "preserve kind feelings toward Russia and her people." (Author's collection)

Putin welcomes me and other Western journalists to his first roundtable interview in Kremlin Library, June 2001. (Kremlin photo)

A woman in Kyiv bows in front of an improvised memorial to people killed during the Revolution of Dignity, 2014. (Author's collection)

One of my last live shots from Moscow, March 2, 2022. (Author's collection)

The selfie I took my last night in the CNN Moscow
Bureau, March 6, 2022. (Author's collection)

To Jill Dougherty
With best wishes. → ~~Good luck~~ in Russia. We'll miss you!

Bill Clinton

My last White House news conference with Bill Clinton, 1997. (White House photo)

My bosses at CNN were fantastically supportive, and, more than anything, I wanted to get back to Moscow. Yet, I could see that something had to change. "I hope this can help me to break through, break out of my 'chipmunk-in-a-cage' approach to life," I told my diary, "working so hard to prove I am 'worthy,' exhausting myself in the process."

Just like my struggle with live shots, I approached most things as an enormous challenge. My first job during college was as a receptionist at a law office. It required answering the phones and greeting guests. Every time the phone rang, my heart sank. Such a simple thing, as I look back on it now, but it became a test of whether I could say the right thing, provide the correct answer to any question, even keep my voice steady. Oddly, I seemed to look for things that were difficult, things that would force me to prove myself. I almost always came through, got the job done, but I paid a price in quiet suffering. With CNN, I had gone to conflict zones, interviewed world leaders, shouted questions at presidents, and yet, there was always that quiet electric hum in the background, preventing me from relaxing. Could going through cancer change me? I hoped so, but I wasn't convinced.

I decided to film my experience of treatment for CNN. A camera crew recorded my checkups with my New York surgeon, and, back in Florida, another crew drove up from Miami to record my last chemo. With CNN editors, we turned that into a televised report, and, later, I began speaking publicly about my experience to groups across the United States, Canada, and, eventually, Russia. I tried to convince women that if you caught the disease at an early stage, you could recover. In Russia I found that many people were reluctant to even discuss the issue, but I was grateful to a friend and colleague, Russian TV journalist Elena Khanga, who invited me to go on her show and discuss my experience.

On April 24, 2000, I had my big checkup with my oncologist, Dr. Elisabeth McKeen, who was supervising my chemotherapy. I asked her, "How do you know this stuff is working?"

"We don't," she said. "All we know is statistics on how it works." Then she went through the numbers, a mathematical prognostication of my future. "With your type of cancer, you have X chance of having it come back in the same breast. With chemo and Taxol and Tamoxifen, that is reduced by X percent." She mentally did the figuring in her head. "You have a 2.5 percent chance of cancer in the left breast because of your mother. So, you're almost normal."

"Very strange sitting there hearing your percentage of living or dying," I wrote in my diary. I had imagined she would be able to tell me whether my cancer was "in remission" or "not active" or even "gone." That's not the way it works. There was no 100 percent definition. But it all sounded much better than I'd expected. "Almost normal." Well, I had never felt "normal" anyway.

A WIG CAN KEEP YOU WARM

There I was in Florida, I thought, and back in Moscow, with Yeltsin's surprise resignation, Vladimir Putin was acting president. He still had to run for election as president. The date was originally set for June or July, but the Kremlin moved it up earlier, to March 26, 2000. I told Atlanta I could not sit this one out. Even as I said that, I was uncertain I really could do it. Television journalism is a physically demanding job—very little sleep, missing meals, running down the street after a candidate—and Moscow would be bone-chillingly cold. I would, no doubt, end up doing live shots while standing on the street in subzero temperatures for hours at a time. And yet, as a friend of mine told me: "There is no downside to this trip; simply making it is an accomplishment."

I flew to Atlanta to see my bosses and discuss how we would cover the election. Everyone was supportive, complimented me on looking "great." Back in the hotel that night, I wrote in my diary: "As I sat in the newsroom, I did feel tired, wondering if my body is up to this. I think the most important thing is to keep limited, specific goals: Try to stay well during the trip. Write some good stories. Do as much of the live-shot routine as I am capable of. But I feel tossed on the sea. No guarantees, a lot of unknowns about how I'll feel, what I can accomplish. No guarantees—that's the hardest part about the illness too."

I called my mother and asked her how she got through her early days of breast cancer and a mastectomy. She said she was very depressed, "out in the weeds" at their house on Cape Cod. My father wasn't even there when she had the operation—he was traveling somewhere on a business trip—but, she told me, "We're strong, we're survivors."

I knew she was, but I wasn't so sure about myself. She had a marvelously down-to-earth approach. After she'd had her second mastectomy, she said, "Well, they only got in the way of my golf shot."

I flew back to Florida, borrowed a warm shearling coat from Valucha, put on my new wig—very similar to my natural hair as a brunette, although in my real hair I'd noticed an increasing number of gray hairs. Valucha had painted a small picture for me, very modern in style, with a large streak of dark red in the middle, and what looked like yellow and blue daggers attacking it. "The red is the cancer," she explained, "and that's how we're going to kill it!"

As I prepared for the flight to Moscow, I wrote myself a note listing "My Objectives." There were three: "1. To do as good a job as I can covering the election. 2. To prove to myself I can still do my job. 3. To prove to Atlanta I can still do my job."

Then I added: "Why do I need to prove this? These are old motivations. New motivations: 1. To work hard, but in a balanced way. 2. To be kind to myself and stop driving myself."

That part was a quote from a nurse with whom I'd had a long discussion about work. She told me: "Listen to your body . . . be kind to yourself." I told her I understood the words she was saying, but really had no idea what they meant. "I tell my body what to do. It doesn't tell me what to do." She looked at me and shook her head. Years later, I understood what she meant.

I packed doses of Neupogen, a drug that helps stimulate the growth of white blood cells, that I would inject in my thigh. Not my favorite. It was effective, but my bones ached.

My bags packed, Valucha and I sat down together in silence as we always did before traveling, a Russian tradition that I had adopted years before. The idea is to settle one's thoughts, prepare yourself for a journey. I found it a beautiful, meditative practice, even if it is short. I breathed in deeply, slowly exhaled, closed my eyes, and saw Moscow and the snow, one of those magical, crystalline days when the sun transforms snowflakes into diamonds.

On the plane to Moscow, I sat there, thinking about our apartment. I hadn't been back since the day in October when I'd left for the United States to get a surgical biopsy. Everything would be there in our apartment on Kutuzovsky Prospekt, everything from my old life, before I learned that I had cancer. I had expected to return in five days; the biopsy, I presumed, would show the tumor was benign, but it didn't turn out that way. Now, six months later, I thought, I'll be walking into that apartment, frozen in time. It was March 10, sixteen days before the Russian presidential election. I would spend the next two weeks in Moscow.

After the usual long drive from Sheremetyevo airport to Kutuzovsky Prospekt, I took the tiny Soviet-era lift to the ninth floor where Valya, our housekeeper, was waiting. I stepped over the threshold, careful not to embrace her until I had fully entered the apartment. (An old Russian superstition, never to shake hands, kiss, or embrace over a threshold, since the house spirits live there.) I was crying, but Valya—eternally optimistic—just hugged me and said that everything would be fine.

I could not have done the work I had to do in the bureau without Valya. Our days often stretched into the wee hours of the morning, and there was no time to clean the apartment, iron clothes, or wash the windows. Valya assured me I would simply pick up where I'd left off, and I found she was right. All the signs of my previous life were there: running clothes, exercise equipment, my home office with a treadmill . . . our "dacha" room where we watched TV, decorated with antique Russian farm implements that we had found at a secondhand shop. It was all somehow comforting, and I thought that when I finished with chemo in May or June, I really could go back and live as normal a life as possible. "Or at least I can come pretty close!" I wrote in my diary. I opened my computer to find 763 new messages, all of which I erased.

The Kremlin, meanwhile, was racing to eliminate any rivals to Putin and to solidify public support for the war in Chechnya. Some fringe candidates, like the Chechen businessman who campaigned in discos, or the ultranationalist Vladimir Zhirinovsky, were quickly eliminated. Other more serious ones, like Yevgeny Primakov, former prime minister and foreign minister; Grigory Yavlinsky, a liberal politician and economist who played an important role in Russia's transition from the Soviet planned economy; and Sergey Kirienko, another former prime minister, all were eliminated. Yavlinsky complained: "It's impossible to have fair elections in Russia under the system created in the last ten years, but if you don't take part, you can't improve things."

The only candidate with half a prayer was the Communist leader Gennady Zyuganov, but he complained that Putin was co-opting some of the Communists' issues: "We've been saying all along that Russia needs a strong government; now *they're* saying it. We've been calling for a pay hike for government workers; now *they're* saying it. But for them it's just words; we're prepared to take action."

PUTIN LIKES TO TALK

The Kremlin PR team quickly set about introducing the relatively unknown Putin to the Russian public, but it needed something new, something to round out the portrait of a tough-guy architect of an antiterrorist campaign. A more human approach was needed, a portrait of an "average" man who had grown up in the Soviet Union, a man with whom his fellow citizens could identify.

The result was the book *First Person: An Astonishingly Frank Self-Portrait by Russia's President Vladimir Putin.* It was based on twenty-four hours of interviews with Putin by three Russian journalists: Nataliya Gevorkyan, Natalya Timakova, and Andrey Kolesnikov. Natalya Timakova began as a correspondent for *Kommersant* newspaper, went on to become deputy head of Putin's Press and Information Office, and finally became Dmitry Medvedev's press secretary, both as prime minister and as president. Andrei Kolesnikov (not to be confused with Andrey Kolesnikov of the Moscow Carnegie Center) became a correspondent for *Kommersant* and went on to become the best-known member of Putin's press pool reporters, covering the Russian president with both loyal devotion and acerbic wit. Nataliya Gevorkyan, who at the time was a special correspondent for *Kommersant*, has lived in France since 2000.

The cover for the English translation declared that "no Russian leader has ever subjected himself to this kind of public examination of his life and views. Both as a spy and a virtual politician unknown until selected by Boris Yeltsin to be prime minister, Vladimir Putin has been regarded as a man of mystery. Now, the curtain lifts to reveal a remarkable life of struggles and successes."

The short book, just 206 pages in its paperback version, has become a sort of Bible for Putin watchers. Gevorkyan gave me a bird's-eye view of its genesis in a Skype interview I did with her in September 2014, six months after Putin illegally annexed Ukraine's Crimea region. It was one of the most interesting interviews I've ever conducted, a graphic, detailed description of the incestuous relationship between Kremlin power and the Russian media in the late Yeltsin and early Putin period.

Nataliya Gevorkyan's father, General Pavel Avetovich Gevorkyan, was a member of the KGB Fifth Directorate, in charge of countering political dissidents. That personal background provided a unique understanding of Putin and his public persona. During the interviews, Putin, she told me, was "doing everything possible [to ensure] that we would like him."

"It was obvious . . . I'm the daughter of a spy," she said. "I know the tricks. I know the tricks! And for me, it was absolutely understandable."

Gevorkyan said the story of the book, for her, began in Paris in December 1999, when she got a phone call from Valentin Yumashev, a former journalist who served as Yeltsin's adviser on media relations and as head of Yeltsin's presidential administration. He ghostwrote two books by Yeltsin, and later married Yeltsin's daughter, Tatyana.

"Are you in Moscow?" he asked her.

When she told him she was in Paris, he said, "What a pity. It would be better if you were in Moscow."

Soon after, she got a call from her editor at *Kommersant*, asking her to return to Moscow. She agreed and, back in the Russian capital, she went to the Kremlin, where she met with Yumashev; Kseniya Ponomaryova, *Kommersant*'s chief editor; and Yeltsin's daughter Tatyana, Yeltsin's "image adviser" (whose last name at the time was Dyachenko). Putin was not there for the first meeting, but, Gevorkyan told me, "it was quite obvious that they were moving him to the presidency, it was not necessary to explain it to me."

"They said, 'We have this guy for president, but nobody knows anything about him . . . so we need a book about him.'" And they needed it fast. "We need this book to be done [by the end of] February, so one month," they told her. "And to be published in February because the elections are in March."

After some persuading, Gevorkyan agreed, and showed up with her fellow journalists for the first session—a pre-interview—with Putin, then acting president. They met in a private room near the president's office. "Putin was very nice at that meeting," she recalled. "Very open, he was talking too much. On, and on, and on! And then he asked if we had ever tried Kremlin piroshki [small pastry with sweet or savory fillings]."

"Do you want to try it?" Putin asked.

Gevorkyan said she accepted the offer because she wanted to see how Putin would handle it—would he call the servant? But he went and brought the piroshki himself.

"He was smiling from time to time," she recalled. "He was doing everything possible so that we would like him . . . I felt that he was pretending to be good at that moment."

She quickly saw that Putin liked to talk about himself. "He talked a lot! Believe me, he enjoys talking about himself. He likes himself . . . I don't know anybody else who likes to talk about himself as much as he does." Gevorkyan explained that her journalistic style includes not changing any words, or "cleaning up" any quotes. She puts it all down verbatim. "I must tell you that the book actually was not edited at all."

They didn't record that first meeting and they didn't take notes, she said. "KGB people do not like journalists. You know that, I know that. The moment you take a pen and notebook, they stop being open."

The actual interviews were held in the Moscow suburbs at what she said was called the KGB Special Building, the same place the organizers of the 1991 coup against Gorbachev gathered. Yumashev, she said, took the building from the KGB and put it under the administration of the president. It was where he wrote the Yeltsin books.

Putin was always late for the interviews, she told me, and I was not surprised to hear this since Putin, throughout his presidency, has been notorious for arriving late to any meeting, including summit meetings with other world leaders. The journalists and Putin met, she says, four or five times for several hours. "It was always a table with food, usually dinner. It was always wine and vodka. But he didn't drink." Yumashev videotaped the entire series of interviews, she said.

Gevorkyan described how she had a moment of insight into Putin's thinking. As the interviews were taking place, the FSB arrested a Chechen terrorist. Putin couldn't stop talking about it, she recalled, despite Yumashev's efforts to get back to the interview. Putin insisted he had the correct information on how the terrorist was captured: It came from the secret file the president was given for his daily security briefings. "This file, top secret, is the main thing about Putin. It is so important to him!" she said. "Even if someone told Putin they had witnessed something personally, Putin would insist he knew the real truth because he had read his briefing report."

Gevorkyan sat next to Putin through all the interviews, she said, and she was convinced: "He was still trying to recruit me!" When she later wrote a separate article that criticized Putin, she said, without giving details, he fumed: "She betrayed me . . . She was *our* person. *Ours.*" It reminded me of something another Russian journalist once told me: Putin respects his enemies, strong people who oppose him. But he despises "traitors."

So, is the *First Person* book true? Many Russian—and Western—journalists and experts have asked that question. Gevorkyan told me: "I don't quite believe all the stories about his childhood. I have no reason not to believe, but I do not believe . . . I mean, I don't have any proof he was lying. But it was something in the way he was talking that didn't just—that let me hesitate."

But the "hooligan" part? Yes.

"He was not from some high-society family," she said, "so a lot of his time he was in the courtyard and in the park, fighting, and so on. And I think, and this he will never say, but he was a small guy, and it is always easy to push a small guy . . . So I think it's quite possible that, since his childhood, it was his idea to find something very strong, like an organization, or [to] learn to fight."

After hours of talking with Putin, sitting next to him, eating with him, seeing him up close, Nataliya Gevorkyan was convinced that Putin "has never trusted anybody." That, she said, is why he will never leave office. He stepped aside to allow a "nothing" like Dmitry Medvedev to take his place, she scoffed, but only because it was a constitutional necessity. And because, when Putin came back in power, people would say in relief, "For God's sake, it's good he's back!" Putin, she thought, was more distrustful than ever. The Kremlin might have created an image of a tough guy, a strong leader, a crafty ex-KGB officer. But Gevorkyan insisted Putin is "a very emotional person" and a "bad spy."

"He was not a spy! . . . He wasn't a spy in the true meaning of the word! He was really a zero as an intelligence man. Big hole. Zero."

"So, what is 'Putinism'?" I asked her.

She said I should try the phrase *Putin—his way.*

Putin does everything "his way," she said. "Believe me, this is a change. Before [in the beginning of his rule] he had a couple of people for consultations around him. I'm absolutely sure that now [in 2014], all the decisions are taken by him, personally, alone, without any consultations with anybody . . . He doesn't want to hear 'no' to anything he suggests."

"America used to be, and still is, Enemy Number One. And it was never any different," she went on. He simply hid that feeling, she said, just as, under Yeltsin, he pretended to be a reformer.

My conversation with Nataliya Gevorkyan confirmed some of my own feelings and opinions about Putin. I, too, had sat next to him and observed him. I saw that emotional side. I saw him try to charm people, how one day he could play the role of back-alley brawler, the next, that of a pious religious believer. Gevorkyan didn't buy his Zelig-like image either: "I don't think he's religious. But he knows that this is a good thing to show. So, the problem is where he stops playing and where he is real. So, we don't know."

MINISTRY OF MIRACLES

Just six days before Russians went to the polls on March 26, 2000, Putin, the "Man of Action," was back. In a stunning PR move, Putin streaked into Chechnya at the controls of a Sukhoi Su-27 fighter jet, the same plane the Russian air force was using against Chechen rebels. Sounding like a horseman praising his steed, Putin pronounced it a "good machine, beautiful, powerful, and obedient."

The lightning visit to an airport near Grozny was unannounced, but the videotape was a sensation on Russian TV—yet another illustration of Putin's carefully curated image. On the ground, he continued his macho rhetoric, warning rebels that Russian troops would pursue them into the mountains: "Those who want to hide in the caves can do as they wish, but I'm not going to be responsible for those who don't manage to hide."

Back in Moscow, Putin and his staff were running a kind of anti-campaign, refusing to debate his rapidly dwindling list of opponents, not running any political ads, and not unveiling any specific campaign platform. Instead, he appeared nightly on TV in his role as acting president, visiting schools and factories, outlining a general idea of where Russia should be headed. This became his political template: campaigning by *not* campaigning. Too busy running the country and doing the people's work to have a moment free for such frivolity.

Inside his public reception office, dubbed by some Russian journalists the "Ministry of Miracles," Russian citizens lined up. Fed up with bureaucracy and incompetent, corrupt regional officials, they turned to Putin, just as Russians, for centuries, had turned for help to the czar, their "tsar batyushka" ("czar little father"). We talked with one of those supplicants, retired colonel

Alexander Vokhrushev. "Before Putin, my comrades went all the way to the Constitutional Court and still didn't get it resolved. How many years they spent on it! And I come here and get it straightened out in a half-hour!"

Letters poured in from all over the country, a litany of typical modern Russian problems: people whose savings were wiped out in bank failures, people in need of better housing. The office director told us that "there are no miracles here," but added: "We don't have the right not to hear people out. Even if it's something we can't solve, we analyze all this information."

"For many Russians," I reported, "Vladimir Putin is an empty slate on which they can project their hopes and dreams," a strategy Putin and his aides would pursue throughout his decades in office.

Some political analysts saw in Putin a reformer. Vyacheslav Nikonov, a political scientist (and, interestingly, the grandson of Stalin's foreign minister), told me that, although Putin's career was mostly spent in the KGB, "he also was known as quite a reformist, the first deputy mayor of St. Petersburg at the time that Anatoly Sobchak was mayor."

Loyalty to the president was one of the key advantages Putin brought to the job as prime minister. Yeltsin himself gave an intriguing explanation for why he chose Putin as his prime minister. In his book, *Presidential Marathon*, published in Russian in 2000, Yeltsin says that Putin "had the will and the resolve" necessary to undertake the fierce political battles that would take place after Yeltsin resigned the presidency, as he intended to do in a surprise move. But, Yeltsin explained, "it would be premature to bring Putin into the political ring at that moment. He had to appear later. When there's not enough time to take a political running jump, it can be bad. When there's too much time, it can be even worse. I didn't want the public to get too used to Putin in those lazy summer months. We mustn't let his mystery disappear; the surprise factor needed to remain intact."

Yeltsin said he didn't even tell Putin—who, at that moment, was serving as head of both the Security Council and the FSB—of his decision. He wanted to pass on to Putin his political legacy, but he wanted to do it through democratic elections, and Putin, he said, disliked "public politics."

Yeltsin also included in that book a discussion he had in Moscow in June 2000 with Bill Clinton, six months after he had stepped down as president. By then, the two leaders were friends. "How do you like Putin?" Yeltsin asked Clinton.

"He's a good, strong leader," Yeltsin quotes Clinton as saying. "I know he has enormous authority in Russia. But he's just taking his first steps, and in order to become a great politician, he needs to trust his heart more, and trust his feelings."

VOTING FOR PUTIN

Five days before the March 26 presidential election I was feeling much stronger, and I was grateful; we were doing live shots every night and it would get only more intense in the last days of the campaign. "I guess I feel it's kind of a miracle I'm even doing live shots," I wrote in my diary. I was glad my brain seemed to be functioning okay, after what they call the "brain fog" people sometimes experience after chemotherapy.

TV live shots are short, usually lasting just a minute or two, but intense. You have to convey a lot of information in a compressed manner without making it too dense to understand for people watching. At the same time, there's a performance aspect to it, too, for which you must be focused and energetic—but not so energetic that the audience is paying more attention to your delivery than to the substance of what you are saying. To make it more challenging, you have a show producer talking to you in your earpiece, telling you to "Wrap!" if you go on too long.

When I started my career in TV, I found live shots nerve-wracking; I wanted them to be perfect little gems of reporting. Under that pressure it was easy to freeze and lose my train of thought. And there was another challenge to my equanimity in doing live shots from the Moscow bureau. In the early 1990s, we did live shots from the roof of the building where our office was located. It had a picture-postcard view down Kutuzovsky Prospekt, with the Russian White House toward the left; the former Comecon building, which always reminded me of an open book, in the middle; and Novy Arbat Street, leading down to the Kremlin. But, more importantly, it was the route Vladimir Putin's motorcade took almost every morning as he streaked into work.

To gain access to the roof, we had to take the elevator to the ninth floor, then climb up a rickety metal ladder, through a kind of hatch, and clamber onto the roof. It was flat, but filled with pipes, wires, and a forest of satellite equipment. The camera operator, sound tech, and I had to stand there, close to the edge, with its fabulous view, braced against the wind, rain, snow, and sleet. To begin with, I am scared of heights, and fearing that I would be blown off the roof with the next gust of wind, I felt my heart pounding out of my chest.

It was a bird's-eye view, all right, but it was a security risk, the FSB explained to us. They ordered us to stop doing live shots from that location. Editorially, I was miffed, but personally, I was relieved. We moved into our other office a couple of flights below and installed a large window with almost the same view.

As the years went on, and especially in the Moscow bureau, with its unending rotation of live reporting, I eventually got used to it, and even began to enjoy it. I loosened up and tried to concentrate on the people at home, as if I were telling a friend what had just happened. Those years of experience paid off as the camera crew and I worked around the clock in the last days of Putin's 2000 "un-campaign" for the presidency.

In the roughly three months since Yeltsin had stepped aside and named Vladimir Putin his successor, we had not seen the acting president in person. This was a media campaign fought—if that is the correct word—on TV, with Putin traveling the country, playing the role of a man already doing the job of president, not just a candidate for the position. It was a "Rose Garden" strategy, but in Russia, there was no Rose Garden. Covering the White House for six years, I had reported on several elections, watching candidates hungry for more airtime, more rallies, more "rubber chicken" dinners with supporters. Putin's election was preordained, so he didn't have to campaign, or face challenging questions from his opponents. Russian voters saw a man hard at work as acting president, not rolling in the mud with other, lesser candidates. Let them debate, let them scream and fight; Putin—in his public image—had only one priority: to protect the Russian people and improve their lives.

The day before the election was very quiet; election laws forbade any type of last-minute campaigning, and election posters around the city were covered with new commercial advertising. In one of my first live shots of the day, I reported that Putin had gone off to a soccer match. "He was sitting there looking as if he's somebody who has no care in the world," I said, "and, in fact, in a sense, he doesn't, because his ratings, at least according to the latest polls, are about 50, 55 percent, and that should be enough to guarantee him a first-round victory."

The anchor, Bernard Shaw, asked me what the issues were.

"Well, there actually aren't a lot of issues," I replied. "If you dispense with Chechnya—which is what catapulted Vladimir Putin to where he is right now—there are no debates."

But Putin could not afford to be a one-issue candidate. Up to now, thanks to his war in Chechnya, he had been spared dealing with economic matters—an albatross that had sunk a succession of previous prime ministers. But life for most Russians was still hard, and discontent was growing.

"Here's what concerns average Russians far more than Chechnya," I explained in another live report: "their own poverty. What does it mean to be poor in Russia? Some retired people have to live on pensions as small as $15 a month, enough to buy a little bread and milk. Fifty-one million Russians officially live below the poverty line; that's 36 percent of the population."

Putin said poverty could be solved only by economic growth, but the question was, how to spur that growth? Across Russia, aging factories struggled to survive, and start-up businesses were drowning in taxes and regulations. Putin said he wanted to lower taxes, but a more specific reform plan wouldn't be ready until May.

Two days before the election, in a TV address, Putin laid out the clearest list of his priorities as president: "Let me repeat that we are electing the president, whose duty is to ensure economic recovery, restore the country's prestige and leading role in the world, make Russia governable again, and deliver stability and prosperity to everyone."

One of his top advisers, German Gref, however, admitted there was a lot of cynicism. "Today, I think, very few people trust us. We not only have to have the right plan, we have to show by our actions we can do something, then they'll begin to believe us, both international investors and our own people." Yeltsin's prime minister, Sergei Stepashin, said people were asking him, "Can Putin really do something?"

"What's to stop him?" Stepashin told them. "He's not financially tied with anyone. He doesn't owe anyone anything, and after this election, he'll be able to take some very harsh steps." Already, though, skeptics were saying Putin had yet to truly distance himself from the oligarchs. Would Putin stand up to Russia's special interests?

Today, with more than two decades' hindsight, it seems strange, even ludicrous, that the man whom many Western observers call a "kleptocrat" could be considered as someone outside of the corrupt inner circle that ruled, and still rules, Russia today. At that early point, however, Putin's direction did not seem clear. Yeltsin was out of the president's seat, but many of the elite with special ties to the Kremlin remained.

Putin was known for his loyalty, and one of his first official steps as acting president was to grant Yeltsin immunity from prosecution for any alleged corruption, a move of critical importance to Yeltsin and his family, who were being investigated for alleged financial improprieties. But that didn't stop him from firing Yeltsin's daughter, Tatyana Dyachenko, Yeltsin's image-maker, and closest adviser. Investigations into alleged money laundering by people close to Yeltsin were under way in the United States, so it was a publicly popular move, but one that could be interpreted as a shot over the bow of the Yeltsin camp.

It was precisely this kind of delicate political balancing act that some analysts in Moscow predicted would be the hallmark of Putin's early time on the job as prime minister, and as acting president: taking steps to guarantee he could take over the presidency for real without burning bridges with the people who'd put him in power in the first place. After all, Putin had no political base behind him when Yeltsin plucked him from political obscurity. Even the political party he supported, Yedinstvo (Unity), had been created out of thin air by the Kremlin just three months previously.

So, Vladimir Putin, like the master judo wrestler he was, was forced to thrust and retreat, leveraging all his strength to keep in balance. And it worked; nearly two hundred of Russia's movers and shakers, businessmen and politicians, jumped on board the Putin presidential bandwagon, formally asking him to run.

The question I kept asking myself at that time was: Will he be their political captive, or their master? The only answer that seemed to make sense on those frigid nights in Moscow on the eve of the election was that nothing would be clear until Putin had won the "black belt" of politics—election in his own right.

He did, of course, garnering more than the absolute majority he needed to avoid a runoff. Looking confident as he voted at a local polling station, he announced, "Tomorrow is Monday, a hard day," he said, "and I will have to get to work." But already there were fears that Putin would lead the country back to Soviet-style authoritarian rule, and those concerns were echoing beyond Russia's borders.

"It's a mistake to prejudge him," US Secretary of State Madeleine Albright told CNN. "His words are okay, but we have to watch his actions."

"He's an enigma," said US Senate Majority Leader Trent Lott, R-Mississippi. "He seems to be moving forward . . . opening up, and some reforms, and yet there is a throwback quality that's got to worry us."

Even before his victory was official, Putin was taking out an insurance policy, warning Russians that, even if he won, things would not improve overnight. "There are many people in the country who are not satisfied with the state of things," he said. "People are tired, things are tough for them, and they expect better things from me. But, of course, miracles don't happen."

ELECTION NIGHT

I got my first glimpse of Vladimir Putin on election night, March 26, 2000, at a post-midnight news conference in the atrium of Alexander House, a modern building featuring a glossy red-granite entrance hall with polished brass hardware, located across the Moscow River, south of the Kremlin. We arrived at 8 p.m. and I grabbed a seat at the large conference table where he would speak with reporters. Four hours later, Putin came through the doors, wearing a dark gray cable-knit sweater and a ski jacket—not a business suit—surrounded by his election team. It was the first time I had seen him in person. He was compact, smaller than I expected, athletic-looking, the embodiment of the generational change under way after Boris Yeltsin.

I took note of the distinctive Putin walk—some call it the "gunslinger's gait"—in which he holds his right arm a bit more stiffly than his left, which swings free. Some ascribe it to his KGB training, which dictates that officers hold their right arm near their body so they can quickly whip out their handgun. Perhaps. Or could it be Putin's many years of judo training? Whatever the reason, he walked vigorously, athletically, but slightly inclined, giving a slightly jerky quality to his gait.

That night, for the first time, I heard Putin's speaking voice in person. His quick, staccato delivery, paced with pauses, his Leningrad accent, his breathy sighs. Putin still sighs at certain points, a phenomenon I have never understood. Is he tired? I don't think so. Bored? Frustrated? Perhaps, but I don't think that is it either. But it creates an odd dissonance: rapid-fire delivery, then a sigh, then another stream of words. To me, it's one of the only things Vladimir Putin does that seems unintentional.

I checked my notes. I was following vote totals, and I noticed the strong showing by the Communist candidate, Gennady Zyuganov, who captured 30 percent of the vote. That was significant, and I decided I would ask Putin about it—that is, if I managed to get a question in amid the crush of journalists.

"Good evening," he began, "or rather, good morning. As acting president, I can already say it is a good morning. Because I had asked voters to come to the polling stations and we can now report that it has happened. That is the main thing."

One of the first questions, predictably, was about Chechnya. Voting took place there, despite the fighting, and Putin said firmly that the terrorists had failed to disrupt the process. "The very fact that the people in the republic have voted in the election of the Russian president," he said, "shows that the overwhelming majority of the Chechen people see their republic as part of the Russian Federation. That is of critical importance, and it cannot but give us a sense of joy."

I raised my hand and jumped in: "Mr. Putin, many people have voted for the Communist Party's candidate. How do you account for that?"

Putin admitted, surprisingly, that the Communists' access to the media was limited, although he did not say who was responsible for that. "The Communists do not have too many opportunities or too much access to the media, especially the electronic media. Nevertheless, a lot of people regularly vote for them." He also admitted the Communist Party's strong showing was a message to the government: "It means that many people in Russia are unhappy with the current state of affairs. It shows that the government's policy should be more balanced, should address the reality in Russia, and should be aimed at raising the living standards of the ordinary people. The rank-and-file Russians should become aware of the advantages of the policy pursued by the government, and then there will be no need to oppose the Communists as a party. One should not fight against the Communists; one should fight to win over the people who vote. I think that can be achieved."

At 2 a.m. we packed up our equipment and headed back across Moscow to the CNN office and a long, intense night of reporting on air. But I felt good; we were on top of the story, I got a question to Putin, and I had plenty of energy—undoubtedly the adrenaline from witnessing Russia's second peaceful transition of power. Years later, my surgeon told me she had been sitting in her kitchen in New York with her husband when she saw me pop up on CNN air, reporting on the election. "Wait a minute!" she laughed, "we just operated on her!"

Walking back to my hotel as the sun was just beginning to rise, I thought about Putin's balancing act: acknowledging the economic pain his fellow Russians were feeling, and assuring them he would try to do something about it, while at the same time reminding the world that Russia—even in its weakened state—still had a vast store of nuclear arms. In my mind, I kept hearing his address to the nation just a few days previously, as he had urged Russians to go to the polls:

"I think I should remind you that on March 26 we are electing not only the head of state but also appointing the supreme commander, because the president, by virtue of his office, is simultaneously the supreme commander of the armed forces. Russia is one of the biggest countries in the world and a strong nuclear power. This is something that not only our friends remember."

On the way back to the hotel, in the pedestrian underpass that connects one side of the vast thoroughfare of Kutuzovsky Prospekt, I encountered two old men playing balalaika and guitar, the guitarist wearing fingerless gloves against the cold. I was the only person in view, but they played on, strumming a Russian folk song. "So beautiful!" I wrote in my diary. "It reminds me of why I'm hooked on this place."

· 9 ·

Vodka

I left Moscow the next day for West Palm Beach, Florida, always a jarring transition, but I needed to get back for more treatment. Taking off from Sheremetyevo airport in the dark, snowplows clearing the runways of snow, and then landing in the blinding sun and tropical humidity. Hulking, stolid Moscow; pastel, evanescent Florida.

A quick trip to New York for a checkup with my surgeons. Everything looks great, one of them told me, adding that he had developed a steady stream of Russian patients. They're very grateful, he told me, and they showed that by giving him what was quickly turning into a museum-size collection of matryoshka dolls, the wooden nesting dolls so emblematic of Russia. He finally told them there was no need for matryoshka dolls, and they started giving him vodka.

Ah, yes, vodka. If there's one thing outsiders identify with Russia, it's that clear, transparent liquid so tied to the very definition of the country. I have had my fair share of vodka, and so I think it's only fair to devote a few words to it.

My parents raised my sister Pam and me in the "Mad Men" era of the 1950s, so it's not surprising that, when I began drinking "adult" drinks in college, my favorites were scotch, gin and tonic, and gin martinis with a twist—no need to add "of lemon." Vodka, it seemed to me, was a more exotic drink, and also a more utilitarian one; drinking vodka seemed, at least to me, to imply that one was doing it for a purpose. And that purpose, I was convinced, was to get intoxicated. Which is why, a few years later, I stopped drinking.

In the Russian language, "vodka" literally means "little water." The root of the word, "voda," means "water." The ending, "ka," is what's called in linguistics a "diminutive suffix," an ending that connotes physical size—in this case, small—but also familiarity or affection.

Vodka. A word of elemental simplicity. Water, the source of all life, a deep, mysterious, and ancient word, but with that little twist of intimacy at the end. "My little water," it seems to say; "darling little water," it whispers.

There are many myths about vodka. "It has no taste," some people say. They are wrong. Vodka looks so clear, so limpid, so light. But when it fills the mouth, bathes the palate and throat, it assumes another form, viscous and warm, and the flavor of the source from which it is fermented—wheat, or rye, or rice, corn, potatoes—wafts through the nose.

I don't remember my parents drinking vodka. My first alcoholic drink was what they drank: scotch on the rocks. I still remember the moment when I took my first sip of scotch. I was a freshman in college and my parents allowed Pam and me to have a party with school friends in our family living room. I felt vaguely nervous, hoping that everything would go okay, but when I raised my glass, sniffed the pungent woodiness, then let it slip down my throat, I felt—no, I *knew*—everything would be all right. Feeling a bit less nervous, I slipped into the bathroom. A deep pink blush was crawling up my neck, from my chest to my face. It seemed to signify something, but, on that cold day in Worcester, Massachusetts, just what it meant wasn't clear. It would take a while, and a lot of drinking, to understand.

My vodka drinking began in Ann Arbor, Michigan, in the Russian-language dorm, Russia House, at the University of Michigan. Pam and I and our fellow students were convinced that culture was the key to really knowing the language, and, we thought, what could be more Russian than vodka?

Every Thursday we would buy the best of the cheap American vodkas, along with some dark rye bread, and celebrate our weekly vodka "vecherinka" (party). The vodka initially burned as it went down, but it did the trick for me, loosening my tongue, freeing me to pronounce those tricky Russian vowels, filling me with a warm, comradely glow. I don't remember many details from those parties, except for my occasional declamatory speech from the top of the stairs, expressing my undying love for the Russian language, Russian culture, and my fellow students.

For many years, I presumed that Pam had similar memories, although she was never much of a vodka drinker. I once texted her some recollections of the Russia House parties and was shocked to find that she had no recollection of what had transpired on those evenings.

"Do you remember my being at those parties?" she quizzed me. "I never drank vodka. Did I carry you back to the room? No recall at all. Red wine, yes, I love Spanish red wine."

"I usually collapsed and slept on the floor until the next morning," I texted back.

Pam replied: "I can't imagine I left you lying on the floor at night. I wouldn't have done that."

"You were probably fast asleep like a good girl," I teased her.

"No way. I would have gone looking for you if you hadn't shown up," she assured me.

My memory is a bit dim from that period, but I do remember that I spent many a Thursday night on the floor, curled up next to a fellow student. It didn't seem that strange to me, although I wondered, sometimes nervously, what had transpired in the hours before dawn.

If the Russia House was my undergraduate study program in vodka, our time in Leningrad as exchange students was grad school. Our "professors" were our Russian friends, Tanya and Sergey. It didn't take long after we arrived at their one-room apartment, brushing the snow off our coats, pulling off our boots, and putting on some "tapochki" (slippers) from the pile at the door, before Tanya would take the bottle out of the bookcase and pass it to Sergey. He would pause, smile devilishly, then open it with a flourish. It was a deliberately theatrical gesture, like the moment in a play when the main character intones his soliloquy, or at Mass, when the priest raises the chalice.

And, in the deepest sense, it was a sacrament—the mystery of a drink that transports its communicants into a sacred world of oblivion, one that cannot be entered without mutual trust. As we raised our glasses and downed our vodka in one gulp with a shouted "Dodna!" ("To the bottom!"), no one quite knew what would happen. We might move on to a deep conversation about music, or art; or Tanya and Sergey might start quarreling; or Sergey might throw open the window in the midst of a snowstorm and shout deliriously into the night air; or we all might start dancing like whirling dervishes; or one of us might pass out. All inhibitions vanished and, because we might embarrass ourselves, or someone else, we entered into an unspoken pact, affirming that we were in this—whatever it was and wherever it might lead—together. There would be no holding back.

One thing, however, was always predictable: The bottle would be drunk until the last drop. We would never consume just part of a bottle and put it away until the next time. Who knew when the next time would be? Sergey would take the empty bottle and, jokingly, wring its neck, forcing out the very last drop into our empty glasses.

There is a phrase in Russian that men who drink vodka together use: "Ti menya uvazhayesh?" ("Do you respect me?"). It is usually pronounced with a little slur and, sometimes, because it's so well known, as a joke. Essentially, it's an invitation to drink, even a way of challenging someone into drinking. It's an act of intimacy that requires a special language. More aptly, it could be translated as "Don't you respect me?"

When my sister and I drank with Tanya and Sergey, Sergey usually poured the vodka into "ryumochki," small, stemmed glasses. Occasionally, we drank from regular glasses that Russians call "stakanchiki," which Sergey would fill with a good two to three inches of vodka. We were expected to drink it to the bottom—"Dodna!"—starting with a toast, "Za zdoroviye!" ("To your health!"), followed quickly by salty chasers, "zakuski" ("nibblies"), like sausage, herring, pickles, and smoked salmon that punctuated our drinking with what felt like an exclamation point at the end of a sentence. "Ah, *yes!*" Sergey would laugh like a sleigh driver cracking a whip on a troika, and we were off.

Our little circle wasn't the only one to be swept up in the unpredictability of vodka. In 1992 an inebriated president Boris Yeltsin played the spoons (a Russian folk instrument) on the head of Askar Akayev, president of Kyrgyzstan. In another infamous affair at Ireland's Shannon airport, he snoozed aboard his plane as the Irish prime minister waited below on the tarmac for a meeting that never took place.

The crowning touch came in September 1994 in Washington, DC, when Yeltsin was staying across the street from the White House at the official guest residence, Blair House, preparing for his first meeting with President Bill Clinton. As author Taylor Branch tells the story in his book, *The Clinton Tapes: Wrestling History with the President*, Yeltsin sneaked out of Blair House in his underwear and made his way to the corner of Pennsylvania Avenue. Secret Service agents found him alone, drunk, "yelling for a taxi." He apparently wanted to go out to get a pizza.

When I first came to Moscow as CNN's bureau chief in 1997, I ended up reporting on several drownings in local lakes and rivers. It was a regular summer occurrence. The number of victims was far higher than in the West, and I soon learned that most of it was due to swimming after drinking vodka.

Throughout the centuries, Russian leaders have tried to control their people's urge to drink, even though the state, for centuries, made money from its monopoly on alcohol. In 1914, during World War I, the czars tried to stamp out vodka drinking. In the 1950s and 1970s, Russia's Communist rulers periodically restricted the sale and availability of vodka. In the mid-1980s Soviet president Mikhail Gorbachev imposed the "dry laws" that raised the price of vodka, wine, and beer and cracked down on public drinking. In 2010, then Russian president Dmitry Medvedev limited the hours in which Russians could buy vodka.

But the most effective tactic that I witnessed was Putin's own power of example. Perhaps due to the five years he worked as a KGB officer in Dresden,

East Germany, he does drink beer, but, when it comes to vodka, he is not your average Russian male. Publicly, at least, he drinks very little, and the transformation I witnessed from Boris Yeltsin to Vladimir Putin was striking.

During the Yeltsin years, our camera crew once visited a site outside of the capital where "chemical troops" were practicing decontamination efforts. We arrived at 9 a.m., and, after about an hour of shooting video of the soldiers hosing down vehicles, and then interviewing them, we were directed by our military guides to a large, camouflaged Quonset hut. As we entered, expecting to see bins of supplies and equipment, I was surprised to see a long table stretching for what seemed to be the entire length of the hut. It was laden with plates of smoked salmon, deviled eggs, pickles, sausages and meats, grapes, a variety of cheeses, and an entire collection of every form of alcohol known to mankind: vodka, whiskey, cognac, champagne, sweet wine.

Our guides were instantly transformed into our hosts, as they greeted us with wishes for a Happy Defender of the Fatherland Day—a kind of Russian combination of Veterans Day and Father's Day.

Knowing what was likely to come, I thanked them profusely but insisted we had to get back to work. They insisted right back. And so, my producer, camera crew, and I sat down and soon found ourselves raising a glass to toast Russian–US friendship. Having experienced many hours of toasts during my life in Russia since 1969, I was well versed in the etiquette of such encounters, and so I launched into a few tales of my student days in Leningrad as well as my own father's service in World War II. Our CNN team sipped as abstemiously as possible under the circumstances. I explained that I didn't drink, that I was a "sportsmenka" ("sportswoman") who never touched the stuff when I was in training. I did, however, meet the moment rhetorically with a florid but sincere toast to the famous April 25, 1945, meeting on the River Elbe when Soviet and US forces clasped hands shortly before the victory over Nazi Germany. Our hosts joined in wholeheartedly with vows of eternal friendship.

That morning drinking encounter was only one of many during that late-Yeltsin period. When he suddenly resigned on December 31, 1999, naming Vladimir Putin as his successor, the vodka-drinking rituals changed almost overnight. Gone were the vodka breakfasts with Russian government officials. No more predawn cognacs. Vladimir Putin drank green tea, and magically, just as in a short story by czarist-era satirical writer Nikolai Gogol, those officials developed a taste for tea.

I would arrive for an interview at a faceless government office, and immediately, the official I was about to talk with would ask his assistant—almost invariably a young woman—to make a cup of tea or perhaps coffee for me. It made my interviews both easier and shorter, as well as more coherent.

Vodka drinking was a rich source of anecdotes, and I even did a video report on techniques Russians use to survive hangovers. One morning we headed for the "Shot Glass" bar in downtown Moscow where I encountered three men who obviously had thoroughly researched the subject. They told us to use just their first names.

"Coffee, of course! We used to have good pills under the Communists, but I don't trust 'em anymore," Sergey told me. His buddy Vladimir opined: "I don't drink nothin', only mineral water. Not much to eat, no tea with lemon like Dr. Zhivago."

But my favorite remedy recipe came from Mikhail, who was sure "the best way to take the hair of the dog that bit you is to split a pint of vodka with three guys. We're giving ourselves a little extra here."

Then, there was the traditional remedy: drink the juice from your pickle jar. They call it "rassol," and a Russian company had just started canning it. It was made from fermented cabbage, beet juice, and spices. They told me it had a lot of vitamin C. We gave it to Andrey, another man who was imbibing before noon. "It's actually pretty tasty," he told us. Next year, the company said it planned to add a dash of pickled carrot juice.

I could laugh as we videotaped this story because I was not drinking; I had stopped more than a decade before. I am convinced I could not have kept up the travel and intense work schedule if I had been drinking.

Alcoholism never stopped being a health problem, or a political problem, in Russia. More than two decades after he first was elected president, Putin even worked it into his annual presidential address to the Federal Assembly, right up there with threats to the West that he might have to use nuclear weapons. "By the way," he added, "on the subject of drinking, we have achieved a noticeable, positive result. In fact, we have significantly reduced the consumption of alcohol, primarily strong alcohol, without imposing any extreme restrictions, which should certainly improve the health of the nation."

Then, reviving an old Soviet saying, he urged the audience: "Stop drinking and get on your skis!"

PREMONITIONS

In 2000, I spent my fifty-first birthday in Moscow, shooting a story on the Moscow Marathon, inwardly cheering on hundreds of serious runners, many of whom didn't even have proper running shoes, wearing old-fashioned Soviet sneakers instead. There was, however, one young man I noticed among the runners who looked out of place. He was smoking!

I had to return to the United States that summer of 2000 for several weeks of radiation in New York. It seemed easy, at first, just lying there as they directed radiation at the site where the lump had been, but it turned out to be tough. You lie there in a contorted position with one arm over your head, hand on forehead, locked into that pose by a specially fitted mold that makes it impossible to move, a crucial condition for aiming the radiation at the precise spot. My arm fell asleep and my neck hurt.

In my diary I wrote: "I wanted to be a model patient but even I ask, 'Can I move my head?' 'No!' was the firm answer from the technician." And yet, I was running every day in Central Park and getting letters from viewers who had seen my cancer special on CNN and were sending their support and prayers. It touched me deeply and gave me strength to know there were so many others who had been diagnosed with cancer and were going through the same thing. It was like a giant family, united by pain—and hope.

We returned to Moscow in early August, a month filled with premonitions of bad things to come. August, even in Washington, always seemed filled with unpredictability, and in Moscow you could experience the point/counterpoint of Russians relaxing on summer holiday at their dachas juxtaposed against a coup—or an attempted one, like the 1991 August Coup against Mikhail Gorbachev.

As the CNN driver navigated the sea of cars back from the airport to our apartment, I felt uneasy. There was no particular reason, but during my three decades of studying, traveling, and living in Russia, and the Soviet Union before it, I had picked up some of the superstitions and premonitions that are part of Russian tradition and which many Russians share.

I thought of the saga of Moscow's original Cathedral of Christ the Savior, which stood on the northern bank of the Moskva River, downstream from the Kremlin, constructed over forty years, consecrated in 1883, at the time the largest Orthodox church in the Russian empire. In the 1930s, as part of the Communists' vicious war against religion, Josef Stalin ordered it removed to make way for a massive wedding-cake-style Palace of the Soviets, topped with a statue of Lenin.

The authorities dutifully dynamited the cathedral, but the 1941 German attack on Moscow stopped construction of the Palace, and the foundation sat empty until 1958, when a huge outdoor swimming pool—the "Moskva" pool—was installed, the largest in the Soviet Union, heated year-round. Happy Soviet citizens frolicked in the warm water, but the babushki said the pool was cursed. Because of the sacrilege of destroying a house of God, they said, nothing would ever rise again in the Cathedral's place.

Finally, in 1994, three years after the USSR had collapsed, a new Cathedral of Christ the Savior was constructed, partially with donations from more than a million residents of Moscow, thus ending the superstitious whispers of doom.

THE *KURSK*

I couldn't shake my feeling of unease. August always seemed to be the month that something bad happened.

A week after we returned from the States, on August 12, 2000, in the frigid northern waters of the Barents Sea, a huge explosion tore apart the inside of the nuclear-powered submarine *Kursk*. This was followed by a second explosion, and the sub plunged to the bottom of the sea. Some of the 118 sailors aboard were killed instantly, but most were trapped in the surviving sections of the sub, their air running out, slowly asphyxiating, waiting desperately for help.

The Kremlin initially would not even confirm the sinking had taken place. Putin was on vacation at the Black Sea, and for days he made no public comment on the sinking. To make matters worse, when the navy finally confirmed the explosion, Putin appeared before news cameras in a golf shirt.

Distraught families of the sailors were desperate for news. The entire country was transfixed by the agonizing wait and infuriated by the lack of information. We were doing constant live shots from the CNN bureau, and every hour brought more agonizing details. Some of the sailors were still making SOS signals, banging on the hull of the sub. Some Russians told us it was just like the Chernobyl nuclear plant explosion in Soviet times: silence, lies, a cover-up. A retired captain whom we interviewed said he had had his fair share of close calls aboard submarines and felt a kinship with the *Kursk* sailors.

"It's completely dark. It's cold, they're probably thirsty, they're probably lying down so they don't use too much oxygen. Are they praying? Writing final letters? We can only guess."

After five agonizing days Putin finally gave the go-ahead for British and Norwegian divers to launch a rescue mission, but by that time, all the sub's crew were dead. In one town-hall-style meeting between distraught families and the head of the government inquiry into the disaster, one of the submariners' mothers, beside herself with grief and fury, screamed at officials.

This was a human disaster, but for the Kremlin, it was a PR disaster as well. Putin showed no emotion and remained at his vacation spot in Sochi instead of returning immediately to Moscow. Even Putin's media adviser, Gleb Pavlovsky, conceded: "Of course, Putin should have been more emotional and supportive of the people in this situation, and we should have advised him of that. I think we made a mistake. We should have met people's expectations—[he] should have been less of a technocrat and more of a psychotherapist."

In his election campaign, and in his first days as president, Putin's team had carefully curated his public image as a "man of action," but now what was needed was empathy, not a characteristic that Putin was known for. He finally met with the families, telling them his "heart ached"; he went further in an interview: "In spite of the fact that I've been in the Kremlin for hardly more than one hundred days, I feel completely a sense of responsibility and guilt for this tragedy."

Newspapers were blaming him for the slow response and the deaths. Meanwhile, the families were holding memorial services for their loved ones. In the military town of Vedyaeva, the cries of mourning women drowned out the sound of martial music. As the families laid flowers, one bereft woman threw herself to the ground. Another woman collapsed as a naval officer broke off his speech in mid-sentence. "Doctor! Right now!"

Most shocking of all, at another memorial, the mother of one of the dead sailors screamed at officials: "I'll never, ever forgive you! Take your medals off and shoot yourselves! We'll never leave you in peace, you bastards!"

The footage, recorded by a local Russian television station, shows officers trying to calm her, then a medic in civilian clothes injects her with something and she sinks toward the floor.

August ended with one more portentous event: a fire at Moscow's gigantic Ostankino Television tower. It was a symbol of the capital, a Russian version of the Eiffel Tower, built in 1967 of metal and concrete, a testimony to the scientific prowess of Communist Russia. With a restaurant and an observation tower on top, it was the highlight of many visits to Moscow for Russians and foreigners alike. Coming on the heels of the *Kursk* disaster, and a bombing in a Moscow underground walkway that killed twelve people, it deeply disturbed many Russians, who wondered what the next catastrophe to hit Moscow would be.

Putin blamed the fire on the country's desperate economic condition: "This last emergency shows the state of our vital installations and the state of the entire country," he said.

Looking back at the first year of Putin's presidency, I never could have foreseen that, a quarter of a century later, he would still be in power, or that he might be able to stay in power—legally—until he was eighty-three.

Vladimir Putin was a central focus of my reporting, of course, but there was the unrelenting daily dose of breaking news on other subjects, and even news about Boris Yeltsin kept popping up. There were recurring rumors that he was dying, just as there had been when he was president. His death would be a major news event, so we had to track down each news eruption, and I was continually forced to revise my obituary of the president. One day in March 2001 a Russian journalist friend called my cell phone and whispered: "It's time to finish writing your Yeltsin obit." But Yeltsin wouldn't die until 2007.

POLITICAL MATRYOSHKA DOLLS

By November 2000, after all my treatment and checkups, I was back in Moscow for good. Russians were watching the US election, always, it seemed, more interested in American politics than their own, debating whether Al Gore or George W. Bush would be better for Russia. Gore meant continuity; Bush could be a "new wave," especially on arms control issue. Some Communists were itching to go to America as election observers, convinced that hardly any country was less democratic than the United States.

I headed for Moscow's Old Arbat Street to check out what the souvenir shops were saying—my gauge: matryoshka dolls painted with the faces of politicians and other celebrities. They were still selling Bill Clinton dolls (one set had a tiny Monica Lewinsky and an even tinier cigar), but in a sure sign of capitalist entrepreneurship, they told me they would be happy to make either a Gore or a Bush doll—if there was a buyer.

George W. Bush was elected, and the matryoshka doll makers went to work, depicting him in a Stetson hat, but tension already was brewing between the Putin administration and Washington. Every year, the Russian military held exercises to test its preparedness for conflict. Russia's military was in seriously bad repair after the fall of the Soviet Union, and Putin had set about rebuilding his armed forces. This year, symbolically, he turned the war games into a potent message that Russia, despite its weakened military, could still fight battles on land, on sea, and in the air.

A highlight of the exercises this year was a test launch of two Topol-M intercontinental ballistic missiles, Russia's most modern and sophisticated ICBM. Russia might no longer be a superpower, but it sure wanted to act like one. It was an obvious warning that, if Washington went ahead with a national missile defense system, against which Putin personally was lobbying, Moscow would equip the Topol-M with multiple nuclear warheads.

There was another blast of the Cold War blowing through relations: the US arrest of a career FBI agent on charges of spying for Russia, followed quickly by the arrest in Moscow of an American student on a drug charge.

Just two months before, an American businessman, Edmond Pope, was found guilty of espionage, then was pardoned by Putin.

I was surprised by the rapid deterioration in relations, and it was a rude awakening for Moscow too, as Lilia Shevtsova, an expert in Russian politics on whom I often relied to explain the intricacies of Kremlin intrigue, told me: "Even one month ago, there was a strong illusion in the Kremlin that it would be much easier to deal with a Republican president, but not with a Democratic president." Not anymore.

At many junctures over the coming years, I would be confounded by official Moscow's lack of understanding of the American political system. When Donald Trump ran for president in 2016, for example, several Russian officials told me they were sure Moscow and Washington would finally see eye to eye on many issues, but they were blindsided by the domestic US backlash against Trump, and by Trump's own chaotic blend of personal praise for Putin contradicted by the harsher policies of his administration. In an off-the-record meeting with some Russian officials, I could see their obvious confusion and disappointment that Trump could not just wave a wand and put an end to economic sanctions against Russia.

But in December 2000 there were other stories we had to cover, and one of them took us to Ukraine, and the Chernobyl nuclear power plant. Authorities were shutting down reactor No. 3, ceasing operations at the plant for good. It was a surreal visit, as my camera crew filmed the carcass of the plant and reactor No. 4, where the nuclear nightmare began on April 26, 1986. We drove to the nearby town of Pripyat, where 45,000 people once lived; it was now abandoned, with Soviet-era concrete apartment buildings rotting to their foundations. We had a dosimeter with us to measure the radiation. As we passed empty storefronts, we were careful to walk only on sidewalks being reclaimed by moss and grass, checking the radiation levels every few minutes. Over the years, the streets and sidewalks had been washed many times and the radiation level was low, but in the houses, we were told, it was still dangerously high.

We drove to the neighboring town of Slavutich, where almost all the residents worked at the Chernobyl plant. Everyone we interviewed knew the danger Chernobyl had created but, nevertheless, they were torn about shutting it down. We met Alexander Veshkin standing across the square downtown with a sign that said: "Work and a salary, not an unemployment check." He told us he was forty years old, that he and his wife Svetlana worried that the Chernobyl accident might affect their son Misha, who was born two months after it happened. Their fears didn't come true, but, he said, closing the nuclear plant was a "personal tragedy" for him and his family.

"For the world community, shutting down Chernobyl is getting rid of the ghost of a dangerous nuclear facility," he explained. "But I gave the best part of my life to the station."

I thought of the radiation treatment I had just had back in New York, so carefully calibrated, with all possible precautions taken, and of how the local people here in Pripyat who lived near the nuclear power plant had no idea they were being exposed to radiation that would, in the years to come, kill some of them or leave many with thyroid cancer. As Serhii Plokhy relates in his masterful chronicle, *Chernobyl: The History of a Nuclear Catastrophe*, the Gorbachev government initially kept the explosion a secret and then, downplaying the rising radiation levels, ordered the annual May Day parade in Kyiv to go forward, thus exposing thousands of marchers to the unseen danger.

There was a word so many Ukrainians used during our trip to Chernobyl, the same word I had heard over the years from Russians who had survived serious accidents, or terrorist attacks, only to be injured or even killed by incompetent attempts by government authorities to respond: "khalatnost"—"negligence."

I heard it as I reported on the sinking of the *Kursk* submarine. I heard it as we traveled to a remote Russian town to report on a terrible fire in which many people died because the building's emergency exit doors were bolted shut to keep out burglars and bums. I heard it in 2002 when terrorists attacked the Dubrovka Theater in Moscow, taking almost 1,000 people hostage, only to have 130 of them die—not because of the terrorists, but because of a gas that government security forces pumped into the theater to incapacitate the attackers. I saw it in 2022—two decades later—in social media postings by Russian soldiers, furious they were being sent into battle in Ukraine with rusty weapons and faulty body armor.

In so many tragic events, average Russian people ended up suffering the most, due precisely to official carelessness, negligence, or incompetence. It was something I remembered from the Soviet days: sidewalks with holes in which you could sprain an ankle or break a leg; electrical outlets exposed to the rain just waiting to electrocute someone. In the West, negligence was prevented, or at least mitigated, by the right to sue someone in court. But in post-Communist Russia, now beset by waves of terror attacks, many people felt they were on their own, left to fend for themselves. This, I believe, explains some of the approval President Putin received from his fellow citizens. Here, finally, they thought, was a man who promised to protect them, a strongman who would go after the terrorists with a vengeance. They often supported Putin while expressing a complete lack of faith in his government. This, of course, has deep roots in Russian history, with the "narod" (the "people") keeping their faith in the czar while blaming his corrupt courtiers.

Invariably, there were promises this would never happen again, the perpetrators would be punished, justice would be done. But the attacks didn't stop, and neither did the khalatnost.

Putin, meanwhile, was busy making the case to the West that he was fighting the same war in Chechnya that the United States and other countries were fighting against international terrorism. Even before becoming president, when he was still Yeltsin's prime minister, Putin penned an editorial for the *New York Times* making common cause with Americans: "The same terrorists who were associated with the bombing of America's embassies have a foothold in the Caucasus. . . . No government can stand idly by when terrorism strikes. It is the solemn duty of all governments to protect their citizens from danger."

More than two decades later, he made the same argument to justify his invasion of Ukraine: He had "no choice" but to launch a "special military operation" against Ukraine: "Let me remind you that in 2000–2005 we used our military to push back against terrorists in the Caucasus and stood up for the integrity of our state. We preserved Russia. In 2014, we supported the people of Crimea and Sevastopol. In 2015, we used our armed forces to create a reliable shield that prevented terrorists from Syria from penetrating Russia. This was a matter of defending ourselves. We had no other choice. The same is happening today. They did not leave us any other option for defending Russia and our people, other than the one we are forced to use today."

In those early days of covering President Putin, I began to see patterns of behavior that I eventually would describe as "classic Putin," like simultaneously playing the role of both "arsonist" and "firefighter"; that is, fueling a conflict, then offering to mediate a peace agreement. There is, of course, the time-tested remnant of Soviet thinking, "whataboutism," in which Putin counters criticism of his actions by blaming the criticizer for doing the very same thing. A striking example came during an awards ceremony at the Kremlin in December 2022 as Putin raised a toast and sneeringly admitted Russia was deliberately bombing Ukraine's civilian infrastructure: "There is a lot of noise right now about our strikes against the energy infrastructure of the neighboring country," Putin said. "Yes, we are doing this. But who started it?"

I had other Russian friends, however, who took a benign view of Vladimir Putin. One of them was a young Russian diplomat whom I both liked and respected. He was, for me, the best example of a diplomat: honest, dedicated to his country and to promoting its best interests, which meant bringing Russia out of its isolation and integrating it into Europe. He told me he was frustrated with his job, that there were a lot of old "nomenklatura" (Communist bureaucratic elite) types left over from Soviet times who were suspicious of him because he spoke English. During a dinner conversation one evening he told me there was a lack of coordination in Putin's administration and in the government, with very few smart, Western-oriented staff. Everyone in the presidential administration, he said, had his own personal agenda and helped only himself, with little sense of doing a professional job. He chalked that up to holdovers from Communism. And yet, he insisted: "Putin's instincts are democratic. He's very much a lawyer."

Part of me believed that. After all, Putin was educated as a lawyer and often claimed that he was acting strictly according to the letter of the law. But as I watched more closely, I began to discern yet another pattern: Publicly professing a fastidious adherence to the law, Putin took actions that ultimately perverted the meaning and intention of the law. As time went on, if the law didn't allow him to do something, he simply had his increasingly rubberstamp parliament pass a new law. When his actions violated international law, such as annexing territory that belonged to another country (e.g., Crimea), he would accuse European countries or the United States of doing the same thing.

In order to realize his dream of joining the KGB, Vladimir Putin had studied law at Leningrad State University, so we decided to talk with some law students. We headed for Moscow State University. One student there told us it was hard to find anyone who dreamed of becoming a judge. "Judges are influenced by gangsters, the mafia," he said. "It's very dangerous for them, and they're sometimes murdered."

In the early years of Putin's presidency, I was buoyed by reforms in the new Criminal Procedure Code and the Land Code, but I was troubled by Putin's pledge to create a "dictatorship of law." The phrase had a definite Soviet-era ring to it.

A MAN WITHOUT A COUNTRY

Reporting on Vladimir Putin's first term as Russian president allowed me, in a way, to start from the beginning. Boris Yeltsin already was in his second term when I began my job as bureau chief, but Putin—although he served briefly as Yeltsin's prime minister and then acting president—was opening a new chapter in Russia's history as an independent nation.

Examining my own experiences in the USSR, especially in Leningrad, as well as in post-1991 Russia, I tried to put Putin in both historical and personal perspective. Immediately, one major factor stood out: The country in which he was born, the USSR, no longer exists. I've pondered the meaning of that for years, what it might mean for him, and for other Russians.

It's one thing to say, "The USSR no longer exists; the Russian Federation is a successor state to the Soviet Union." That, of course, is a fact. The USSR, with its massive size—eleven time zones, fifteen republics, population of 286 million people—and its nuclear weapons, was formally dissolved into fifteen independent nations on December 22, 1991. Its legal successor was the richest and most powerful former republic, the Russian Federation.

But the heart sometimes rebels against facts, or alters them to soften the sting of reality. I imagine saying, "The United States of America no longer exists; New England (or the West Coast, or the South) is the successor state to the United States." It's incomprehensible. I can feel the shock, the disbelief, that the nation in which I grew up is no more, that my brothers and sisters who live in New York, Massachusetts, and Virginia, now live in different countries, that I must cross an international border to visit them. Almost impossible to imagine that the power and might of America would dissolve, too—its purpose, its mission in the world, suddenly meaningless.

I was born in the United States four years after World War II ended. The war had devastated Europe, Russia, and parts of Asia, but the US mainland was unscathed. Men were back at work. Women who had joined the labor market during the war mobilization were continuing to work. Factories that once had produced weapons were churning out washing machines and televisions. Thanks to the GI Bill, 8 million veterans pursued an education in college and vocational schools, and Uncle Sam picked up the tab. The country's first planned communities were springing up. My parents rented an apartment in Stuyvesant Town, an 80-acre private residential development on New York City's East Side, financed by the Metropolitan Life Insurance Company. The company's president said he wanted to give its middle-class residents an opportunity to "live in a park—to live in the country in the heart of New York." It opened two years before I was born.

Twenty or so blocks north, the sleek modernistic United Nations building now stood, symbol of hope for a peaceful future. The Marshall Plan was rebuilding Europe, solidifying American influence and liberal values. The United States was now the world's military, economic, and geopolitical superpower. Dangers were just down the road—the Cuban Missile Crisis, Vietnam—but, for now, America was an optimistic place for a white, middle-class young person to grow up.

Vladimir Putin, born in 1952, was growing up in the shattered city of Leningrad. The war had decimated the city's infrastructure. Almost a million inhabitants were dead, victims of constant bombardment and starvation caused by the 900-day siege by Nazi Germany. When the war ended in 1945, approximately 600,000 survivors were living in the ruins. By 1952 the city was coming back to life, but even in 1969, when I first arrived as an exchange student, it was a dark and dreary place, much of its imperial splendor hidden beneath drab and peeling proletarian paint.

Beyond the physical destruction, there was emotional trauma. Like so many Soviet citizens, Putin, from childhood on, lived in a world of threat and instability. His father was severely wounded at the front. His mother almost died of starvation. His older brother, then a child, died during the siege. That is, of course, if you believe what Putin told his *First Person* interviewers.

Between 1949 and 1951—just a year before Vladimir Putin was born—Josef Stalin unleashed a murderous purge on Leningrad's Communist Party leadership and their families. Twenty-three were executed; others were jailed or fired from their jobs. Putin, as a young man, seemed undeterred by that horror. He dreamed of becoming part of the very system that had repressed and murdered so many of the people who lived in his hometown.

It started when he was a teenager. In an interview with *Kommersant* newspaper two weeks before his first election in 2000, Putin related his story about being mesmerized by the movie *The Shield and the Sword* and trying to volunteer at the KGB's Leningrad headquarters. "It wasn't just a whim," he told the reporter.

Putin has repeated this tale several times, and it has become part of his personal mythology. In the *Kommersant* interview he moves from mythology to ideology, justifying the role that intelligence agents perform: "They didn't even try to recruit me as an agent, although at the time that was widespread. There were a lot of people who worked with the 'organs' [a Soviet term for organs of state security]. This is an important instrument for the life of the state—cooperation with normal citizens. The main thing is on which basis it is built."

Putin, in what I came to know as his Soviet question-and-answer style, turns the tables on the reporter and begins to cross-examine him: "You know what a 'seksot' [a Soviet acronym for paid informer] is?"

The reporter, Andrey Kolesnikov, answers: "A secret agent."

"Good," Putin says. "And why did it get such a negative connotation? Do you know? Because these people performed certain functions. Which functions?"

"Ideological," says Kolesnikov.

"Yes," Putin continues. "This is an ideological investigation. You know, we're talking about spying. That's interesting. Do you know that 90 percent of all intelligence was collected with the collaboration of Soviet citizens? Agents act in the interest of the state. It's not important what you call it. It's important on what basis this cooperation is taking place. If it's based on betrayal and material gain," he said, "that's one thing. But if it's based on ideological principles, that's another thing."

In Yeltsin's Russia, being an informant for the security services was considered a shameful legacy of Communism. In Putin's Russia, especially in the wake of the 2022 invasion of Ukraine, informing on anyone suspected of being disloyal to the state, even friends and relatives, once again was praised as simply doing one's duty as a loyal citizen.

THE MASTER OF THE ROOM

Why does Putin think the way he thinks? What explains his "mirovozrenie" ("worldview")? The CIA, of course, carefully analyzes world leaders, and in 2015 I had a chance to interview two of their Russia analysts at the agency's Langley, Virginia, headquarters. The analysts allowed me to use only their first names, "Rachel" and "Chris."

"The key to understanding Putin," they explained, "is that his life has been marked by personal loss and deprivation. He was weak, small, and sickly. He grew up with a sense that he was special, yet vulnerable. His parents were very cautious, but they doted on him. He carried these feelings into adulthood. He studied judo and sambo [a Soviet martial arts discipline] and learned control, discipline, and strategic use of force."

They told me the CIA studies what Putin says and how he behaves. "We also look at his behavior, at photos, videos, speeches. You don't need to take everything he says at face value, but his words are very important. We do take his words very seriously. They are helpful in understanding his decision-making."

On his body language, they said, Putin is "not one for emotional displays. That stems from his childhood. He covers up his emotions to protect himself and keep threats at bay. . . . In the early videos he was awkward. He didn't handle himself well. He now is the master of the room. He makes everyone wait for hours."

Our discussion took place one year after Putin annexed Crimea, so I probed the CIA experts on his motivation as president. "When a person is under stress," they said, "they revert to comfortable things, and he has become more insular, more rigid in his thinking. . . . He surrounds himself with loyal people. Any kind of opposition is the enemy.

"He identifies himself with Russia. He believes that Russia didn't get a fair shake, just like him. He wants to restore Russia to its former glory and believes he is the only person who can do that. He takes things as a personal insult. Insults to Russia are insults to him. He has grown into that idea . . . He has become more fixated on an identity tied to Russia. This identification has gotten stronger. He feels he is irreplaceable. . . . He has ambivalent feelings about the West. Ties are important, but he also is highly suspicious of the West's motives."

How does the CIA evaluate what Putin might do? The analysts said they look at external events, interesting scenarios, and compare them with Putin's worldview. "Much of what he does is improvisational, reactive," they said. "There is a high degree of relativity."

A VERY CONTEMPORARY MAN

Psychoanalyzing Vladimir Putin can be a perilous yet tantalizing endeavor, and I've pursued it with alacrity for many years. One of the most compelling visions of Putin came from a man whom he ran out of business and imprisoned: Mikhail Khodorkovsky, once the richest man in Russia, former head of the Yukos Oil Company, which was broken up and destroyed on Putin's orders. I met him in Moscow in 2003, shortly before he was arrested at the airport in Novosibirsk, charged with fraud, tax evasion, and other financial crimes. He struck me at the time as a deep, even philosophical thinker, not what I expected from one of Russia's oligarchs. He was sentenced to prison in 2005 but was pardoned by Putin in 2013. He went into exile in Europe shortly thereafter.

I talked again with Khodorkovsky in October 2014 at the coffee shop at the Mayflower Hotel in Washington, DC. I wondered whether he could be objective about Putin, and he admitted: "You understand that I have no reason to love him. But I worked very hard to treat him objectively. I think I succeeded. I convinced myself that it's nothing personal and that I should not take it too close to heart. It's a fight. In this fight there may be one situation or another, but all this should not be taken personally."

He told me he was introduced to Putin when Putin was Russian prime minister and that he had met him several times, one-on-one and with others. "I formed a certain opinion of him, which later turned out to be false," he said. "He seemed to be a very contemporary man who not only understood the current state of affairs but also accepted the European perspective regarding the development of the country and its future. He said . . . the country is more important than the state.

"He understood the state is just one part of society. An important part, but just one part. There is also a second part, and a third part, and so on. At that time, I could not imagine that he would want to stay alone at the top of the pyramid."

Some say Putin has changed, I said to Khodorkovsky. Did he agree?

"Yes, I know many people who know him, and they see that he has changed dramatically. . . . He stopped listening to the opinions of other people. He trusts only himself. And he believes that only he knows what is right. People can influence him only indirectly, only when he doesn't understand they are trying to influence him. People who know him very well can do it."

Putin "believes he has access to different sources of information," Khodorkovsky explained. "But, in reality, the bulk of the information comes from a controlled environment. And everyone around him knows what sources of information he considers the most important, and these people try to ensure that only these sources of information are made available to him. People know that he may be emotional and make decisions under the influence of his emotions. So, they know how to trigger these emotions."

I felt as if I were in a psychiatrist's office, hearing the therapist talk about a patient. Mikhail Khodorkovsky described how he began to understand Putin, and what he called Putin's "talent."

"I am a person who recognizes people's talent over time, but not right away. I agree with those who think that Putin is a recruiter of the highest order. What he can do better than anyone else is see the mask on a person he is talking to and put it on himself. To become whoever the person wants to see. This is his unique talent." Another side of that talent, he said, is that Putin "can see this person's weaknesses, what he wants and what he is afraid of. . . . The majority of people he has dealt with have been self-interested, he looks out for this in people. And if someone has it, Putin sees it and uses it effectively. He is very good at it."

THE "RUSSIAN WORLD"

One of the most deeply held principles of loyal Soviet citizens was their belief that they were part of something big and powerful and important—geographically, the largest nation in the world, melding more than a hundred different peoples and ethnicities into one, united Soviet people.

In the 1950s and '60s, the United States was richer, but the Soviet Union, bristling with nuclear weapons, was the other superpower, even if the standard of living in the USSR lagged far behind that in the United States.

By the late 1980s the Soviet superpower was failing. In 1989, when the Berlin Wall was torn down, Putin was a thirty-seven-year-old KGB officer serving in Dresden, East Germany. In the book *First Person*, he describes his shock as he desperately sought direction from Moscow: "Moscow was silent."

Two years after the Soviet Union collapsed, Putin had returned to Russia and was using his car as a taxi, or so he later claimed, in order to make ends meet amid the economic chaos. Putin has, of course, politically exploited the fact that he was raised in modest circumstances, but today, by most estimates, he is one of the richest people in the world. His scornful references to "elites" ring hollow; he *is* the elite.

When the Soviet Union ended, millions of people across the country were left rudderless, forced to grapple with the profound loss of their country and their own self-definition. For some people, especially in the newly independent Baltic nations of Estonia, Latvia, and Lithuania, it was a liberation from the bonds of Soviet oppression, a rebirth of the deeply held idea that they were returning to their rightful place in Europe. For others, including Russians who supported the Communist system, it was as if a skeleton inside a body had suddenly dissolved, leaving nothing to prevent it from collapsing. The Communist Party had provided not only employment but also access to health care, extra rations, summer camps for children, and social activities. It also provided a system for understanding the world: Marxism–Leninism. That is long gone.

The loss of an ideology, even if many Soviet citizens had lost faith in it or rejected it outright, left other Soviets adrift, fearful of where their country was headed. State-controlled TV in the early 1990s was filled with fortune-tellers and psychics predicting the future. The disorientation persisted for years after the Soviet Union collapsed.

Putin famously called the breakup of the Soviet Union "the greatest geopolitical catastrophe of the century" that left behind millions of ethnic Russians in what were now independent countries. In a 2021 documentary, he told interviewers the collapse was a "disintegration of historical Russia," that it had "turned into a completely different country." One year later, as Russian tanks invaded Ukraine, he described his personal mission as undoing that "tragedy," taking back what he claimed "belonged" to Russia.

None of this justifies the depredations that Putin has visited on his neighbors. But it is instructive to note that most of Putin's early comments about the end of the Soviet Union are tinged with a feeling of humiliation that has only deepened with the years, fueled by resentment of the West, not only for "ignoring" Russia's interests and concerns but also for trying to impose its values on Russia.

The very day he announced what he termed his "special military operation" against Ukraine, he contemptuously challenged the United States: "The so-called collective West and its fifth column are accustomed to measuring everything and everyone by their own standards. They believe that everything is for sale, and everything can be bought, and therefore they think we will break down and back off. But they do not know our history and our people well enough."

PUTIN'S IDEOLOGY

Over the years, if anything, Vladimir Putin has become even more focused on ideological "principles," and there is vigorous debate among Putin-watchers as to whether he has an "ideology" on the level of Marxism–Leninism. In 2022 I asked Marlene Laruelle, director of the Institute for European, Russian, and Eurasian Studies at The George Washington University and an expert in populism and illiberal movements who closely studies Russia's ideological landscape, to explain it.

"I think Putin does not have an ideology in terms of [having a] text," she told me. "He has emotion and resentment, and then he has aspiration for what should be done for Russia. And I think he believes in his role, in his own destiny for Russia."

Putin, now in his seventies, says he is fond of reading biographies of Russian military and political leaders, men like Alexander Kerensky, head of the Russian provisional government that was overthrown by the Bolsheviks in 1917, a personalized approach to history that is reflected in his current beliefs and actions. If he has any ideological principle, Laruelle said, it's that "Russia should survive, and he's the one to do that."

As we talked, I recalled the early days of Putin's rule, when he appeared to believe that Russia could be a great power linked to the world by economic globalization, respected not only for its hard power but also its "soft power," the ability to attract or co-opt others by diplomacy and other non-coercive methods. In 2013, in fact, studying for my master's degree at Georgetown University, I wrote my thesis on Russia's "Soft Power Diplomacy." Ironically, I published it four months before Russia invaded Crimea.

Choosing Russia's soft power as a subject just a short while before Russia used its hard military power (albeit deviously) to annex Crimea may seem, well, not very smart. In fact, during my research phase, I consulted Lilia Shevtsova, my Russian friend and colleague in Moscow. When I told her about my subject, she nearly exploded: "Russia has no soft power!"

After the street protests of 2011–2012, Putin, she explained, began using the term "soft power" as he desperately sought a way to increase Russia's influence in the world. "They started to look around, their speechwriters and analysts, they started to read everything, to steal ideas: 'What can we invent?'" she scoffed. "This doesn't mean that they mean the real thing. The box of instruments is so narrow. They play with ideas without meaning anything."

Harvard's Joseph S. Nye Jr., in his book *Soft Power: The Means to Success in World Politics*, defined soft power as "the ability to get what you want through attraction rather than coercion or payments." It arises, Nye said, "from the attractiveness of a country's culture, political ideals, and policies. When our policies are seen as legitimate in the eyes of others, our soft power is enhanced."

The Soviet Union, Nye explained, "once had a good deal of soft power, but it lost much of it after the invasions of Hungary and Czechoslovakia." In fact, he continued, "Because of its brutal policies, the Soviet Union's hard power actually undercut its soft power."

To be sure, with its world-class ballet, opera, and music, Russia did have enormous cultural soft power, but polls, such as those conducted by the Pew Research Center internationally in 2013, 2015, and 2023, showed Russia's contemporary image in the world was increasingly negative. There was, realistically, no way the Kremlin could make Russia attractive or persuade other nations that Russia should be emulated, or that it had solutions to problems that others should adopt. As one of my Russian colleagues, an expert in domestic Russian politics, put it: "He [Putin] is smart enough to understand that he's talking bullshit."

In his early years as president, Putin attempted to integrate with the West but soon abandoned that strategy, convinced that Russia was not being treated with the respect due a superpower, even if it no longer was one. Russia joined numerous international organizations but quickly made it clear it would not be content to be simply a member, like the rest; it intended to run them. Influencing the West with soft power, making Russia look attractive, was impossible. Instead, Putin turned to a kind of negative power; Russia began to measure its soft power success by the extent to which it was able to undermine the soft power of the United States.

Russia's competitors, like the United States, did have effective soft power. So, Putin and his government simply defined their own version of soft power: top-down and prescriptive, created and controlled by the government. As I recounted in my thesis, they began rebuilding some of Russia's public diplomacy instruments that had collapsed along with the Soviet Union. Believing that Russia was serious about Western-style soft power might have been my mistake, but observing how Vladimir Putin began redefining it helped me to see the outlines of his strategy to preserve Russia's influence—political, economic, and, ultimately, military—in the former Soviet space. Years later, he would try to exploit this influence to win support in the so-called Global South.

The Soviet Union had two main public diplomacy agencies: the "All-Union Society for Cultural Relations," and the "Union of Soviet Societies for Friendship and Cultural Relations with Foreign Countries." Putin created "Rossotrudnichestvo," a tongue-twisting name even in Russian. According to its official website, one of its aims was to "assert abroad the objective presentation of modern Russia, its material and spiritual potential, and the content of the internal and external political course of the country."

Part of this sounds a bit touchy-feely ("its material and spiritual potential"), but Putin soon made Russia's "spiritual potential" a central part of his nascent ideology, both as a means of uniting Russians, and as a way of influencing parts of the world—for example, Africa—that were rejecting "liberal Western values," especially on gender and sexual issues.

As professor Angela Stent, my thesis adviser, explained in her book, *Putin's World: Russia Against the West and with the Rest,* "Putin's Russia has defined its role in the world as the leader of a 'conservative international,' supporting states that espouse 'traditional values' and as a protector of leaders who face challenges from 'color' revolutions against authoritarian governments, which Putin believes are orchestrated by the West."

This mission was so important to Putin that the new-and-improved Rossotrudnichestvo was put under his direct authority, with a separate line in the Russian federal budget, giving him the right to approve the agency's head and his deputy. The new agency's mission was to maintain connections to the Russian diaspora, the so-called "compatriots." In an interview I conducted in 2013 with Konstantin Kosachev, the head of Rossotrudnichestvo and former diplomat and chairman of the Foreign Affairs Committee of the State Duma, he introduced me to the "Russky Mir" ("Russian World").

"I am trying to develop a new concept that is called, very conditionally, the creative concept of a 'Russian World,'" Kosachev said, claiming the concept was similar to what the French had been doing for many years with Francophone programs, and their focus on language, history, and culture.

It also, he said, was a way of strengthening Russia's humanitarian presence in the former Soviet Union. "Not because of Soviet-style 'agitation and propaganda,'" he insisted, "but because of our humanitarian presence, educational programs, youth exchanges, cultural events. It's a normal part of the foreign policy of any nation."

This interview with Kosachev introduced me to the Russian World's conceptual framework. "It's not necessary to swear allegiance to a nation," he explained. "It's not political; it remains in the humanitarian sphere . . . Our dream is to try to initiate a union, a consolidation of the 'Russian World' in which the center would be people who are Russian, but then, radiating out from that, include those who studied in Russia, married Russians, created families, have business interests, are in some way connected professionally or personally. Then there is another layer of people who are simply interested in Russia, in its literature, the ballet, the cosmos."

The Russian World, however, became much more than just a way to win friends and influence people. It became the core concept of Putin's worldview: reuniting Russians and Russian speakers, no matter where they are in the world—culturally, politically, and, if he deemed it necessary, militarily to "protect" them.

That is precisely the rationale Putin exploited when, in 2023, Russia began handing out passports to people living in regions of Ukraine seized by Russian forces. Anyone who refused faced deportation. Announcing his decision to "liberate" Ukraine from what he declared were neo-Nazis, Putin wrapped the concept of the Russian World into an emotional—and false—justification for attacking Ukraine: "We had to stop that atrocity, that genocide of the millions of people who live there and who pinned their hopes on Russia, on all of us. It is their aspirations, the feelings and pain of these people that were the main motivating force behind our decision to recognize the independence of the Donbas people's republics."

The Russian Orthodox Church is another tool of Russian soft power, employed to influence not only religious beliefs but also political ones. As Russia expert Thomas de Waal has noted, Russians consider the head of the Church, Kirill I, Patriarch of Moscow and All Russia, a "political figure," not just a religious one. In one poll published by the newspaper *Nezavisimaya Gazeta* he was rated as the number-six political leader in the country, coming in five places ahead of the foreign minister, Sergey Lavrov. Throughout his career Kirill has been closely tied to Vladimir Putin, and before assuming his position as Patriarch, he was chairman of the Russian Orthodox Church's Department for External Church Relations, a powerful post with broad influence in the former Soviet space. Thomas de Waal calls him a "shrewd political figure," "untouchable," adding: "Although he wouldn't see it that way, the Moscow patriarch is probably the most effective instrument of Russian soft power in the 'near abroad.'"

The Patriarch endorsed the prosecution of members of the band Pussy Riot, who were arrested and sentenced to prison in 2012 after performing a punk rock song at Moscow's main cathedral, praying to the Virgin Mary to save Russia from Vladimir Putin. He has spoken out forcefully against abortion and equal rights for homosexuals, including the right to marry or adopt children. He has been an avid supporter of Putin's war against Ukraine, telling believers that "sacrifice in the course of carrying out your military duty washes away all sins."

Russia's "soft power," I could see, had a hard edge.

· 10 ·

Putin's Kiss

I had my own soft-power encounter with Vladimir Putin at the 2013 Valdai Discussion Club conference, just a few months before I left CNN after thirty years as a correspondent.

The invitation-only Valdai Discussion Club, established in 2004, was considered the Russian government's preeminent intellectual conference. I had attended it for several years. I enjoyed being a kind of fly on the wall as Russian and foreign experts on the country opined on Russia's view of itself and its role in the world. The evenings were a chance to have a drink and chat more informally with the participants, especially Russians, who were more willing to share their personal views offstage. Since Moscow's full-scale invasion of Ukraine in 2022, almost no American or European academics or experts have attended the conference—a sign of Russia's increasing isolation in the West.

The highlight at Valdai pre-2022 was the chance to hear from Russian president Vladimir Putin directly, and at length; he invariably spoke and answered questions for hours (at this conference in 2013, it would be almost four hours).

"I'll try not to bore you unduly," he began wryly. "For us—and I am talking about Russians and Russia—questions about who we are and who we want to be are increasingly prominent in our society. We have left behind Soviet ideology, and there will be no return. Proponents of fundamental conservatism who idealize pre-1917 Russia seem to be similarly far from reality, as are supporters of an extreme Western-style liberalism."

I was intrigued. Putin was talking about "national identity," a subject I had explored for my master's thesis. Russia, he said, had suffered two "national catastrophes" in the twentieth century: the Bolshevik Revolution and the

185

1991 end of the USSR. But he quickly veered off topic and launched into a diatribe, railing against "multiculturalism," "political correctness," and European countries that he claimed were "implementing policies that equate large families with same-sex partnerships, belief in God with the belief in Satan."

And he wasn't finished. "The excesses of political correctness have reached the point," he said, with disgust, "where people are seriously talking about registering political parties whose aim is to promote pedophilia."

It was a theme he would return to relentlessly in succeeding years, even using it to justify attacking Ukraine in 2022: "They sought to destroy our traditional values and force on us their false values that would erode us, our people, from within, the attitudes they have been aggressively imposing on their countries, attitudes that are directly leading to degradation and degeneration, because they are contrary to human nature. This is not going to happen. No one has ever succeeded in doing this, nor will they succeed now."

Putin's Valdai comments were a fascinating, if somewhat disturbing, glimpse into his moral universe. It was completely at odds with the reality of Russia, at least in its big cities, and even inside the Kremlin, where I had encountered plenty of homosexuals over the years. Suddenly, they were personae non gratae.

But I had another mission at Valdai.

After the president's talk there would be a cocktail party, and a chance—if I was lucky—to make a pitch directly to him for an interview with CNN. Our Moscow bureau had a standing invitation to the Russian president to speak with us, but Mr. Putin, obviously, was in high demand.

There was another reason I wanted to lobby the Russian president directly for an interview, whether it would be conducted by me or by one of CNN's well-known anchors. It had to do with an unfortunate incident concerning Larry King, who had been CNN's star interviewer for more than twenty-five years.

The August 2000 sinking of the *Kursk* submarine was a public relations disaster for Putin, and when the Kremlin agreed to an interview with Larry King just one month after it happened, we were amazed by their willingness to make the president available for an interview by an American journalist. The first question Larry asked on air was his usual get-to-the-point style: What happened to the submarine? "It sank," Putin answered laconically.

The response seemed so blunt, so unfeeling, that I winced when I heard it. I knew it would reflect badly on Putin, and a few minutes after the interview was taped, a Kremlin official called me. "You can't put that on the air," he said. I explained that I was not Larry King's producer and I had no influence over the show. The official was insistent, but there really was nothing that I could do, nor would I. The interview aired in full, and the Kremlin was furious. Although our bureau continued to have relatively positive relations with the Kremlin press service, it was a long time before we were granted another interview. Now I had a chance to make the pitch to Putin to give CNN another try.

At the Valdai conference, as I sat in the crammed auditorium, a forest of television cameras planted in the back rows, I plotted how I could fight the crowd after Putin's Q&A session was over and get close enough to speak to him. At the conclusion of his session, my fellow audience members and I quickly made our way to an adjoining hall where tables were set with drinks and hors d'oeuvres. I mingled a bit, but my eye was on the door through which Putin would enter the room.

In a few minutes he walked in, surrounded by a scrum of security men and trailed by the conference participants, normally reserved professors and other foreign policy experts, now eagerly jockeying to get close to Vladimir Vladimirovich Putin.

I saw a small opening and made my move, bracing against a phalanx of security guards with bulging muscles and dark suits. I quickly deduced my plan was not going to work, so I scrunched down to half their size, pushed through in a sort of a one-yard-line football maneuver, and suddenly found myself face-to-face with Mr. Putin.

"Vladimir Vladimirovich!" I said in Russian. "Perhaps you remember me. I was CNN's Moscow bureau chief until 2005. It's very nice to see you again. CNN would be honored to invite you to join us for an interview, anytime."

Putin smiled, almost sweetly, and replied that of course he remembered me, and it was nice to see me again. "As for an interview," he said, "you have to ask my press secretary," and he gestured toward Dmitry Peskov, whom I knew quite well, standing to my left.

As I turned toward Peskov, I felt warm lips on my right cheek. It was a kiss. A brief one—not an embrace, no Slavic three-cheek greeting—just a soft, fleeting smack. For a second, I wasn't sure who had kissed me—or why. But there was only one possibility, and that was Vladimir Putin, who stood there smiling at me.

I felt almost frozen in place. I had just been kissed by Putin and I didn't know how to react. My journalist mind kicked in, going over the sequence: I'd asked for an interview; he kissed me. Yes, that actually happened. But why? And what comes next?

The crowd was swirling around the president; no time for second acts. The only word that came to mind that seemed appropriate was a brief "Spasibo" ("Thank you"), and I stepped aside. Mr. Putin already was almost submerged by a wave of admirers.

Later that evening, I spoke with a Russian friend of mine, a fellow journalist, and told her what had happened. It all seemed so unreal.

She brought me back to reality. "Oh, he kissed me too!" she said matter-of-factly.

"What?!" I exclaimed.

"Yes, I think he just wanted to unnerve me," she said.

And so began our half-hour exegesis of a Putin kiss. We developed several theories of why the Russian president would kiss a woman, at least in public, all of them based on the presumption that nothing Mr. Putin does is unintentional. Even before his first election, and certainly after that first major public relations blunder during the sinking of the *Kursk*, the Kremlin had been hyperaware of Putin's image. His aides carefully crafted it. There was a reason, we concluded, that Vladimir Putin had kissed my friend and me, at different times and in different places.

My friend used a word in Russian that perfectly describes what she thought lurked behind her Putin kiss: "sniskhoditelnost" ("condescension"). And yet, she said, Putin had kissed her even as she was shouting at him about another Russian journalist who had been kidnapped by Russian forces and handed over to Chechen rebels. She admitted that while Putin might "hate" her, "he respects someone who is strong enough to be a fighter."

When it came to my Putin kiss, we worked up a few theories. Number 1: The same "condescension" he had shown her.

Number 2: He was happy to see me—an entirely plausible hypothesis. After all, many Western journalists were critical of Putin, depicting him as a criminal puppet master, especially as he racked up more years as president. I had begun my assignment as bureau chief in 1997 during the leadership of Boris Yeltsin, and, after he was gone, the early days of the Putin presidency, when Mr. Putin appeared to be a proponent of economic reform and opening to the West. The Kremlin allowed us access to most of the president's public events and news conferences where he willingly answered our questions. So, by kissing me, Mr. Putin might have been simply recalling the good ol' days when he felt Western journalists had treated him fairly.

Number 3: He was being courtly. Also a possibility, especially since Mr. Putin, like most Russian men of his age, combines a certain retro-Soviet courtliness with a dismissive, oozingly misogynistic friendliness. If I had been younger, he might have patted me on the head and said, "Charming little girl!" But I was a grown woman, and an American, to boot. An unexpected kiss would do the trick. Especially if you are a former KGB agent trying to get someone on your side by trying to make them like you.

Number 4: He was trying to knock me off balance, to gain advantage by discombobulating me, in this case, with a kiss. After all, Mr. Putin is a former

KGB officer who once described himself to cellist Sergey Roldugin, a close friend and confidant, as "a specialist in human relations," as quoted in *First Person*. In a now-infamous meeting with German chancellor Angela Merkel, he allowed his large black Labrador into the room, knowing that she is deathly afraid of dogs. He later denied he wanted to scare her, explaining he just "wanted to do something nice for her." With me, no dog was necessary, just an unexpected kiss on the cheek.

There was one more possible explanation—Number 5: A Mafia "initiation." Not in the literal sense, but as a symbol of welcoming one into the "family," along with its attendant responsibilities to keep the family secrets. Similar to journalist Nataliya Gevorkyan's phrase, "She was *our* person. *Ours.*"

My journalist friend and I laughed as we subjected the president's kiss to a battery of psychological tests. In the end, we agreed we really didn't know why he had kissed either of us, and we probably never would.

I also checked in with another Russian friend who had held senior positions in Russian state broadcasting, telling him about the kiss and my attempts to decipher just what it meant. He looked at me mischievously and asked "What do you think? Is it a blessing or a curse?"

Throughout my time as a journalist covering Vladimir Putin, I often did try to psychoanalyze him, precisely because he is so opaque. Beginning in 1999, I observed him, talked with him, interviewed him, photographed him, questioned him, and studied him. Any attempt to do this, naturally, is a losing proposition; we are not likely to get any psychological reports from the Kremlin. But over the years, I was able to meet with and ask questions of him, the first encounter, a nearly four-hour discussion he held with nine journalists for US media outlets. It took place on June 18, 2001, in the Kremlin Library.

I was invited to sit next to him, to his right. As we sipped tea and nibbled on piroshki, he was deliberate, even in the way he ate, breaking his pastry into little pieces, sipping his tea slowly. Watching Mr. Putin up close, just a foot or two away, his face, his hands, his gestures, his voice, his demeanor, gave me a visceral feel for how he interacts (perhaps "operates" is a better term) with other people.

In contrast to most politicians, Vladimir Putin doesn't fill a room with his presence, or even try to. I once watched a fascinating piece of video in which President Putin arrives at a former czarist palace. Members of the military honor guard, impossibly tall, are dressed in uniforms straight out of a fashion designer's vision of real-life toy soldiers: dark blue double-breasted jackets with gold buttons, peaked hats dripping in gold braid. The guards, in precise coordinated movement, cock their heads in an exaggerated arc as he walks by. Putin, however, almost seems to hunch forward, as if he would rather arrive unnoticed.

In some sit-down meetings he emotionally retreats, preferring to draw out his interlocutor, leaving them to fill in the spaces in the conversation. Some observers have described Putin as a mirror reflecting to the other person whatever that person wants to see. It's also an effective way of making the other person feel uncomfortable. This is not to say that Putin is passive or doesn't make his points, and in some cases, as I saw in the Kremlin Library, he can suddenly switch gears into heated rhetoric.

During this 2001 meeting, I asked the first question, about missile defense. He obviously knew the subject well, and launched into a lecture about missile technology:

"Do you know the speed at which a ballistic missile flies? Seven to seven and a half kilometers per second. To knock it out, an antimissile must fly at the same speed, which makes fifteen kilometers per second, when combined. It's like hitting a bullet with another bullet."

We went around the table, each correspondent asking his or her questions. The *Washington Post*'s Susan Glasser raised the subject of his war in Chechnya. His calm and cool demeanor suddenly evaporated, replaced by boiling fury.

"What would you suggest we do? Talk with them about biblical values? They even interpret the Koran in their own way. And they consider everyone who wears a cross to be an enemy. I told the president [George W. Bush]: 'Imagine that some armed people come along and want to grab half of Texas. Can you imagine that?' And yet, that was exactly at issue in Russia. And you know it!" Putin began stabbing the air with his index finger, almost accusing us reporters.

"I sometimes think about what is happening in the media," he went on, "and I don't believe that nobody understands it. If a campaign is being mounted, I think it is simply a deliberate attempt to use the situation in Chechnya in order to destabilize the Russian Federation. I can think of no other explanation."

With other world leaders, especially from countries at odds with Russia, Putin can be cutting and sarcastic, even boorish. "Manspreading," legs apart in a feudal-ruler pose, is another technique he uses, a corporal semaphore, placing his interlocutor in a supplicant position. President Barack Obama downplayed Putin's poses, but the fact that he even noticed it is significant. "I know the press likes to focus on body language," Obama said at a news conference in 2013, "and he's got that kind of slouch, looking like the bored kid at the back of the classroom." Over the years, Putin has become even more petulant and, at times, insulting.

Putin speaks grammatically correct Russian, which a friend of mine, a confirmed member of the Russian intelligentsia, described to me once this way: "To me he always sounds like a Soviet apparatchik who is trying hard to be a bit folksy. His 'accent' is definitely urban [unlike Khrushchev's southern Russia village accent] and Leningradish. Profanity is his KGB 'accent.'"

Mr. Putin does, on occasion, have a presidential potty mouth that he uses to great advantage. Sometimes it's to create the image of a "muzhik" ("a real guy"); at other times it's to look tough, not taking shit from anyone. The most famous example was in September 1999 when Russia was hit with a series of deadly apartment bombings, as described in an earlier chapter. Vowing revenge, Putin, at the time Russia's prime minister, unleashed his famous expression that signaled a major political shift: "We'll go after them everywhere. Excuse my language, but if we catch them in the toilet we'll rub them out in the outhouse."

Of course, translating this phrase with the full force of the original Russian requires a high degree of linguistic savoir faire. The words he used—"rub them out" ("mochit'") and "outhouse" ("sortir")—are crude, gangster expressions, not the kind of language expected of a president. That tough talk shocked many Russians; they'd never heard anything like it from a leader before. But many applauded it. No more drunken Yeltsin stumbling his way through a speech; finally, a tough, vigorous young leader who had their back and would give the finger—and more—to terrorists.

His off-color expressions only seemed to burnish that image. At a summit meeting in 2002 that I covered for CNN, a foreign journalist asked the president whether Russia was repressing human rights in Chechnya, where most people are Muslim. Putin snidely shot back: "If you're really ready to become an Islamic radical, and you're ready to have yourself circumcised, I invite you to Moscow. We have a multi-faith country, and we have experts in that. I'll recommend doing the operation so that nothing grows back."

Over the more than two decades he has been in power, Putin has only strengthened this "regular guy" image. The message: He is one of us.

Putin is a decidedly un-sexy man, at least in the Western context of attractiveness, but he and his Kremlin PR handlers burnished a Soviet-style masculinity to raise his macho quotient. In April 2013, protesters from FEMEN (which describes itself as an "international women's movement of brave topless female activists") with bare chests and "Fuck you, Putin" written in large black Cyrillic letters on their backs, rushed toward Putin and German chancellor Angela Merkel at an industrial fair in Hanover, Germany. The video shows Putin's eyes bulging in what looked like gleeful approval as he gave the first topless woman two thumbs up.

In 2002, on Putin's fiftieth birthday, the Kremlin added a little sex appeal. A blonde singing duo with the retro-Soviet name of "Singing Together" released a bouncy electro-pop song extolling the qualities of "A Man Like Putin." The song seemed geared to teen girls, but the image of Putin the heartthrob had broader appeal, promoting the president to the masses, especially women who often had to put up with men who were definitely not like Putin.

It was an instant hit. The songwriter said he wrote it almost on a bet, but more likely it was a Kremlin attempt at image-making for the president, one of many to come. The lyrics begin with a girl complaining that her boyfriend is drinking and she's sick of it:

> And now, I want someone like Putin.
> Someone like Putin, full of strength
> Someone like Putin, who doesn't drink
> Someone like Putin, who doesn't offend me
> Someone like Putin, who won't run away.

The Kremlin constantly polls the Russian public, closely guarding the results for use by the president's PR advisers, but polling by other companies at the time showed Putin with a steady approval rating of 70 percent. Asked what they liked about Putin, Russians described his "honesty . . . decency . . . work ethic . . . intelligence . . . and purposefulness."

One young girl we interviewed said, with a giggle: "He's young, he's clever, he's very diplomatic—can I say that? He's just very . . . [laugh] He's a beautiful man, that's what I think."

Eventually, Putin no longer was young, so the Kremlin revised his image. From young and vigorous, he morphed into the more mature "adult" in the room. Then there were photo ops with little children, the Kremlin's modern take on revolutionary-era propaganda images of Vladimir Lenin with little children at his knee, which, of course, echoed even earlier religious imagery of Jesus and children.

But Putin wasn't always the pure-as-the-driven-snow reincarnation of sanctity. His sense of humor often had an ironic and sometimes earthy, sexual twist to it. "If a grandmother had certain sexual indicators, she would be a grandfather," he said in June 2006, answering a question about sanctions against Iran. In 2003, explaining how the law works, he said: "Everyone has to understand, once and for all, that you've got to obey the law all the time, and not just when they grab you 'in a certain place.'"

During the December 2011 protests, young people wearing white ribbons on their coats gathered on the icy streets of Moscow to reject what they said were rigged parliamentary elections. Putin smirkingly derided the symbol of their protest movement. "Frankly speaking," he said, "when I saw those little ribbons, I thought it was some sort of action against AIDS. I'm embarrassed to say I thought they were wearing condoms."

All of this could seem off the cuff, just more of this muzhik-speak. But, just as with my kiss from Mr. Putin, it can be interpreted variously as an expression of who he really is; as a premeditated act designed to make a point; to artificially create an image; to set an opponent on their back heel; to elicit information; or the embodiment of whatever the viewer wants to see.

STUCK IN THE PAST

Anyone who has visited Moscow or St. Petersburg is familiar with Soviet kitsch. Walk down Old Arbat Street in Moscow and you'll see a plethora of objects for sale: fake fur army hats and leather belts with a hammer-and-sickle insignia, matryoshka dolls with depictions of Stalin, red Soviet flags, even an occasional Lenin impersonator. (Once, at Christmastime, outside the Kremlin walls, I encountered a modern-day "Lenin" taking a break and drinking a latte with a Father Frost [Santa Claus] impersonator.)

That's just the cheap, tourist-trap version of Soviet nostalgia. But there are deeper veins of post-Soviet nostalgia that Putin is mining, exploiting some Russians' longing for their lost empire.

For older Russians, it can be nostalgia for the days when jobs were guaranteed by the state (even if, as the old Brezhnev-era saying goes, "They pretend to pay us; we pretend to work"). It can be as simple as remembering their youth—or their first love affair. Like people everywhere, some older Russians miss the days when they were young, even if most Soviet citizens at the time lived in poverty, compared with life in the West. They may remember the queues in which so many Soviet citizens, especially women, spent hours waiting for food or clothes that would suddenly appear in stores for one brief moment, to be scooped up by the lucky ones who had gotten a tip in advance, or simply walked by at the right moment. They even had a nickname for the string shopping bags they used to carry with them at all times: "avozka" ("a little just-in-case bag"). A few years ago, shopping in a chic Moscow clothing store, I saw that string bags were back, updated in bold colors with leather trim.

All that waiting in line seemed like such a colossal waste of time, and it was. But it also offered an opportunity to socialize, to be together, in one common experience that everyone—willing or unwilling—had to share, a rare occurrence amid the anonymity of life today in Moscow and other big Russian cities. And it is a graphic reminder of the inequality of life in today's Russia.

Their grandparents may have been hauled off to the Gulag by Stalin's henchmen, but for some Russians, that was only part of their lives, the part they want to forget. Many Russians don't even know their own family history. The Russian government, under Vladimir Putin, has whitewashed Soviet history, eliminating the horror of Stalin's repression, turning the heroism of Soviet citizens who fought and died in the millions during World War II into a cult of suffering. The Russian government has shut down the oldest and most respected human rights organization in the country, Memorial, that was dedicated to the preservation of historical memory and to the history of political repression, declaring it a "foreign agent." The government is rewriting school textbooks. Young children are dressing in World War II–style uniforms and assembling rifles, just as they did in Soviet times.

For some young Russians with no memory of the suffering inflicted on their grandparents and even their parents, the attraction of post-Soviet nostalgia may be the pride—the hubris—they associate with being citizens of a superpower, a country that matters, a country that tells other countries what to do, a Russian version of the Americans who boisterously chant "USA! USA!"

Putin feeds that emotion with his muscle-flexing insistence that a country is either sovereign or it's a victim of stronger nations: "There is no middle way between being a sovereign country and a colony, no matter what you call a colony," he said in 2022. "If a country or a group of countries is unable to make sovereign decisions, it means that it already is a colony to a certain extent, and colonies historically have no future and stand no chance of surviving a tough geopolitical fight."

Throughout my time reporting on Vladimir Putin, I wondered whether he could make a final break with the past, if he could free himself from the straitjacket of his totalitarian upbringing that convinces some Russians that they are surrounded by enemies, that no one can be trusted, that loosening the reins is dangerous. Two decades ago, I listened to his first inaugural address, in which he told his fellow citizens: "We have proved that Russia is becoming a modern democratic state." I wanted to believe it. In the first two years of his presidency, Putin introduced economic reforms, and it buoyed my hope that the country could emerge from the wreckage of the early 1990s in which so many Russians had lost so much.

But some Russians still live, mentally and emotionally, in the USSR, and I am forced to conclude that Putin is one of them. I had a graphic illustration of that mentality once, while killing time with other reporters, waiting for a brief meeting with the president at his residence outside of Moscow. I asked a senior Putin aide whom I had gotten to know relatively well, whether he truly believed, as he said he did, in democracy for the people of Russia.

"Of course, I do!" he assured me. "But right now, our people are naive and vulnerable. If we let people vote the way they want, they're likely to choose the wrong candidates, Communists and the like. Eventually, we'll have full democracy, but they're not ready for it right now. It's dangerous; there could be chaos."

It was a moment of clarity for me. I understood that the magical day when Russians would be "ready" to make their own decisions, to make their own mistakes on the road to democracy, just as Americans have done in our slow road to freedom and equality—that day would never come. It would be like the old joke about Communism, the "bright future" that was always beyond the horizon. My colleague, Putin's aide, didn't trust the Russian people. Not yet. And, as it seems to me, he never would.

Two years after I left my post in Moscow, I listened as Vladimir Putin, on February 10, 2007, at the Munich Security Conference, delivered a snide riposte to what he described as America's attempt at "unipolar" control of the world. It began, in typical Putin style, with an attempt at humor that left a menacing aftertaste: "This conference's format will allow me to say what I really think about international security problems. And if my comments seem unduly polemical, pointed, or inexact to our colleagues, then I would ask you not to get angry with me. After all, this is only a conference."

"One state and, of course, first and foremost, the United States," he went on, "has overstepped its national borders in every way. This is visible in the economic, political, cultural, and educational policies it imposes on other nations. Well, who likes this? Who is happy about this? . . . One single center of power. One single center of force. One single center of decision-making. This is the world of one master, one sovereign."

Suddenly I felt I was back in the 1980s, as an aging Soviet general secretary inveighed against the United States. The Vladimir Putin whom I had reported on in the early 2000s, who had spoken of cooperation with Washington, had vanished. That old Soviet instinct for control dies hard. And Putin, as I've been convinced during the more than twenty-five years I have spent reporting on him, remains, essentially, a Soviet man.

· *11* ·

9/11

September 11, 2001, was my sister Joan's fortieth birthday, and I woke up that morning making a mental note that I would call her after 9 a.m. in New York, where she lived—eight hours behind us in Moscow. I headed for the office and looked at our schedule for the day, which included a press briefing by Douglas Feith, President George W. Bush's undersecretary of defense for policy. He was in the Russian capital to discuss nuclear arms reduction and missile defense issues at the Russian Defense Ministry with his Russian counterpart, Colonel-General Yuri Nikolayevich Baluyevsky.

Midday we headed for the Marriott Hotel and waited, along with the other news crews, in a corridor outside the briefing room for what seemed like an unusually long time. My mobile phone buzzed unexpectedly. It was our senior producer, Maxim Tkachenko.

"Jill," he said, "Atlanta just called. There's some breaking news: A plane just crashed into the World Trade Center in New York City."

I was confused. "Was it an accident?" I asked. I couldn't imagine any other scenario.

"It's unclear," Maxim replied.

I told some of the other reporters what he had relayed, and a few minutes later Maxim called back.

"Another plane flew into another tower," he said.

"What?" I yelled.

Maxim was a very controlled and serious person, and he sounded concerned. I knew right then it could not be an accident, but what was it? Maxim told me what he knew, which was very little.

Suddenly, they opened the doors to the briefing room, and we were ushered in. I took a seat in the second row.

In his book, *War and Decision: Inside the Pentagon at the Dawn of the War on Terrorism*, Feith recounts that he had a meeting with Russian journalists that morning, and as he headed for the car, a US embassy press officer informed him that a plane had hit the World Trade Center. Feith said that he was skeptical: "First reports are almost always wrong."

Just as he arrived at our briefing hotel, Feith said, the embassy press officer told him that a second plane had hit the World Trade Center. He listened in on a cell phone to a CNN broadcast of President Bush speaking from an elementary school in Sarasota, Florida: "Terrorism against our nation will not stand."

As soon as Feith was seated and began taking questions, I asked him what he knew of the attacks. He said all they knew was what they had seen live on CNN.

A few minutes into the briefing, my phone vibrated again. I leaned over and tried to keep my voice low. It was Max. "They've hit the Pentagon," he told me.

I quickly raised my hand and told Feith that CNN was now reporting that another plane had hit the Pentagon and there was some type of fire. Feith looked shocked. He said he knew nothing about it. Suddenly, his aides stopped the briefing and hustled him out of the room.

We raced back to the bureau and were soon reporting around the clock. I called my sister Joan, but her cell phone didn't answer. The horror of even thinking about something happening to my youngest sister was almost too much to contemplate. It shattered the distanced approach I'd always tried to take when reporting on terrible things that I had witnessed as a journalist; my mind was running on two tracks, experiencing the moment in all its shock and pain but, emotionally, trying to keep it at a distance, not allowing it to overwhelm me.

Within hours of the attacks on New York and Washington, Vladimir Putin was on the phone, the first international leader to call President George W. Bush to express his condolences and support. In a televised address later that day, Putin said: "Russia knows directly what terrorism means. And because of this, we, more than anyone, understand the feelings of the American people. In the name of Russia, I want to say to the American people—we are with you."

The image of Putin on the phone, talking with George W. Bush, stuck in my mind, and I recalled another moment less than three months before, at Brdo Castle in Slovenia, as I sat at a news conference, watching Bush and Putin, side by side, pledge to build a "constructive, respectful relationship," Bush saying he had "looked the man in the eye . . . I was able to get a sense of his soul." Putin, more measured, but agreeing with Bush that "Russia and the United States are not enemies, they do not threaten each other, and they could be fully good allies."

With this 9/11 phone call, I thought, they really are allies. I was witness-ing the proof.

By evening Moscow time, I was able to get through to my sister Joan on her home phone. She was, thank God, okay. She told me she had been running late for work and was outside her office building on Fifth Avenue, Midtown, as the first plane hit the North Tower. Then she saw the second plane plow into the South Tower. Her first thought, she told me, was, "That was no accident." Joan walked home to Brooklyn over the 59th Street Bridge, looking back over her shoulder at a column of black smoke filling the sky. Years later, she told me, amid the horror, one of her strongest memories was how clear and brilliantly blue the sky had been that morning, just before the planes struck.

Night stretched into morning. When the live shots ended, I walked across the parking lot to our apartment building and fell into bed.

The next day, I awoke feeling—as I usually do in the morning—invigo-rated and positive. Then, like a heavy blanket, the memory of what had just happened smothered me. In my diary I wrote: "a feeling that it can't be real, that I dreamed it—that life will never be the same."

PUTIN'S "PREMONITION"

Two days before 9/11 our CNN Moscow team had noted an ominous event: Ahmad Shah Massoud, the top commander of the Northern Alliance, a coalition of anti-Taliban militias, was assassinated in Afghanistan by two Al-Qaeda suicide bombers disguised as journalists. Our bureau had followed Shah Massoud's military efforts against the Taliban, and we had, in fact, trav-eled to neighboring Tajikistan to report on it. I remembered standing in the mountains, looking over into Afghanistan, thinking of how Shah Massoud, an outstanding military tactician, had led the fight against the Soviet occupation of Afghanistan two decades before.

Months later, Putin revealed he'd had what he described as a premonition about terrorists and September 11. In an interview with Russia's NTV, he said that on September 9, he called Bush and informed him of Shah Massoud's assassination. "I told my American colleague, 'This really worries me,'" Putin said. "I have the feeling something is going to happen, that they are apparently preparing something."

Soon after news of the 9/11 attacks broke, Russian citizens made their way, in sad pilgrimage, to the US embassy in Moscow, a large, buff-colored building on one of the capital's main thoroughfares, a short drive from our bureau. On the sidewalk in front they left flowers, cards, and handwritten notes, some of which described their own recent experiences with terrorist bombings in the Moscow metro and in a shopping mall. As we filmed the scene, I choked back tears.

President Putin was attempting to make common cause with the United States, noting that both countries were the objects of terrorist attacks. The question now was, how should Russia respond? On September 12 Putin conferred with a group of Russian politicians. Their advice, one source told us, was mixed. Most agreed that Russia and the United States were facing a common enemy. Some counseled Putin to stick with the United States; others said Russia should remain neutral. Still others argued that Russia should oppose any US moves.

A few days later, in Sochi, Putin huddled with his security and foreign policy advisers. It was obvious the Bush administration would soon retaliate for the 9/11 attacks, but there was ample reason for some Russians officials to question why Moscow should get involved in any US military action. After all, in the 1980s, as Soviet troops fought a useless Cold War battle in the treacherous mountains of Afghanistan, the United States had supported their enemy, the Mujaheddin (which later evolved into the Taliban). The Soviet Union finally retreated from Afghanistan in 1989 after ten long years of fighting and at least 15,000 military deaths. It was a painful lesson for the Soviet Union, and one that led to the collapse of the USSR.

Alexey Arbatov, member of the Russian parliament and an expert to whom I often turned for guidance on Russia's foreign and defense policy, described the stakes: "Russia's direct participation in American military action, providing its facilities or bases, or even taking part in some of the operations, would make Russia an object of new terrorist attacks."

Vladimir Putin was at the crux of a momentous decision: How far should he go in helping George W. Bush's war on terrorism?

Standing firm with Washington could score diplomatic points for Mr. Putin, and maybe even win him some economic benefits from the West—a priority for Putin—but should he offer Washington the use of Russia's airspace? Or the use of former Soviet military bases and defense facilities it still had in Central Asia?

Central Asian nations bordering Afghanistan—countries like Uzbekistan, Kyrgyzstan, and Tajikistan, which, twenty years before, had been part of the Soviet Union—were barely able to contain their own radical Islamic movements, including the Taliban. Now, they said, they were ready to cooperate with any country—including the United States—that would help combat terrorism. Talk like that made Moscow nervous; introducing US military forces to Central Asia would place them squarely in Putin's backyard, and any military action might destabilize an already fragile region.

Although Putin appeared to be moving toward more cooperation with the United States, his decision, nevertheless, astounded me. He had been speaking out forcefully against the attacks on America, but now, as the United States prepared to attack Al-Qaeda in Afghanistan, he was offering more than words of support, even going beyond what several of his top officials had advised him to do.

With the Bush administration preparing to attack Al-Qaeda in Afghanistan, Vladimir Putin offered to provide intelligence that Russian security agencies had collected on the infrastructure, location, and training of international terrorists. In a stunning decision, he coordinated with Central Asian nations to allow US forces, for the first time, to operate two military bases in the region.

And he did even more. One year later, when the Bush administration pulled out of the landmark 1972 Anti-Ballistic Missile Treaty, Putin—initially, at least—took it in stride, suddenly ending a quarrel that had once threatened to disrupt US–Russian relations. And when Washington sent US military trainers to Georgia, near the border with Russia, preparing for deployment in Afghanistan, Putin didn't bat an eye.

"I think what he did was a revolution in terms of Russia's foreign policy," Dmitri Trenin, at the time director of a leading think tank, the Moscow Carnegie Center, told me. "But that revolution did not happen overnight, and it did not happen because of September 11. He [Putin] used, he seized upon September 11 as an opportunity to leapfrog in his foreign policy, the outlines of which by that time had been complete." Putin, he said, was leading his own foreign policy and defense advisers in a new direction, toward full partnership with the United States and the West.

But Trenin injected this caveat: "It's not that he wants to be friends with the U.S. for friendship's sake, he does it for Russia's sake—as he sees it."

As I reported on the breaking news, I tried to keep my eye on the broader significance of the history that was unfolding in front of me. Vladimir Putin was pivoting westward, but, as I would learn over the coming years, his true motivation for taking action could be quite different from what it appeared to be on the surface. "Evil must be punished," Putin said after 9/11. "[But we] should not become like bandits that act from behind a corner. We should consider our decisions and proceed from correct facts."

The Russian president had been trying to link his fight against rebels in Chechnya to the United States' fight against international terrorism, and now he had succeeded. The Bush administration began urging Chechnya's leadership to break ties with Al-Qaeda and its leader, Osama bin Laden. In an interview I conducted with FSB director Nikolai Patrushev, he claimed the security service knew where bin Laden was hiding before the attacks on the United States, and it had informed "other" special services. Bin Laden, Patrushev said, had since changed his location but was still in Afghanistan. The FSB, he vowed, would find out where he was and pass that information on to its "Western colleagues."

"Russia has never tried to kill Osama bin Laden," he said. "We usually deal with infiltrating criminals, arrest them, and turn them over to the courts to be punished. That's what I think should be done. However, we have experience where, when a suspect offers armed resistance, in order to avoid casualties, it is possible to kill him."

We interviewed Patrushev at Lubyanka, the building that houses FSB headquarters. In the first flush of post-9/11 mutual support between Moscow and Washington, we conducted several interviews and video shoots there. Officers opened their files to show us intelligence, including photos, passports, and weapons seized from terrorists fighting in Chechnya and bombing apartment buildings in Russia—the same kind of international terrorists, Putin argued, who had attacked New York and Washington.

Putin took a "We told you so" approach after 9/11, insisting he had been warning the West since he took office that there was a worldwide network of fanatical terrorists, funded primarily by drug money. The number-one criminal suspect for both countries: Osama bin Laden. The attacks on the United States, he said, "could be compared in scale and cruelty to what the Nazis were perpetrating.

"I feel guilty for what has happened," he added. "We spoke so much about this threat, but apparently not enough." What did Putin mean? Ostensibly, he was blaming himself for not being vociferous enough about the threat, for not making it clear to the United States. Indirectly, however, he was blaming the United States for not listening to him, a complaint that would fester and grow as time went on.

THE PAYOFF

Putin's support for the United States did pay off, however, and not only by convincing the Bush administration to publicly reevaluate its position on Russia's fight against what it considered international terrorism. In May 2002 President Bush flew to Russia to sign the Strategic Offensive Reductions Treaty (SORT), in which Russia and the United States each agreed to limit their nuclear arsenals to between 1,700 and 2,200 operationally deployed warheads.

Putin also won the promise of a new role for Russia in NATO, one of the thorniest and most complex issues I covered in Russia or in Washington. It remains a subject that can ignite vicious debate between Russians and Americans, as well as between American experts on Russia. And yet, in those early days of reporting on Vladimir Putin, I hoped that Russia and NATO could work toward a common understanding of how to structure security in a world no longer divided by the Cold War.

Boris Yeltsin and Bill Clinton began the process, signing the NATO-Russia Founding Act on Mutual Relations, Cooperation, and Security, a formal cooperation agreement with the organization, in 1997.

French president Jacques Chirac captured the drama of the moment: "This summit is one of those appointments that history has made with itself. Today we are building peace. By signing . . . the Founding Act of a new European security organization in which Russia will occupy its full place," he said, "we will be turning the page on half a century of misunderstanding, of confrontation, of division on our continent." It didn't quite turn out that way.

Moscow soon became convinced it had no real voice in deliberations with NATO's other members—it was "19 against one." With three new NATO members—Poland, Hungary, and the Czech Republic—waiting in the wings, NATO pledged to Russia that it had "no intention, no plan, and no reason" to install nuclear weapons on the territory of new members. Putin didn't believe it.

The low point in the relationship during Yeltsin's presidency was 1999. As NATO launched its air war against Yugoslavia, Russians pelted the US embassy in Moscow with paint balloons. I could feel the ground shifting as several Russian officials whom I had gotten to know, as well as foreign policy experts whom I counted among my colleagues and friends, were infuriated by NATO's attacks on the Serbian capital of Belgrade. It tore a hole in the relationship between Russia and the United States that never healed.

NATO's plans to accept the Baltic States on Russia's border to join the alliance was another flashpoint. NATO expansion had always been the biggest single irritant in the Russia–NATO relationship, but now, Putin, in a major post-9/11 policy shift, seemed to be changing the equation: "We are fully prepared to go as far in developing our relationship as the alliance is," he said. Improve Russia–NATO relations, he suggested, and the issue of NATO expansion will cease to matter.

Two and a half months after September 11, Putin was poised to sign a new agreement with NATO that, some predicted, could bury the Cold War forever. Moscow would have a seat at the table on issues ranging from terrorism to arms proliferation, and NATO was promising that Russia would have an equal voice.

During two days of talks in Moscow with senior Russian officials, Secretary General George Robertson tried to begin "mapping a way forward," creating, perhaps, a new council within the alliance where Russia would be equal to NATO's other nineteen members. It was all "exploratory," Robertson said, and after what he called a "fascinating" discussion with Putin, he reported that the Russian president had assured him this was not an attempt by Russia to "slow down or neutralize" NATO's work, or for Russia to try to have a veto over NATO decisions.

Putin himself, in the first few years after 9/11, continued to take a positive approach toward NATO, even meeting with NATO leaders in Rome in 2002, signing a joint declaration on "NATO-Russia Relations: A New Quality," pledging to "intensify efforts in the struggle against terrorism, crisis management, non-proliferation of weapons of mass destruction, arms control and confidence-building measures, theatre missile defense, search and rescue at sea, military-to-military cooperation and defense reform, and civil emergencies, as well as in other areas."

There were doubters in Moscow like retired general Leonid Ivashov, who predicted, "It will be a big discussion club. They'll listen to each other, but I'm convinced they won't make any decisions on any serious matters."

I asked for an interview with Sergei Karaganov, a dapper, acerbic adviser to Putin whom I often consulted for interpretation of the opaque Kremlin decision-making process. Putin, he told me, could not agree to simply a new version of the old "symbolic" relationship with NATO: "I think Putin wants as close cooperation with the West as possible; however, there is always the problem that some types of cooperation we've had have been 'facelifting.'"

Left unsaid were the concerns the United States and its allies had about Putin's scorched-earth tactics in Chechnya.

I wanted to know what the Russian public thought about NATO. A new poll of Russians living in the heartland was out, and more than half of them still thought the alliance was aggressive and a security threat, tracking closely the way Putin himself described it at a news conference with President Bush three months before 9/11: "We ask ourselves, 'Is this a military organization?' Yes, it's a military organization. 'It doesn't want us in it?' No, they don't want us. 'It's moving toward our border?' Yes, it's moving toward our border. Why?"

There might, however, be another view among Russians living closer to Europe, I thought. We flew to Kaliningrad, the Russian enclave in the heart of Europe, formerly the German city of Konigsberg.

I was surprised to find that people there were more hopeful. The terrorist attacks on the United States had had an impact, but there was an even stronger factor: NATO was not just some abstract concept dreamt up by military planners. Kaliningrad's neighbor, Poland, already was a NATO member, and, if Lithuania were to join, Kaliningrad would be surrounded by NATO.

And yet several people told us they didn't feel threatened. If Russia joined NATO, they said, it could bring them closer to their European neighbors. That desire to be part of Europe, to enjoy a better standard of living, was growing stronger. They wanted Europe and, even more importantly, they thought Europe wanted them.

But, as NATO expanded, Putin's suspicions grew. The divide between Russia and NATO, as I saw on a trip to Tallinn, Estonia, was deeper than just a military border. We went to sea—the Baltic Sea—with twenty-five-year-old navy lieutenant Lauri Tumm, the Estonian navy's chief of operations. Like most things in the tiny Baltic nation, the navy was small—just eight ships. But, as I reported for CNN, Lieutenant Tumm and his minuscule fleet were Russia's worst nightmare, not because of the ships they had but because of the friends they kept.

Estonia won its independence from the Soviet Union in 1991, and the Russian navy pulled out in 1994, vindictively sinking ships and ripping out electrical wiring. The Estonian navy wasted no time beginning cooperation with NATO, even though it would not become a member of the alliance until 2004. As soon as it got its first ship, it took part in combined naval exercises—just 187 miles from neighboring Russia. Its soldiers were serving with NATO in Kosovo, and Lieutenant Tumm told me his navy was ready for full NATO membership. So were the people we spoke with in the capital, Tallinn, who said they would feel "much more secure" as NATO members.

For Putin, however, expanding NATO to the Baltics was a nonstarter: "In Europe they talk about destroying old boundaries," he said. "How can the expansion of NATO resolve that issue?"

I interviewed Estonia's president, Lennart Meri, a meeting that I cherish to this day. Meri was a true statesman. His father, Georg Meri, was a diplomat between World Wars I and II, when Estonia enjoyed a brief period of independence. Lennart was educated in Berlin, London, and Paris. Like many Estonian families, the Meris were exiled to Siberia. His father was sentenced to a labor camp in Moscow.

In our interview at the presidential palace in Tallinn, President Meri insisted that expanding NATO's borders to Russia was not a threat to Moscow: "We will give a firm guarantee to ourselves, to our children, to our grandchildren, that there will be stability."

In March 2004 all three Baltic nations—Estonia, Latvia, and Lithuania—along with four other former Soviet satellites—Bulgaria, Romania, Slovakia,

and Slovenia—did become members of NATO, bringing the alliance right up
to Russia's borders, but, as Steven Pifer, former US ambassador to Ukraine,
put it: "Putin did not raise a fuss."

Leading Russian politicians like Mikhail Margelov, a member of the
Russian parliament and, later, chairman of the Foreign Affairs Committee of
the Federation Council, was surprisingly sanguine: "Well, I would rather have
NATO on Russia's borders than Al-Qaeda. I would prefer to have NATO
bases than Tora Bora."

But there were dark clouds on the horizon. Estonia's foreign minister,
Harri Tiido, described it to me this way: "Nations are positioning themselves
on this or that side of an imaginary line in Europe and the line is according to
the choice of western values."

Two months after 9/11, Vladimir Putin gave a brief speech at the Russian embassy in Washington. Recalling his first meeting with George W.
Bush in Slovenia, he sounded like a nineteen-year-old boy on his first date:
"We were nervous, which was quite natural, but, most importantly, we were
ready for dialogue, and the dialogue took place, we had a conversation that
was very important for us and for our countries. We said then that the Cold
War had receded into the past, that our countries were no longer each other's
enemies, and we said that the very nature of our relations was changing;
they should be founded on common interests, common values, and mutual
respect."

"Today," he vowed, "Russia is a country whose integration in the community of free and democratic countries has become irreversible."

That all sounded positive and promising, but, like the sound of an
orchestra with just one instrument out of tune, I kept hearing an off-key note
in Mr. Putin's statements. There was no way I could imagine, at that point,
how deeply discordant Moscow and Washington eventually would become.

Two weeks after the 9/11 attacks, Putin delivered a speech at the Bund-
estag in Berlin—in German, which he speaks fluently, thanks to his years as
a KGB officer in Dresden. He began on a positive note. "Russia is a friendly
European nation." It had a relationship with NATO, he noted. Yeltsin had
signed the Founding Act on Mutual Relations, Cooperation, and Security in
1997. But, Putin said, it was not a "partnership." "In reality, we have not yet
learned to trust each other. . . . In spite of a plethora of sweet words, we are
still surreptitiously opposed to each other."

Then, he zeroed in on what really galled him. "Today decisions are
often taken, in principle, without our participation, and we are only urged
afterwards to support such decisions. After that they talk again about loyalty
to NATO. They even say that such decisions cannot be implemented without
Russia. Let us ask ourselves: Is this normal? Is this true partnership?"

BEHIND PUTIN'S WORDS

Putin sounded angry. His views on NATO, on the West, on Russia's role in European security, were hardening. Years later, after he had ordered his troops to invade Ukraine, I wrote in an opinion piece for CNN.com, a kind of "mea culpa."

"I admit it," I said. "During the twenty-two years I reported on Putin, I didn't listen to him as closely as I should have. Or, rather, I listened to the parts I wanted to hear, the parts that sounded good to the ear of a Westerner." Listening to Putin was like watching a foreign-language film—hearing the dialogue all right, but without understanding the subtitles. And those subtitles offered clues not only to what Putin was thinking but also to the direction in which he was evolving.

By 2007, when he addressed the Munich Security Conference, he had crossed the Rubicon. He began with a snide, Putinesque comment: "Incidentally, Russia—we—are constantly being taught about democracy. But for some reason those who teach us do not want to learn themselves." Then, he upped the ante: "One state and, of course, first and foremost, the United States, has overstepped its national borders in every way. This is visible in the economic, political, cultural, and educational policies it imposes on other nations. Well, who likes this? Who is happy about this?"

When I first read that speech, I admit, I discounted some of Putin's hard edge, chalking it up to mere rhetoric. And I wasn't the only one; as former Latvian president Valdis Zatlers put it, years later, "We heard, but we didn't understand." Nevertheless, I began my personal list of several themes that seemed to harden with every speech that Putin delivered:

Russia was driven to its knees under Gorbachev and Yeltsin.
It's time for Russia to stand up, restore its power, and influence in the world.
I am the leader who will do that.
The West says nice things about Russia in public, but privately deceives us.
The West ignores Russia's security interests; it does not respect us.
Russians are kind people, but naive; weak people are taken advantage of, beaten.
The West looks tough, but it is weak. We in Russia are tough, and we will outlast it.

Resentment was the keynote. The United States, powerful nation that, on one level, he respects as a worthy enemy, yet deeply resents. A country that must be confronted. A country that, as he sees it, stabbed Russia in the back.

By February 2022, Putin's bitterness was at full boil: "We have always sought to be part of the so-called civilized world. So, following the collapse of the Soviet Union, which we allowed with our own hands, it seemed to us for some reason that any day now we would become part of that so-called civilized world. But it turned out we weren't welcome there, despite all our efforts and attempts. I'm saying this, having in mind my own work as well. I also made these efforts, our efforts to be closer, to be part of it—No!"

THE GATHERER OF THE RUSSIAN LANDS

Vladimir Putin is not unique in feeling unwanted by the West. *Are we part of the West? Do we belong?* These recurring questions have haunted Russians since at least the time of Peter the Great.

For centuries, Russia has been drawn to the West, to its technological superiority, to its lifestyle, to its creature comforts, and yet, on another level, Russia has always considered itself morally superior to the West—a "spiritual culture" based in communal values, not rank individualism. Putin, a twenty-first-century man, has been channeling those eighteenth-century debates since becoming president, and I believe he has not substantially changed any of his opinions; if anything, his view of the United States, his view of the world, has only calcified.

But this is my view from the outside. To get a better perspective on Putin, during my years in Moscow, I would occasionally talk with Alexey Venediktov, one of the most well-known journalists in Russia, a friend and colleague. As former editor in chief of Echo Moscow radio, Venediktov not only reported on Putin, he also knew him and his Kremlin staff and talked with them frequently. (It didn't protect him from Putin's wrath. Facing Kremlin pressure, like so many independent media outlets, Echo Moscow decided to shut down in March 2022, after the law on "fake news" about the Ukraine war went into effect.)

"It seems to me that a picture has formed in his [Putin's] mind," he told me in 2014, after Putin illegally annexed Crimea. "There were two destroyers, Gorbachev and Yeltsin. And they went down in history as destroyers— 'sometimes with a plus sign, because there were some things that needed to be destroyed.'" He told me that was a quote from Putin himself.

"Then came the time for building. Gathering the lands. The real Russia, not the empire! And his historical role, as I understand it, is to gather together. . . . And it doesn't necessarily mean gathering territory. It can be spiritual . . . the so-called 'Russian World.' He understands that is his historical mission."

But, I asked him, Putin understands, doesn't he, that these people now live in sovereign countries?

"The spiritual," Venediktov replied, "is higher than borders."

Putin often talks about the importance of protecting Russia's "sovereignty," but Venediktov told me that, for Putin, "higher than sovereignty is his historical mission."

"He thinks of it from the point of view of a history book, as opposed to what he will leave his family. The children are grown, he is free. What will he leave the world? What will they write about him? This is very important for him, that he leave to history the concept of the two 'destroyers,' and one 'gatherer.' This is a concept which he personifies—it's his legacy. He is working on his legacy."

How Putin will formulate that legacy depends, to a large extent, on his view of the world. Venediktov shook his head. "Internally, we see isolationism," he said, and it was coming directly from Putin himself.

"The people who surround him, they are people from the past, even from the nineteenth century. . . . We didn't believe in that before, or it didn't get expressed a lot. But Putin, like me, is part of a generation that is not very educated. We have a Soviet education in the humanities. And on top of our Soviet education there is now a layer of this imperial consciousness. So, a skilled manipulator exploits this."

In spite of his grand ideas, Putin was forced to deal with Russia's current reality. In just the first few years of his presidency, Vladimir Putin would be confronted with his own 9/11s. Terror struck Russia again, and again. And Putin would use that threat to solidify his power.

· 12 ·

Dubrovka

There were some days in Moscow when life felt normal. Not lighthearted but even-keeled, not constantly on edge, waiting for the next tragedy to unfold. But tragedy did come, on October 23, 2002, sixteen days after Putin's fiftieth birthday.

The second act of the musical *Nord-Ost* had just begun at Moscow's Dubrovka Theater, a story of love and heroism during World War II. Suddenly, in a moment captured on an in-house security video, an armed man in camouflage commandeered the stage and began kicking the actors off it. At first, the audience thought it was part of the show. A doctor sitting in one row said some people even applauded. "We couldn't imagine! We just couldn't imagine that's reality!" he later recalled.

Inside the darkened hall, more men rushed onstage brandishing guns. Armed women in long black garb stood along the walls, bombs strapped to their bodies. A few people in the audience managed to escape. One of them, a woman, told reporters "They yelled at us: 'Don't you understand what's happening?'"

Moscow's emergency numbers lit up as terrified hostages called from cell phones. One man, panicked, screamed "I'm calling from the theater! They want to kill us! Help!" A woman who worked in the theater whispered to police: "I can't talk long . . . there's a guard outside my door. It's not a Russian. It's probably a Chechen and he's wearing a mask. Help me! I'm so scared!"

Russian special forces surrounded the theater as desperate relatives of the hostages gathered outside in the freezing rain. "I have two children in there! How can this be happening?!" someone screamed.

More than nine hundred hostages were trapped. The orchestra pit soon was turned into a toilet. There was almost no food and little to drink.

211

The leader of the hostage-takers, Chechen fighter Movsar Barayev, allowed in a television crew from NTV to record a statement. "Our group is called the Suicide Squad of Islam," he announced. "Our aim—and we've said this many times before—is to stop the war and get Russian troops out."

The hostage-takers called for a journalist who had chronicled the Chechen wars to act as go-between with Russian authorities. That woman was Anna Politkovskaya. She bravely entered the theater and talked with the terrorists and their prisoners. "I've never heard or seen anything as horrifying," she said as she emerged from the theater. One of the hostages said 'We're ready to die. We're praying, but we know you've abandoned us.'"

In another call to emergency services a man told the operator: "They're really planning to blow everything up!" The terrorists demanded that relatives of the hostages, along with other Russians, quickly organize a large protest supporting the Chechens' demands and that the media broadcast it on all channels. Frantic relatives complied and, eventually, some children were freed, but others remained inside.

One desperate protester cried "Please! Peace! We want our kids to come home! Resolve your problems any way you want but just let the kids go!"

On the third day, there was the sound of explosions. Government security forces had filled the theater with a "knockout" gas. They refused to tell emergency rescue teams what the substance was; it later was revealed to be a fentanyl derivative. Security forces killed most of the terrorists, but there was chaos as rescuers rushed comatose hostages from the hall and carried them to buses. When it was over, the theater was littered with the bodies of terrorists and unexploded bombs.

After three days held at gunpoint, more than 700 hostages left the theater alive. Officially, 130 of them died, although independent journalists put that number at 174; 5 were shot by the terrorists, and the rest were victims of the gas used in the "rescue" operation.

I was in the United States when the crisis broke out. Valucha was ill and we needed to return home for a series of doctors' visits and testing. I flew back to Moscow in time to report on the aftermath of the hostage-taking, and on the plane, images of shocked, grieving families tormented me. Once again, Russian civilians paid the price for wars, and for their own government's incompetence.

President Putin tried to turn the *Nord-Ost* hostage siege into Russia's 9/11. In an address to the Russian people, he apologized for the deaths of the hostages: "We were unable to save everyone," he began. "Please forgive us." Then he thanked people around the world for their expressions of support against what he called a "common enemy." "This enemy is strong and dangerous, inhuman, and brutal. It is international terrorism. As long as it remains unbeaten, people cannot feel safe anywhere in the world. But it must and will be beaten.

"Russia will not . . . give in to any blackmail," he vowed. "International terrorism is becoming more impudent, acting more cruelly. Throughout the world terrorists voice threats to use means comparable to weapons of mass destruction. I declare, with full responsibility, that if anybody ever tries to use such means against this country, Russia will respond appropriately against all the places where the terrorists, the organizers of these crimes, and their ideological and financial supporters find themselves. I emphasize, wherever they may be."

President George W. Bush supported Putin's actions in resolving the crisis, despite the number of hostages who died. Bush blamed the terrorists for their deaths. Putin himself drew broad lessons from the attack: "We are paying a heavy price for the weakness of the state and inconsistency of actions," he said, ordering his general staff to develop a new doctrine to fight terrorism at home and abroad, mirroring Bush's war on terror.

The *Nord-Ost* hostage siege was a turning point for the Russian media. For the first time, Russian journalists were covering—live—a breaking news story that raised ethical and legal issues some of them had never considered: Do you put a hostage-taker on the air if you think it will save lives? Do you show the location of security forces surrounding the theater? Galvanized by media coverage of *Nord-Ost*, the Russian parliament, in record time, approved controversial amendments to Russia's law on the media.

One of the amendments prohibited the media from broadcasting information that could hamper an antiterrorist operation. Echo Moscow Radio's Alexey Venediktov told me they did broadcast an interview with a hostage-taker during the crisis. The press ministry threatened to shut down Echo's website. "This is a very dangerous amendment," Venediktov said, "because it allows any bureaucrat or court to interpret it so that if there's any attempt to explain why there is terrorism in Russia or why there's a war in Chechnya, they can immediately shut down any media outlet."

As Putin's presidency wore on, Alexey's words would only ring truer. Bush's war on terror transformed American society; Putin exploited the threat of terrorism to tighten his stranglehold on Russia.

OUR CHECHEN "TOUR"

A month later, in November 2002, the Kremlin announced a "journalist tour" to Chechnya. In our bureau we were trying to decide how to cover

Putin's Second Chechen War. The previous bureau chief, Eileen O'Connor, and her team had carried out the risky mission of covering Boris Yeltsin's First Chechen War, which lasted from 1994 to 1996. It was a vicious, brutal conflict in which thousands of civilians died in massive Russian artillery strikes and air attacks.

Even as the fighting diminished, the region was plagued with kidnappings for ransom and large-scale hostage-taking. The most notable incident occurred in 1995, when Shamil Basayev took more than 1,500 people hostage at a hospital in the town of Budyonnovsk. But Russian forces engaged in their own human rights abuses, including "enforced disappearances," in which they abducted civilians suspected of cooperating with the rebels, as well as their relatives. The person simply disappeared, to be tortured or executed in secret.

The Chechen rebels and terrorists soon responded in kind, kidnapping and, in some cases, killing foreigners as well as their fellow Chechens. The Russian government estimated that, in just three years, approximately 1,000 people were kidnapped by Chechens. In 1998 four British telecommunications workers were seized and later beheaded by kidnappers.

In this second war, which Putin started in 1999, the Kremlin made it difficult for foreign news crews to travel to Chechnya, warning that crews would be on their own if anything happened, which members of the press interpreted as a veiled threat to stay away. Explaining how the journalist tour would work, the Kremlin assured us that Russian forces now controlled the republic, but, "just in case," we would be accompanied every step of the way on this three-day trip, watched over and controlled by government "minders" and burly SWAT teams from the Russian Interior Ministry. We knew that this would limit our access to civilians, but we decided that at least we would be on the ground, able to observe some of the reality of the war.

In the decimated capital, Grozny, we experienced what "peace" looked like. As we drove through the city, we passed block after block of blackened, shattered buildings, electrical wires dangling from what once were windows, broken gas lines protruding from piles of concrete rubble. We spent the next two nights on the base of the 46th Brigade of Interior Ministry troops, and each night we heard gunfire and shelling. When daylight broke, sappers patrolled the streets, as they did every morning, clearing mines laid by rebel fighters the night before. But there was progress, our guides insisted: Previously, there were roughly thirty terrorist acts a day; now there were only one or two.

The smell of diesel fuel hung heavy in the air. Tanks and armored personnel carriers rumbled through the streets; trucks spewed a smoke screen to make it harder for rebels to shoot down Russian helicopters with heat-seeking missiles. On Minutka Square everyone we saw was dressed in camouflage and had a weapon: Defense Ministry troops, Interior Ministry troops, riot police, local police—just like the rebels, hiding in the mountains.

We stopped at a roadside stand to talk with the merchants, and it was clear they did not agree with our minders that "things were coming back to normal." A woman wearing a headscarf and mittens against the cold told me: "Right now, it's not dangerous. We know if we come to work here we'll get back okay, but in the center of the city, it's fifty-fifty. They're blowing up buses, putting bombs under cars; there are shootouts."

The city felt deserted; many residents had fled to refugee camps in neighboring republics, but those camps were being closed, and the Russian government was urging residents to come home, despite the destruction. We saw one apartment building that seemed to have signs of life and climbed up the rubble-strewn stairs to find a woman named Lilia who had come back after three years living in the camps. She still didn't have running water, but there was gas for cooking, which she shared with another family.

As she put a battered pot on the stove, she told me: "Yes, they're shooting, people go missing, they're taken off to places, people come in the middle of the night. Yes, that all happens, but somehow you just hope it will get better, and all of this will stop."

People going missing was a phrase I heard a lot on that brief trip. Chechen men were rounded up by federal forces during so-called "zachistki"—"cleansing operations"—to find suspected terrorists. Some were never seen again, human rights workers said.

We loaded up our bus and were moving on through the streets when, suddenly, our vehicle was halted, swarmed by women protesters holding up pictures of missing men and signs that said: "Give us back our Chechen sons!"

We wanted to talk with the women, but our government minders wouldn't let us off the bus—"Too dangerous," they told us. "They could have bombs under their skirts." What's more, they claimed, the women were being paid by rebels to protest.

We arrived at Grozny Hospital #4, the maternity ward. A young woman comforted her two-day-old daughter. Thanks to a gas stove, the room was warm, but the water pipes were frozen. Nurses carried buckets by hand; there was one toilet for forty-five women. The deputy director of the maternity ward told us the zachistki were shameful: "The men disappear without a trace, just disappear. I could understand if they were involved in something, but they aren't, they're innocent. And then the families have to buy back the bodies for a lot of money, so they can at least bury them."

Yet again, the people were paying the price for the brutal war. As Anna Politkovskaya said in her book, *Putin's Russia*, "We are ground to dust between the millstones of terror and anti-terror."

BESLAN

There are moments when journalistic objectivity and emotional detachment feel impossible, when the sheer horror of an event, and the unimaginable pain its victims feel, can't be shut out. Every part of you screams that this can't be happening—that it is too much to bear.

I've experienced such moments in several places from which I've reported. In Afghanistan, as crews using backhoes and shovels unearthed decomposing bodies from a mass grave, the stench of death permeating the cloth mask I wore. In Lithuania in 2023, as I walked through a former KGB prison, now a museum, where people resisting Soviet occupation were tortured unmercifully and executed. In conversations with elderly Jewish people who survived monstrous cruelty in Nazi death camps.

But "Beslan," just that one word two decades later, still fills me with horror. Officially, it's known as the 2004 Beslan School Siege, but it was not just a horrendous, monstrous terrorist attack on innocent children and their parents, mostly mothers. It was also a turning point in Russia, another moment when Russians, traumatized, lost faith in their government's ability to protect them, a panic that Vladimir Putin seized upon and exploited in order to convince Russians that only he could save them.

In late August 2004 I returned home to the States for another post-cancer medical checkup. As usual, I followed the news from Russia, checking in with the Moscow bureau daily, but I was feeling increasingly uneasy. Chechen militants were changing their tactics, using female suicide bombers, dubbed "Black Widows." On August 24, two Chechen female suicide bombers downed two airliners, killing everyone aboard. Another Black Widow killed ten people and wounded fifty outside a Moscow subway station.

And then, the unthinkable.

It was the first of September, traditionally in Russia the opening day of the school year. It's a happy day when children, dressed in their freshly ironed best, take hold of their parents' hands and set out for school, carrying flowers for their teachers. Many of them walked to School #1 in Beslan, a city of 40,000 in the autonomous republic in North Ossetia, part of the Caucasus region, not far from Chechnya. They stood in the school yard, hugging and greeting friends.

Suddenly, two vehicles drove up. Bearded men in camouflage and black shirts, brandishing machine guns, fired warning shots into the air and forced everyone inside. Some people escaped and alerted police. The terrorists, 32 Islamic militants from the region of Chechnya and Ingushetia—almost all men, but including 2 women—herded everyone into the gym. There, 1,128 parents, children, and teachers would endure three days of being held at gunpoint, in temperatures so hot they stripped down to their underwear, with nothing to eat or drink. Several male hostages were shot in cold blood. At one point, there was an explosion in a nearby room when one of the women terrorists' suicide vests detonated, killing her and the other female terrorist, a male terrorist, and several male hostages. I was later told by the parents that the terrorist leader, whom his band called "The Colonel," decided to kill the woman, who apparently was not told they were attacking a school and objected to the operation.

In consultation with senior CNN supervising editors, we dispatched two correspondents to Beslan. I watched their televised reports from the United States, feeling helpless. I left for Moscow as soon as I could.

The terrorists, meanwhile, had mined the school, installed tripwires, and hung explosives from basketball hoops in the gym. Hostages, especially the children, were fainting from the heat. Desperate, they began to drink their own urine. The government tried to conduct hostage negotiations, but they broke down.

On the third day, there was a series of explosions, ignited by Russian security forces. A group of hostages began to flee the building. The hostage-takers pursued them outside, opening fire on women and children. Russian security forces fired back, but many hostages were shot, and then were carried, bleeding, to ambulances and even private cars. Some terrorists, trading camouflage uniforms for civilian clothes, escaped. Russian forces set out in pursuit.

Many hostages were still trapped in the gymnasium. The roof of the gym, apparently ignited by incendiary devices launched by Russian forces, caught fire and collapsed, the fiery debris falling onto the people below. When the raging fire was extinguished, authorities found at least 100 bodies. More troops stormed the building, firing grenades, machine guns, and antitank rockets—all while women and children were desperately trying to escape—making their way from room to room, engaging in firefights with the terrorists.

When it was over, fifty hours later, more than 334 people were dead, 186 of them children, and 783 were wounded. All but one of the militants were killed.

By that time, I was back in Moscow, locked in an unending series of live shots, trying to make sense of the obviously chaotic operation by the Russian security forces. I prepared for a trip to Beslan but also tried to focus on Vladimir Putin's response. Had he learned from the debacle of his slow and unfeeling response to the sinking of the *Kursk* submarine four years before? This was a searing human tragedy and a threat to the Russian state. How would he handle it?

In the end, like the *Kursk*, it turned into a political and public relations disaster for the Kremlin, but for different reasons. In the *Kursk* tragedy, Putin responded slowly and, at the beginning, unfeelingly. The families of the victims were irate and blamed him personally. There was no "enemy" that Putin could blame; he himself had rejected help from other countries.

With Beslan, Putin began in somewhat the same fashion as *Kursk*, ignoring the attack on the first day, and then, after the deadly ending of the crisis, flying to Beslan to meet with the families. He began with brief words of solace: "All of Russia is now with North Ossetia at this time, grieving together with you, thanking you and praying for you."

He quickly pivoted to his "Vladimir Putin, Man in Charge" image.

"This is not a challenge to the president, parliament, or government," he said. "It is a challenge to all of Russia, to our entire people. Our country is under attack."

From the beginning, the Kremlin tried to control media coverage of the Beslan siege. CNN and BBC were broadcasting from the scene, but Russian authorities prevented Anna Politkovskaya and Russian war correspondent Andrei Babitsky from traveling to the region.

As I reported on air from Moscow, I kept recalling the first hours of 9/11 and the response of the American president, George W. Bush, to the attacks on America. The Russian president responded to Beslan in some of the same ways that Bush had responded to 9/11, but there were clear differences, from the beginning, in how each leader interpreted the attacks.

The evening of 9/11, George W. Bush urged Americans to unite, proudly summoning the national will. "A great people have been moved to defend a great nation," Bush said in an address to the nation that evening. "Terrorist attacks can shake the foundations of our biggest buildings, but they cannot touch the foundation of America. These acts shattered steel, but they cannot dent the steel of American resolve. America was targeted for attack because we're the brightest beacon for freedom and opportunity in the world. And no one will keep that light from shining."

President Putin, in an address to the nation on September 4, after the siege had ended, turned to the seminal theme of his presidency: the collapse of the Soviet Union. Beslan, he seemed to be saying, was yet another national humiliation.

"Russia has lived through many tragic events and terrible ordeals over the course of its history," he said. "Today, we live in a time that follows the collapse of a vast and great state, a state that, unfortunately, proved unable to survive in a rapidly changing world. . . . We all hoped for change, change for the better. But many of the changes that took place in our lives found us unprepared."

Presenting a litany of failures by post-Soviet Russia, he seemed to blame the entire country and its citizens:

> We stopped paying the required attention to defense and security issues and we allowed corruption to undermine our judicial and law enforcement system . . .
> We need to admit that we did not fully understand the complexity and the dangers of the processes at work in our own country, and in the world. In any case, we proved unable to react adequately. We showed ourselves to be weak. And the weak get beaten.

The weak get beaten. It became one of the most famous phrases ever uttered by Putin.

Both presidents vowed they would respond, Bush saying, "The search is under way for those who are behind these evil acts. I've directed the full resources of our intelligence and law enforcement communities to find those responsible and to bring them to justice. We will make no distinction between the terrorists who committed these acts and those who harbor them."

Putin, claiming that one of the terrorists' aims was to "foment interethnic hatred and send the North Caucasus into an explosion of violence," vowed: "We will consider anyone who gives in to this kind of provocation as an accomplice in this terrorist act and a supporter of the terrorists."

Bush, in those early hours, did not specify who had attacked the United States. Putin, in contrast, presented Beslan not only as an act by militants from the Caucasus region of Russia but also as directly linked to international terrorism. And he went even further: "Some would like to tear from us a 'juicy piece of pie,'" he declared. "Others help them. They help, reasoning that Russia remains one of the world's major nuclear powers, and as such still represents a threat to them. And so, they reason that this threat should be removed. Terrorism, of course, is just an instrument to achieve these aims."

There was little doubt what Putin meant. The West was using terrorism to eliminate what it saw as a nuclear threat from Russia. The idea seemed preposterous. Yes, the United States had granted asylum to Ilias Akhmadov, the "foreign minister" of the Chechen separatist movement, and, yes, US officials had met with Chechen separatist representatives. Russian and other intelligence agencies, including those of the United States, believed there was at least, in part, a connection between the Chechen rebel movement and an international web of terrorists.

But at least one Chechen leader condemned the Beslan attack, and early claims by Russian authorities that the terrorists at Beslan included citizens of foreign countries proved wrong.

A few days later, Putin was blaming US officials for undermining Russia's war on terrorism: He insisted that each time Russia complained to the Bush administration about meetings held between US officials and Chechen separatist representatives, the US response had been "We'll get back to you" or "We reserve the right to talk with anyone we want." Some US officials, he claimed, still had a "Cold War mentality."

The Beslan attackers were not "freedom fighters," he jeered. Taunting Western officials, he asked: "Would you talk with Osama bin Laden? . . . Why don't you meet with Osama bin Laden, invite him to Brussels or to the White House and engage in talks, ask him what he wants and give it to him so he leaves you in peace. . . . You find it possible to set some limits on your dealings with these bastards, so why should we talk with people who are child-killers?"

And yet, Western leaders, for the most part, supported Russia during the Beslan siege. In Moscow, the Russian chief of staff, Colonel-General Yuri Baluyevsky, stood side by side with his NATO counterpart, vowing that Russia would "take steps to liquidate terror bases, in any region."

In London, British foreign secretary Jack Straw called the Russian position "understandable," adding, "The United Nations' charter does give a right of self-defense, and the United Nations itself has accepted that an imminent threat or likely threat of terrorism certainly entitles any state to take appropriate action."

In November, R. Nicholas Burns, the US permanent representative to NATO, visited Moscow, pledging cooperation. "You . . . who watched the horrible and tragic events unfold at Beslan this past September, do not need me to remind you that North America, Europe, and Russia are engaged in a common struggle against terrorism. And it is only by working together that we can prevail."

But, in a step that echoed his rejection of Western aid during the *Kursk* tragedy, Putin focused on the West's criticism of his government's position on human rights and democratic reform. "We'll do this at our own pace," he declared. "In Russia, democracy is who shouts the loudest," he said. "In the U.S., it's who has the most money."

Grieving parents in Beslan, meanwhile, blamed the government for the deaths of their children and turned out in protest, one woman crying, "We want a government that can protect us! That thinks we're worth something!" But, just as with the botched operation to reach the submariners who died in the *Kursk* submarine in 2000, and the *Nord-Ost* theatergoers killed by security personnel using secret poison gas in 2002, the families of Beslan never got justice from their own government. The Putin administration convened a parliamentary commission to investigate but, two years later, it exonerated the authorities of any blame for the deaths that occurred during the school siege.

The residents of Beslan called it a whitewash and eventually filed two suits against the Russian government in the European Court of Human Rights. The families did get some vindication: The court awarded the victims $3.1 million in damages and excoriated the Russian government for using excessive force in employing military-style weapons. The Russian government appealed the ruling.

Putin modeled his response to Beslan on the Bush administration's response to 9/11, the Global War on Terrorism, which fundamentally transformed domestic US security laws and institutions.

Putin quickly instituted his own series of sweeping proposals. "Terrorists are trying to break apart the state, to destroy Russia," he declared. "I am convinced the unity of the country is the main prerequisite for victory over terror." But the purpose, it seemed, was to concentrate power in his own hands.

It took only three months after Beslan for parliament to pass, and for Putin to sign, a law eliminating direct gubernatorial elections across Russia, calling it a "counterterrorism" measure, and giving Putin the right to appoint those regional leaders. Russians would no longer vote for individual members of parliament; they would vote for political parties, instead. Russia's security services would be joined in a US-style Homeland Security agency. Liberal opposition political leaders decried the moves, but, by now, democratic forces were divided and weak. One liberal member of parliament, Vladimir Ryzhkov, maintained: "There is no more doubt that this is an authoritarian regime, and the harshness of this regime is intensifying."

Putin's actions sparked some indirect criticism from the former president, Boris Yeltsin, who urged that, in responding to the Beslan crisis, "We will not allow ourselves to abandon the letter—and more importantly—the spirit of the Constitution."

Russians were now grappling with the same tough questions Americans faced after 9/11: How does a country defend itself against terrorists—without destroying its citizens' political and civil rights? In the United States, the president, Congress, and civil society would debate and seek answers. In Russia, Vladimir Putin would decide.

In the ensuing years, after each crisis, Putin would seize the moment to constrict political opposition and strengthen his grasp on power, justifying it as vital to protecting national security. After the 2011–2012 "Bolotnaya" protests, the Kremlin introduced "foreign agent" legislation that ramped up the process of shutting down independent NGOs and opposition media. In March 2022, as his invasion of Ukraine rained down terror on civilians, Putin targeted Russians who criticized the war, reviving the Stalinist concept of a "Fifth Column."

"The West will try to rely on the so-called 'Fifth Column,' on national traitors, on those who earn money here, but live there," he warned, "and I mean 'live there,' not even in the geographical sense of the word, but according to their thoughts, their slavish consciousness."

But that was all in the future. Wrapping up my live shots in Moscow, we headed for our flight to Beslan.

We arrived late in the afternoon and drove to School #1. The sky was black and so was the building. It was hard to distinguish where the road was. But, as we came closer, we could hear what sounded like an animal—a dog? a wolf?—baying mournfully.

Then I saw it. The inside of the school was illuminated by a dim light and I could make out the silhouette of a man walking slowly past the shattered windows. The cry was coming from him. I had never heard a human being make a sound like that—a howl, a scream of complete despair and desolation. We stayed outside and took no pictures, leaving what I presumed was a father who had lost a child to his unimaginable grief.

At daylight, we set out again for the school. Local people, some of them holding the hands of their children, already were walking slowly through the charred remains of the building, leaving flowers and stuffed animals in classrooms they passed. The gymnasium was being cleared of smoldering rubble. It looked like a bombed-out church, and it felt like a sacred place, where so many souls had suffered, then perished. Families, loved ones, and neighbors of the victims were bringing bottles of water and plates of food, things the terrorists deprived their captives of in the last hours of their lives. On a shattered windowsill relatives had placed the victims' shoes, along with icons of saints.

"Someday," I wrote, "on this place, there will be a memorial to the men, women, and children who died here. But the wreckage of Beslan's Public School #1 already is a memorial to grief."

I met two twelve-year-old boys, friends who had survived the massacre. I was shocked to see them there, but they insisted on showing me everything, guiding me through the blackened halls of their school.

"We were trying to climb out when there was the first explosion," one boy said. "I fell backwards on the little kids, then we tried again and there was another explosion. We broke out this window and ran barefoot in that direction and they started shooting at us, at our backs." Awed by the miracle of their own escape, the boys returned to the school again and again, they told me, trying to help others learn the fate of their loved ones.

"Here, under the floorboards, that's where the terrorists hid guns," they said. "And this is where they shot people."

As we passed a door covered in dried blood, I thought of the parents now walking through with their children, explaining to them what had happened.

How can parents expose them to this horror? I asked myself. But then I saw what someone had written on a chalkboard: "This can never be forgotten, or forgiven."

There was one room I will never be able to forget. It was where the two female terrorists were killed when one of their suicide vests exploded. On the ceiling was a tangled mess of darkened skin, blood, and hair. The stench was unbearable.

The majority of Beslan's residents at the time were Muslims, and, following Muslim tradition, the dead had already been buried. We visited the cemetery, where groups of women stood, keeping watch over the mounds of dark earth, each one covered with flowers and stuffed toys, here and there an Orthodox Christian icon of a saint. In the distance we could see the snow-covered peaks of the Caucasus Mountains.

Grief mingled with anger. The men gathered in groups in courtyards between their apartment buildings, tending outdoor fires where the families cooked communal meals. We met a mother, Tamara, who invited us to her apartment. She told us she prayed that, someday, her little boy, seven-year-old Damir, would forget what had happened that September morning. He was in the next room, playing a video game, but she whispered to us that he was afraid of every noise, especially the sound of footsteps.

"It reminds him of the sound of the terrorists who were approaching the tiny room where we were hiding," she said. "We were silent, we didn't even breathe, hoping maybe they wouldn't notice us. Then we heard those scary steps of the fighter in his boots. He broke down the door, we saw him all dressed in black with a mask on his face and a huge gun in his hands." For some reason, she said, the fighter turned and left.

Tamara told me she had tried taking Damir back to school, but the noise of the children running in the hallway terrified him. "He was covering his ears," she said, "and begging me to take him home."

She told me she had asked a relative, a policeman, if the schools were now any safer.

"What are you talking about?" he said. "We haven't been paid in three months. Forty people have resigned. They have no weapons, no flak jackets. And if they have them, they're so bad they don't even wear them."

I went back to Beslan in January 2005, right after Russian Orthodox Christmas. I met three mothers visiting the graves of their children. It was the birthday of Alana, who would have been ten years old. Her grave was marked with a wood cross onto which was affixed a photograph of a young girl with light brown hair and bright eyes. Below that were carefully placed red, pink, and yellow roses, along with white carnations. "She used to play the piano," they told each other, "and she loved to dance."

The winter wind had blown over the Christmas tree they had brought for their children. One mother, Susanna, stood the tree back up and put the ornaments on once more, just as she used to do for her son, Daur, who was thirteen when he died.

"Is it any comfort," she asked, "that they are little angels in heaven?"

Two decades after the tragedy, the gymnasium at Beslan School #1 still stands as a horrifying reminder of the attack, its walls black with soot, messages of condolence scratched into that ghastly concrete canvas. On September 1, 2024, families gathered to remember the victims, holding photographs of those who had died. On the exterior of the building hung a sign, as if those dead were speaking to the living: "Remember us? Remember us! As long as you remember, we're alive."

· *13* ·

Ted Comes to Town

In the spring of 2000 I got news from Atlanta that Ted Turner, founder of CNN and then vice chairman of Time Warner, Inc., was coming to Moscow. He would arrive May 11. The highlight of his visit would be a private meeting with President Putin.

I was still back in Florida, finishing up months of treatment for cancer, but I got to work, making phone calls and helping with schedules. My final day of chemo was scheduled for 10 a.m. on May 5. The day began earlier than expected with a 2:30 a.m. call from the Kremlin—Putin's protocol chief, telling me the meeting we had requested was "almost scheduled." Good news! That evening, Valucha and I stood on our balcony and watched the SunFest fireworks over the Intracoastal Waterway between Palm Beach Island and West Palm Beach. It felt like a positive sign for Ted's trip, and we clinked glasses to celebrate that, plus the end of my chemo journey.

Although I still had several weeks of radiation ahead of me in June and July, I thought it was important to be in Moscow to troubleshoot Turner's visit and make sure everything went smoothly. Besides, I wanted to see Ted again. To me, he was a visionary who had revolutionized journalism, a peacemaker intent on solving conflicts around the world by giving viewers access to the unvarnished truth about what was happening.

I arrived just in time for the May 9 fireworks marking Russia's most important holiday, Victory Day, celebrating the Soviet Union's victory over Nazi Germany in 1945. The weather was glorious, thanks to Moscow mayor Yuri Luzhkov, who had "seeded" the clouds with chemicals to chase away any possibility of rain.

On Red Square, 5,000 elderly male veterans in their seventies and eighties, chests bursting with medals gleaming in the sun, marched in formation.

Putin stood at the podium on Lenin's tomb, Yeltsin seated behind him, and told the crowd that Russia's victories in World War II would help it survive challenges in peacetime.

Ted Turner had met Vladimir Putin back in 1994 when Putin was deputy mayor of St. Petersburg. The Carter administration had boycotted the Olympic Games to protest the Soviet Union's invasion of Afghanistan, but Turner organized the "Goodwill Games" as an alternative. It won Turner recognition and respect in Russia.

Putin had been inaugurated as Russian president just four days before, and Ted would be one of his first guests at the Kremlin. The day before he landed in Moscow, I went to the Kremlin to discuss final details of his meeting with Putin with Alexei Gromov, a Putin aide whom I knew relatively well from his time as head of the Yeltsin administration's press service. He was now Putin's press attaché and, twelve years later, would become Putin's deputy chief of staff.

Thin, slightly balding, with a buzz cut and a deep voice, smoking Dunhill cigarettes, he seemed to me more like a bodyguard than a press secretary, but for more than two decades he had been an influential figure behind the scenes in Russia's media universe, an éminence grise who was the co-founder of Russia's top international broadcaster, RT, originally known as Russia Today. I didn't hold that résumé against him, and I enjoyed our interactions.

When we arrived, I saw that he was working in the same office that Yeltsin's previous press secretary, Dmitry Yakushkin, had occupied. Even the furniture was the same. The only new touch, incongruously, was little clown statues on the desk and tables.

The plan, Gromov told me, was for Putin and Ted to meet one-on-one. Ted's staff seemed a bit worried about what he might say. He always said exactly what was on his mind, with no concern for diplomatic niceties.

During my conversation with Gromov, he turned the subject to the Internet, which was relatively new at the time; I'd gotten my first e-mail address only three years before, when I came to Moscow. "It's new," he said. "We don't know a lot about it." We need to study it, he told me, but there is a chance to start "s nulya" ("from zero") by creating new laws to deal with it.

"The Communists used to say: 'Give the people a little bit of leeway and you never know what they'll come up with,'" he continued, and although the Communists aren't in charge anymore, he said, it still was true. The Russian people, Gromov told me, aren't sufficiently developed for all this freedom and lack of control, as they have in the United States. "We need to control the Internet," he told me, "in the good sense of the word."

Ted's plane arrived the next day at the new business wing of Vnukovo International Airport. "His body language was so loose, he almost looked a bit unhinged, crazy, but friendly crazy," I wrote in my diary. We climbed into two black Mercedes and headed downtown. Ted would freshen up and we would drive to the Kremlin. At Borovitsky Gate I jumped out, and the cars entered the giant redbrick walls of the Kremlin.

Later, the interpreter filled me in on the meeting, which was one-on-one as planned. It turned out to be a fascinating discussion of nuclear weapons, a subject in which Ted Turner was deeply interested. In two weeks, Bill Clinton would arrive in Moscow for a summit with Vladimir Putin, and at the top of the agenda was arms control. As the interpreter gave me details of the conversation, it struck me that Putin might have been trying out some negotiating lines on Ted.

They began with START II (Strategic Arms Reduction Treaty II), the nuclear arms control agreement signed by President George H. W. Bush and President Boris Yeltsin in 1993, and agreed there was hope for a "START III" agreement. (Although START III was proposed, negotiations ran into difficulty and it was never signed.)

That led directly, the interpreter explained, to the subject of the ABM (Anti-Ballistic Missile) Treaty. The connection was important: The US Senate had ratified START II in 1996, and the Russian parliament had just done so in April, but it made ratification contingent on preserving the ABM Treaty, which limits anti-ballistic missile systems that could protect a country against nuclear attack. So, two years later, when the United States pulled out of the ABM Treaty, Moscow immediately withdrew from START II.

During this meeting with Ted Turner, the interpreter told me, Putin took a sheet of paper and drew a series of boxes in horizontal rows, representing several countries that the United States would term "rogue nations," including North Korea and Iran, which had nuclear weapons. This was a threat to the United States, Putin noted, and one option was to put a reconnaissance satellite in orbit over each nation. Another option would be a satellite system that would protect the entire country. Sounding quite reasonable, Putin, according to the interpreter, said Russia could accept that.

But then, in what I soon learned was classic Putin style, he destroyed his own argument. There is only one country capable of jeopardizing the security of the United States, he said, and that is Russia. A plan to protect the whole of the United States would break the strategic balance between our countries, something with which Putin said he could not agree. "My people in the military said you have to take adequate measures, and this means we would have to take out our old deactivated missiles and refurbish, rearm them."

At this point, the interpreter said, Ted Turner interjected: "Let's rid the world of nuclear weapons. Why keep them?"

Not surprisingly, in his discussion with Ted Turner, Putin raised the subject of Chechnya, the breakaway region the Russian leader was obsessed with at the time. Putin said that before he launched the Second Chechen War in 1999, Chechnya had de facto independence, but it had invaded another country—a comment replete with irony twenty-two years later, when Putin invaded Ukraine.

The interpreter described Putin as analytical and intelligent. In discussions, he said, he waits for the translation, which gives him time to think. Some people think Putin is cold, the interpreter said, but he didn't agree.

Ted finally emerged from the Kremlin, and we headed for the Moscow mayor's office, an imposing red building on Tverskaya Street, a thoroughfare that flows elegantly downhill toward the Kremlin. We entered through the formal hallway and walked up the staircase to the elaborate vestibule. The mayor greeted Ted and invited us into a large room. We sat down at an enormous white table.

Yuri Luzhkov was a politician in the mold of Chicago's Richard Daley: He never missed an opportunity to exploit any event covered by the media to get his message across, precisely the kind of scenario that gave Ted's aides heart palpitations. Cameras rolling, Luzhkov launched into a ten-minute diatribe about TV Center, his station, which was about to lose its license as the federal government invented challenges to its ownership. Those challenges had been ruled illegal, he said, but they had proceeded with plans to put the station up for sale.

When Luzhkov was finished fulminating, Ted said there are people in America who try to manipulate the media, but the most important thing is to protect the freedom of the press. "Rupert Murdoch tells lies about me," he said, "but I don't want to shut him down."

Luzhkov was on a roll, complaining about consumerism and even admitting (out of nowhere) that he didn't need as many suits as he owned. Ted finally got a word in about his main preoccupation: nuclear weapons. "Why do we need them if the Cold War is over?" he asked. "We should point them at the Germans," Ted said. "They're the ones who cause all the trouble!" I could feel the collective gulp from Ted's aides.

The cameras finally shut down and the two men proceeded to the large balcony that overlooked Tverskaya Street. Luzhkov told him that everyone, including Lenin and Yeltsin, had delivered speeches from that balcony. "Maybe I'll say something!" Ted announced theatrically. Everyone laughed.

There was one more stop for Mr. Turner: the Russian Defense Ministry. We arrived on time—a miracle in Moscow's traffic—but were informed that the minister had just been called to the Kremlin so we would have to wait. An officer led us into a room and stood by. Ted immediately began engaging him in conversation. I was helping out as interpreter.

Ted asked him whether anyone could buy a Russian nuclear missile. For a minute, I thought I didn't understand, but that was precisely what he was asking, so I dutifully translated. The officer looked confused. He asked me to repeat the question. When I did, he laughed, obviously thinking it was a joke. It wasn't.

So, the officer began explaining that you can't just buy a missile, there's a whole technical crew that maintains it and makes sure it is working properly. You'd have to buy the crew too, so it's not that easy, he explained. But I knew what Ted Turner was driving at: He wanted to rid the world of nuclear weapons, buy them up and destroy them, and he pursued that objective with passion. A year later, he co-founded the Nuclear Threat Initiative, a global security organization working to reduce threats from nuclear, biological, and chemical weapons, along with another proponent of arms control, Senator Sam Nunn.

Ted Turner and his team drove back to his hotel, and I headed for the CNN bureau. A story was breaking, and I had to report on it as quickly as possible. Russian tax police and other federal officers, wearing masks and toting submachine guns, had raided the offices of Media-MOST, the country's largest independent commercial media company. For several hours, employees were not allowed to leave. News cameras descended on the scene and NTV, owned by Media-MOST, reported the raid live, calling it an "attempt at political intimidation."

Media-MOST's vice chairman told reporters: "It's an attempt to punish NTV for its coverage of the Chechen war, for its coverage of corruption in the highest echelons of Russian power."

Russian officials immediately denied that, claiming the raid was part of a criminal investigation of Media-MOST, which prosecutors accused of "illegally receiving and disseminating evidence from commercial and bank secrets, invasion of privacy, illegally accessing secret memos . . . telephone conversations . . ."

Media-MOST, headed by the Russian media magnate Vladimir Gusinsky, was a television, press, and radio empire that had its own satellite system. Its run-ins with the Russian government had begun six years previously when its security force was disarmed by President Yeltsin's bodyguards. For the past few months, NTV's well-known anchor, Yevgeny Kiselyev, had been attacking Putin and his administration for alleged "dictatorial tendencies."

Ted Turner had a personal interest in the raid unfolding in Moscow. As part of Gusinsky's deal with his creditor, Gazprom, they were to look for an international investor to buy a stake in NTV. Turner was interested and, along with a team of investors, began negotiations. He struck a deal with Gusinsky to buy his shares but failed to complete the other half of the deal with Gazprom.

Now, the takeover of NTV and the dispersal of its journalists had all but killed Turner's interest. Putin's war on the Russian media was just beginning. The fate of NTV—and the fate of Russian journalism—became a central issue in my reporting from Moscow, as well as my post-CNN academic career.

SILENCING THE MEDIA

As the Soviet dictator Josef Stalin said, "Ideas are more dangerous than guns," and no one knows that better than Vladimir Putin. Undoubtedly, that is why the ex-KGB officer has tried to control ideas, and the freedom to express them.

I became a fan of the NTV television channel when I first came to Moscow as bureau chief in 1997, attracted by its factual and brave reporting, as well as its sense of humor. I became a regular fan of *Kukly* (the word in Russian means "dolls" or "puppets"), NTV's satirical show that first aired in 1994. Calling it a satirical show doesn't begin to explain the phenomenon that *Kukly* became. It starred life-size puppets, caricatures, whose faces and mannerisms bore an uncanny resemblance to well-known politicians and other personalities. They acted out exaggerated fables that took reality to its outer limits. It was hilarious, bawdy, at times obscene, and it was a sensation, the most popular show on Russian TV, as it relentlessly made fun of Boris Yeltsin and his entourage.

When Putin came on the scene in the late summer of 1999, the show's doll-makers crafted a latex version of the prime minister "born," in one episode, as a deformed man-child wailing in his cradle, being rocked by his "father," Boris Yeltsin. "Oh! He's so unattractive," Yeltsin bemoans, "and his origins—God forgive me!—are dark, and his eyes are blurry . . ."

Humor and satire were potent forces back in the Soviet Union, where people could not openly express opposition to the Communist government. Jokes, "anekdoti" (anecdotes), were the weapon of choice, indirect but bitingly true expressions of what Soviet citizens were really thinking.

One of my favorites: A man goes to a news kiosk and says, "Can I have a copy of *Pravda*?" (*Pravda* was the Communist newspaper, and the word "pravda," in Russian, means "truth.") The vendor says, "There is no *Pravda*." The man asks, "Well, then, can I have *Rossiya*?" (*Sovietskaya Rossiya*—"Soviet Russia"—was another publication.) "*Rossiya* is sold out," the vendor replies. "All that's left is *Trud*." (*Trud* was yet another Party-controlled newspaper. The word means "labor.")

Yeltsin, as president, complained about *Kukly's* sarcasm, but Putin, Kremlin insiders said, was infuriated by it. It wasn't just his *Kukly* double that Putin detested; it also was NTV's critical coverage of his war in Chechnya. In June 2000, a month after Putin was inaugurated, Vladimir Gusinsky, the owner of the holding company to which NTV and several other media outlets belonged, was arrested, accused of being part of a shady privatization deal that allegedly pilfered $10 million from the Russian government.

Putin professed to know nothing about the arrest. Gusinsky, imprisoned and under duress, sold Media-MOST to the partially government-owned Gazprom. He denounced the deal after he fled to his villa in Spain. The story behind the story, as always with Russian oligarchs, was complicated and murky, but the pattern was clear: Vladimir Putin was intent on controlling the media in Russia; independent outlets and individual journalists who dared to investigate or criticize the Putin government would not be allowed to exist.

By early spring of 2001, thousands of supporters of NTV were jamming Pushkin Square in downtown Moscow, a show of support for the embattled network, but also for freedom of expression in Russia. As we pushed through the crowd, I spoke with one protester who told me "NTV is the only channel that tells the truth! All the others are under government control." The network's general director, Yevgeny Kiselyov, put it more bluntly: "I don't believe a single word that comes out of the Kremlin these days. They are a bunch of liars. . . . Mr. Putin, he is in charge of the whole operation. I don't know what the code name for the operation is, but the ultimate goal is to take over NTV."

The government insisted the case had nothing to do with press freedom; Gusinsky was simply trying to defraud his creditors.

NTV pulled out all the stops in its public relations battle that day, broadcasting live from the rally and including its *Kukly* puppets, this time showing President Putin in a sailor suit saying, "Nothing threatens freedom of expression in Russia. It's guaranteed in the Constitution!"

NTV staff were now convinced the police would soon invade the network's offices and install new management. They manned the office round the clock for eleven days, and my crew and I stayed with them a couple of nights, discussing the situation with them and with others who converged on the office as a show of moral support. On April 15, at home in bed at 4 a.m., I was awakened by a call on my cell phone. The voice was high-pitched and frantic. I thought it was a kid prank-calling and hung up, but immediately there was another call. It was Masha Kiselyova, wife of Yevgeny: "We are being held at NTV by the Omon [riot police]. They got here at three a.m."

My cameraman Sergey and I raced to Ostankino TV tower where NTV had its offices. Armed security guards hired by the new director were at the door, brandishing Kalashnikovs. I could see why Masha thought they were riot police.

Journalists were everywhere, crowding the halls, a forest of cameras. Standing in a hallway at NTV, I called Robert Wussler, a former president of CBS television and Turner Broadcasting System. He was negotiating a possible deal for Turner to buy a stake in NTV in order to preserve its independence. One of the people he had been in discussions with was Dmitry Medvedev, Putin's deputy chief of staff and, as so often happens in Russia's incestuous political and business world, chairman of the board of Gazprom. (He would later go on to be Russian president.) When I described to Wussler the scene unfolding before my eyes, he told me NTV's owners had promised they would not use force. "They lied to us!" he yelled.

NTV journalists were pouring out of the building, refusing to sign loyalty oaths to the new Kremlin-friendly owners, and crossing the street to the studios of TNT, an entertainment cable channel owned by Gusinsky, where they set up a kind of NTV-in-exile operation. They even tried to broadcast a pirate version of a news bulletin on the airwaves of NTV, but engineers still loyal to NTV shut them off mid-sentence. NTV was the first TV network to be politically neutered, and there would be others.

A day later I flew to Sotogrande, Spain, to interview Vladimir Gusinsky, a jowly, energetic man wearing thick, oversize eyeglasses. Gusinsky was a true self-made man who created a media empire from scratch in the rip-roaring early days of post-Soviet Russia. His résumé included a stint as a theatrical director, a cab driver, and investment consultant. He started a newspaper, then branched out into magazines, radio, and TV. Sitting at his villa in the Spanish sun, he pointed the finger squarely at Putin for the takeover of NTV.

Putin, he told me, "pulled the plug" on the channel in order to silence its critical voice. "I am sure that every major decision, including the nighttime takeover of NTV, was sanctioned, unfortunately, by the president. I am sure Putin knows and is directing all the details of what is going on. This so-called 'Operation NTV' is really like a special operation of the KGB, which Putin represents.

"The government is in a dilemma," he went on. "They have to decide the problem of Chechnya. They have to decide the problem of heat, pensions, crime, and corruption. It's much easier to unplug NTV, and then there won't be any problems. It's obvious the Russian government will not rest on its 'successes.' The opponent must be destroyed."

As I had learned to do when dealing with Russian oligarchs, I took a double-track approach: I understood that what they said was usually motivated by their business interests or potential for political influence, but I still listened carefully, trying to be objective. Even oligarchs, I learned, can sometimes tell the truth. And Russia's maverick media were being eliminated, one by one. As Putin's "friendship" with the West cooled, the repression of journalists only intensified.

In July 2004 the American editor of *Forbes* magazine's Russian edition, Paul Klebnikov, was shot in cold blood. An unknown gunman opened fire from a passing car as he left his Moscow office. Two days later, I went to a local church where friends and colleagues had gathered for a private service in his memory. The Russian prosecutor said Paul did not lose consciousness after the attack and was able to talk for a little while. He said he saw the attacker and was able to describe him, but did not recognize him, and had no idea why he was shot.

The authorities were operating on the theory that Paul was killed because of his work. Four years previously he had written a book about Boris Berezovsky, titled *Godfather of the Kremlin*. Then, he published a list of Russia's billionaires, the oligarchs, many of whom had made their money in the country's murky privatization deals of the early 1990s. Some of them reportedly were furious. In another book he profiled a Chechen warlord-turned-businessman, calling him a "barbarian."

Klebnikov's friends and colleagues told me that day that, as a result, he had a lot of enemies. Russia, after all, could be a very dangerous place for a journalist who tells the truth about powerful people, and he was delving into the shady world of Russia's so-called "bandit capitalism."

His work was dangerous, but, his friends said, Paul loved Russia and was optimistic about its future. He joined a growing list of journalists killed in Russia whose murders were never solved. In 1994, the young investigative journalist Dmitry Kholodov was blown up at his office. Five months later, prominent TV host Vladislav Listyev was shot in cold blood on his doorstep. Four other journalists had died in 2004 while carrying out their professional duties.

The same day as the church service I went over to Echo Moscow Radio to see my friend and colleague Alexey Venediktov. I found him yelling, as he often did, at an editorial meeting with staff. Echo journalists also were looking for answers in Klebnikov's death, but so far, Venediktov said, the investigation seemed "wrapped in secrets and lies."

"There was preliminary information that Paul died in the ambulance," he explained. "Then came the version that he died in an elevator that got stuck, or in the operating room. Investigators have forbidden doctors to talk with the media. There are too many questions and too few answers!"

Standing outside his studio, Venediktov told me, "One of our journalists was on the air and got a call saying, 'We know where your son is playing right now . . . you should think about his health.' I saw her as she came out of the studio, completely pale. So, it's a very dangerous profession."

And it continued to be. In October 2017, Tatyana Felgenhauer, the station's deputy editor in chief and a colleague and friend, was stabbed in the neck by a man who forced his way into the Echo Moscow offices. Five years later, I saw her in Vilnius, Lithuania. The scar had healed but was still visible.

• _14_ •

Stalin's Definition of Writers

"Engineers of the Human Soul"

Vladimir Putin's concept of the media is a far cry from the First Amendment to the US Constitution. For him, it's a simple transactional equation: Whoever owns the media controls what it says. "There should be patriotically minded people at the head of state information resources," Putin told reporters in 2013 at his annual news conference, "people who uphold the interests of the Russian Federation. These are state resources. That is the way it is going to be."

As one Russian journalist explained it to me: "As Putin sees it, the media are not an institution of civil society, they're propaganda." All media outlets under control of the state, he said, are "instruments for reaching a goal inside the country, and abroad."

If, within Russia, Putin's Kremlin has waged a domestic war on independent media, outside of Russia he has been waging an information war, with state-controlled media his weapon of choice. Just as he depicts most conflicts, Vladimir Putin invariably claims the West started it. Moscow's mission, he claims, is to break the "Anglo-Saxon monopoly on global information streams."

I'm not sure who, exactly, invented the term "Anglo-Saxon media," but it's a phrase that, despite its antiquated imagery, has become an integral part of the Kremlin's strategic messaging. When I first heard it, images of Angles, Saxons, Huns, and Vandals swinging maces and pickaxes immediately came to mind, but Putin and his minions who employ it to this day are serious. A reporter once asked Putin why the world "doesn't see the truth"—meaning Russia's truth—about the war in Ukraine. Putin's answer: "The worldwide media monopoly of our opponents allows them to behave as they do."

Putin's press secretary, Dmitry Peskov, once told me that Russia was locked in "informational confrontation, ideological confrontation" with the

West. "Sometimes, information begins to dominate reality and change it like a broken mirror. . . . You have to have a very sophisticated and a very developed system of communication of your ideas and your point of view to an international community."

I heard the same thing from Margarita Simonyan, the head of RT, the Russian government's international broadcaster. "When was the last time you saw something non-critical about Russia anywhere in the mainstream media? Show me!" she complained. "I haven't seen anything, ever, in my life! Show me a single piece that is positive about Russia, a single piece about anything in the mainstream media. Can you remember any?" Like Peskov, Simonyan used the expression "mainstream media" (in English), adding a touch of Fox News to our conversation.

RT, originally named Russia Today, was founded in 2005. Simonyan was appointed to her position when she was only twenty-five. I knew her then, and we stayed in touch until the 2022 invasion of Ukraine. Sitting at her computer during a conversation in 2014, nine months after Russia illegally annexed Crimea and instigated fighting in the Donbas region, she told me that she had trouble sleeping, thinking about the carnage in Ukraine, and she blamed it all on the United States, a charge she leveled in excellent, American-accented English, thanks to a year she spent in 1995 as an exchange student living with an American family in Bristol, New Hampshire. "We feel like we're at war," she said angrily. "What are we supposed to think? That's exactly the opinion of many Russians—that the conflict in Ukraine is a result of American meddling."

But it didn't just start with Ukraine, she said; Russia had felt under threat for fifteen years, ever since NATO bombed Belgrade. "I mean, we were completely in love with the United States before that. Completely!" she sighed. "You had Russia wrapped around your little pinkie! Then, for some ugly reason, you bombed our little brother. We more or less hate you ever since, I mean, as a country."

Her anger was boiling. "Who gave you the right to do that? Was it under international law? Why do you think you are the wisest, the fairest, the most, the best? Whenever Obama says 'We are an exceptional nation,' seriously, people here in Russia want to take out a gun and shoot him! Because the last person we heard such words from was Hitler."

Simonyan, it seemed to me, harbored the same resentment that fueled Vladimir Putin's view of the West. Her complaints in 2014 were almost verbatim to Putin's in 2022: "If you talk with anyone in Russia," she told me, "all of them will tell you that America is out to get us, to expand NATO to all our borders, to get Ukraine into NATO, Georgia into NATO. To have their bases all over the place, to make us weak—basically, to destroy the nuclear parity."

Simonyan told me the Russia Today supervising editors quickly gave up on the idea of promoting Russia and its soft power. "What is going to make me watch a TV station? Not too many people out there are interested in Russia so much that they really want to watch things about Russia and only about Russia. How many people are there? Ten, twenty thousand? Fifty thousand across the world? That's not nearly enough that it's worth spending so much money." She conceded that RT is not trying to make the case that Russia is the main force for good in world—"No. Been there, done that! We're over with that. We don't think that works."

So Russia Today died, and was reborn—rebranded as RT, an innocuous name with almost no hint that it was a Russian broadcaster. That was on purpose. Russia, Simonyan told me, has a problem that goes to the core of its culture: It wasn't able to explain itself adequately to the world, and "sometimes it doesn't have the desire to explain itself."

"You know, we in Russia have this mentality: If I do something and start to explain myself, it looks bad. You know the Russian word 'opravdivatsya' [to justify oneself]; this is something that Russians hate to do, as you know, so they'd rather raise their chins and say 'Okay, if you don't understand me, I'm not going to explain it to you.' "

In America, Simonyan said, it was absolutely different: "I remember how surprised I was that a person thinks it's necessary to explain his or her image, especially if a lot of people think he or she did something wrong. Whereas in Russia you always hear: 'Don't explain.'"

It would be easy to brush off Simonyan's comments and counter them by pointing to Russia's notorious use of propaganda, but I think she was right. Russia does not engage in a debate over whether its actions are right or wrong. It does not admit to failure, or to moral failure. It creates, instead, an alternative universe, complete with its own set of rules, presenting Russia as the paragon of righteousness, and America as the source of evil in the world. Undermining American soft power was, and remains, the goal. RT's airwaves are filled with conspiracy theories, reports on Americans abandoned or exploited by their own government, and news designed to present US leaders as weak and corrupt.

SHOW ME!

At a December 2022 Kremlin ceremony, Vladimir Putin stood by and applauded as a deep-voiced announcer invited Margarita Simonyan forward to receive an award for her "major contribution to state informational policy, for the active preparation and conduct of societally significant activities, service in health care, education, and development of national culture and for her long, conscientious work."

Wearing a deep blue suit that matched the blue of the Russian flag, Simonyan strode forward, stood at the podium, and with an ironic smile, told the president: "I've been working under your direction for many years. I always wanted to tell you something and, it seems to me, this is the most appropriate moment to say what I always wanted: Thank you for 'rubbing out the cannibals.'" (Simonyan used the same crude Russian verb "mochit" that Putin used to promise he would "rub out" terrorists in the "outhouse" when he started the Second Chechen war.) "You promised us twenty-some years ago—remember that unforgettable phrase of yours—to 'rub them out.'"

She ended her emotional panegyric, turning to Putin and saying: "Thank you, yes, with pain, with blood, thank you for pulling our people out of the bloody mouths of those cannibals. And we are going to help in this, to 'rub out' the cannibals as much as you need us to. I serve Russia!"

In Putin's takeover of the Russian media, he often combined brute force and financial machinations. But I soon began to understand that he employed another, bloodless, modern technique: Apply pressure, and wait. Pass laws that constrict the space available for independent media. Set legal traps, citing antiterrorist legislation. Send the tax police to carry out endless inspections of a recalcitrant broadcaster or their business associates, denying that political views have anything to do with the investigation. Don't kill them, just maim them. Try to squeeze them into irrelevance. Now, after the 2022 full-scale invasion of Ukraine, I would add: Declare independent media "foreign agents" and hound them out of existence—or out of Russia.

That's what happened to TV Rain (TV Dozhd), once Russia's last remaining independent TV channel.

RAIN CLOUDS

The TV channel Dozhd—the word means "rain" in Russian—attracted viewers from the hip, young world of Moscow's successful middle class, the group that the Kremlin eventually gave up on attracting to its political ranks. Founded in 2010, the privately owned channel originally was broadcast on cable, private satellite, and on the Internet; its news included criticism of the government, and it gave airtime to well-known Putin critics like Alexei Navalny, reported on allegations of corruption and human rights abuses during preparations for the 2014 Olympic Games in Sochi, and provided extensive coverage of the

2013 Euromaidan uprising in Kyiv, also called the "Revolution of Dignity," against the pro-Russian Ukrainian president Viktor Yanukovych.

But in January 2014, Dozhd crossed Putin's red line. On the eve of the seventieth anniversary of the lifting of the Nazi Blockade of Leningrad, the channel conducted an online poll, asking its viewers: Should the Soviet government have surrendered Leningrad during the infamous World War II Nazi Blockade "in order to save hundreds of thousands of lives"?

The question, for many Russians whose families had lived—and died—in those nine hundred days of starvation, including Vladimir Putin, was a sacrilege. The political uproar was immediate. The government's media agency accused Dozhd of breaking the law, noting that Article 49 of the law on media requires journalists to "respect laws and the legal interests of citizens."

"Such questions and statements," the agency said, "could be interpreted as insulting to veterans of the Great War of the Fatherland and to residents of Leningrad during the Blockade, who exerted all their efforts to achieve victory in the battle with Nazi Germany."

Dozhd's editor in chief, Mikhail Zygar, publicly apologized, but cable and satellite operators quickly dropped Dozhd from their lineups, severing the channel, it said, from 90 percent of its outlets and 80 percent of its income. The general director and co-founder, Natalya Sindeyeva, a tough-as-nails media entrepreneur, announced that Dozhd had only enough money to survive another month. The staff resorted to Internet fundraisers to keep going.

In December 2015, the channel's landlord broke its office and studio lease. I was visiting Moscow that month, and one of Dozhd's anchors invited me to do a live interview on Ukraine. When I asked where the studio was located, he gave me an address that I knew, from nearly a decade living in the Russian capital, was in a residential area. "Yes, it's an apartment building," the staff told me. "Just come up to our floor."

With a light snow falling, I walked to the neighborhood, located the building, took the elevator up, and found myself in a tangle of bikes, baby strollers, and sneakers. Yes, it was a private flat, and yes, it was now also a studio. Inside, to the right, a young woman was seated at a computer. To the left, in the living room, separated by heavy black curtains, was the studio, complete with a camera, lights, and a TV news desk where an anchor and his guest were discussing the economy. I took some pictures, but the staff asked me not to reveal the location of the apartment.

They asked if I wanted makeup. "Down the hall in the bathroom," they told me. That's where I found a professional makeup artist, her powder and lipsticks arrayed near the sink. "My friends ask me where I work," she laughed, "and I tell them, 'In a bathroom!'"

The anchor, political journalist Mikhail "Misha" Fishman, took it all in stride. "Just like Soviet times," he quipped. Dozhd was broadcasting from a private apartment, he told me, because the Kremlin had made it clear that no one should rent space to the channel. It was the second time the staff had been forced to move. Fishman was convinced that Dozhd's travails were orchestrated by the Kremlin. "There were some reasons, formal reasons, having to do with economics," he said, "but no one has any doubts it was a decision issued from above."

"Does President Putin himself give the order?" I asked him.

"That could be," he said, "but I don't think that's really crucial. There is not a significant event in the media business that can happen without the direct sanction of President Vladimir Putin. So, in that sense, as an experienced journalist, I have no doubt that, before shutting Dozhd off from the cable system, [the authorities] got permission from Putin."

Putin sets the direction; his bureaucrats, eager to please him, relentlessly shut down what remains of free media, Fishman said. "In that sense, we are all in a position of threat. I think, in the next year or two, it will be very tough for journalists in Russia, very tough."

Misha Fishman had no idea of how tough it ultimately would become for TV Rain, and for any independent journalist in Russia. In 2015, however, the channel's founder, Natalya Sindeyeva, had a somewhat different take. I met her in New York in a coffee shop during a trip to the United States. She told me she was sure that, if the Kremlin really wanted to eliminate Dozhd, "they would have shut us down. We would have been one of the first it would happen to. There was no mission to shut us down, no," Sindeyeva told me. "But to make us, let's say, weak—yes, there was that task. They squeezed us."

No knock at the door by the police? No armed men?

"No, of course that's not the way it is," she explained. "At least not yet, and I hope it will never happen."

Like Fishman, Sindeyeva said Putin sets the course at the Kremlin but doesn't issue direct orders to stifle the press. "It's definitely not coming from the president," she said. "Let's say, he's not exactly a nice guy, but he doesn't know about all these details. It does come from the presidential administration, however. It's not his order, though. It's the general context."

Dozhd managed to survive in Russia until early March 2022, a week after Putin unleashed his full-scale war against Ukraine. On March 3, the channel shut itself down. It already was blocked by Russia's regulators, but until that point it had continued to broadcast on YouTube. The summer before, it was officially declared a "foreign agent" and was required to include an announcement in every broadcast or website report: "This report [material] is created and [or] distributed by a foreign mass media outlet, carrying out the functions of a foreign agent, and [or] a Russian legal entity carrying out the functions of a foreign agent." With characteristic brashness, the channel began selling T-shirts with the words "Foreign Agent."

But ten days after Russian tanks rolled over the border into Ukraine, I sat in the CNN Moscow office and watched online as Sindeyeva, seated at the news desk, announced that Dozhd was closing. She took a deep breath and said, "We need strength to exhale and understand how to work further. We very much hope to return to the air, and we will continue our work." The image on the screen cut to a gallery view of staff joining a Zoom call from different locations. In the studio, other staff crowded around the news desk behind Sindeyeva. One young man stepped forward. "We all feel such pain and we're afraid," he said. "We are crazy scared! And I know many of you are afraid right now, but a coward is a person who gives in to fear.

"We've lost this fight, but sometimes in a fight, you have to step back. And I think right now we've made the right decision to keep the most treasured thing we have. It's our life, it's our duty. They tried to call us the worst names ever, to blame us for some imaginary crimes, but why do we need to be afraid of the new law about 'fakes'? We tell the truth here on TV Rain."

TV Rain's final broadcast ended with Sindeyeva saying "no to war" as everyone walked off the set.

As they filed out of the studio, the channel began broadcasting black-and-white film of Tchaikovsky's ballet, *Swan Lake*, just as Soviet TV did during the 1991 coup against President Mikhail Gorbachev, after the death of Soviet premier Leonid Brezhnev, and at other destabilizing moments, playing the ballet over and over again, the Kremlin's version of "Nothing to see here!"

Most of TV Rain's staff fled Russia, to any place they could get a plane ticket: Tbilisi, Istanbul, and then to the Baltic region, and Riga, Latvia, where a wave of independent journalists set up their operations-in-exile. The station eventually found a home in the Netherlands, where, in December 2022, the Dutch media licensing authority granted it a five-year TV broadcasting license. Speaking with CNN in March 2024, on the eve of the Russian presidential election that would put Vladimir Putin back in office for six more years, Ekaterina Kotrikadze, TV Rain's media manager and on-air host, sounded more optimistic about TV Rain's future and its ability to continue reporting on the situation within Russia.

We are going to produce a big report tomorrow about remote regions of the Russian Federation where we interviewed people who live there, talking about what they think, what their problems are, and why they vote for or against Vladimir Putin. It is possible to work while you are abroad, and it's really important to see what's going on there. For example, [at] Alexei

Navalny's funeral, we saw tens of thousands of people lining the streets in Russia. I mean, it gives me hope and gives me strength, and I know there are millions of Russians who know that they're not alone, and this is the main mission that we have right now.

In December 2022 I talked with Katya on my podcast, *KennanX*, which I host for the Kennan Institute in Washington, DC. She was convinced that Putin's war against Ukraine would be a turning point for Russian journalism.

"We can see how people are getting to understand that they are fooled, and that reality is different. They are asking for answers, and they will get these answers eventually. Some of them are already watching TV Rain or reading Meduza or others. . . . The truth means a lot. The truth still matters."

EVERYONE LIES

The template for Putin's 2022 war against Ukraine—not just the kinetic, military aspect but the information war—was forged in the earliest days of the Putin presidency as he took over, shut down, or forced into exile the independent media of Russia. I could see his strategy clearly in 2014 as Russia annexed Crimea and a motley group of Russian-controlled "separatists," along with Russian "special operations" forces, began taking over Ukrainian government buildings in the Donbas region.

I had retired from CNN in 2014 and was granted a fellowship at Harvard Kennedy School's Shorenstein Center on Media, Politics and Public Policy. I started researching Russia's use of disinformation and, in August 2014, published the results in a paper called "Everyone Lies: The Ukraine Conflict and Russia's Media Transformation."

The 2014 conflict in Ukraine unleashed a massive and sophisticated propaganda war which, in its intensity, rivaled peak moments of the Cold War's battle for hearts and minds. Some of the methods employed were traditional, including disinformation, half-truths, and labeling, but the battle also was waged with a dizzying array of modern weapons, including digital communications, blogs, and social media. Dmitry Kiselev, Russian television anchorman and head of a new Russian government information agency, was clear about the Kremlin's strategy: "Previously, there was artillery preparation before an attack," he explained. "Now, it's informational preparation."

Most major countries employ some form of propaganda in conflicts and wars, but for Moscow the conflict in Ukraine accelerated profound changes already under way in the Russian media. The centralization and mobilization of information resources in the hands of the state provided the Kremlin—and

President Vladimir Putin—the means to eliminate any information sources that opposed his rule, as well as to galvanize public opinion domestically, in the "post-Soviet" region, and internationally.

In this information war, which continues today, Putin did not need a crushing victory, although he has succeeded in dominating the media landscape within his own country and parts of Ukraine. He was engaging in a series of tactical skirmishes that challenged the "rules of the game" established by the West. By questioning, demeaning, and attacking American and European moral "hypocrisy," he was positioning Russia as the "Un-West," a power that defined its own rules.

For Putin's new propaganda chief at the time, Dmitry Kiselev, one battle already was won: "We've switched roles," he says. "Russia is for freedom of expression and the West is not.

"Objectivity does not exist. There's not one publication in the world that's objective. Is CNN objective? No. Is the BBC objective? No. Objectivity is a myth, which they propose to us and impose on us."

THE STEALTH STRATEGY

In late February 2014 men in green camouflage military uniforms carrying weapons took up positions in the Crimean Peninsula, a region of Ukraine populated primarily by Russian speakers. It seemed obvious to me that the men were Russian security forces, but Vladimir Putin denied it, telling reporters at a March 4 news conference, "The post-Soviet space is full of such uniforms." You can buy them anywhere, he claimed.

Russian officials steadfastly insisted the men were not Russian troops, with Defense Minister Sergei Shoigu telling the media the reports were "complete nonsense."

In the blogosphere the sparring reached epic proportions. Western reporters tweeted photographs of Russian license plates. Pro-Ukrainian bloggers sarcastically referred to the uniformed forces as "little green men." Pro-Russian bloggers and journalists used the catchword "polite men" and released pictures of them in camouflage, cradling automatic weapons, chatting amiably with little children.

Russia's explanation for the "little green men" was a classic example of the Soviet technique of military deception called "maskirovka"—literally, "camouflage"—and during his annual call-in program in December 2015, Putin himself "unmasked" the operation, admitting that Russian troops were, in fact, on the ground in Crimea. "Of course, Russian servicemen backed the

Crimean self-defense forces," he explained, but insisted they were needed to protect the lives of Russian-speaking Crimeans.

That life-or-death scenario—rescuing Russians and Russian speakers from the depredations of "fascists"—became the driving narrative in the Kremlin's campaign to justify its incursion into Crimea, and it was broadcast relentlessly on all state-run media in Russia, especially television, which reaches more than 90 percent of the Russian population. Russian state television was filled with images of swastikas and bloodshed, fanning an atavistic panic that the bloody World War II battle against fascism was back again.

Propaganda or not, viewers in Russia who watched the broadcasts were primed to accept the government's narrative that Nazis had carried out the Revolution of Dignity in Kyiv. World War II—which Russians commonly refer to as the "Great War of the Fatherland"—elicits deep, patriotic emotions.

On March 16, 2014, voters in Crimea—at the barrel of a gun—passed a referendum to join Russia. Two days later, Vladimir Putin stood on a giant stage erected on Red Square, framed by a military chorus in crisp white uniforms, and looked out on a sea of joyous faces. "After a difficult, long and exhausting journey, Crimea and Sevastopol have returned to Russia," he proclaimed, "to their home harbor, their home shores, their home port!"

"Glory to Russia!" the crowd roared. The strains of the Russian national anthem—a stirring blend of Soviet-era melody and post-Soviet lyrics—filled the square. "From the southern seas to the polar regions, lie our forests and our fields. You are unique in the world, one of a kind—This native land protected by God!"

The TV cameras, broadcasting the celebration live on state-controlled networks, panned the audience, lingering on young, bright faces, then focused on the Russian presidential standard, the czarist double-headed eagle on a field of white, blue, and red, unfurling in the chill breeze. A heart was projected on a giant video monitor at the back of the stage and it glistened with the words: "Crimea is in my heart!"

As I watched the TV broadcast of the rally, I immediately was struck by its similarity to the production of Nazi film director and propagandist, Leni Riefenstahl, *Triumph of the Will*—the same kind of martial music, the heroic depiction of the leader, the adoring crowds mesmerized by their devotion to the cause.

The military incursion into Crimea and the illegal referendum to join Russia sent Vladimir Putin's ratings sky-high. In an April 2014 poll by Russia's Levada Center, reported by the *Moscow Times*, 82 percent of Russians surveyed approved of Putin's leadership, and 58 percent said their country was heading in the right direction, the highest number in more than two decades.

The 2014 war in Ukraine spawned a flurry of legislation restricting the media in Russia. One law allowed the government to block any website, without a court order, if it contained "extremist" information. "Extremism," however, was defined broadly.

The Kremlin's stranglehold on the media is based in Vladimir Putin's suspicious view of the Internet. In 2014 he told a media conference the Internet originally was a "special CIA project." Russia's "special services," he said, are responding by "introducing special security systems" of their own. Putin's pliant parliament immediately produced a law requiring social media websites to keep their servers in Russia and to save all information about their users for at least six months.

Crimea, and the war in Donbas, ignited during an equally fierce cultural war within Russia. Putin's Ministry of Culture began developing the principles of what is being called the "Foundations of State Cultural Politics," the basic concept of Putinism, which demanded Russia be considered a unique and distinct civilization, not reduced to "West" or "East." In a word, it decreed that "Russia is not Europe"; it is a moral center of gravity in its own right.

Multiculturalism and *tolerance*, two words that had entered the Russian language with often negative connotations, were now taboo. The government's task, the Ministry said, was to create a "single cultural policy" to be promulgated in all spheres of society: "education, youth policies, migration policies and, especially, the mass media."

For Vladimir Putin, Ukraine—and the culture war—was a turning point, the moment in which the true state of events had suddenly become crystal clear, at least as he understood it: Russia was surrounded by enemies. Yugoslavia in 1999, the Western bombing of Belgrade, the invasions of Iraq and Afghanistan, and especially the "color" revolutions in Ukraine and Georgia, which he claimed had their origins in the "chaos" of the Arab Spring; all of it, he said, was part of a "war to the finish" against Russia.

Putin was intent on striking back. He was using every weapon in his "hybrid" arsenal to do it: military, political, economic, psychological. Putin, the former KGB officer, was trained in methods of influencing people, and, as the old expression goes: "There is no such thing as a former KGB agent."

• 15 •

Another Home

In the CNN Moscow bureau there's a painting that I gave to the office staff as a gift. It's an oil painting of fruit, luscious and ripe, with intense colors, painted by my partner Valucha in Moscow, in a style she called "not-so-naive primitive."

Valucha had a long career as a singer and composer, and she turned to painting about a decade before we moved to Moscow. Although she initially rebelled at the idea of moving to Russia, after almost a decade she had fallen under its spell. Yes, she did think it was somewhat coarse compared to life in her native Rio de Janeiro, but she was deeply attracted to Russian culture. She managed to visit almost every major museum in Moscow. She quickly found out where she could buy good-quality art supplies, and which shop would do a good job of framing.

She bought what seemed like tons of art books, especially ones on her favorites: Wassily Kandinsky, Kazimir Malevich, and other members of the Russian Avant-Garde, a period of extraordinary creativity that transformed the world of art, just as the 1917 Russian Revolution overthrew the czar.

We painted our apartment in deep, vivid colors. The dining room was a saturated red. The painters told me they were convinced we were Communists.

We set up a painting studio for Valucha in one of the large rooms where she spent hours every day. Her not-so-naive primitive style began to change, incorporating some of the influences from Russian artists.

But the Russian winter was too much for a Brazilian and, after a year or so, we bought a small apartment in Florida. Like an international snowbird, she would gather her sketches and head for Miami where she would paint, study, and read about art. "Home," however, was still Moscow.

247

But in 2005, after more than nine years in the Russian capital, I got a call from my boss in Atlanta. "Have you ever thought of Asia?" he asked. I said no. My beat was Russia. I knew nothing about Asia. My boss assured me I would be fascinated by the region. He offered me the job of CNN's managing editor, Asia-Pacific, based in Hong Kong. I would be in charge of seven bureaus spread across the Asia-Pacific region, from India to Australia.

My heart said: "Stay in Moscow." I couldn't imagine being anywhere else. But this was a unique opportunity that might never open up again. I thought of my father's time in China. My head said: "Go east." It would be challenging, certainly. I knew none of the Asian languages, I knew little about the wide variety of cultures, and, although I had run the Moscow bureau, I had never supervised that many people. I would direct editorial coverage but I, myself, would rarely be reporting.

Valucha and I talked it over for several days. Once again, I was asking her to pull up stakes, move thousands of miles away to yet another country. Although Hong Kong was beautiful and intriguing, she had grown to actually love Moscow. She once told me that, and I broke out laughing. "But you said a Brazilian couldn't live in Russia!" I teased her. "Well, I changed my mind," she replied.

We had a whole Russian life to pack up. We had collected some furniture that we bought in antique stores, not valuable pieces, but handmade in traditional Russian styles. I had found a nineteenth-century "shkaf," a cupboard from the city of Vologda in Russia's northwest, constructed of thick, hand-sawn slabs of wood, hand-painted with colorful folk designs, including a "kindly lion" depicted on the side, believed to protect the home and keep it peaceful.

I had a small collection of little cabinets made by artisans who were part of the nineteenth-century Abramtsevo Colony, an artists' collective founded to revive traditional Russian national styles. It reminded me strongly of the Arts and Crafts style that flourished in many countries in the late nineteenth century, especially England and the United States. I fell in love with the cabinets, each one unique, with depictions of sleighs bounding through the snow, or a partridge perched on a grapevine.

Packing each one, I was struck by the exuberant colors and voluptuous designs. Russians are often described as drab and dowdy by Westerners, but I knew they were completely the opposite. Russian folk art, I was convinced, with its ancient, pagan roots, truly expressed the soul of Russian people. Memories flooded back of the villages I had traveled to over the years, photographing dachas with their intricately carved "nalichniki" (wood window frames). I never quite gave up on my dream to build my own dacha someday.

Valucha and I planned a farewell party for early June. We invited friends, colleagues, even Foreign Ministry and Kremlin officials with whom I had worked over the years. The afternoon it took place I was surprised to see Dmitry Peskov, Putin's press spokesman, arrive carrying a box and a letter from President Putin.

The box contained a porcelain tea set, with two cups, on which were depicted the famous bridges of St. Petersburg. "I studied in Leningrad!" I told Peskov. He laughed and said, "Jill, we know!" I realized how naive that sounded; he, the Kremlin staff, and the FSB undoubtedly knew a lot more about me than where I had studied.

The letter was printed on thick paper with the red presidential seal at the top and the title "President of the Russian Federation." It was addressed to me in a formal but friendly style.

> Respected Jill,
>
> I am expressing gratitude to you for your many years of fruitful work in Moscow, for your objective reporting on events taking place in our country.
>
> I am certain that the great professional and lived experience will allow you to successfully continue your activities in a new post. I hope that you will continue to preserve good feelings for Russia and her people.
>
> From my heart I wish you creative success and all the very best.

It was signed with Vladimir Putin's distinctive signature and a number on the back: IIII ★ 04289.

I had the letter professionally framed, with double matting and protective glass. It still hangs on the wall in my apartment. I walk past it frequently and, occasionally, I stop to read it again, to study Putin's signature, to think about what he said, how he said it, and especially when he said it.

Part of it is predictable polite verbiage. Part of it, no doubt, is flattery. Most of it would be utterly impossible for a Russian president to say to any American journalist today.

But then there's that phrase in the letter: "continue to preserve kind feelings for Russia and her people" (Надеюсь, что Вы и впредь сохраните добрые чувства к России и ее народу). That felt different; not like boilerplate, or flattery. I did have "kind feelings" toward the Russian people, and to the Soviet people before that. Even at the worst moments of Vladimir Putin's cruel war against the Ukrainian people. Even when Alexei Navalny died, possibly murdered, in prison. Even when the Kremlin used every devious "administrative measure" to engineer Putin's reelection to a fifth term.

I remembered my Russian friends, who refused to be intimidated by him or by those who carried out his orders or his whims. Friends who fled Russia, friends who stayed behind. Many of them had warned me over the years just what kind of a man Putin was. In my heart, I believed them; they had grown up in the Soviet Union. I hadn't, and I heard what I wanted to hear.

If I had changed my mind about Putin, it was not because of what I did. It was because of what Vladimir Vladimirovich Putin himself did.

HONG KONG

In 2005 we moved to Hong Kong, to an elite, forty-story apartment building right in the center of the city. It was chic, modern, beautiful. Valucha asked me where we could set up our dacha room, like the one we had in Moscow, a kind of retreat. With our modern Hong Kong decor, I saw little chance we could create the same ambience.

We visited the Tea Museum near our apartment building. It was interesting, but after a few visits, we had no desire to return.

"Where are the art museums?" she asked.

It became painfully obvious that Valucha was suffering from what I facetiously termed "Sino-Soviet" culture shock. And Russia had won.

I soon was traveling across Asia—to Japan, India, Indonesia—astounded by the variety in cultures, and by CNN's global reach. In each bureau we had staff, most of them citizens of the country in which they were working, who understood the issues and could provide crucial context when news broke.

One of the most intriguing countries I visited was South Korea. It was so technologically advanced that I felt I was catapulted into the future. Then, suddenly, there was a chance to visit North Korea. One of our senior staff, a South Korean, was set to go on the trip, but the North Koreans, at the last minute, rejected her visa application. I presumed it was because, since she spoke Korean, she would understand more than the North Koreans wanted to reveal. I immediately jumped at the opportunity.

The correspondent who would lead the trip was Mike Chinoy, a CNN foreign correspondent for twenty-four years, author of two books on North Korea. When I asked him to prepare me for the trip, he described it concisely: "Jill, it's a mind fuck."

North Korea was beyond anything I had experienced in the old Soviet Union. In the level of deception, it left the USSR in the dust. In Pyongyang we stayed in a hotel where we could sip a cappuccino while the North Korean people in the countryside starved. One evening, I decided to explore the city by myself. I was sure I was being followed, but the chance to see adults and children on the streets, to peer in store windows, to hear the sounds and sniff the air, was too tantalizing.

The first thing I noticed was the North Koreans were short and thin. Even the men seemed to be no taller than I was, at five-foot-four. I chalked that up to their limited diets. The store windows were worse than anything I had seen in the Soviet Union. Cans of tinned food were piled in little pyramids. A few carrots and potatoes were arranged in neat rows.

The people spoke Korean, of course, but it was a radically different version than the language of South Koreans, more high-pitched and emotional, especially when referring to the leader at the time, Kim Jong-il. Our minders took us to the Juche Tower, a massive 550 feet high, topped by a red glass torch symbolizing the Juche ideology, stressing self-reliance and independence. I was convinced the female guide was about to have a heart attack as she described, in rapidly escalating tone and volume, the spiritual union between the people and the man they referred to as their "Dear Leader."

We had two minders: one, a young man who appeared to be in his early twenties, with a stern expression and an oddly voluptuous swirl of black hair; the other, a man roughly my age, with a smoother manner. He had served abroad in the foreign service, including in Russia.

We drove two hours north to the mystical mountain of Myohyangsan to visit the International Friendship Exhibit, a gigantic museum complex built into the side of a mountain. Along the way, I asked our guides if we could stop and take some pictures of the countryside. It took a while to win the debate, but eventually we pulled over. I had noticed what appeared to be agricultural workers, all of them barefoot and very thin, toiling away, and we quickly took out our cameras to shoot it. But when our minders saw what we were up to, they quickly hustled us back into the car.

We were the only visitors at the museum. I felt like Dorothy in *The Wizard of Oz*, walking through massive doors, opening on cue, through gigantic, silent halls (we were not able to visit all two hundred of them) filled with more than 250,000 gifts presented from all over the world to "Dear Leader" and to his father, President Kim Il-sung ("Great Leader").

Throughout the visit, our guides harangued us on what they considered unfair video that CNN used whenever it referred to North Korea. "All you show are missiles, and men marching," they complained. "Why don't you show peaceful North Korean people?" I explained that they did not allow us to take video of the people, and it would be a good idea if they did. The older minder said there was a solution: That weekend there would be a celebration in the central park of Pyongyang, and we could shoot pictures there.

When we arrived at the park on the appointed day, our cameraman started shooting. I decided, just as I had decades previously in Russia, to walk as fast and as far as I could to see what I could see. I set out and, within fifteen minutes or so, I came upon a charming scene. Inside an open-air pavilion, elderly North Koreans, dressed in traditional clothing, were dancing, swaying to traditional music played by other elderly North Koreans. I hoped that Mike and our cameraman would get there to record it.

And they did. As the cameraman searched for better angles, I asked the older minder, "Is this for real?" I remembered the numerous times in Russia when what I thought was real had been arranged far in advance. He smiled at me and said, "You'll never know."

DANCING IN PYONGYANG

The highlight of my trip to North Korea was the Arirang Mass Games, a massive gymnastics show in an equally gigantic stadium, featuring 100,000 dancers and gymnasts. We were hoping to catch a glimpse, and take pictures, of Kim Jong-il. Rumor had it he was going to attend. There was an excited buzz in the air, but suddenly, the crowd fell silent. In the next section of seats, close enough to focus on him, Kim Jong-il entered. He was portly, but a bit thinner than usual, I noted, sporting a shock of dark hair standing straight up, and wearing glasses. As he took his seat, the people in front of us sprang to their feet and began to frantically applaud. There were audible sighs of excitement. Make that awe. It felt as if they were witnessing the second coming of Christ.

I returned to Hong Kong full of tales of North Korea, but it was hard to capture the out-of-body experience of it all. Living and studying in the Soviet Union had prepared me to a degree, but the Kim family took the art of despotism to new heights.

A SHOCKING DIAGNOSIS

Four times a year Valucha and I returned to the United States for a break. On one of those trips home, I had a medical checkup. Valucha had been feeling a bit off, too, so we made an appointment with her doctor in New York as well. We were not prepared to hear the word "cancer" yet again. But it was true. We were devastated to hear Valucha's diagnosis: She was terminally ill.

This time, just as she had cared for me during my bout with breast cancer, it was my turn to care for Valucha. We began what turned into a year of consultations with a series of doctors in Washington, Chicago, and New York. We researched every treatment we could find, but her case was advanced, and there was little time left.

CNN was extremely supportive and allowed me to work from wherever I was. Every day I had conference calls with Hong Kong. Soon, however, it was clear: We decided to return to Washington, to the same apartment building where we had lived before Moscow. But it was not a happy homecoming.

Valucha died February 12, 2006. She always insisted she be cremated and that I scatter her ashes in places that were dear to her. Along with her daughter Gigi, I flew to Rio de Janeiro. We decided to hire a boat and sail offshore from Copacabana beach where she had spent her childhood. We found a fisherman who promised to take us out, but a storm blew in overnight. When we arrived at the beach, the boat was there but the fisherman was not. We found him in a local bar.

"I am not sailing when there's a *resacca*," he told us firmly. The word in Portuguese means "a storm with waves and an undertow." It can also mean "hangover." Maybe the fisherman meant both. But the wind, indeed, was fierce and the rain pelted us as we ran back to our car. We would come back the next day. This time, we took the subway and promptly got lost. A man approached us and asked whether he could help. Gigi and I both spoke some Portuguese, and he asked where we were headed. For some reason, I trusted him. We explained that we intended to scatter Valucha's ashes in the waters off Copacabana beach.

"Then you should know what to say as you do that," he said. When we asked what he meant, he told us he was a sociologist, and an expert in Candomblé, the Afro-Brazilian religion that combines traditional African beliefs with Catholicism. He said that, according to the Afro-Brazilian culture, which was so strong in Brazil, even among many white Brazilians, we should pray to Iemanjá, the goddess of the water, as we sprinkled the ashes. He wrote out the Yoruba words on a small piece of paper.

We returned to Copacabana the next morning. A soft rain was falling, but the waters were a bit calmer than the day before. We climbed out on the rocks that jutted from the beach into the shallow waters. We repeated the words the man had taught us. I laughed as the wild wind danced with Valucha's ashes, then sank to the waves below. I turned to Gigi, held her close, and we wept.

A year later, on a trip to Moscow, I took a small box of her ashes with me. One summer's night I headed down the street to the small park near our apartment that Valucha, years before, had defended against the recalcitrant Mercedes driver. I stopped at the fountain, topped by a golden statue of a woman running, trailing a banner behind her. I took out the box, opened it, and gently poured the ashes into the water.

"Well, you're back," I whispered.

LEAVING CNN

I never returned to Hong Kong. CNN assigned me to the State Department, covering Hillary Clinton and, later, John Kerry as secretaries of state. After my six years reporting on presidents George H. W. Bush and Bill Clinton, my "Hillary trips," my near-decade in Moscow, and my time in Asia, I felt on top of my brief.

Mrs. Clinton embarked on nonstop travel, and my passport soon was bulging with visas: Egypt, Burma, Georgia, China, Brazil, Pakistan, Israel, Oman, Japan, India, Ukraine, Mexico, China, and more. I also volunteered to do temporary duty in Afghanistan and Iraq. Of all the countries I encountered for the first time, Afghanistan affected me most deeply. The people, with their astounding beauty; the dun-colored mountains; the sense of history and adventure—I felt drawn to it with a fierceness that surprised me.

And yet, amid the excitement—and exhaustion—another emotion was stirring within me. My body was in motion, but my mind was restless. I decided to go back to school to get that master's degree I had set aside back in my twenties. In 2010 I enrolled in a graduate liberal studies program at Georgetown University.

I wanted to open up my brain and think differently. Yes, my job as correspondent at the State Department entailed a lot of thinking, but it was always on deadline, with a specific purpose. School, I figured, would give me free rein to explore things in which I was interested, and Russia—still—was at the top of the list. But in one course the professor challenged us to write a paper in which we would have to decide whether it was right for the United States to bomb Hiroshima. In other courses I examined the influence of art in propaganda. I studied early Soviet films. And, because it was Georgetown, a Jesuit university, at the core of those issues was the moral dimension.

There were times during the four years it took me to complete the required courses that I almost gave up. I would return from a State Department trip, drop my bags, and head for my computer. I lugged textbooks with me as I followed Secretary Clinton to China. I wrote papers early in the morning. One of them, on political developments in Russia, I sent to Clinton, who, in turn, shared it with the Russia experts within the Department.

I was surprised to receive a detailed letter from Secretary Clinton in response:

> Russia is once again undergoing a period of change, and the ultimate outcome resides in the hands of the Russian people, particularly the generations born and educated since the fall of communism. You are right that this past spring's demonstrations show that Russians, especially the urban middle class, are not apathetic, they want to choose their leaders and to have a say in how they are governed. The protests showcased both the power of civic action and its limits as an instrument of political change.
>
> It is unfortunate that Russia's leadership took measures over the summer to counter what it wrongly perceives as foreign inspired and financed civic action. You may want to address reactions to the protests in your paper; our Russia experts also suggest that you consider the impact of the return to direct elections of Russia's governors, and the possibility that the impetus for political evolution could come from the regions where many remain dissatisfied with the delivery of public services and lack of decentralized decision making and accountability.

At the end of the letter, Secretary Clinton added: "I am delighted to know you are pursuing a master's degree, although I cannot imagine when you find the time!"

Yes, I was still hooked on Russia. And now, armed with a master's degree, I felt confident enough to follow my heart, end my thirty-year on-air career with CNN, and pursue academic research on Russia. In August 2013 I told my bureau chief I was leaving CNN. I was sure I was doing the right thing, even if I was unsure of what, precisely, that "right thing" was. Nonetheless, I knew I'd found exactly what I was hoping for: a different way to understand what Russia was all about.

From my journalistic career I knew information was key—a resource more important than oil and gas, more powerful than an army. It could change hearts and minds, ignite revolutions, incite genocide. Now, I could use academic tools to research how Russia was exploiting information, including disinformation and propaganda, for its domestic and foreign policy goals.

That fall I got the first sign I was on the right path: the fellowship at Harvard. I found a small apartment to rent in Cambridge, Massachusetts, and that February, sitting in the living room, watching Vladimir Putin on TV presiding over the opening of the 2014 Sochi Winter Olympics, I observed propaganda in action.

A news report from CBS said the Olympic Games might as well be called "The Putin Games," highlighting not only Putin's public image as a "man of action" but also, as Russia expert Stephen Sestanovich put it, "Russia's reemergence on the international scene." The Games also highlighted corruption in Russia; Moscow spent an eye-popping $50 billion. There were numerous questions about where all the money had gone.

There also was the issue of Russia's repression of the LGBTQ community. The country's "gay propaganda" law sparked international calls to boycott the Sochi Games. On February 7, opening day of the Olympics, Russian police arrested four gay rights activists in St. Petersburg.

Just a few weeks after the Games ended, Russia illegally annexed Crimea and invaded the Donbas region of Ukraine. Local militias, under the direction of Russian forces, declared the independence of two "people's republics." It was a watershed moment, not only for Ukraine but also for Russia.

"All sides are using propaganda: Ukraine, Russia, the United States, and other Western countries," I wrote in a research paper, "but, for Moscow, the conflict in Ukraine is accelerating profound changes already under way in the Russian media: the centralization and mobilization of information resources in the hands of the state, providing the Kremlin—and President Vladimir Putin—the means to galvanize public opinion domestically and in the region, as well as forcefully assert Russia's policies, views, and—increasingly—values internationally."

Back in Washington, I applied for the next step in my academic career: I was accepted as a public policy scholar at the Woodrow Wilson International Center for Scholars in Washington, DC. Its Kennan Institute was devoted specifically to the study of Russia and the region, and it became for several years my "home base," where I continued my research on Russian propaganda.

IS NARVA NEXT?

In 2015 I packed my bags for Tallinn, Estonia. I was given the chance to work with an Estonian think tank, funded by the foreign ministry, the International Centre for Defense and Security. I chose Estonia deliberately: In 2007 it was the target of what NATO called "the first major attack of cyber warfare in the world." The Distributed Denial of Service (DDoS) attacks lasted for three weeks and were blamed on Russia, which denied the claim, but there was evidence that it was carried out by Russia or by Russian-speaking hackers.

The project I proposed was to observe Russian speakers in Estonia and how they were influenced by Russian media and propaganda. Almost a quarter of Estonia's population is Russian-speaking, and many of them were watch Russian TV and following Russian websites.

My research partner was Riina Kaljurand, who later became Estonia's ambassador to the Republic of Georgia. Finally, I was on the ground, seeing the concrete results of information warfare. We called our report "Estonia's 'Virtual Russian World': The Influence of Russian Media on Estonia's Russian Speakers."

The country's Russian speakers are concentrated in several regions of Estonia, most notably in Narva, a town that sits directly on the border with Russia, just 100 miles from St. Petersburg. We drove two and a half hours across the green, flat expanse of land from Tallinn to Narva. It's the third-largest city in Estonia, but in that tiny country, population just 1.3 million, "large" is 53,000 inhabitants.

When we arrived, we headed to the east side of town to the medieval Hermann Castle that towers over the west bank of the Narva River. On the east bank, high on a hill, stands the fifteenth-century fortress of Ivangorod, Russia. I stared in amazement; it is the embodiment of the Cold War. A heavily fortified bridge with secure checkpoints, built in 1960, straddles the river between them. It is called the "Friendship Bridge," but it didn't feel very friendly. NATO calculated that if Russia ever were to invade Estonia, which is a member of the Alliance, this is where Russian tanks would come rolling through.

Riina and I had come to Narva searching for the answer to the subject of our paper: "Could the Ukraine scenario be repeated in Estonia?" Russia had just illegally annexed Crimea, employing new, innovative forms of warfare, and this raised troubling issues for Estonia. How vulnerable was Estonia to those kinds of unconventional attack? Would Russia try to manipulate Estonia's Russian-speaking minority, giving Moscow the incentive to create instability? Would Putin exploit his false justification to "defend" Russian speakers, no matter where they lived?

As we later described it in our paper, "A war narrative hangs in the air, creating suspicion and even panic among Estonians, whatever language they speak." The Russian speakers had less trust in the Estonian government and were more isolated from the general population. Importantly, Estonian and Russian speakers lived in different information spaces; Russian speakers watched Russian TV channels, and as a result, they were exposed to Moscow's skewed interpretation of events.

In our report, Riina and I explained that Russian TV often is described as "propaganda," but, in reality, it's a couch potato's dream: an attractive, even mesmerizing mix of high-decibel discussion shows, tearjerker serials, and singing contests, peppered with news bulletins and current events programs that toe the Kremlin line. In my apartment in Tallinn, I watched it with my morning coffee and found it entertaining, a Russian version of American TV's frothy morning shows.

On Saturdays, for example, there was a series called *I'm Losing Weight*. A woman checked her bathroom scales and happily discovered she'd lost two and a half kilos. But, sandwiched in during the commercial break, there was an advertisement for an upcoming news show, *Blockade of Crimea*. The voiceover asked menacingly why a country with "European values" (the implication that the country was Ukraine was clear) was blockading truck traffic to Crimea and causing such misery to its people.

Two months of research in Estonia opened my eyes to the complexity of "identity." I remembered vividly—from my early days as a student in the USSR, and from my later travel to various Soviet republics—the differences in language, dress, and culture. Estonia, even under Soviet repression, was thoroughly European. Georgia was proudly Caucasian. Uzbekistan looked, felt, even smelled exotically Central Asian.

But the Russian-speaking Estonians we were interviewing seemed to define their "Russian" identity culturally, not politically. After all, they were no longer living in the Soviet Union; they were living in independent Estonia. Yet some of them said they still felt like their country was part of Russia because their relatives lived there, or their ancestors were buried there.

In Kohtla-Järve, a mining town in northeast Estonia, we met seventeen-year-old Elizaveta Silina. "In spite of the fact that I was born in Estonia," she told us, "I consider myself Russian because all my relatives are in Russia, my native language is Russian, so I definitely consider myself Russian."

Other Russian speakers seemed to defy linguistic or ethnic categorization. Marina Jerjomina, who was born in Rostov-on-Don, Russia, moved with her husband to Estonia when she was twenty-three. She remained proud of her Russian origin and education, but said when she first saw the trees and natural beauty of Estonia and the "intrinsic culture" of its people, she fell "head over heels in love." Marina founded Studio Joy in the southern Estonian city of Valga, on the border with Latvia, and began teaching singing to the studio's members, regardless of ethnic background or language. "I never divide people into nationalities," she said. "I divide them into whether they are good or bad, and who I would like to have contact with and who not. I always say, there are no good nationalities or bad nationalities, there are good and bad people."

Marina said she had no concern that Russia would try to exploit ethnic tensions. "What I am more worried about is the future of our young people," she explained. "We have problems with drugs and alcohol. Kids are sitting at the computer for eight hours, playing computer games, and they don't want to do anything else. That's what's scary! I'm not worried about some external threat; I'm worried about internal threats that we have to solve."

Then there was the seventeen-year-old we interviewed in Narva. He spoke Estonian, Russian, and English. I asked him where he got his news and information. As soon as I asked the question, I realized it probably sounded strange to him. He, like most teenagers, was not searching for the latest article to explain Estonia's foreign policy; rather, he obtained information about what was happening in the world from social media, music videos, and viral posts. He said he followed English and Russian sources more than Estonian.

"Who do you believe?" I asked him.

"Oh, I don't believe anyone," he said, matter-of-factly. "They all lie."

THE HALL OF MISSILES

Leaving CNN gave me more time to devote to programs that tried to improve relations with Russia. That may seem like a benighted idea today, but, even under Vladimir Putin, before the 2022 invasion, there was some hope that if citizens of both countries could come together and share their experiences, their views, their hopes with each other, it might lead to something good for both countries.

I was invited to join the Dartmouth Conference. It was what diplomats call a "track 2" group whose members were civilians, many of them former Russian and American government officials. Their common purpose was to find ways of bridging differences, solving problems, and building mutual trust. The conference was started in 1960 by Norman Cousins, editor of the *Saturday Review of Literature*, who discussed the possibilities of person-to-person diplomacy, even in the depths of the Cold War, with President Dwight D. Eisenhower. The name of the organization came from the location of its first meeting on the campus of Dartmouth College.

Yes, both sides were grounded in the foreign policy of their respective governments, but in our off-the-record discussions there was room for genuine dialogue and even out-of-the-box ideas, not just on issues like arms control, but on matters like health care and even religious values. Sitting for several days around a table, listening, commenting, debating, eating meals together, taking tours of the Russian and American cities in which we met, we got to know and respect each other.

In December 2019 we met in Dayton, Ohio, where the Kettering Foundation, which sponsors the Dartmouth Conference, is based. After a day of meetings, we set out for the National Museum of the US Air Force at Wright-Patterson Air Force Base, the world's largest military aviation museum. It had a mind-bogglingly large collection of Cold War technology, ranging from the most important US photo reconnaissance systems (spy satellites) used from the 1960s to the 1980s to a US "Minuteman" intercontinental ballistic missile (ICBM), which became operational in 1962, a year before I began studying Russian in high school.

Our group, made up of Americans and Russians, was awestruck as we walked through the Missile Gallery, stopping to crane our necks and peer up into its 140-foot-high silo-like structure. Titan I and II and Jupiter missiles towered over us like silver fingers of giants. The Minuteman 1A—at almost 54 feet high, weighing 65,000 pounds, and able to travel at 15,000 miles an hour—was simultaneously terrifying and stunningly beautiful. It could be launched in less than a minute and hit Moscow in less than a half-hour. Moscow had its own missiles on hair-trigger alert, aimed at American cities.

It would have been easy to shrug it off with black humor, the consequences too horrible to imagine, but all of us stood there together, in our fragile humanity, realizing that our two nations, in order to defend ourselves, were ready to leave the other country—and the world—in ashes.

· *16* ·

Kids on the Streets

Russia really is a country of possibilities, and young people have a huge expanse in which they can realize their potential, and make their dreams come true.

—Vladimir Putin, November 21, 2023

Throughout my years in Moscow, I tried to follow what young people were up to. After all, I was twenty when I first went to Leningrad, and I knew how the Russian government, and the Soviets before that, were fixated on keeping young Russians in line.

In early December 2011 a series of small street protests broke out in Moscow. The organizers dubbed them "For Fair Elections." The people who took to the streets—soon, tens of thousands of them—were furious at what they charged was massive fraud in the State Duma elections. Others were still seething at what had happened that past September, when Dmitry Medvedev, who had been president for one term, announced he would not run again. He was, in effect, handing the presidency back to the man who had put him in office: Vladimir Putin.

It was a political trick that many chess-loving Russians dubbed the "castling maneuver." Putin had served his first two four-year terms, from 2000 to 2008, and, by law, he could not run for a third term. Medvedev became his placeholder from 2008 to 2012, creating a kind of legal fig leaf that allowed Putin to return to office. And not just for four years. The Kremlin has engineered an amendment to the Constitution that extended the presidential term to six years. So, Putin, if he were elected—and there was little doubt he would be—would have another six years in office, and he could run for another six-year term after that.

"Prime Minister Putin is definitely the most authoritative politician in our country and his rating is somewhat higher [than mine]," Medvedev explained, in a monumental understatement.

It was humiliating for Medvedev, who once had been viewed as a Western-oriented, reformist moderate. In June 2010 he visited Silicon Valley in hopes of learning how to modernize Russia's high-tech economy. A CNN crew and I were allowed close access to Medvedev's tour of America's tech capital. He met with Apple CEO Steve Jobs and Cisco Systems chief John Chambers. He even sent his very first tweet (in Russian): *Hello everybody, I'm now on Twitter and this is my first message.*

Medvedev became an avid tweeter. In June 2010, after a summit with Barack Obama, he posted a happy tweet: *Haven't had a burger in a while. Lunch with Obama at Ray's Hell Burger.*

But then, there was the not-so-happy tweet from December 7, 2011, that seemed to accuse opposition leader Alexei Navalny of bestiality: *It has become clear that if a person writes the expression "party of swindlers and thieves" in their blog then they are a stupid sheep getting fucked in the mouth.* The Kremlin called it an "improper retweet" and took the post down, blaming an unnamed official. "The guilty will be punished," it warned.

Twelve years later, as Vladimir Putin launched his military invasion of Ukraine, Medvedev was busy tweeting again, this time comparing Ukrainians to "cockroaches," making not-so-veiled threats to use nuclear weapons and bizarrely defining Russia's aim in the war as stopping "the supreme ruler of hell, whatever name he uses—Satan, Lucifer, or Iblis."

Medvedev's transformation over the years from educated and hip to unhinged and just plain weird was disappointing, even shocking. He became a laughingstock. His opponents chalked it up to alleged alcoholism; his supporters described it as political cosplay, a "good cop / bad cop" routine with Putin.

The 2011–2012 protests became known as the "Bolotnaya" protests because they took place at Bolotnaya Square, about a half-mile from the Kremlin. They were a turning point, spreading to almost 100 cities across Russia. In Moscow, as many as 60,000 people turned out on the streets. I was back in Washington as foreign affairs correspondent, covering the State Department, but I watched our CNN reports from Moscow carefully. The crowds included people of all ages, but I especially noticed the young ones. They had an air of self-confidence that seemed new and different. Alexei Navalny was leading the protests, and many in the crowd, referring to the Putin government–endorsed political party, United Russia, chanted Navalny's "party of crooks and thieves" epithet.

Putin, without naming the United States, tried to blame the protests on outside forces: "a developed scheme to destabilize society that did not rise up on its own." He claimed Hillary Clinton had given a "signal" for the protests to begin. Then he reverted to the crude, off-color humor he often employs.

As described in an earlier chapter, many of the protesters were wearing white ribbons on the front of their jackets and coats. "Frankly, when I saw on the screen that thing that some of them had on their chest," he said coyly, "Honestly, I'll tell you, it's indecent, but nevertheless: I thought it was propaganda in the fight against AIDS, that it was, pardon me, that they were these condoms." It didn't take long before the protesters were trolling Putin back, spreading memes of Putin with a condom on his chest.

The Bolotnaya protests ebbed and flowed for several months. In May, the opposition announced what they called the "March of Millions" to protest Putin's upcoming inauguration for a third term. This time, unlike the relatively peaceful December protests, the police cracked down violently, injuring dozens of people and arresting at least four hundred. But the protests did not stop.

In June 2017 Navalny urged his supporters to hit the streets again. CNN asked me to fly to Moscow to provide analysis on what was now a nationwide protest against corruption.

The day after I arrived, we headed for Navalny's campaign headquarters. We found ourselves in a large room bustling with young staff on a mission. It felt ad hoc, and yet professional, the closest thing I had seen in Russia to the political "war rooms" in US elections.

The woman who met us at the entrance wasted no time with small talk. I perched on a chair and waited for Navalny. As he walked over to us, I could sense it: Here was a real political animal. Tall, handsome, charismatic, with an engaging blend of humor and seriousness of purpose. A Russian friend of mine, who knew Navalny well, said he was eager to learn as much as he could about running a political campaign and had studied American TV shows like *The West Wing* for cues.

We parked our van near Tverskaya Street, a broad, elegant thoroughfare in downtown Moscow, and set out on foot. It was a national holiday, Russia Day, and the Moscow mayor's office had organized a daylong reenactment of historical events, complete with actors in costume, that stretched up and down Tverskaya. Alexei Navalny urged his protesters to "crash" the party.

As we passed through the police security checkpoints, I could see what I believed were protesters, one by one, or in small groups, doing the same thing. They gathered in the middle of the street. Some were carrying little yellow rubber ducks, a symbol created by Navalny to troll Dmitry Medvedev for allegedly building an elaborate, expensive duck house on one of his properties.

As more and more protesters arrived, they began to unfurl signs, along with tricolor Russian flags, and started chanting "Russia without Putin!" It was a bizarre scene: young protesters in jeans and T-shirts rubbing elbows with seventeenth-century soldiers in long red coats carrying lances, while a Peter the Great impersonator looked on. Bolshevik Revolution–era soldiers in sandbagged forts manning machine guns as World War II soldiers twirled their girlfriends around, dancing to 1940-era hits. Young women in modern dress out for a pleasant sunny day in downtown Moscow pushed baby carriages, as police in Ninja-style riot gear and black helmets waded into the crowd of protesters, grabbed them, and hauled them away to police vans.

When I asked one young man, who said he was seventeen, what he hoped to accomplish, he told me it wasn't to ensure Putin was removed from office so Navalny could become president; it was to have a chance to live the way he wanted to live, to have a good future, which he bitterly said was being stolen by Putin and Medvedev. His aims were simultaneously amorphous and heartfelt, and, to me, inspiring.

I recalled something Hillary Clinton had said about the young Arab Spring protesters who turned out by the thousands seven years earlier in Tunisia, Egypt, and other Middle Eastern countries. "What are you going to do when the protests are over?" she had asked them. "Go back to the streets!" they replied. Wrong, she said. The next step, Clinton told them, should be political organizing.

This was precisely what was lacking in Russia. The Kremlin suppressed opposition politicians, undermined any political parties that challenged Putin's rule, and worked assiduously to "infantilize" voters—pacify them, convince them that politics was a dirty business, a useless endeavor that should be avoided.

I talked with more of the young protesters, again, more teenagers. Although Navalny had called for the demonstration, most of the young people I spoke with admitted they did not necessarily support him, although Navalny did, they said, stand for ideas they shared. They were attracted by his modern, irreverent humor, as well as his very active social media presence: He had millions of followers on YouTube and other sites.

Our cameraman wanted to get a wider shot of the street, which now was teeming with protesters. Across from us I noticed some people standing on a third-floor balcony of one of the buildings that faced the street. I yelled up to them in Russian, asking whether we could join them. They gave us a thumbs-up. We pushed our way through the crowd to the entrance and climbed up a few flights. I was surprised to find a public workspace with comfortable chairs, desks, and a bustling coffee bar, much like you would find in any big city in the United States. Our cameraman headed for one of the windows for a better view, and I went to an adjoining room. It was quiet; I presumed whoever had been there was down on the street, taking part in the rally. I moved over to a large window and looked down on a sea of young people carrying signs and banners, shouting in unison "Russia without Putin!" Here and there I could see police in force, corralling young men, and occasionally a young woman, yanking them off to side streets.

A young fellow who looked like a teenager came into the room and moved toward the far side of the window, ignoring me, apparently transfixed by the scene below. Unexpectedly, the crowd started singing the Russian national anthem. It was the last thing I expected to hear, but the young man near me began singing along quietly with them. The protest was anti-Putin, anti-corruption, but not anti-Russia.

I was intrigued. This was a different kind of young Russian. Devoid of ideology or any "isms," including Putinism. Seemingly uninterested in politics, and yet apparently patriotic enough to sing along to the Russian national anthem. Not on the street shouting anti-Putin slogans, but seemingly one in spirit with the people who were. I wanted to learn more.

YOUNG PIONEERS

Among my Soviet memorabilia I have three little pins from the early 1970s depicting the three stages of life under Communism for a good Soviet child. Russians call the pins "znachki" ("badges" or "membership pins"). Every organization, factory, sporting event, Communist hero, or historical event had its own znachok, often red in color, with an illustration of the person or an inspiring slogan like "Hero of Socialist Labor" or "International Day of Workers' Solidarity."

The first of my three pins is a ruby-red five-pointed enamel star with a white circle in the center, atop of which is a raised depiction of a little boy with curly hair. That boy is Bolshevik leader Vladimir Lenin at a very young age. It's the symbol of the first stage for a loyal young Soviet child, the Little Octobrists (founded in 1924, and named in honor of the Great October Socialist Revolution in which the Bolsheviks took power). Little kids from ages seven through nine joined the Little Octobrists, and the pin reminded them that Lenin, too, was once a child, but with the proper socialist values, he grew up to be the leader of a great nation.

The next stage in a child's communist development was the Young Pioneers, founded in 1922. It was compulsory for middle school students ages eight to fifteen. The Pioneers' znachok is red, of course: a five-pointed star with a burst of flame coming from the top. In the middle is a white bust of Lenin, now a balding adult man. Across the bottom of the star is a sash with the slogan, in gold: "Always prepared!"

If you were a good little Pioneer, at age fourteen you could go on to the next level, the Komsomol (the All-Union Leninist Young Communist League, founded in 1918). If you weren't, you ended your Communist Party trajectory at age fifteen. Komsomol membership continued until age twenty-eight, and from that point on, you were on your way toward membership in the Party. The Komsomol pin has a profile of Lenin in gold, depicted on a large red flag, with the initials of the organization (VLKSM) in gold.

Komsomol members, like the Boy Scouts, were supposed to be clean in thought, word, and deed. There was to be no smoking, drinking, or "hooliganism." The Boy Scouts were banned in Russia after the Bolshevik Revolution and replaced by the "Young Pioneer" organization, effectively prohibiting any form of traditional scouting within the Soviet Union. At its peak, the Komsomol had 44 million members. By July 1991, as the USSR was crumbling, it had shrunk by half, to 21.3 million. After the failed hard-line coup against Soviet president Mikhail Gorbachev in August of that year, it was disbanded.

Vladimir Putin did not become a Young Pioneer. In the book *First Person*, he said, "I was a hooligan, not a Pioneer." The interviewer asked him, "Are you being coy?" Putin countered: "You insult me. I really was a bad boy."

As president of Russia, however, Putin has tried his darnedest to revive Soviet-style youth organizations. One of the first groups was called "Nashi," founded in April of 2005 by a circle of businessmen, a professor, and youth group leaders. Chief among them was Vasily Yakemenko, thirty-six at the time, an economist who once worked with Putin's presidential administration. The word "nashi," in Russian, means "ours." It has a chummy overtone of "our guys." Nashi members, however, were not particularly chummy.

I did a report on them in June 2007, as Nashi members turned out in force in front of the Estonian embassy in Moscow, throwing stones, using bullhorns to blare angry slogans, and holding Estonia's ambassador, Marina Kaljurand, prisoner in her own embassy. Back in Estonia's capital, Tallinn, the government had moved a bronze statue of a Red Army soldier, commemorating the Soviet Union's role in World War II, from downtown to another location. The Nashi protesters in Moscow threw stones at the embassy, broke windows, and chased cars carrying Estonian diplomats. We managed to get into the embassy to interview the ambassador. The Russian police outside seemed to be doing little to control the crowd, and the atmosphere was threatening. As we left the embassy, I could hear them yelling "Fascists!" When the ambassador held a news conference, the youth tried to shut it down. Guards had to repel them with tear gas.

We left the embassy and drove to Nashi headquarters, where I interviewed Vasily Yakemenko, who had created the first pro-Putin youth group,

"Walking Together" (Idushchiye vmeste) in May 2000, the month Putin was first inaugurated. He told me Nashi's core values were freedom and fairness. Nashi's critics had a different take: They compared Nashi to Nazi Germany's Hitler Youth, and called them "Nashists."

The headquarters had a military, masculine feeling to it, but we were introduced to seventeen-year-old Masha Drokova, one of Nashi's 5,000 commissars, or core activists, a true believer in its mission.

"I always had inside of me a spark of patriotism," she recalled. "I wanted to improve things. I had all this energy, but it was all just potential. When I joined the movement, came to meetings, and I heard the leaders, and I'm thinking, 'This is it. These are my thoughts exactly.'"

Masha was studying at the prestigious Moscow State University, but commissars also could study for free at Nashi's own university. And there were other perks, like internships at major Russian corporations, and summer camps. Masha told me she spent hours doing activist work, like gathering signatures for a petition or organizing a blood drive, and, as a reward, she was chosen to appear on TV during a Nashi-sponsored concert on Red Square. She was, I could see, a perfect member of the Putin Generation. "We are the generation that was born at the same time a new Russia was being created," she said, right on cue. "It's in our hands to make her great."

Making Russia Great Again was, indeed, the cause. Other members told me its goal was to make Russia a global leader of the twenty-first century. To do that, they had to sweep away the old generation of leaders, the "losers," as they call them, the ones who weakened Russia, and replace them with a new generation who would take Russia in the right direction.

With its unswerving devotion to country, its terminology, its red jackets, and its boost for a young person's career, Nashi invited comparison to the Komsomol, but Nashi's leader called the Communist period repulsive.

"Nashi is not part of the government establishment," Yakemenko insisted, "and it doesn't get government funding. Money comes from donors and large Russian corporations." But, he admitted, Putin met regularly with the group. "Any meeting we have is a signal both to the government structures and to the business community that the president and, to a certain extent, the government, considers this project a priority."

Estonian ambassador Marina Kaljurand was sure the organization functioned "if not with the permission, then at least with the silent consent of the Kremlin, because they are a pro-Kremlin youth organization and they have very direct and close ties with the high officials in the Kremlin."

As my camera crew and I prepared to leave, Yakemenko handed me a glossy Nashi brochure. On the cover there was a photograph of a soldier in night-vision goggles superimposed on Moscow's Red Square. But the soldier didn't have a Russian uniform; he was from NATO. When I asked Yakemenko what a NATO soldier was doing on Red Square, he explained: "If we are not strong enough, then the American soldier who is now in Iraq or in the Republic of Georgia will be in our country."

THE KREMLIN'S HARD/SOFT SELL

I kept my focus on the youth group movement, as more and more organizations came into existence, almost always held at arm's length legally from the Kremlin, for deniability's sake, but obviously tightly controlled.

The Kremlin tried both hard sell and soft sell. One group I visited in 2017 wasn't really an organization at all. It was a hangout place for young people, hip and modern, located in a renovated factory building in Moscow. The teenagers and people in their early twenties who frequented the place had the opportunity to learn computer programming, painting, and graphic arts, even costume design. There were earnest political discussions for those who wanted that. Posters were everywhere. One had a depiction of Russian cavalry officers during the Napoleonic War, alongside an image of a Red Army soldier in World War II. "The Russians have been impossible to defeat for hundreds of years," the inscription said—a quote ascribed to Otto von Bismarck. In another section of the club there were T-shirts for sale, with the face of Vladimir Putin, and another poster with a photo of Putin that boasted: "For the first time in thirty years someone has abolished one of the Anglo-Saxon rules."

Putin-era youth groups had their origin in the early days of political protests, known as "color revolutions," that swept countries of the former Soviet Union and the Middle East and North Africa: Georgia's 2003 Rose Revolution; Ukraine's 2004–2005 Orange Revolution; the 2011–2012 Arab Spring uprisings.

Vladimir Putin accused the West, specifically the United States, of fomenting those rebellions. In November 2014 he warned: "In the modern world extremism is being used as a geopolitical instrument and for remaking spheres of influence. We see what tragic consequences the wave of so-called color revolutions led to," he said. "For us this is a lesson and a warning. We should do everything necessary so that nothing similar ever happens in Russia."

Enrolling Russian young people in state-sponsored youth groups was a way not only to solidify support for Putin and his government but also to suppress any unofficial youth groups, rebellious youth, or budding revolutionaries.

By 2022, after Putin had ordered the invasion of Ukraine, the Kremlin had abandoned any pretense to "soft" indoctrination of young Russians. On June 14, 2022, five months after the invasion, and conveniently the 100th anniversary of the founding of the Soviet-era Young Pioneers, a new organization appeared: the "Movement of the First" (Dvizheniye Pervykh). "We consider ourselves PIONEERS of the Fatherland!" the group's website proudly announced. "We want to be the FIRST in knowledge and creativity, in defending the Motherland, in science and technology, in work and sports, in preserving nature, and wherever we want to fulfill our dreams!"

Notably, Movement of the First did not replace existing youth organizations like Yunarmiya but rather joined forces with them. Yunarmiya, the official name of which is the "All-Russia Young Army Military Patriotic Social Movement," was founded in 2016, under the direction of the Russian Defense Ministry. It is one of the best examples of Putin's drive to foster patriotism among Russia's young people with what it calls "military-patriotic upbringing," a Kremlin strategy that has become even more entrenched since Russia's full-scale invasion of Ukraine, which required mobilizing more young men to join the military.

The government is dedicating major resources to such youth organizations. Movement of the First, for example, reportedly was funded with the equivalent of almost $205 million. Part of that money was to be used to spread the movement throughout Russia, and by October 2023, it had councils not only in every region of Russia but also in occupied regions of Ukraine.

TEACHING "THE PUTIN GENERATION"

Reporting on these youth groups, talking with Russian teenagers and other young adults, I was intrigued and wanted to learn more about Russia's youth culture. I had just been hired as an adjunct professor at Georgetown University's Center for Eurasian, Russian, and East European Studies, and I had the germ of an idea, luckily supported by the Center's director, Angela Stent, to teach a course with the working title "The Putin Generation." In it, I would explore this young generation of Russians, roughly twenty years old, who had grown up knowing no leader other than Vladimir Putin.

I soon discovered that Russian sociologists had been examining the subject of the "Putin Generation" for about twenty-five years, trying to understand whether these young people were different from Russian citizens of other generations, and if so, how. After all, Putin was the only president they had ever had (with the brief interlude of Dmitry Medvedev). One of the top researchers was Elena Omelchenko of the Center for Youth Studies at the National Research University, Higher School of Economics, in St. Petersburg. Finally, I would be able to explore the subject based not only on my own impressions, observations, and interviews with young Russians but also on concrete sociological data.

The book Omelchenko edited, *Youth in Putin's Russia*, is the only one of its kind I have found in English, and I chose it as my textbook. Omelchenko and the other researchers in the book describe how young Russians identified themselves, who they hung out with, what "subculture" they belonged to, how they viewed their society and their government, how religious they were, and what their hopes and aspirations were for the future. These young people were the "Putin Generation," but Vladimir Putin, in his own youth, definitely had not been one of them.

Judging by photographs of a teenaged Putin from the 1960s, he was not a "stilyaga" (Soviet "fashionistas" from that period), nor was he a hippie or a punk in the 1970s mode (yes, the Soviet Union had hippies and punks), or, indeed, a rapper of the 1990s. He looked more like one of the average Russian kids I saw on the streets of Leningrad back in the early 1970s, wearing nondescript clothing, maybe a nylon track suit, walking the streets endlessly with friends, trying to get away from the cramped flats where they lived with their parents and grandparents. The teenaged Putin sported a bad haircut, proletarian attire, and a rather forlorn look. He was intent on becoming a KGB officer, not a revolutionary.

I now had a fair amount of material for my Georgetown course, and I began compiling a syllabus—a challenging and fascinating venture. Understanding young Russians was only part of it; seeing how my students—the very same age as the young Russians we were studying—understood the lives and aspirations of their counterparts in Russia gave me new ways of looking at members of this generation.

They had so much in common, regardless of political system or geography. At least, in 2019, when I began teaching the course, they did. Almost none of them watched TV (so young Russians ingested less state propaganda than their parents). They were on the Internet and on social media. A study by the Levada Center showed that in 2001, a year after Putin became president, only 2 percent of Russians were daily Internet users. By 2024, four out of five Russians, primarily young but including a growing number of older Russians, were using the Internet daily.

Not watching TV, however, did not mean they were exposed to less news and information; it was just coming at them from different sources, like music, art, popular culture, social media—which were not only sources of entertainment but also means of transmitting information about the world, and about values shared by youth around the globe. They dressed the way most Western young people dressed; they listened to some of the same music, like rap (in Russian). They shared posts on Instagram and TikTok.

I pored over academic studies from Russian and European think tanks that concluded this generation of young Russians, as a group, were more tolerant and open to differences, like being LGBTQ, than previous generations. Knowledge of foreign languages and the opportunity to travel broadened their outlook. They were more involved in civic life, volunteering in pet shelters or hospices, cleaning up their neighborhoods—a major difference from the forced "volunteerism" of Soviet days. They were concerned about war, about climate change, about pollution in their cities and towns. They had little trust in their government, but at the same time, support for Vladimir Putin remained comparatively high.

I found myself hoping that this young generation, born after the Soviet Union died, might ultimately change Russia in some profound way, and I had numerous discussions with my students about it. At the same time, I was worried about my innate optimism, the naiveté that had led me to believe Vladimir Putin's early promise as president to protect "freedom of speech, freedom of conscience, freedom of the mass media, ownership rights, these fundamental elements of a civilized society."

In her book, Elena Omelchenko added a note of caution: "Complete liberation from the birthmarks of Soviet sociality, despite generational change, has not occurred to this day." Young people still had some "Soviet" traits. Those traits would grow stronger as Putin tightened his control of Russian society.

A closer read of the studies and polls, like a 2020 report on Russian youth and civic engagement by the Center for European Policy Analysis, revealed deeper, more troubling signs. "While calling for cooperation with Europe and the United States, many young Russians who took part in focus group discussions argued that Russia should remain 'sovereign,' 'a separate territory,' and be independent of international structures. Such isolationist tendencies cannot be attributed simply to state propaganda. They are probably rooted in opinions popular among the Russian youth that 'no one is waiting for Russia' in the West and that 'they do not like us there.'"

I heard that expression, *They do not like us there,* in other post-Soviet countries. In Tbilisi, Georgia, for example, I talked with a government official who said the biggest challenge he encountered was trying to convince people that both they and the country could succeed, dissuading them from their feeling of rejection, their gut feeling that "the West doesn't want us." It was a powerful emotion, a chip-on-the-shoulder resentment that Vladimir Putin had been gnawing on for years. In February 2022 he used it to justify his invasion of Ukraine: "Where did this insolent manner of talking down from the height of their exceptionalism, infallibility and all-permissiveness come from? What is the explanation for this contemptuous and disdainful attitude to our interests and absolutely legitimate demands? . . . They just do not need a big and independent country like Russia around."

Vladimir Putin is not unique in feeling unwanted by the West. That question has haunted Russians since at least the time of Peter the Great. *Are we part of the West? Do we belong?* have been recurring questions for hundreds of years. Peter dragged his countrymen into Europe, ordering men to shave off their beards, directing state officials and boyars to throw away their medieval-style robes and dress in European styles. The Russian aristocracy spoke French, the servants spoke Russian, until Pushkin installed Russian as the country's literary language.

I witnessed a modern version of this in the early days after the fall of the Soviet Union, when increasingly rich "New Russians" flocked to European capitals and to the designer stores opening their doors in Moscow.

I even heard jokes about their ostentatious wealth: Two Russian men meet in Moscow, and one says to the other: "I like your tie; where did you get it?" The other man proudly replies: "Paris. I paid 200 euros for it." The first man scoffs: "Oh, that's nothing! I paid 300 euros for that same tie."

Yes, young Russians were traveling and studying abroad, watching Netflix, posting on TikTok. They were becoming, I thought, citizens of the world.

And then, Russian tanks plowed west, over the border, in a full-scale invasion of Ukraine.

· *17* ·

A Headless Body

During my years in the Moscow bureau, there was no subject, other than Russia, to which we paid as much attention as we did to Ukraine. It was the second most powerful republic in the USSR, its breadbasket, a scientific powerhouse. It was the center of a significant portion of the Soviet defense industry. When the Soviet Union collapsed, Ukraine had 1,700 nuclear weapons on its territory. When I began my job as bureau chief, six years after Ukraine had declared its independence, it already had become a political battleground, balancing between West and East, with parts of the country yearning for ties with Europe, other parts still clinging to Russia.

There were personal ties, too. It's only a slight exaggeration to say that almost every Russian I knew had a relative in Ukraine, and, for me personally, every trip we took to Ukraine brought back poignant memories of my previous experiences in the country: the month in 1972 that I spent in the city of Donetsk, in Ukraine's mining region, back when I was a guide on a US Information Agency exhibit; the freezing streets of Kyiv in the earliest days of post-Soviet independence; meeting a former ballet dancer selling her family's exquisite red-and-white woven towels in order to put bread on the table; a wonderful museum where I discovered a treasure trove of works by some of my favorite artists, like Alexandra Exter and Sonia Delaunay.

For years, I wore an embroidered shearling vest from the Carpathian Mountains that I bought from a man at a flea market in Kyiv. It was miles too big for me, but it was filled with mystery—the same feeling I had when I watched my first Ukrainian film, *Shadows of Forgotten Ancestors*, by the film-maker Sergei Parajanov.

Then there was Kyiv itself, with its chestnut trees and cafés, a lovely city just to stroll in, or take a morning run, as I always did, up the steep hills that

273

rose from the elegant main street, the Khreshchatyk, pausing on the paved terraces that provided an opportunity to admire the view.

There was a different atmosphere, one that I couldn't quite define. A gentleness among people I met, quite different from the hustle and bustle of Moscow. Yet all of this was tinged with a history of the horrors the Ukrainian people had endured, from Stalin's forced starvation, the Holodomor, that killed millions of Ukrainians in the 1930s, to Babyn Yar, where in 1941 Nazi soldiers shot to death nearly 34,000 Jews.

In the autumn of 2000, I saw reports of a murder, a particularly gruesome one, in Ukraine. Georgiy Gongadze, thirty-one years old, a prominent and controversial investigative journalist, had disappeared in mid-September. One month later a burned, headless body, with distinguishing marks linking it to Gongadze, was found buried in a shallow grave in the woods near Kyiv. His wife Myroslava was allowed to identify the corpse, and she said it appeared to be the body of her husband.

Gongadze was harshly critical of President Leonid Kuchma and several top businessmen from the president's entourage, and Gongadze's journalist colleagues immediately suspected he had been killed because of his reporting. Before he disappeared, he staged public protests, in one deliberately taping his mouth shut, holding a sign proclaiming "Freedom of Speech."

Then, a sensational development: The leader of the Socialist Party made public a tape recording which he said proved that President Kuchma, along with some key officials in his administration, had taken part in what turned out to be Gongadze's kidnapping. On the tape, Kuchma allegedly told two top aides to "do something" about Georgiy Gongadze. Kuchma called the cassette tape a "provocation," an attempt to blackmail him and plunge Ukraine into chaos.

My producer, Maxim Tkachenko, and I, along with our CNN cameraman, flew to Kyiv. We located Myroslava Gongadze, a journalist herself, with a degree in law, who was caring for their twin daughters. She seemed shattered by her husband's horrific fate, but firm in her belief of what should come next. "Who did it?" she said. "I want the truth. I don't care who gave the order." Eventually, four police officers were sentenced in the murder, but whoever ordered the killing was never apprehended. Myroslava and her children were granted political asylum in the United States in 2001.

When my crew and I returned to Kyiv in March 2001, signs demanding Leonid Kuchma's impeachment were hanging from balconies throughout the capital. The scandal over Gongadze's death had mushroomed into what was dubbed "Kuchmagate." A tent city sprang up along the Khreshchatyk (a form of protest that would be repeated over many years of political upheaval to come) and stayed there for two weeks, but the political opposition remained divided. Police moved in, tore down the tents, and arrested forty-four activists.

Kuchma's scandals were straining relations with the United States. Ukraine, at the time, was the third-largest recipient of US aid, but the Bush administration was treading carefully, trying to avoid pushing Ukraine back into the arms of Russia.

As I write this, it all seems so familiar—especially the balancing act performed by successive American administrations when it came to Ukraine. President George H. W. Bush, along with future presidents, hoped Ukraine could overcome its internal divisions and prosper as an example, even to Russia, of what was possible if democracy could take root. But to Russians, Ukraine was always more than another now-independent former Soviet republic. As Vladislav M. Zubok explains in his masterful history of the USSR, *Collapse: The Fall of the Soviet Union*, millions of Russians, and Ukrainians, "could not imagine Ukraine and the Russian Federation as separate entities. For the Russians, Ukraine was like Scotland to the English, only closer."

I had graphic proof of this in November 2004 when, as Ukraine's Orange Revolution began, I raced to the airport in Moscow with the CNN camera crew and our Russian producer for a flight to Kyiv. To speed things up at customs I collected everyone's passport—everyone except our producer, who was a Russian citizen. He had forgotten his international passport, he told me. Exasperated, I asked him how he could do such a thing. "I'm really sorry, but I still can't get used to the fact that Ukraine is another country" was his reply.

THE ORANGE REVOLUTION

Viktor Yushchenko was a made-for-TV presidential candidate: tall, handsome, and understatedly charismatic. But it wasn't just superficial; in the early days of post-Soviet independence, he was governor of Ukraine's central bank and, later, prime minister under President Leonid Kuchma. The country was on the verge of default, and Yushchenko introduced 100 days of major reform, including privatization of agricultural land and business deregulation. The economy began to grow, but in 2000, amid Ukraine's roiling political warfare over economic reform, Kuchma dismissed Yushchenko, who went on to become head of the opposition coalition, "Our Ukraine."

Ukraine sits on a fault line between Russia and the West, and Kuchma, during his two terms in office, was balancing both, maintaining friendly relations with Moscow while sending 1,600 Ukrainian troops to join the US-led coalition in Iraq.

Viktor Yushchenko wanted Ukraine to join the European Union, the World Trade Organization, and, eventually, NATO. On July 4, 2004, he announced he was running for president. His opponent was Kuchma's prime minister, Viktor Yanukovych, a Moscow-supported candidate who had had a hardscrabble childhood in the mining region of Donetsk, including two run-ins with the law as a teenager. Drawing support from the heavily industrialized Russian-speaking regions in eastern Ukraine, as well as from the country's tycoons and oligarchs, Yanukovych promoted the idea of dual citizenship with Moscow, as well as making Russian Ukraine's second official language. He even did some campaigning in Russia.

When the votes from the October 31 election were counted, neither candidate reached the required 50 percent or more, and a runoff was held in late November. Ukrainian voters were glued to their TVs as the two candidates squared off in a rare American-style debate.

Vladimir Putin played a role in the election, too. In a not-so-disguised attempt to bolster Yanukovych, Putin made two trips to Ukraine during the race. Yanukovych ran up huge vote totals in the regions that supported him and, once again, there were charges of fraud. He won, but Yushchenko's supporters were adamant that the vote was rigged, and most international observers, except for those from Russia, agreed. Anger was growing across the country, fueling what became the "Orange Revolution."

But it wasn't just the stolen election that galvanized the country. His supporters still were seething about the poisoning of Yushchenko, a shocking event, even in the rough and tumble of Ukrainian politics. In September, just as he was beginning his election campaign, Yushchenko fell ill. His face became swollen, pockmarked and yellowish-gray. His symptoms were so severe that he was transported to a hospital in Vienna, Austria. The international team of doctors treating him said there was no doubt he had been poisoned with the chemical dioxin. In samples they took from his body, they reported finding concentrations more than 1,000 times the norm. It had likely been administered orally, they concluded, in food or in a liquid, by a "third party."

Yushchenko maintained all along he was poisoned by political enemies who were trying to kill him. His supporters suspected it had happened at a dinner with the leadership of the Ukrainian security service, and claimed the plot might have been carried out with help from "outside" Ukraine, which meant, of course, Russia.

More and more people, unfazed by the cold, were turning out on the streets of Kyiv. The Kuchma government accused Yushchenko and the opposition of trying to foment an uprising like Georgia's "Rose Revolution," which had put a new, Western-leaning president in power in Tbilisi.

Reporting from the streets of Kyiv the evening of December 3, I explained that the most remarkable thing was that, even after the Central Election Commission ruling that Yushchenko had lost, his people were still calling him "president," and, if anything, there was a festive atmosphere downtown where they had been holding demonstrations for several days. But could it stay peaceful?

After that live shot, we drove down the cobblestone street leading to Independence Square, the "beachhead" of the Orange Revolution, as one opposition leader put it. Our van was quickly surrounded by a sea of protesters, young people mostly, muffled in parkas and heavy coats, sporting orange armbands, banners, and ribbons, the symbol of the opposition.

Rule number one for journalists covering a civil disturbance—however calm it looks—is to avoid getting into a situation like that. With the icy roads, however, there was no way to make a quick retreat. As I looked at the protesters' faces, I was reassured. They were laughing, cheering, blowing noisemakers—as triumphant as if Ukraine had won the World Cup. I suddenly remembered we had left a CNN sign in the back window of our van, and as we passed through the crowd, many of them cheered and gave us a thumbs-up. We eventually found a place to leave the van and, with camera and microphone, we moved slowly through the crowd on foot.

We found Tatyana, a computer programmer, huddled in a fur hat. Why was she here? "So my children won't have to leave for America and Canada and Germany to find jobs," she told me. "I want them to stay in Ukraine."

We spoke with Lucy, a university student. She said she would stay on the streets "as long as it takes" to make sure the candidate she voted for was declared the rightful president. I heard that over and over in the coming days.

We moved on to the tent city that was mushrooming on the Khreshchatyk. Thousands of people were setting up tents, bringing in sleeping bags, obviously preparing for a long stay. Everything was still peaceful, but the threat of violence or a police crackdown was constantly in the air. At times you could almost smell it.

Across Ukraine, there were hundreds of thousands of pro-Yushchenko demonstrators on the streets. On Kyiv's main square a giant stage was erected, and a nonstop rotation of politicians and musicians alternately rallied and entertained the crowds. From time to time, they sang along to the movement's rap song: "We are many, we're together, we are going to win!" I asked one of the organizers why they chose orange as the symbol of Yushchenko's campaign, which was now obviously a revolution. He gave me as good an explanation as any: that it was a "happy" color.

I took up a position right in front of the stage so I could see the faces of the people. The music was excruciatingly loud, but I will never forget looking deeply at those faces. There were old people who, I'm sure, had lived through World War II and Stalin's rule, but whose eyes were shining with hope. There were teenagers cheering and laughing, caught up in the excitement and power of the crowd. There were families with kids, the little ones dressed in snowsuits, scarves tied snugly around their necks, their parents looking expectantly toward the stage at the political leaders they hoped would bring more opportunity.

Suddenly, Yulia Tymoshenko, the impossibly elegant yet tough-as-nails economist and politician, co-leader of the Orange Revolution, took the stage, dressed in a blindingly white coat, with her thick blonde braids perfectly coiled around her head, like a snow maiden. Tymoshenko supported all of the policies Yushchenko endorsed—joining the EU and, eventually, NATO—but she was a more polarizing figure, inconsistent in her pro-Western position, a factor that would eventually destroy her relationship with Viktor Yushchenko and erode the opposition's fragile unity.

But the Orange Revolution was now, and Viktor Yushchenko walked out onstage to join her, looking out at a sea of yellow and blue Ukrainian flags, mixed with orange banners. He seemed strong but, from just below the front of the stage, with the blinding lights illuminating his face, I could see the pockmarks, the bags under his eyes, the disfigurement caused by the poison that would be with him forever. Later, we were able to interview him. The dioxin not only scarred his face but damaged him internally. He was very ill. As he spoke with us, I was struck by the savagery of poisoning a political opponent. Yushchenko was a casualty in Russia's titanic battle to keep Ukraine under its control.

On one level, the Orange Revolution was an unequaled television story: thousands in the streets, a charismatic opposition leader who almost died from poisoning, a firebrand female opposition leader urging protesters to blockade government buildings, row after row of riot police in black uniforms and black helmets. Snow, cold, and hot emotions swirling about us as history was being made.

The opposition was very media-savvy, and obtaining an interview with Viktor Yushchenko was relatively easy; getting one with the other Viktor was not. Viktor Yanukovych's staff finally promised us an interview, and we set off for his office in the government building, only to cool our heels for two hours and then be informed the interview was canceled.

For days, we looked for Yanukovych's supporters on the streets, but they were nowhere to be found. Finally, one night, we found a group of miners from Donetsk who had come to the capital by train and were huddled around a campfire outside the parliament building. I struck up a conversation with Yura, a man in his mid-forties who looked quite a bit older. He told me why he supported the prime minister: Under this government, he said, they were finally getting paid on time. Before, Yura said, his family couldn't even afford to buy enough bread. "I feel like crying when I talk about it," he told me.

What did he think about the protesters across the street?

"We were marching along, expecting the worst," he said, "all sorts of provocations, but we just waved at each other," he said. "They have their opinions, we have ours. In the end, we drank some beer together and had a great time."

Yura had no anger that I could see. Like so many people in the young countries that once were part of the Soviet Union, all he wanted was a better life. He, and millions of others, had been cheated of that. But there was no doubt he loved Ukraine.

Later that night, I watched the crowds gathering outside the parliament building, waving flags. Both sides of the political divide flew the blue and yellow flag of Ukraine. We arrived in Kyiv carrying our flak jackets and helmets, prepared for the worst. We never had to use them. For all of President Leonid Kuchma's massive corruption and alleged masterminding of Georgiy Gongadze's murder, he did not call out the military to subdue the Orange Revolution. It was a peaceful transfer of power.

This time, there was a happy ending for millions of Ukrainians who wanted their country to become part of Europe. Based on the vote fraud by Prime Minister Yanukovych, Ukraine's Supreme Court annulled the November runoff and ordered a repeat runoff for December 26. Viktor Yushchenko won, with 52 percent of the vote, pledging to overcome corruption and join Europe. He was inaugurated as Ukraine's third post-1991 president.

Ukraine seemed on its way toward membership in the European Union and, perhaps, NATO.

STUNNING REVERSAL

It was not to be. Viktor Yushchenko was unable to carry out reforms and restore Ukraine's economy. In fact, during his five years in office, the economy deteriorated. By 2005, fueled by that crisis, Yanukovych's Party of Regions was back again, stronger than ever. In the 2006 parliamentary elections, Yushchenko's reform party finished third. In a sign of ignominious defeat, the Europe-oriented president had to approve the nomination of his archrival, Viktor Yanukovych, for the post of prime minister. By 2010, amazingly, Yanukovych, once again, was running for president.

The rough-around-the-edges, Russian-speaking, Soviet-style politician in a bad suit, Yanukovych was given a makeover by the American political consultant Paul Manafort, paid for by an oligarch friend of Yanukovych's. (In 2016, Donald Trump hired Manafort as campaign manager for his run for the US presidency. In 2018 Manafort was convicted of bank and tax fraud and sentenced to prison, but he was pardoned by Trump shortly before Trump left office.)

This time, Yanukovych won, and immediately set out to undo Yushchenko's efforts to tie Ukraine to the West and lash it ever more tightly to Moscow.

REVOLUTION OF DIGNITY

The next revolution was not peaceful. Once again, thousands of Ukrainians were marching in the streets of Kyiv. This time, however, President Viktor Yanukovych ordered riot police to subdue protesters. Deadly clashes broke out in which more than 100 protesters were killed and 13 police officers died. Many more were wounded when special Berkut police opened fire.

The popular uprising, which began in late November 2013 and ended in late February 2014, was called the "Revolution of Dignity," or the Maidan Revolution, "Maidan" referring to Kyiv's Independence Square (in Ukrainian, "Maidan Nezalezhnosti"). As in the Orange Revolution, Ukrainians were fed up with corruption, abuse of power, and violations of human rights, and having their chance to join Europe snatched, yet again, from their hands.

So much of it seemed so achingly familiar as I arrived in Kyiv, but this time I flew in the evening of March 3, 2014, from Washington, not Moscow. Just two months before, I had "retired" from CNN, although the word seemed, at that point, ridiculous, since CNN continued to send me to Moscow and other places in the region when news broke. Breaking news is rarely happy news.

The CNN driver took me immediately from the airport to Maidan Square. I was shocked by what I saw. I walked downhill, pushing my way through crowds of people, past piles of still-smoldering wood, twisted metal, and other debris, mountains of tires piled high as barricades, alongside mounds of flowers placed near where the hundred shooting victims, already called the "Heavenly Hundred," had died. Makeshift memorials that looked like altars were covered with red carnations, Ukrainian flags, European Union flags, votive candles, pictures of saints, and photographs of the men who had died, draped with rosary beads. One handwritten note said: "Heroes never die." Another, in Russian: "Believe us, we wanted to live, to create, to love, to raise children, but we offered our lives in sacrifice to save Ukraine from the bastards."

Below, on the square, I could see the tall, elegant Independence Monument, its white marble gleaming, the figure of a woman representing Ukraine atop a gold Corinthian capital. She held aloft a gilded guelder rose branch, seemingly untouched by the fighting below. But around the square stood buildings scorched by fire. Smoke curled from windows.

All the joyful excitement that I had witnessed during the Orange Revolution nine years before was gone. Men in fatigues hurried about. One of them used a chain saw to cut wood for a makeshift stove. Women stirred large vats of soup and ladled out coffee. Kyiv now looked like a city after a war.

Eight years later, attacked by Russia in a full-scale invasion, it would be, in fact, a city at war.

The next day I visited the tents that had been set up near the Independence Monument. I spoke with two women psychologists who were offering counseling to people who had experienced sniper attacks by police. One enterprising person had even set up a souvenir stand with mugs depicting Kyiv's mayor, the former boxer-turned-politician Vitali Klitschko, along with tiny boxing gloves in the colors of the Ukrainian flag.

The protesters, once again, had won the revolution. After the shooting was over, European diplomats convinced Yanukovych to sign an agreement with the opposition. But on February 22 he abandoned the country and fled to Moscow. Parliament named an acting president and prime minister, and Ukraine was back on track, once again, its sights set on integration with Europe. I left for home, relieved, yet unsettled.

LITTLE GREEN MEN

But Vladimir Putin reacted quickly. Five days later he dispatched masked troops without insignia to seize Ukraine's Crimean Peninsula. Putin, at first, denied the "little green men," as Ukrainians dubbed them, were Russian forces.

"They were local self-defense units," he assured the reporters. Russian social media took the trolling a step further, renaming the "little green men," "Polite People."

A year later, Putin was boasting about his exploit. "I gave orders to the Defense Ministry—why hide it?" he said in an interview, a smug smile curling his lips, "to deploy forces of the Main Intelligence Directorate, along with marines and commandoes, under the guise of reinforcing security for our military facilities in Crimea."

In mid-March Putin signed a treaty of annexation with the Russian-backed leaders of Crimea. In his speech that afternoon, he laid out—almost verbatim—themes he would use in 2022 to justify his total invasion of Ukraine: "Nationalists, neo-Nazis, Russophobes, and anti-Semites executed this coup."

Trying to justify his illegal annexation of Crimea, or his all-out war against Ukraine, he insisted he'd had no choice but to act: "The residents of Crimea and Sevastopol turned to Russia for help in defending their rights and lives, in preventing the events that were unfolding and are still under way in Kiev, Donetsk, Kharkov, and other Ukrainian cities. Naturally, we could not leave this plea unheeded; we could not abandon Crimea and its residents in distress. This would have been betrayal on our part." (Putin, along with other Russian officials, still clung to the Russian spelling of the Ukrainian capital, "Kiev," instead of the Ukrainian spelling, "Kyiv.")

In 2022, on the verge of invading Ukraine, he repeated that claim: "The People's Republic of Donbas appealed to Russia for help."

The disconnect between Putin's rhetoric and reality became a mind-warp.

"We want to be friends with Ukraine," he claimed, "and we want Ukraine to be a strong, sovereign, and self-sufficient country."

Russian bombers were pummeling civilian apartment buildings, yet Putin insisted: "These are our comrades, those dearest to us—not only colleagues, friends, and people who once served together, but also relatives, people bound by blood, by family ties."

As always, he blamed the West: "They are constantly trying to sweep us into a corner because we have an independent position," he said in 2014, "because we maintain it and because we call things like they are and do not engage in hypocrisy. But there is a limit to everything."

TOTAL WAR

In February 2022 I was at home in Washington, watching statements from the White House that claimed Putin was about to order his troops to attack Ukraine. The Biden administration, in an unprecedented preemptory revelation of national security intelligence, warned of a "very distinct possibility" that Russian forces would attack within the next few days.

President Joe Biden's National Security Adviser, Jake Sullivan, told reporters the United States was convinced Russian military action was imminent. CNN dispatched news teams to Moscow and Ukraine. A senior CNN editor soon called, asking me how quickly I could get to Moscow. I immediately booked a flight, packed, and, on February 15, headed for the Russian capital.

Working out of CNN's Moscow bureau, I watched the "special military operation," as Putin insisted on calling it, unfold over its first two weeks, a methodically choreographed propaganda operation camouflaging a deeply flawed military strategy and a massive political miscalculation.

In the days leading up to the invasion, the Kremlin and the Russian Foreign Ministry scoffed at the very idea that Russia would attack Ukraine. "Nonsense!" declared Putin's spokesman, Dmitry Peskov. Foreign Ministry spokeswoman Maria Zakharova dismissed the US warning, calling it "absurd," and insisting that Russia and Ukraine "are a people that has a common history."

Russian officials, TV commentators, and even some individual Russians I spoke with dismissed any chance there would be an invasion. One TV show displayed a clock as the anchor mocked Washington's warning: "They say there's going to be an invasion. I'm still looking at my watch. So, where's the invasion?"

Moscow already had a different, more strained atmosphere. Up to now, each time I returned to Russia I felt almost as if I were going home. After all, I had lived in Moscow for almost a decade, I had friends there, and I enjoyed life in the city. This time, I felt a vague uneasiness that reminded me of the old Soviet days.

The Kremlin already was crafting the pretext for war, and it unfolded in the best Soviet-style tradition. The Donetsk and Luhansk regions of Ukraine, depicted by Russia as statelets that broke away from Ukraine in order to gain their freedom, had declared their independence in 2014. In reality, the two regions were controlled by separatists supported by Moscow, which engineered an unofficial "referendum." The day I arrived in Moscow, the Duma, the lower house of the Russian parliament, voted unanimously in favor of a resolution calling on Putin to recognize those self-declared "people's republics" as "sovereign and independent states."

Would he? Wouldn't he? In classic Putin style, the Russian president kept the country—and the world—hanging on his decision. There was, of course, no doubt he would follow through, but it gave an already-made decision the gloss of legality.

On February 21 Putin appeared on TV to announce that he was signing a presidential decree recognizing the independence of the statelets. His long and rambling speech, filled with references to Russian and Soviet history, was focused on Ukraine but, over and over, he returned with a vengeance to the gnawing issue that lay at the heart of his argument: the perfidy of the United States. As always, he blamed others for "forcing" him into a decision he already had decided to make.

"We demand that those who took over and retain power in Kiev immediately cease military action. If they do not, all responsibility for the possible continuation of bloodshed will be entirely and fully on the conscience of the leaders of the Ukrainian regime."

Putin alone would decide whether there would be war or peace. All decisions—military and diplomatic—were in his hands. In one extraordinary TV broadcast that reminded me of the movie *The Godfather*, Putin humiliated his own director of foreign intelligence, Sergey Naryshkin, forcing him to go on the record publicly to pledge support for Putin's decision to attack Ukraine.

As I watched the sneer on Putin's face as he twisted the knife deeper into Naryshkin, I thought of Putin as a young boy in Leningrad, pummeled by the other boys because he was smaller and weaker. Now, he had a triumphant gaze. And that name—Naryshkin. It's one of the most famous noble families in Russia, going back at least to the sixteenth century. The family tree is adorned with ambassadors and grand marshals, chamberlains and commandants.

Whether Putin thought about all of this when he was skewering Naryshkin is dubious, but that is how I understood it that day: Vladimir Putin, raised in a tough Leningrad neighborhood, poor, bullied, had shown Naryshkin who was boss. Next, he would try to show the world.

Like clockwork, the leaders of the rebel "republics" magically appeared at the Kremlin in suits and ties, each seated at a desk yards away from Putin in the cavernous hall, for a formal signing ceremony. Wasting no time, Putin immediately ordered Russian "peacekeepers" into the region. It was pure kabuki theater.

Over the years, I had heard Putin criticize the United States, but this time, he was overflowing with bitterness and spite. Like an angry husband on the brink of divorce, he hurled recriminations at the country he once described as a "partner." America had deceived Russia, he rattled on, in vindictive stream of consciousness, pretending it was not going to expand NATO.

"They have deceived us, or, to put it simply, they have 'played' us. Sure, one often hears that politics is a dirty business. It could be, but it shouldn't be as dirty as it is now, not to such an extent. This type of con-artist behavior is contrary not only to the principles of international relations but also, and above all, to the generally accepted norms of morality and ethics. Where is justice and truth here? Just lies and hypocrisy all around."

Yes, that love affair with the West, if there ever had been one—a brief flirtation?—was over. And Vladimir Putin would have his revenge.

Despite all the assurances from Russian officials that Moscow would never, ever attack, all the deprecating remarks about Western "paranoia," Russian tanks were rolling across the border into Ukraine. But this war would not be called a "war." Less than a week later, the Duma passed a law making it a crime to use the words "war" or "invasion," or to disseminate any information about the conflict that did not come from the military, violations to be punished by up to fifteen years in prison. Putin's phrase "special military operation" would be the only way to legally refer to his war.

Until, one day, nine months later, in comments to reporters in Moscow, Mr. Putin himself used the word "war."

"Our goal is not to spin the flywheel of military conflict," he said, "but, on the contrary, to end this war. We have been and will continue to strive for this."

Was that word "war" a slip of the tongue? A bit of trolling? A final recognition of reality? It wasn't clear. Like his kiss on my cheek years ago, his true motivation would remain a mystery.

· 18 ·

Fleeing Putin

Even in the midst of an imminent conflict, I tried to meet with friends in Moscow. Soon after I arrived, I texted Mikhail Fishman, a well-known independent journalist with TV Rain. It had been a long time since I'd seen him in person, and we agreed to have coffee in a few days. But on February 22, Russian tanks rolled over the border into Ukraine and Putin announced his "special military operation."

I got a cryptic text from Misha: "My family and I are going on vacation to Baku." My old Soviet-era instincts kicked in. Going on vacation was the last thing Misha would do as a war was breaking out. But I knew it was best not to ask any questions—just stop texting and wait. I soon learned that my friend and his family had fled Russia, as had many of the channel's journalists, fearing for their safety.

Russian journalism no longer exists in Russia. Yes, there are real journalists still working behind the scenes, often anonymously, in danger of arrest and imprisonment. And there are people in Moscow sitting behind anchor desks or hosting talk shows, but in reality, they are part of a massive propaganda machine controlled by the Kremlin. Real Russian journalism now exists only outside of Russia.

Almost all independent journalists fled the country after Vladimir Putin ordered his troops to invade Ukraine in February 2022. So, in mid-May, I traveled to Estonia, Latvia, and Lithuania—three Baltic nations where many Russian journalists now work.

On the plane, I thought: What do I call them? Expats—émigrés? Not refugees—but what? Would they be able to return to Russia? I thought of the Russians who fled the 1917 Bolshevik Revolution, some of whom, like my

287

colleagues and friends, hoped they would return to Russia after Lenin and his cohorts were gone.

But the USSR lasted for almost seventy years, and most of them lived their lives abroad and died in exile.

WISHFUL THINKING

A day after I arrived in Vilnius, Lithuania, I got a text in Russian: "Jill, hi, we heard you're in Vilnius. Would you like to join us for our morning show?" The text was from Tatyana (Tanya) Felgenhauer and Alexander (Sasha) Plush-chev, both of whom were anchors on Echo Moscow Radio.

Echo Moscow had chronicled the earliest days of post-Soviet Russia, and during the Putin years it had hung on, despite increasing Kremlin pressure to toe the line. Now it was gone, shut down by its board of directors after Russia's censorship watchdog, Roskomnadzor, blocked its website for allegedly disseminating "deliberately false information" about the Russian military and for supporting "extremist activity" and "violence."

I had been interviewed by Tanya and Sasha via Zoom several times over the past few years, from Washington, DC. So, newly arrived in Vilnius, I agreed to come by and join them on their new YouTube channel. In Russia, YouTube has become a kind of alternate television; most young Russians no longer watch state TV, which is increasingly irrelevant to them.

Their studio turned out to be a large room in a commercial building which their friends were allowing them to work from, complete with LED studio lights, a "green screen" behind them, two cameras, and a square black "anchor desk" in the middle, at which sat Tanya and Sasha, each with a laptop and microphone. They already were involved in a live conversation with viewers about the war, and they waved me in to sit at a third microphone. We chatted on air for a half-hour or so. Sasha happily reported that, that morning, 25,000 people were watching our YouTube discussion.

When the show was over, I switched on my phone and interviewed them. We spoke in Russian. Tanya had just arrived in Vilnius. She told me she had "hung on" in Moscow for the first three months following the February 24th invasion of Ukraine.

> Well, at first, it was adrenaline. They're shutting down Echo Moscow, everyone's leaving, you have trouble understanding what's happening, and on the one hand . . . you want to witness everything, plus, foreign journalists are constantly calling you and saying "Well, how can this be happen-

ing?" and you feel yourself very much needed . . . and then one month goes
by, and then a second month, and then you understand you have absolutely
no work, you have no perspective, you have a YouTube channel where
you continue to say the things you've gotten used to saying, but every day
you're reading reports that yet another journalist has been arrested or put in
jail. So, there's no work and there are a lot of risks, and you think, "Why
am I staying here?"

I had the idea that I wanted to see it right to the end. How is it going to
end? But a thought came to me: "Tanya, if they put you in jail, you won't
see how this ends because in prison they show First Channel [state] TV,
and they won't show any bit of how it will end.

I asked her how Alexey Venediktov, Echo Moscow's former editor in
chief, was doing. The last I had heard, some unknown persons had left a
pig's head, along with scrawled anti-Semitic slurs, at his Moscow apartment
door.

"Yes, there were several incidents, she answered. "They threw the pig's
head. Then they closed Echo Moscow, the media were liquidated, and after a
bit, they put Venediktov on the register of 'foreign agents.'"

I asked Tanya and Sasha if they planned to return to Russia.

"Without a doubt," Sasha said.

"After the war?" I asked.

"Of course," they replied, "as soon as it's possible."

"For me, this is a long business trip," Tanya added. "We continue to
work, and we'll return in order to work."

Sasha agreed.

"And can you return with Putin in power?" I asked them.

"No, absolutely [not]! It's impossible," Sasha almost yelled at me.

"Even if Putin wrote us a letter and said—"

Tanya finished his sentence: "Yeah, we'd write a letter to him: 'Vladimir
Vladimirovich, it's better if you go directly to the Hague. We'll meet in court!'"

STAYING BEHIND

In Vilnius I saw Yevgenia Albats, one of Russia's most respected investigative journalists, and one of the last to leave Russia. She is the longtime editor
in chief and CEO of *The New Times*, a weekly political magazine. Just days
after the invasion of Ukraine, Putin blocked it, but she continued it online
as newtimes.ru. Russians still in the country can access it, along with other

websites from abroad, by using a VPN (virtual private network). Like most independent Russian journalists, she also has a YouTube channel.

Until the very end, Albats remained defiantly in her hometown of Moscow. But, in September 2022 she finally left for the United States, where she accepted a teaching job.

"Why did I, at last, make this decision?" she said on her YouTube channel. "I will tell you: because I already had four administrative cases against me, I was labeled a 'foreign agent,' and it became clear to me that just three or four weeks were left before I will be arrested."

Yevgenia was a close personal friend of Alexei Navalny. She said she discussed with him her decision to leave Russia, and that he supported it. Knowing Zhenia (the Russian nickname for Yevgenia) personally, as I do, I am sure it was a wrenching decision for her. She believes in being on the ground, close to the action, able to talk with sources. If you are outside of Russia now, she told me, you no longer can call somebody and say: "Can you give me a comment?"

"I know for sure that no one speaks over the phone anymore," she explained. "Just no one! You have to meet with people in person. . . . And they're afraid, and they meet with you in a very constrained environment. You're not supposed to be seen with them—you meet with them in the parks, in the [entrances of] buildings, in the closed clubs, so that no one will see that you entered the same room."

In 2014 Albats's foundation was the third in Russia to be declared a "foreign agent," and she was forced to pay large fines to the government. She had numerous encounters with security officials. She kept a bag packed with clothes and supplies, in case they came after her.

"It's not pleasant," she said.

"So why stay?" I asked.

"Because somebody has to!" she exclaimed. "Because it's a shame! It's a shame! My country, Jill, I'm a citizen of the Russian Federation. My country started the war of attrition, the war of choice, the war of conquest, against another country. We are journalists. Our job is to cover this."

WHO'S LISTENING?

As I spoke with colleagues and friends now living outside of Russia, I asked: "Are your fellow Russians back in Moscow and other cities still listening to you?"

I thought back to the aftermath of the Bolshevik Revolution, when waves of Russians fled to Europe, to China, to the United States. The journalists and writers among them set up Russian-language newspapers and other publications. As the years passed, however, they lost touch with what actually was happening back in Russia. Technically, they had challenges: Their publications were printed on paper, difficult to ship back to Russia, so they were read, for the most part, by fellow Russian exiles.

This new wave of exiles, whether they left after Russia's 2014 annexation of Crimea or after Putin launched his full-scale invasion of Ukraine in 2022, can continue to be "part of the conversation," thanks to the Internet, digital media, and VPNs.

But what I really wanted to know was: Are Russians back home still listening?

SMELLING THE CORPSES

None of the journalists I spoke with in Tallinn or Vilnius knew what would happen next. All of them said they intend to return to Russia, but they couldn't say when. What this means for their profession, and for them personally, is unclear.

In Vilnius, I ran into Sergey Parkhomenko, a longtime journalist, publisher, and political commentator. Many of Russia's journalists, right now, he told me, are in a "professional crisis."

"First of all, [there's] exhaustion from the subject generally, and the feeling that the war started, and it's a catastrophic event, and in three days it will be over. . . . Then it was three days more, then three weeks, then three months, and no one knows how long this is going to continue, and it's impossible to prolong that level of attention."

Some journalists who fled Russia, he predicted, will rethink their profession. "Some will have that first reflex, 'Ah! They kicked us out! They shut down, destroyed my media! But you can't stop me!' Some despair, some get tired, some calm down, and some think, well, there are other professions I can work in. I can teach, or I can try to work in business or to write a book."

Russian journalists can have an impact working from Europe, the United States, or other countries, but Parkhomenko insisted they need to be on the ground, in the place from which they are reporting:

> You need to live in Irkutsk in order to make a tour of small towns and villages in Tuva, Buryatia, or the Baikal region and see how they are burying the people who are perishing in Ukraine. It's not happening in Moscow. [They] can't know anything about those burials, they don't know those people, don't talk with them, they don't hear the sounds or [experience] the smell of the corpses.

Putin's Russia is trying to—how did they say it in Nazi Germany? To reach a "final solution." They want a final solution for independent media. "When we win the war," they think, "we'll hunt them abroad, we'll send people with Novichok to poison them. Not immediately, but later. We'll be able to do it. We have time." That is their view of the world, that's how they think of their task, and they are going to achieve it.

But will Russia still be Russia, I thought, if its best minds, its critical thinkers, those who are its moral compass, either have left the country or are imprisoned? With savage fury, Vladimir Putin was turning on his own people, driving them out, threatening anyone who did not support his war. I recalled his words, and the scorn with which he'd said them: "Any people, and especially the Russian people, will always be able to distinguish the true patriots from the scum and the traitors, and just to spit them out like a midge that accidentally flew into their mouths."

I thought of Dmitrii Sergeyevich Likhachev, one of Russia's most esteemed scholars, who spent five years in a Gulag concentration camp, a person who embodied the highest values of Russia. "Nationalism," Likhachev said, "lives in the shadows and only pretends to be based on love for one's country. But, in fact, it is spawned by malice and hatred for other nations and for those people in one's own nation who do not share these nationalistic views."

WHO AM I?

Back in the States, I texted Misha Fishman, my journalist friend with whom I'd planned to have coffee in Moscow. He told me that he and his family now live in the Netherlands.

Fishman's show on TV Rain was always sharply critical of the Putin government, and he was sure he couldn't go back to Moscow. But now that he was outside of Russia, he said, at least "I'm not in a risky position anymore. I'm safe."

When he first left Russia, he told me, "I couldn't open my mouth . . . I'm still in this limbo." He has a new YouTube channel, but admitted, "Now I'm very different from what I was before. For twenty years I was part of my own story. I never separated me from my country. And now I'm not. Who am I? Am I part of Russia anymore? Does my voice matter? I don't have accurate answers to this."

Where is Russia going? I asked him. "It's going backward, back in time to the Middle Ages." Russia, he said, "is dying."

· 19 ·

Last Night in Moscow

I shared dinner with a Russian friend just before I left Moscow. She worked with an NGO. We met at a nearby popular movie theater, built in the Soviet days but remodeled, and welcoming, about a fifteen-minute walk up Kutuzovsky Prospekt from the CNN bureau. It had a café at the far end of the high-ceilinged foyer which, I knew from previous visits, served delicious lattes and a fantastic chicken Caesar salad.

As I entered the theater lobby, I passed a poster advertising the classic movie *Casablanca*, and as I walked past, I snapped a photo. I was intrigued to see Humphrey Bogart and Ingrid Bergman, slightly out of context, the film's iconic name written in Cyrillic letters. I found my friend in the café, and after ordering, we went upstairs to a more private part of the restaurant on the balcony and took a table overlooking the foyer.

As we started talking, despite the warmth I felt for my friend, I could feel myself slipping into that guarded, Soviet-era way of talking, just as I had in my texts with Misha Fishman, concerned that someone might overhear our discussion.

She was planning to leave Russia as soon as possible; for her, too, the writing was on the wall. She told me she had "Plan A, Plan B, and Plan C." Just in case someone was listening, I asked no questions about the specifics—where she would go, how she would get there, what her plans were after leaving.

When the waitress brought our salads, we switched to pleasantries.

I mentioned *Casablanca* and the poster downstairs.

"Such a wonderful film," she recalled. She had seen it recently with friends on the film's eightieth anniversary, and the plight of those desperate to find refuge from the Nazis in a neutral country moved her deeply. "That question: 'Should I stay, or should I go?' It's so real to me right now," she

293

said. Months later, after she left Russia, she would tell me: "We were struck by how relevant it was to our present day and to the horrors of our reality. But the time I truly felt like I, myself, was in Casablanca [was when] I was in Yerevan, on my way to Europe. I went out with friends, and it hit me—it was exactly the same atmosphere: émigrés spending their time in a bar, waiting for something, hoping for some certainty, while there's a war going on."

Suddenly the brutal truth of what my friends—and there would be many more—were experiencing hit me: They were about to flee Russia, the country where they were born, where they grew up, had families, where they had made careers—the language, the country they loved. They were going to leave it all behind. Would they ever return?

TEACHING WHILE THE TANKS ROLLED

In Moscow, trying to explain Putin's war to CNN viewers, I still had my "day job." I had dropped everything to fly to Moscow, but I was in the middle of the semester at Georgetown University, teaching my "Putin Generation" course. The head of the department gave me his blessing to teach online from Russia. During the COVID-19 pandemic I taught almost exclusively online via Zoom, and it worked well, allowing my students and me to talk with experts in Russia, Ukraine, the Baltics, and other regions.

Doing live shots from the CNN bureau on Putin's decision to invade Ukraine, I realized I could not stick with the syllabus I had compiled months before. This was a historic, defining moment. So, I set the syllabus aside and, in one online lecture, I gave my class a tour of the CNN Moscow office, showing them the equipment we used for our live reports, along with the boxes of pizza that fueled our late nights.

I kept thinking about ways I could make my lectures more real, and timely. The CNN bureau had several young Russian interns helping out, and I asked them whether they had any friends who might want to talk with my students. They suggested a few young people, so I called them up and talked with them for a bit. I chose two young women, Natasha and Sofia, and a young man, Dima (to protect their identities, I am not using their real names).

Natasha and Sofia, both in their early twenties, were horrified by the invasion. I explained to my class that it could be risky for anyone to express misgivings or opposition to the war—already protesters on the streets were being arrested in droves—but the two young women seemed eager to talk with my students. Nevertheless, just in case, I used only the audio, no video.

Natasha and Sofia were university graduates, lived in Moscow, had traveled in Europe, and were convinced that the war would cut Russia off from the West, making it impossible for them to pursue their careers. My students didn't need my help to get the conversation flowing; I sat back and watched young people with completely different realities begin to share about their lives.

Natasha's hatred of Putin and revulsion against the "special military operation" were palpable. She spoke about the generational differences within many families in Russia, including hers: "My parents and grandparents are not like us young people," she told my class. "They are Soviet people. They won't protest until they have nothing to eat." Whenever she asked her mother about the invasion, she said, her mother would simply repeat that she was "conditioned to survive." Old people don't want any "uncomfortable" thoughts in their lives, she explained. They have enough to worry about.

Among Natasha and Sofia's friends, they said, there was a lot of anxiety about the future, but it was more focused on how the conflict could affect their personal economic situation. Although both young women were intent on leaving Russia, they seemed, at times, hopeless they would be able to.

"The government is so much more powerful than we are and it's so difficult to leave," Sofia said. Both women seemed scared they would become pariahs in the West, although they saw themselves as simply "prisoners of a regime."

Natasha spoke about the sense of shame she felt for the country she insisted she loved. "The part that connected me to Russia," she said, "is dying." Russia always thought of itself as a country that defended itself against foreign enemies, but now, Russia was doing the attacking, and she was sure that would have a huge impact on Russians' own sense of who they are.

As the conversation continued, Natasha's anger and sadness grew, and she begged my students not to make the mistake of thinking the people of Russia were behind Putin's decision. The conversation ended with a heartfelt promise by my students that they wouldn't forget those two young girls were, indeed, "prisoners of a regime."

It was midnight in Moscow. Because of the eight-hour time difference with Washington, Natasha and Sofia had stayed up very late, but no one seemed to mind. The conversation was so intense, so honest, that when it was over—after I had thanked them, said good-bye to my class, and shut down my laptop—I sat by myself in an office at the CNN bureau and broke down in tears. What had just happened seemed like a miracle: My young university students, in Washington, were talking directly, live, with young Russians their own age, in Moscow, who now faced decisions my students would almost surely never have to make.

Practically every young person I spoke with during my stay in Moscow shared these girls' opposition to, and horror about, the war, but I wanted my students to have a chance to talk with someone who thought the invasion—Putin's "special military operation"—was justified. Dima fit the description. We spoke with him a few days later.

Dima had a radically different view of what Vladimir Putin was doing. His father was a diplomat. Dima had lived abroad, studied at a prestigious university, and, obviously, was on the fast track to success in Vladimir Putin's world. As he saw it, the Russian president had an obligation to protect his country from threats posed by the United States and Europe. The "special military operation" was completely justified, Dima said confidently. Ukraine was filled with nationalists and fascists. NATO was intent on encircling Russia, using Ukraine as a cudgel, and it was just a matter of time before they attacked Moscow.

It was jarring to hear a young Russian so suspicious of the West, especially one who had lived abroad, but as I listened to him, I could sense an undercurrent of cynicism that reminded me of Vladimir Putin: It was sad, he said, that Russia had to take action, that people would die, but, after all, it was the West's fault. Although none of my students could see any justification for what Dima was saying, it was a valuable lesson to hear, almost verbatim, how some Russians were quickly accepting Putin's explanation for the war.

LAST NIGHT IN MOSCOW

Midday, March 5, I arrived at the bureau to prepare for my overnight shift of live shots that began at 11 p.m. (3 p.m. in Washington, the beginning of CNN's primetime news programs). I usually spent several hours in advance, reading Russian wire reports, poring over statements from the Kremlin and the Foreign Ministry, watching briefings by the Defense Ministry, and studying anything Vladimir Putin had said or done.

Putin was constantly on government-controlled TV at this point, in a parallel universe of Zoom-style conferences with his military commanders and security officials. As the days wore on, his appearances became more surreal. French president Emmanuel Macron rushed to Moscow to try to dissuade him from attacking Ukraine, and their Kremlin conversation seemed like a parody of COVID-19-era "social distancing." The two leaders sat at opposite ends of a ludicrously long white conference table, evidence of the Kremlin's extreme measures to keep the Russian president safe from infection. It soon became the subject of mocking Internet trolling.

Working overnights, I usually got back to my hotel, ironically named the "Ukraine," by 5 or 6 a.m. On March 5, I woke up and glanced at my phone. There was a cryptically worded text from the acting bureau chief saying he would be back in a few hours. Something was up.

I quickly dressed and headed across Kutuzovsky Prospekt to the bureau. The bureau chief, I learned, along with the heads of other international news bureaus, had been summoned to the Russian Foreign Ministry's Stalin Gothic building, a short drive from our office. The Duma's new law making it a crime to disseminate any "fake" information about the war—that is, any information that did not come from the Russian government or military—would make our jobs as journalists, or mine as an analyst, impossible.

President Putin's rules still held: The war could not be called a "war." There could be no reference to any "invasion." Russian troops were "successfully and courageously" carrying out the "de-Nazification" of Ukraine. Any deviation from Putin's "special military operation" terminology was illegal.

As soon as our bureau chief returned to the office, we agreed that all reporters and non-Russian producers should leave Moscow as soon as possible. Most other Western networks followed suit. Our newsgathering operation would continue, but, for now, with Russian staff only.

My return flight to Washington, DC, a Lufthansa flight using a Boeing jet, already had been canceled. Boeing announced it was halting operations in Moscow, as well as suspending parts, maintenance, and technical support services for Russian airlines. I managed to book a flight to Frankfurt via Dubai, then on to Washington.

It was late and I had to get back to the hotel to pack, but I wanted a few more minutes to think about what was happening. Everyone had left. I was alone in the bureau.

I walked back to the newsroom, silent at this late hour, with the eerie glow of three TVs on the wall, showing CNN and two Russian state TV channels, the juxtaposition of two different worlds: on CNN—the Russian attack on Ukraine. On the Russian channels—claims of "genocide" against Russian speakers in the Donbas region; no reports about the Russian assault on Ukraine. That divide would only worsen as the Russian government cued its propaganda machine, inundating all media platforms, a river of invective, a torrent of self-justification.

The control room in the bureau was dark, but the tiny red lights on the equipment were glowing, as if reminding me that—regardless of any orders from the Kremlin—the news would not stop. I stood next to the studio door, remembering all the times I had sprinted to do a live shot—tanks rolling down Kutuzovsky Prospekt, the broad thoroughfare on which our bureau was located; Vladimir Putin launching the Second Chechen War; terrorist attacks on the Moscow subway; and, yes, presidential summits when a trusting West had once put its hopes in Putin as a "reformer," perhaps, even, an ally.

Near the camera crews' equipment storage room, I remembered racing to cover breaking news, frantically packing, loading our gear into the van for a heart-stopping drive to the airport, flying off to cover yet another disaster, or war, or revolution, not knowing when we would return. My heart began to race. I felt that old adrenaline rush of excitement tinged with fear. And yet, on that March night in Moscow, stronger than anything was the aching feeling that I might never be a part of that again. For the first time in the half-century I had spent in Russia, I had a premonition that I might never return.

March 5, 2022. My last night in Moscow, perhaps forever. To some, that might seem like a good thing. Russia these days is a country to avoid, a pariah state that attacks and savages its neighbors, a dangerous place for Westerners who might be unjustly arrested and held as hostages for prisoner exchanges.

For me, however, not returning to Russia is almost unthinkable. It's a country that I have studied, lived in, traveled through, tried to understand, obsessed over, sometimes loved, sometimes hated, always wanted more of.

It was time to pack, but I took one more look at my old office and the sofa where I'd slept so many nights, not knowing what the morning would bring. What horrors would this war bring, not only for Ukraine, but for Russia itself? I wouldn't be here to see it. I was being torn from Russia because of this impossible, inevitable war that was the product of one man's will—Vladimir Putin.

I put on my coat and hat, turned off the lights in the bureau, and locked the door behind me. Down three flights of stairs to the street level. I heard the main door buzzer sound behind me. I glanced up across the parking lot to the apartment where Valucha and I had lived for almost a decade, mentally walking through all the rooms, remembering.

I turned right, past the security guard station, and slowly walked down Kutuzovsky Prospekt, half a block to the park that Valucha, years ago, had defended against the Mercedes-Benz driver intent on plowing through the newly seeded grass. I could see her raising her walking stick high in the air, daring him to try it.

I stopped and stood next to the fountain where I had scattered her ashes fifteen years before. In my mind's eye I could see her sitting on the bench nearby, meeting me for a midday break, watching the babushki playing with their little grandchildren.

I had to say good-bye.

The fountain had been drained for the winter, but I touched my fingers to the snow, waited a second until it melted, and made the sign of the cross. Then I turned, felt a chill wind hit my face, and headed for my hotel.

Epilogue

Life has become better! Life has become happier!

—Josef Stalin at the First All-Union Conference of the
Stakhanovites, November 17, 1935

TBILISI

I saw her face before I met her. It was one of eight grim-looking photographs on a poster glued to a fence around a construction site on Rustaveli Avenue, the main street of the Georgian capital, Tbilisi. Someone, apparently, had tried to rip it down, but you could still make out the words "agents who insult the church." It looked like a wanted poster, and it was. All of the people were depicted as enemies of the Georgian people by the ruling political party, the Georgian Dream. It reminded me of similar, much larger posters plastered throughout Moscow several years previously, depicting opposition figures as traitors to Russia.

I was in Tbilisi that March of 2024 for a security conference. Back in Soviet days, Georgia was one of the first republics I ever visited. I found it endlessly intriguing. An ancient, mountainous land, a crossroads of cultures, renowned for its wine, music, and fiercely independent people. Yes, it was the birthplace of Stalin, but his depredations against his own people exceeded anything wrought by foreigners. The day I arrived the streets were full of energy and laughter. Then I saw the poster.

Several colleagues had suggested I contact the woman on the poster, Eka Gigauri, executive director of Transparency International Georgia, the largest civil society organization working on good governance and corruption in

299

Georgia. She was being targeted by the government under a draft "foreign agent" law, a carbon copy of the 2012 Russian law that I was quite familiar with, aimed at shutting down Western-funded nongovernmental organizations. I invited Eka for a quick coffee at the conference hotel. She was quiet, almost gentle, but I sensed a steely core of conviction. Being personally targeted was unpleasant, she told me, but she had no intention of stopping her work.

Two months later, the Georgian foreign agent law was adopted, igniting large protests that were met with tear gas and water cannons.

In late October 2024, I returned to the Georgian capital to provide on-air analysis of the country's parliamentary elections for CNN. I met with Eka again, the day before the ruling party officially "won" the elections, which international observers soon declared rigged. She was locked in an Orwellian pressure campaign by the Georgian Dream—"GD," as opponents called it. The government's anti-corruption bureau had declared her a "political candidate" and Transparency International a "political party." It was ludicrous, she told me, but she explained what was behind the action: "They know we are dependent on foreign funding. It's on our web page. So, they wanted us to not monitor elections." The designation would make it illegal for her to receive any donations from abroad or to spend donor money.

It was also retaliation for her testimony to the US Senate Foreign Relations Committee in September, she explained. On Capitol Hill, she had laid out the stakes: "If Georgian democracy is defeated and the country plunges into the Russian orbit again, this would mean an evaporation of chances for further democratic development of any country eastwards or southwards from Georgia. Geopolitically, this would mean the erection of a new iron curtain in our region, with Russia once again marking its backyard, claiming Georgia as part of its sphere of influence."

"Sphere of influence." It's a phrase I myself use, a sanitized diplo-speak version of how Vladimir Putin is trying to claw back influence and control over countries that used to be part of the USSR. They now are independent nations, but Putin still considers them part of his "backyard." Georgians I met with on that trip had another way of describing it.

"This is a time when our European values are being tested," Saba Buadze, a young opposition politician, told me a few days after the parliamentary elections. "Although the public did massively and overwhelmingly vote in favor of these European values, still there is a significant chance of us remaining in the Eurasian gray zone." If the Georgian Dream, under its billionaire founder, Bidzina Ivanishvili, who made his fortune in Russia, retains control of the country, Saba said, "Democracy will further deteriorate; there will be a massive crackdown on freedom of speech."

"We have only one option, which is to fight with everything we can, to take back what has been stolen," Saba said. "I'm not sure about the success of this. I'm hopeful, I'm optimistic, partly because of my young age. But also because I believe European values are very innate to Georgians. I believe the Georgian society is a truly European society. I believe we have European values. I believe we have the desire to fight for these values. But sometimes this is not enough to change the tragic reality. I hope this will not be the case."

Sitting in a café in Tbilisi, hearing Saba describe how Ivanishvili and his cohorts had captured almost all of Georgia's state institutions, I remembered so many conversations over the years in Moscow, as my Russian friends and colleagues warned me about Putin.

"The signs of what Ivanishvili is were out there, even in 2020, even before that," Saba said, "but our partners refused to believe what we have been saying."

———————

One morning a few weeks ago I woke up in the middle of a dream. Or, rather, a nightmare. I was in Washington, DC, standing on the street, staring up at the Watergate apartment building. Its face had been sheared off by a massive explosion. The charred interiors of the apartments gaped open; curtains flapped in the wind. I saw no people, no bodies.

Later, I remembered that Putin had conjured that very image more than twenty-four years previously, in an opinion piece in the *New York Times*, trying to convince Americans that Russians were facing the same threat from terrorism as they were.

> Imagine something more placid: ordinary New Yorkers or Washingtonians, asleep in their homes. Then, in a flash, hundreds perish in explosions at the Watergate, or at an apartment complex on Manhattan's West Side. Thousands are injured, some horribly disfigured. Panic engulfs a neighborhood, then a nation. Russians do not have to imagine such a calamity. More than 300 of our citizens in Moscow and elsewhere suffered that fate earlier this year when bombs detonated by terrorists demolished five apartment blocks.

My mind fills with images of Ukrainians, fleeing from burning buildings, as Russian missiles tear into apartments, schools, and hospitals.

I'm teaching my "Putin Generation" course again. I collected new material for the syllabus, new polls and research on Russia's young people, new music videos by Russian artists, new memes, photographs I took during my last trip to Moscow, and interviews with Russians who fled the country and are living in Europe. I reached out to one Russian professor, still in Moscow, who talked with my students last year. Perhaps he will do it again. But talking with Americans could get him in serious trouble with the security services that now control life in Russia.

I would go back to Moscow in a heartbeat, but I can't. Americans are imprisoned, arrested on fake charges. They're useful for the Kremlin to barter to get valuable Russians (an FSB officer?) back home.

So how do I really know what young Russians are thinking—about the war, about Putin, about their lives? One of my former students, Claudia, told me she had kept in touch with Russian friends and even reached out to find new ones online. She was part of the class that spoke on Zoom from Washington with three young Russians in Moscow that night in February 2022, as Russian troops attacked Ukraine.

I admitted to Claudia that, after the invasion and devastation now unfolding, I wondered whether I should continue to call my course "The Putin Generation." If young Russians like Natasha and Sofia, with whom we spoke, were so opposed to the war, perhaps it meant that this was no longer the "Putin" generation? What about the antiwar protests on the streets of Moscow and other cities across Russia just after the invasion? How many young Russians feel this way?

Claudia told me of a friend, Kamila, a young Russian already in Europe when the full-scale war began. Kamila thought the "special military operation," as Putin called it, would last for a couple of days, and then she could go home.

> I got really sad because I understood it wasn't going to end. You get so sad because for years you follow Navalny, and people like Navalny, and you think that something will change, you have this kind of hope that there's something coming that will be great and cause the 'Putin Empire' to fall—and with this war you realize that this won't be true anymore. All these people are suddenly going to prison or going abroad; you realize that hope is gone, that's what hits you most, in the moment. There's no hope anymore. It's not like I can go home and believe that there is a greater future coming. There is not.

Kamila did go home to Russia for a short time, to see her parents, Claudia told me. In one of her conversations with Kamila, her Russian friend told her that, back in Moscow, she thought people would be fixated on the war. But that was not the Russian reality Kamila found.

"No, not at all. That's the thing—you read all the news and you think people are freaking out, but that was just before mobilization, like in the first two months. Now, when you try to speak to people about it, they just go: 'Let's just not talk about it. I'm not into politics and I don't want to get into an argument.' It's just this extremely taboo topic. People just don't talk about it."

Kamila insists that she loves Russia, but it's a different type of place right now.

"I never really missed the place itself; I missed the way I felt there, the memories. . . . Most of all I missed that kind of hope that was all around you. We were all working for a better future, we were talking about it a lot. And that's the thing—because there was so much censorship, you feel like you really came together with your friends, like: 'This is going to change.' There was so much hope. And there's no hope there right now. I'm still waiting for this to change, but I don't see myself going back there if it doesn't, because it might be the same Russia in terms of the physical place, but it's not going to be the kind of Russia I always dreamed of."

When the war is over, Kamila wants to go back to Russia.

There is a long silence.

"I'd love to go back," Kamila said. "That's the thing—I love my country so much that I would love to go back. But . . . to a different one. To the one that I was hoping it was becoming."

Kamila is crying now. "It literally feels like there's a hole inside of me that will never heal. And you don't know what to do next with your life. I don't know what's going on, what's going to happen tomorrow, how to continue living life. Because I love Russia. And seeing it like that is so heartbreaking. And you feel that every day. It doesn't go away. It's a huge loss."

I told my student Claudia that I was considering changing the name of my "Putin Generation" course. Putin, I explained, was so toxic. And, in Russia, everything seemed to be in flux.

But Claudia told me I shouldn't. "The name is accurate," she said. "The war showed you that it's the only name that can truthfully describe them. Because this complexity of ideas and actions—being technically against the war, but not politically minded enough to care about it or change it—is only the symptom of having grown up under a dictator who 'numbed' them. Putin made them politically helpless, and it's showing now, especially as the war goes on. They are Putin's Generation more than ever."

I did keep the name of the course. And I thought a lot about what Kamila had said: Russia is no longer the same. Her Russia is gone. Is mine?

Navalny is dead. I talk with old friends from Russia who are still in shock. They still cannot believe he is gone.

Putin has been "reelected" for the fifth time. He could be in power until 2036. I watch the video as he stands there, after the votes were counted, a picture-perfect image, flanked by a row of young people. He thanks them for being "comrades-in-arms . . . warriors who rose to defend their Fatherland, who thought about their Motherland today—and about future generations."

That is what Putin is offering young Russians these days: the glory of dying for the Fatherland.

The semester at school is almost over. I ask my students what kind of Russia—and young Russians—they think they will be dealing with in the future. After all, they're the same generation. My students aren't very optimistic. They've seen the new textbooks the Russian government requires students to read, books claiming Russia is in an existential conflict with the West, that Ukraine is a "neo-Nazi" state, that Russia doesn't start wars—it tries to end them. They see a new poll: Half of Russian young people agree democracy is preferable to any other kind of government, but 20 percent of them are open to the idea of an authoritarian government. Another 20 percent don't think it really matters for them.

But I remind my students that, even in the dark years of Communism, Mikhail Gorbachev appeared, prying open the USSR with *glasnost* and *perestroika*. Maybe another Gorbachev can emerge? My class doesn't seem convinced.

I message my friend, Zhenia Albats. She was a close friend of Navalny's.

"Navalny was everything Putin was not," she says. "He believed in the virtues of freedom, the rule of law, and free and fair elections. He dreamed about turning Russia into a normal, friendly, democratic country capable of being part of the Western world—he called it the "Beautiful Russia of Tomorrow." She quoted from a letter he wrote to her from prison: "Zhenia, everything is okay. It's a historical process. Russia goes through it, and we go along with it. We will get there. Probably."

I want to believe that.

I see pictures of mourners, thousands of them, many of them young, standing for hours in long lines, bringing flowers to Navalny's grave. They know the FSB is watching them, using facial recognition technology to record them. They come anyway.

On Election Day, I see more young Russians turning out at noon, queuing up to vote—but not for Putin—in a silent protest organized by the opposition. They look around at the people next to them in line and they understand: Other people think the way I do. I'm not alone.

I am rereading George F. Kennan's "Long Telegram," which the American diplomat sent to President Truman's State Department on February 22, 1946, an effort to explain the forces that molded the Soviet Union's behavior. One paragraph rivets my attention. Almost four decades later, it seems to capture the essence of Vladimir Putin and the country he's trying to hammer into existence for Russia's young people:

At the bottom of Kremlin's neurotic view of world affairs is traditional and instinctive Russian sense of insecurity . . . this latter type of insecurity was one which afflicted rather Russian rulers than Russian people; for Russian rulers have invariably sensed that their rule was relatively archaic in form fragile and artificial in its psychological foundation, unable to stand comparison or contact with political systems of Western countries. For this reason they have always feared foreign penetration, feared direct contact between Western world and their own, feared what would happen if Russians learned truth about world without or if foreigners learned truth about world within. And they have learned to seek security only in patient but deadly struggle for total destruction of rival power, never in compacts and compromises with it.

Russian rulers? Yes. Russian people? No. The young people I got to know in Leningrad fifty years ago grew up under Communist rule. But they helped to end it.

Archaic? Yes. Vladimir Putin is pulling his country back into the past. He's on a mission, as a Russian colleague once put it, "a mission that is maybe not given by God, but something that God must approve. . . . He doesn't have any peers in his own country. And when you sit in that position, then the only interlocutor you have is God."

On Christmas in 2023, Vladimir Putin attended Mass at Annunciation Cathedral, the fifteenth-century church where czars once worshipped, securely located inside the redbrick Kremlin walls. As candles flickered, casting their golden glow on the icons of prophets and saints, a priest in golden robes holding a gold cross intoned the Divine Liturgy.

There was only one worshipper: Vladimir Putin. He stood to the side, bareheaded, wearing a short black overcoat and, beneath it, a white turtleneck sweater and a dark suit jacket. He later removed the coat and stood silently by, a somber expression on his face, crossing himself and bowing slightly, at one point biting his lip. In previous years, he was joined by his family, by other worshippers, families, and children. This year, he was all alone.

A Note on Russian Names

Russian names can be confusing to non-Russians, but they are based on a well-organized system that imparts significant information about the person: their sex, their father's name, their family name.

Russian names have three parts: first name (имя), patronymic (your father's first name) (отчество), and family name (фамилия).

For example, one of Russia's most famous writers is Leo Tolstoy. In Russian, his name is Lev Nikolayevich Tolstoy (Лев Николаевич Толстой).

Men's first names usually end in a consonant: Lev.

Women's names usually end in "a": Natasha.

The patronymic also is gendered. For men, it ends in "ovich" or "evich" (Nikolayevich) (Vladimirovich). For women, it ends in "ovna" or evna" (Nikolayevna) (Vladimirovna).

To make things more complicated, Russians love so-called "diminutives," or the "affectionate" form of names. Diminutives connote small size, but most often, intimacy. The diminutive of Ivan is "Vanya." This is similar to the way English uses "Jack" for "John" or "Ted" for "Edward." They also can be used to tease or insult someone.

Russians use scores of these nicknames: Sasha, Zhenia, Misha, Kolya, Anya, Lena, etc. Then, there's a whole category of even smaller and more intimate names, for example, "Elena" can turn into "Lenochka."

Here's where it gets tricky. Most of these nicknames end in "a," which would normally mean it's a woman's name, but with diminutives, it can be either a man's or a woman's name. For example, Alexander (a man's name) and Alexandra (a woman's name) use the same diminutive: Sasha.

All of this creates a delightfully confusing welter of names that find their way into Russian novels. They are not created to confuse the reader but rather to impart family ties, lineage, and, above all, how the person fits into the emotional context of the moment. A mother, for example, might typically refer to her son Vladimir as "Vova." If she is angry at him, she might revert to a stern "Vladimir!" If he apologizes, she could lovingly call him "Vova," "Volodya," "Volodenka," and an almost endless variety of other affectionate versions.

Bibliography

Alexievich, Svetlana. *Secondhand Time: The Last of the Soviets, an Oral History.* Translation by Bela Shayevich. New York: Random House, 2016.

Andrew, Christopher, and Vasili Mitrokhin. *The Sword and the Shield: The Mitrokhin Archive and the Secret History of the KGB.* New York: Basic Books, 1999.

Belton, Catherine. *Putin's People: How the KGB Took Back Russia and Then Took on the West.* New York: Picador, 2020.

Billington, James H. *The Icon and the Axe: An Interpretive History of Russian Culture.* New York: Vintage Books, Random House, 1970.

———. *Russia in Search of Itself.* Washington, DC: Woodrow Wilson Center Press, 2004.

Bittman, Ladislav. *The Deception Game.* New York: Syracuse University Research Corporation, Ballantine Books, 1972.

Burns, William J. *The Back Channel: A Memoir of American Diplomacy and the Case for its Renewal.* New York: Random House, 2019.

Dobrynin, Anatoly. *In Confidence: Moscow's Ambassador to Six Cold War Presidents.* Seattle: University of Washington Press, 1995.

Dougherty, Jill. "Russia's Soft Power Strategy." Graduate Thesis, Georgetown University, November 1, 2013. https://repository.library.georgetown.edu/bitstream/handle/10822/709790/Dougherty_georgetown_0076M_12414.pdf?sequence=1.

———. "Everyone Lies: The Ukraine Conflict and Russia's Media Transformation." Shorenstein Center on Media, Politics and Public Policy, Harvard University, August 20, 2014. https://shorensteincenter.org/everyone-lies-ukraine-conflict-russias-media-transformation/.

———. "How the Media Became One of Putin's Most Powerful Weapons." *The Atlantic,* April 21, 2015. https://www.theatlantic.com/international/archive/2015/04/how-the-media-became-putins-most-powerful-weapon/391062/.

———. "Putin's Hard/Soft Strategy." *The Wilson Quarterly* (Winter 2016). https://www.wilsonquarterly.com/quarterly/_/putins-hard-soft-strategy.

———. "Fleeing Putin." *The Wilson Quarterly* (Summer 2022). https://www.wilson quarterly.com/quarterly/_/fleeing-putin.

———. The Ambassadorial Series: Nine Ambassadorial Interviews with Jill Dougherty. Middlebury Institute of International Studies, February 2023. https://www.middlebury.edu/institute/academics/centers-initiatives/monterey-initiative-russian-studies/ambassadorial-series/nine.

Feith, Douglas J. *War and Decision: Inside the Pentagon at the Dawn of the War on Terrorism.* New York: HarperCollins, 2008.

Gaddy, Clifford G., and Fiona Hill. *Mr. Putin: Operative in the Kremlin.* Washington, DC: Brookings Institution Press, 2013.

Garrels, Anne. *Putin Country: A Journey into the Real Russia.* New York: Farrar, Straus and Giroux, 2016.

Gessen, Masha. *The Man Without a Face: The Unlikely Rise of Vladimir Putin.* New York: Riverhead Books, 2013.

Gevorkyan, Nataliya, Andrei Kolesnikov, and Natalya Timakova. *First Person: An Astonishingly Frank Self-Portrait by Russia's President.* New York: PublicAffairs, 2000.

Giles, Keir. *Russia's War on Everybody, and What It Means for You.* London: Bloomsbury Academic, 2023.

Gorbachev, Mikhail. *Perestroika: New Thinking for Our Country and the World.* New York: Harper & Row Publishers, Inc., 1987.

———. *Memoirs.* New York: Doubleday, 1996.

Graham, Thomas. *Getting Russia Right.* Cambridge, UK: Polity Press, 2023.

Kennan, George. *The Long Telegram.* New York: Cosimo Classics, 1946.

Klebnikov, Paul. *Godfather of the Kremlin: Boris Berezovsky and the Looting of Russia.* New York: Harcourt, Inc., 2000.

Kostyuchenko, Elena. *I Love Russia: Reporting from a Lost Country.* Translated by Bela Shayevich and Ilona Yazhbin Chavasse. New York: Penguin Press, 2023.

Laruelle, Marlene, and Jean Radvanyi, eds. *Russia: Great Power, Weakened State.* Lanham, MD: Rowman & Littlefield, 2023.

Massie, Suzanne. *Land of the Firebird: The Beauty of Old Russia.* Blue Hill, ME: Heart Tree Press, 1980.

National Security Archive. "Cable from US Embassy Moscow to Secretary of State, Subject: Boris Nikolayevich Yel'tsin: A Mid-Range Political Assessment, January 30, 1992." https://nsarchive.gwu.edu/document/29669-document-7-cable-us-embassy-moscow-secretary-state-subject-boris-nikolayevich.

———. "The End of the Soviet Union 1991." Washington, DC, December 25, 2016. https://nsarchive.gwu.edu/briefing-book/russia-programs/2016-12-25/end-soviet-union-1991.

Nye, Joseph S., Jr. *Soft Power: The Means to Success in World Politics.* New York: PublicAffairs, 2004.

Omelchenko, Elena, ed. *Youth in Putin's Russia.* Cham, Switzerland: Palgrave Macmillan, 2021.

Ostrovsky, Arkady. *The Invention of Russia: The Journey from Gorbachev's Freedom to Putin's War.* London: Atlantic Books, 2015, 2018.

Plokhy, Serhii. *The Last Empire: The Final Days of the Soviet Union.* New York: Basic Books, 2014.

Politkovskaya, Anna. *Vtoraya chechenskaya* ("Вторая чеченская"). Moscow: Igor Zakharov Publishing, 2002.

Pomerantsev, Peter. *This Is Not Propaganda: Adventures in the War against Reality.* New York: PublicAffairs, 2019.

Riasanovsky, Nicholas V. *A History of Russia.* New York: Oxford University Press, 1963.

Rid, Thomas. *Active Measures: The Secret History of Disinformation and Political Warfare.* New York: Farrar, Straus and Giroux, 2020.

Sharafutdinova, Gulnaz. *The Red Mirror: Putin's Leadership and Russia's Insecure Identity.* New York: Oxford University Press, 2020.

Shevtsova, Lilia. *Yeltsin's Russia: Myths and Reality.* Washington, DC: Carnegie Endowment for International Peace, 1999.

———. *Putin's Russia.* Washington, DC: Carnegie Endowment for International Peace, 2003.

———. *Russia: Lost in Transition—The Yeltsin and Putin Legacies.* Washington, DC: Carnegie Endowment for International Peace, 2007.

Shevtsova, Lilia, and Archie Brown, eds. *Gorbachev, Yeltsin, Putin: Political Leadership in Russia's Transition.* Washington, DC: Carnegie Endowment for International Peace, 2001.

Smith, Hedrick. *The Russians.* New York: Quadrangle / The New York Times Book Co., 1976.

Snyder, Alvin A. *Warriors of Disinformation: American Propaganda, Soviet Lies, and the Winning of the Cold War.* New York: Arcade Publishing, 1995.

Sorokin, Vladimir. *Day of the Oprichnik* (originally published as *Den' oprichnika*). Moscow: Igor Zakharov Publishing, 2006. Translated by Jamey Gambrell. New York: Farrar, Straus and Giroux, 2011.

Stent, Angela. *The Limits of Partnership: US–Russian Relations in the Twenty-First Century.* Princeton, NJ: Princeton University Press, 2014.

———. *Putin's World: Russia Against the West and with the Rest.* New York: Twelve, Hachette Book Group, 2019.

Yeltsin, Boris. *Midnight Diaries.* Translated by Catherine A. Fitzpatrick. New York: PublicAffairs, 2000.

Yovanovitch, Marie. *Lessons from the Edge: A Memoir.* Boston, New York: Mariner Books, 2022.

Yurchak, Alexei. *Everything Was Forever, Until It Was No More: The Last Soviet Generation.* Princeton, NJ: Princeton University Press, 2005.

Index

ABM (Anti-Ballistic Missile) Treaty, 201, 227
Academic Travel Abroad, 72
Adriamycin, 144
Afghanistan, 199, 200–201, 202, 216, 226, 254
Africa, 182, 183
African Americans, 52
Akayev, Askar, 164
Akhmadov, Ilias, 219
Albats, Yevgenia, 289
Albats, Zhenia, 304
Albright, Madeleine, 157
alcohol, 12, 14, 161–66
alcoholism, 166
Aldrin, Buzz, 22
Alexandra (empress), 125–27
Alexei (tsarevich), 125–27
All-Russia Young Army Military Patriotic Social Movement, 269
All Things Considered (magazine), 72
All-Union Leninist Young Communist League, 56, 266
All-Union Society for Cultural Relations, 183
Alphabet of Taste, xii
Amanpour, Christiane, 75
American National Exhibition, 43–44
amputations, 51

Andropov, Yuri, 36, 75
Anglo-Saxon media, 235–36
Anti-Ballistic Missile (ABM) Treaty, 201, 227
Apollo 10, 45
Apollo 11, 22, 45
Arab Spring uprisings, 268
Arbat (Moscow), 118
Arbatov, Alexey, 200
Arirang Mass Games, 252
Armenia, 95, 99
Armstrong, Neil, 22
Arnett, Peter, 78
art, 146, 247, 248
Ashkhabad (Turkmenistan), 59
Asia-Pacific CNN bureau, 248, 250–52, 254
assassinations, 16, 135, 199, 233–34
Astoria Hotel, 23–25
Aurelia (ship), 13–14
Aurora (ship), 23
avozka, 24, 193
Azerbaijan, 95, 99

babushki, 19
Babyn Yar, 274
Baer, Jonathan "Smokey," 72
Baghdad, 78, 101
Baker, James, 91, 101

313

Baltic States. *See* Estonia; Latvia; Lithuania
Baluyevsky, Yuri Nikolayevich, 197
bandit capitalism, 233
banyas, 19–20
Barayev, Movsar, 212
Basayev, Shamil, 133, 134, 214
Basayev, Shirvani, 134
Bashkirs, 47
BBC (British Broadcasting Corporation), 49, 65
"Beat the System" (WMAQ program), 70
Belarus, 95, 99, 100
Belgrade (Serbia), 203, 236, 245
Belsan School Siege, 216–24
Beregis' Avtomobilya (film), 8
Berezovskaya, Lena, 112
Berezovsky, Boris, 128–29, 233
Beryozka, 14
Biden, Joe, xi, xiii–xiv, 282–83
Bierbauer, Charles, 78
Birobidzhan, 47
black market, 24
Black Widows, 216, 217
Blitzer, Wolf, 80–81
Blockade of Crimea (television news show), 258
Bolotnaya protests, 221, 262–63
Bolshevik Revolution, 23, 26, 41–42, 125, 265, 290–91
Bolsheviks, 21, 117
Borodin, Alexander, 47
borsch, 38–39
Bosnia, 105
Bosnian War, 105
"Boston Arm" (USIA exhibit), 50–51
Boyle, Charlie, 68
Boy Scouts, 266
brassieres, 56
Brazil, 253–54
breast cancer, 142, 143, 144–46, 161, 167, 225
Brezhnev, Leonid, xiv, 75, 127, 241

British Broadcasting Corporation (BBC), 49, 65
Brodsky, Iosif, 11
Buadze, Saba, 300–301
Budyonnovsk hostages, 214
Bulgaria, 205–6
Burford, Russ, 14, 25–26
Burma, 254
Burns, R. Nicholas, 220
Burns, William J., xii
Buryats, 47
Bush, Barbara, 89
Bush, George H. W.: CNN coverage of, 78–81, 88, 107; economic aid to independent republics, 100; Gorbachev relationship, 89, 92–93, 95; Gorbachev resignation telephone call, 92–93; Kiev speech, 88; nuclear arms treaties, 227; peace conferences chaired by, 90; presidential election, 101–2; Soviet coup, 81–82, 84; Ukrainian aid, 275; US economic aid to Russia, 100, 101, 102; USSR collapse and republic independence, 91; USSR collapse announcement, 95; USSR visit, 89; Yeltsin relationship, 96, 100
Bush, George W.: Chechnya War, 35, 202; as matryoshka doll, 170; 9/11, 198; presidential election, 170; Russian terrorism response, 213, 219; Russia relations, 170, 198–99, 200–201, 206
Byelorussia, 91

Callaway, John, 76
camp excursions, 56
cancer, 142, 143, 144–46, 161, 167, 225, 252
Cancer Ward (Solzhenitsyn), 73
Candomblé, 253
capitalism, 43–44
car-buying systems, 53
carnets, 118

Casablanca (film), 293–94

castling maneuver, 261

Cathedral of Christ the Savior, 167–68

Catherine the Great (empress), 56

Catholicism, 2, 253

Caucasus region, 48, 137, 138, 173, 216–24

Center for European Policy Analysis studies, 271

Central Asia, 59, 60, 99, 100, 104, 200

Chambers, John, 262

Chechnya, 152, 213–15. *See also* Chechnya Wars

Chechnya Wars: first, 133, 214; media coverage and control, 229, 231, 232; as presidential election issue, 155; Putin on, 190, 191; Russian anti-terrorism against, 35, 134, 136, 137–38, 139, 140, 173, 201–2, 214; second, 133–41, 213–15; terrorist attacks, 35, 136, 172, 211–12, 216–24; Turner-Putin discussion on, 228; US involvement, 219

Chekhov, Anton, 37

chemotherapy, 143, 144–46, 161, 167, 225

Chernenko, Konstantin, 75

Chernobyl nuclear power plant, 171–72

Chernobyl (Plokhy), 172

Chernomurdin, Viktor, 130

Chicago, 68–72, 74–77

Chicago Tribune, 72

"Chicken Kiev" speeches, 88

China, 1, 254

Chinoy, Mike, 250, 252

Chirac, Jacques, 203

Christopher, Warren, 102

CIA (Central Intelligence Agency), 45, 177–78, 245

Clinton, Bill: descriptions, 106; Lewinsky affair, 128; as martryoshka doll, 170; NATO cooperation agreements, 203; presidential election, 101–2; on Putin, 153;

Russia relations (Yeltsin), 102–4; White House plane crash, 80

Clinton, Chelsea, 80

Clinton, Hillary: letters from, 255; personality and descriptions, 106; Putin blaming protests on, 263; as secretary of state, 254; speech preparations and style, 105–6; trips to former Soviet republics, 104–5; Tuzla Air Base visit, 105–6; White House plane crash, 80

The Clinton Tapes (Branch), 164

CNN (Cable News Network): broadcasting descriptions, 74; Bush–Clinton presidential election, 101–2; Bush White House coverage, 78–80, 88, 107; cancer treatment reports, 145; Chechnya Wars, 133–41; Clinton White House coverage, 102–7; early years, 74–76; employment with, 74–76, 78–80; executives at, 75; Gulf War reporting, 78; 9/11 attacks, 198; North Korean criticism of, 251; resignation from, 255; Russian relaxation and downsizing of, 117; Soviet coup, 80–88; staff at, 75, 80–81; USSR collapse, 89–92, 93–95. *See also* Moscow CNN bureau

coal miner protests, 123–24

coffee and coffee shops, 114–15, 166

Cold War: African objective, 68; capitalism *vs.* Communism, 43–44; history, 1; Space Race, 5–6, 7, 22, 51; USSR collapse and end of, 93, 94

Cold War Radio (Pomar), 67

Collapse (Zubok), 275

Collins, James F., 82–83, 89

color revolutions, 268, 276–79

Commonwealth of Independent States, 99. *See also* Belarus; Russian Federation; Ukraine

Communism: African objective, 68; capitalism *vs.*, debates on, 43–44; in China, 1–2; consequences of,

xv; insignias of, 22; Lenin's tomb,
124–25; in Lithuania, 2; post-USSR
comparisons, 124; post-USSR
concerns, 122, 129; Russian criticism
of, 73–74; Soviet anecdotes about,
124; US propaganda against, 67; in
USSR, xv; youth indoctrination and
development, 265–66
Communist Party: banning of, 122;
control of, 36, 37; government and
industry influentials in, 24; media
control of, 52; post-coup, 87;
presidential candidates, 148, 158–59;
Stalin purge of, 176; US election
observers, 170; USSR collapse and,
180; vodka restrictions, 164; youth
indoctrination, 266
condescension, 188
Conover, Willis, 66
cooks, 117, 118, 119
corruption, 138, 156
Council on International Education
Exchange, 13, 32
Council on Student Travel, 13
Cousins, Norman, 259
credit system, 53
Crimean Tatars, 47
Crimea (Ukraine), 149, 181, 236, 242,
243–45, 256, 281–82
Criminal Procedure Code, 174
Crouse, Timothy, 101
Cuban Missile Crisis, 10
customer service, 110
Czech Republic, 203

Dagestan, 133–34, 135–36, 139
Dartmouth Conference, 259
Delaunay, Sonia, 273
dental care, 51–52
Deutsche Welle, 65
disappearances, enforced, 214
discrimination, 11, 47, 137–38
Distributed Denial of Service (DDoS),
256

Dobrovolsky, Georgy, 51
Dobrynin, Anatoly, 25
"Dodna!", 163, 164
dogs, 189
Donahue, Phil, 55–56
Donbas region (Ukraine), 58, 184, 236,
242, 245, 256
Donetsk (Ukraine), 58–59
Dougherty, Joan, 197, 198, 199
Dougherty, Pam: address book
confiscation, 38; childhood, 1;
Donetsk visit impressions, 58–59;
education, 3, 11, 12, 30, 31, 44, 45;
Kazan reviews, 49; Russian exchange
student studies, 12–30, 32; Russian
language studies, 3–4, 8, 10, 11, 12;
university drinking, 162–63; as USIA
Russian exhibition guide, 44, 45
Dougherty, Vincent, 1, 2, 6–7, 11,
33–34, 77
Dozhd (TV Rain), 238–42, 292
Dr. Zhivago (film), 26
Drokova, Masha, 267
drownings, 164
Dubrovka Theater, 172, 211–13, 220
Dyachenko, Tatyana, 127, 142, 149, 156
Dzerzhinsky, Felix, 86

Echo Moscow Radio, 86, 129, 213,
233–34, 288–89
economy: North Korean, 251; Russian,
155; Soviet, 46, 51, 55
Eduardovich, Robert, 32
Egypt, 254
employment, 28–29
English language pronunciation, 21
environmentalism, 75
espionage, 170–71, 176–77
Estonia: cyber warfare attacks in, 256;
identity of, 258; independence of,
87, 99, 205; NATO membership,
203, 205–6; propaganda studies in,
256–59; protesters at embassy of,
266; Russian journalists in, 287;

think tanks in, 256; travel to, 59; USSR collapse and liberation of, 180; vulnerability of, 257

"Estonia's Virtual Russian World" (Dougherty, J., and Kaljurand), 257

European Hotel, 23–24

"Everyone Lies" (Dougherty, J.), 242

Everything Was Forever, Until It Was No More (Yurchak), 29–30

executions: African prime ministers, 20; Chechens, 214; royal families, 125–26; Soviet-state, 16, 29, 86, 176, 216

Exter, Alexandra, 273

fakery, xiii, 56–57

fartsovchiki, 24

Federal Security Service (FSB), 34–35, 86, 133, 135, 150–51, 202

Feith, Douglas, 197, 198

Felgenhauer, Tatyana, 288–89

FEMEN protests, 191

femininity, 15

Fifth Column, 221–22

fires, 169, 172

First Person (Putin), 17, 24, 33, 148–51, 176, 180, 189, 266

Fishman, Mikhail, 240, 287, 292

Fitzwater, Marlin, 90, 100

Flock, Jeff, 74

Florida, 142, 146, 161, 225, 247

folk art, 248

food, 118

foreign friendships, 25, 27

Formanek, Ingrid, 78

fortune tellers, 49

"Foundations of State Cultural Politics," 245

freedom of expression, 42, 231, 243

Friendship Bridge, 257

Fromson, Dodi, 61

Fromson, Murray, 61

FSB (Federalnaya Sluzhba Bezopasnosti), 34–35, 86, 133, 135, 150–51, 202

Fuller, R. Buckminster, 49–50

Gagarin, Yuri, 51

Ganić, Ejup, 106

Gazprom, 129, 229, 231

Georgetown University: courses taught at, 269, 270, 294–96, 301–4; graduate program, 104, 181, 254–55; teaching at, 269–70, 294

Georgia: civil society organizations in, 299–300; commonwealth membership, 99; enemies of state, 299–300; identity of, 258; independence and life in, 100; NATO membership, 236; revolutions in, 245, 277; Soviet production controls, 99–100; travels to, 254; US diplomatic relations with, 95; US military trainers to, 201

Georgian Dream, 299–301

Gevorkyan, Nataliya, 148, 149–52, 189

Gevorkyan, Pavel Avetovich, 149

Ghana, 68

gifts: to Americans, 30; from Putin, 249–50; for Russians, 14–15, 27–28

Gigauri, Eka, 299–300

Godfather of the Kremlin (Klebnikov), 233

Gogol, Nikolai, 165

Golden Horde Mongol Khanate, 46

Gongadze, Georgiy, 274

Gongadze, Myroslava, 274

Goodwill Games, 226

Gorbachev, Mikhail: Bush relationship, 88–89, 91–92; Chernobyl explosion, 172; Communist Party bans, 122; coups against, xii, 81–85, 241; death and memorial, 96; legacy, 97; marriage, 96, 97; peace conferences chaired by, 90; post-coup, 87, 90; resignation, 92–94; respect for, 96; USSR collapse, 90, 91; vodka dry laws, 164; Yeltsin relationship, 90, 121–22

Gorbachev, Raisa, 85, 96–97

Gore, Al, 170

gostepriimnost, 28

Grand Ole Opry, 68

Great October Socialist Revolution, 8, 59, 265
Gref, German, 156
grocery stores, 110
Gromov, Alexei, 226
Gromyko, Andrey, 25
Grozny (Chechnya), 139, 140, 214–15
The Gulag Archipelago (Solzhenitsyn), 73
Gulag labor camp, 41, 73, 86, 194, 292
Gulf War, 78
GUPDK, 109
Gusinsky, Vladimir, 129, 229, 231, 232

hangover remedies, 166
Happy Defender of the Fatherland Day, 165
Harvard Kennedy School, 242
Harvard University, 255
health care, 51–52, 145
Heavenly Hundred, 280–81
Hermann Castle, 257
Hermitage Museum, 16
Hersey, John, 1–2
Herzegovina, 105
Hill, Anita, 89
Hiroshima (Hersey), 1–2
Holliman, John, 78
Holodomor, 274
homosexuality, 108–9, 184, 186
Hong Kong, 248, 250, 254
hospital conditions, 143
hospitality, 28
hostage-taking terrorism, 172, 211–13, 214, 216–24
Hotel Volga, 48–49
housing, 54
Humesky, Assya, 11
humor, 230
Humphrey, Hubert, 24–25
Hungary, 203
Hurst, Steve, 82, 85
Hussein, Saddam, 101

identity, 258
Iemanjá (goddess), 253

I'm Losing Weight (television series), 258
In Confidence (Dobrynin), 25
India, 254
informants (secret agents), 176–77
Ingushetia, 134, 141, 215
International Centre for Defense and Security, 256
International Friendship Exhibit, 251
International Women's Day, xiv
Internet, 226, 245, 270
In the First Circle (Solzhenitsyn), 73
Iraq, 254
Israel, 254
Ivangorod, 257
Ivanishvili, Bidzina, 300–301
Ivan the Terrible (czar), 46
Ivashov, Leonid, 204
Ivins, Molly, 72–73
Izvestia (newspaper), 52

Jackson, Jesse, 74
Japan, 254
jazz, 66
jeans, 24
Jerjomina, Marina, 258
Jewish Autonomous Obast, 47
Jobs, Steve, 262
Johnson, Lyndon, 24–25
journalism, 72–74, 76–77. *See also* media; radio broadcasting; television journalism
journalists: foreign correspondents, 61; murders of, 233–34, 274; Russian independent exiled, xiv, 287–92; Russian state-controlled, 287; skills for, 61
Juan Carlos of Spain (king), 90
Juche Tower, 251

Kaiser, Robert, 61
Kalinin, Mikhail, 118
Kaljurand, Marina, 266, 267
Kaljurand, Riina, 257
Karaganov, Sergei, 204
Kazakhstan, 91, 95, 99, 104

Kazan (Tatarstan), 45–50
Kennan, George F., 304–5
Kennan Institute, 256
KennanX (podcast), 242
Kennedy, John F., 10, 22
Kerenksy, Alexander, 181
Kerry, John, 254
Kessler, Glenn, 106
KGB: buildings of, 150; coup and
    aftermath, 81, 85–86; exchange
    student surveillance, 23, 25; insignia,
    36; media relationships, 150; prison-
    labor camps of, 41, 73, 85, 194, 216,
    292; Putin and power of, 135; Putin's
    career plans, 17, 18, 24; recruitment
    process, 18; renaming, 86; training
    institutions for, 33; US exhibitions
    with agitators from, 52–53, 59
Khanate of Kazan, 46
Khanga, Elena, 145
Khodorkovsky, Mikhail, 178
Kholodov, Dmitry, 233
Khrushchev, Nikita, 10, 43–44, 54, 73,
    102, 118
Khrushchyovki, 54
kidnappings, 140, 214, 215, 274
Kim Jong-il, 251, 252
King, Larry, 186
Kirienko, Sergey, 148
Kirill I (Patriarch of Moscow and All
    Russia), 184
Kirov, Sergei, 16
Kiselev, Dmitry, 86, 242, 243
Kiselyev, Yevgeny, 229, 231
Kiselyova, Masha, 231
kissing, 187–89, 193
Kitai-Gorod (Moscow), 113
kitsch, 193
Klebnikov, Paul, 233
Klitschko, Vitali, 281
Kohtla-Järve (Estonia), 258
Kolesnikov, Andrey, 148–49
Komar, Dmitrii, 87–88
Komi People, 47
Komsomol, 56, 266

Korzhakov, Alexander, 128
Kosachev, Ivan, 87
Kosachev, Konstantin, 183
Kosachev, Raisa, 87
Kotrikadze, Ekaterina, 241–42
Kovalev, Valentin, 128
Krasnaya Moskva, 15
kreml, 46
Krichevski, Ilya, 87–88
Kryuchkov, Vladimir, 86
Kuchma, Leonid, 274–75, 279
Kukly (televison show), 129, 230, 231
Kursk (submarine), 168–69, 172, 186–
    87, 220
Kutuzovsky Prospekt (*renamed
    Kalininsky Prospekt*), 109–10, 293
Kyiv (Ukraine), 239, 244, 273–77,
    280–81
Kyrgyzstan, 91, 95, 99, 104–5, 200

bin Laden, Osama, 201–2
Laika (Russian dog), 5
Lake, Anthony, 103
Land Code, 174
lapel pins, 46, 265
Laruelle, Marlene, 181
Latvia: independence of, 87, 99; NATO
    membership, 203, 205–6; Russian
    journalists in, 287; travel to, 59;
    USSR collapse and liberation of, 180
Lenin, Vladimir, 8, 124–25, 193, 265
Leningrad (*now* St. Petersburg): bathing
    traditions in, 19; cultural life in, 37;
    history and descriptions, 16, 17,
    19, 22–23, 35, 175, 239; Putin's
    childhood in, 16–18, 22, 151,
    175–76, 270; residential descriptions,
    26–27; tram travel experiences,
    25–26; USIA exhibition tour in, 45,
    46; vodka, 163; water quality in, 18;
    winter descriptions, 31–32; WWII
    aftermath, 175–76
Leningrad State University (*now*
    St. Petersburg State University):
    African students at, 20; classes at,

20–21, 22–23, 32–33, 37–38; cultural comparisons, 15; dormitories at, descriptions, 16, 18–19, 20; gifts for Russian students, 14–15; Putin's studies at, 18, 33–35, 174; trip to Russia, 12–14; Vietnamese students at, 20; vodka, 163; winter semester at, 31–33, 37–38
letter smuggling, 53
Levine, Sol, 80
Lewinsky, Monica, 128, 170
LGBTQ, 256, 271
Likhachev, Dmitrii Sergeyevich, 292
The Limits of Partnership (Stent), 102, 103, 104
Listyev, Vladislav, 233
literature, subversive, 14, 15
Lithuania: independence of, 87, 99; KGB prisons, 216; NATO membership, 203, 205–6; radio broadcasting interviews in, 288; Russian journalists in, 287; travel to, 59–60; USSR collapse and liberation of, 180
Little Octobrists, 265
Lomonosov Bridge, 26
London, Jack, 40–41
"Long Telegram" (Kennan), 304–5
Lott, Trent, 157
Lumumba, Patrice, 20, 68
lunches, 118
Luzhkov, Yuri, 225, 228
Lyden, Jacki, 72

Macron, Emmanuel, 296
Madrid Peace Conference, 90
Manafort, Paul, 280
"Man Like Putin, A" (song), 191–92
manspreading, 190
Mansvetov, Vladimir, 60–61, 63
marathons, 166
"March of Millions" protests, 263
Margelov, Mikhail, 206
Maria (Grand Duchess), 125–27
marijuana, 14

Maskhadov, Aslan, 139, 140
maskirovka, 243
Massoud, Ahmad Shah, 199
Matalin, Mary, 102
Matlock, Jack, 81–82
matryoshka dolls, 31, 161, 170, 193
McDonald's, 119
meals, in Moscow bureau, 118–19
media: Anglo-Saxon, 235–36; on Chechnya Wars, 139; freelance journalism, 72–74, 76; post-Soviet coup, 86; post-USSR collapse and relaxation of, 117; Russian, controversial practices, 213; Russian independent, 129, 229–32, 238–42, 292; Russian journalist exiles, 287–88; Russian state war on, 129–30, 229–42, 243; Russian youth and, 270–71; Russo-Ukrainian War, 86, 238, 241, 242, 292; Soviet questions on American, 46; in Soviet Union, 46, 52, 65–66, 86, 241. *See also* journalists; propaganda; radio broadcasting; television journalism
Media-MOST, 229, 231
medicine, 109
Medvedev, Dmitry, 151, 164, 232, 261–62
Memoirs (Gorbachev), 121–22
Memorial (human rights organization), 194
menstruation supplies, 15
Meri, Lennart, 205
Merkel, Angela, 189, 191
Mexico, 254
mic fright, 63–64
micro loans, 104–5
Mikkelson, Gerald, 21, 22, 23
Ministry of Culture, 245
Ministry of Miracles, 152–53
Mitkova, Tatyana, 86
Moldova, 95, 99, 100, 103
money laundering, 138, 156
Moscow: American citizens' value in, 302; American National Exhibition

in, 43–44; apartment in, 109–10, 147–48, 247, 248; author's life in, 112–15; Chechnya Wars and explosions in, 136; Chechnya Wars and Operation Whirlwind, 137–38; city descriptions, 113–14, 118; driving styles in, 110–11; farewell party, 249; fast food in, 119; grocery stores in, 110; lifestyle in, 114–15; navigation challenges, 118; relocation to, 108–9, 247; residents of, descriptions, 113; Russian journalists and exile from, 287–92; Soviet kitsch nostalgia in, 193; terrorist attacks in, 172, 211–13, 216; Turner visit to, 225–30; USIA exhibition tour stop, 45; Valucha's ashes in, 253–54, 298. *See also* Moscow CNN bureau

Moscow CNN bureau: anti-Taliban militia commander assassination, 199; bureau chiefs at, 107–8, 147; Chechnya War, 139–40, 141; chemical troops reports, 165; coal mining protests, 123–24; descriptions, 109, 110; downsizing, 117, 119; hangover remedies, 166; labor contracts and meal provisions, 119; news and readiness requirements, 119; presidential election coverage, 154, 155–59; pre-Ukraine invasion descriptions, xii–xiii; Russian bureaucratic demands on, 118; staff descriptions, 112, 117, 118, 119; submarine explosions, 168–69; television live shots, 154; Turner visit, 225; vodka and drownings, 164; workdays at, 119; Yeltsin encounters, 119; Yeltsin reports, 169–70

Moscow Marathon, 166
Moskva pool, 167
Movement of the First, 269
Mujaheddin, 200
multiculturalism, 245
Munich Security Conference, 195, 207

Murgel de Castro, Vera Lucia "Valucha": artworks of, 146, 247; cancer treatment and support of, 144; CNN employment communication, 77–78; death and ashes, 252–54, 298; descriptions, 71; Hong Kong relocation, 248; journalism positions, 76–77; in Moscow, 247, 248, 298; Moscow relocation and visa requirements, 108–9; partnership with, 71–72; real estate, 77; residence, 76; Washington, DC, relocation, 78, 80; reckless driver challenge, 111, 298

Muscatine, Lissa, 105–6
music, 66, 68
muzhik ("real guy" persona), 191, 193
Myohyangsan, 251

name pronunciation, 112
Narva (Estonia), 257
Naryshkin, Sergey, 284
Nashi, 266–68
National Defense Education Act (NDEA), 7
nationalism, 292
nationality, 47–48
National Public Radio (NPR), 72
National Security Archive (George Washington University), 90
National Security Council (NSC), 82
NATO (North Atlantic Treaty Organization), 127, 203–6, 236, 267–68
NATO-Russia Founding Act on Mutual Relations, Cooperation, and Security, 203
NATO-Russia Relations: A New Quality, 204
Navalny, Alexei, 238, 242, 262, 263, 290, 304
Nazi Germany Blockade of Leningrad, 19, 22–23, 35, 175, 239
Nazis: Kyiv revolutions blamed on neo-, 244; Leningrad WWII blockade,

19, 22–23, 35, 175, 239; Russian holidays celebrating victory over, 165, 225; Russian propaganda on Crimea using imagery of, 244; Russian propaganda on Ukraine as neo-, 184, 282, 297, 304; terrorism comparisons, 202; Ukrainian Jewish massacres by, 274; youth groups comparisons, 267

NDEA (National Defense Education Act), 7

New Buffalo Times (newspaper), 76–77

newspaper journalism, 76–77

The New Times (political magazine), 289

New Union Treaty, 81

Nicholas II (czar), 21, 23, 125–27

Night Owl show, 67–68

Nikonov, Vyacheslav, 153

9/11, 197–202

Nixon, Richard M., 25, 43–44, 79–80

North Atlantic Treaty Organization (NATO), 203–6, 236, 267–68

North Korea, 250–52

North Ossetia, 216–24

Novaya Gazeta (newspaper), 133

NPR (National Public Radio), 72

NSC (National Security Council), 82

NTV (Russian television), 199, 229–32

nuclear arms: presidential elections and, 159; reduction treaties, 89, 202–3, 227; Soviet perception of, 179; of Ukraine, 273; US–Russia reduction discussions, 197, 198; USSR collapse and control of, 93; USSR collapse and scientist unemployment risks, 101

nuclear arms scientists, 101

Nye, Joseph S., Jr., 182

Obama, Barack, 190

O'Connor, Eileen, 107–8, 144, 214

Odnoetzhnaya Amerika (Ilf and Petrov), 40

Olympic Games, 226, 238, 255–56

Oman, 254

Omelchenko, Elena, 270, 271

One Day in the Life of Ivan Denisovich (Solzhenitsyn), 73

One-Storied America (Ilf and Petrov), 40

Operation Provide Hope, 100

Operation Whirlwind, 137–38

Orange Revolution, 268, 275–79

Ostankino Television tower fire, 169

"Our Ukraine" (coalition), 275

Pakistan, 254

Palace of the Soviets, 167

Parajanov, Sergei, 273

Parkhomenko, Sergey, 291–92

Pasternak, Boris, 26

Patriarch's Ponds, 113

Patrice Lumumba University, 20, 68

Patrushev, Nikolai, 202

Patsayev, Viktor, 51

Pentagon attacks, 198

Peregrim, Michael, 2–3, 4–5, 6, 7–9, 11

Perestroika (Gorbachev), 92

performance anxiety, 63–64, 70–71, 145, 154

perfumes, 15

Peskov, Dmitry, 187, 235–36, 249, 283

Peter the Great (tzar), 16, 21

photography, 14

pickle juice, 166

Pifer, Steven, 206

Pizza Hut, 119

Plokhy, Serhii, 172

Plushchev, Alexander, 288–89

poisonings, 276, 278

pokazukha, xiii

Poland, xi, 203, 205

Politkovskaya, Anna, 133, 134, 135, 212, 215

"Polovtsian Dances" (composition), 47

Pomar, Mark G., 67

Ponomaryova, Kseniya, 149

Pope, Edmond, 170

Popov, Gavriil, 81

postal surveillance, 36

Potemkin, Grigory, 56

Potemkin village, 56–57
Pozner, Vladimir, 55–56
Pravda (newspaper), 52, 86–87, 230
presidential elections (Russia 2000):
    anti-campaign strategies, 152–53,
    155; campaigning restrictions, 155;
    Chechnya voting, 158; date change,
    146; issues, 155–56, 158–59; Putin
    as candidate, 156–57; Putin election
    night news conference, 157–58;
    Putin public relations for, 148–52;
    rival eliminations, 148
presidential elections (USA Bush–
    Clinton), 101–2
Presidential Marathon (Yeltsin, B.), 153
Primakov, Yevgeny, 148
Prince Igor (opera), 47
Pripyat (Ukraine), 171
Proffer, Carl, 11
Proffer, Ellendea, 11
propaganda: Russian, on Crimea
    invasion, 244; Russian, on Kyiv
    uprising, 244; Russian, on Ukraine,
    xiii, xiv–xv, 126, 173, 242–43, 262,
    282, 283, 301; Russian, on Ukraine
    invasion, 256; Russian, on Ukraine
    invasion classification, xv, 173, 180,
    283, 285, 297; Russian, on Ukraine
    invasion justification, 184, 282, 297,
    304; Russian, on West, 243; Russian,
    studies in Estonia, 256–59; as Russian
    media purpose, 235, 237; US against
    USSR, 67; USSR against US, 46, 50
prosthetic devices, 50–51
protests: coal miner, 123–24; early
    former-Soviet political, 268; election
    fraud, 261, 262–64, 268, 275–77;
    freedom of speech/expression, 231,
    274; government corruption, 191,
    221, 262–64, 274–75; Red Army
    solider statue relocations, 266
Pussy Riot, 184
Putin, Lyudmila, 24
Putin, Vladimir: African objective, 68;
    alcohol and, 164–65; appearance,

157–58; author's perception of, 152,
    249–50; behavior descriptions, xii,
    17, 150, 153, 189–93; biographies
    on, 17, 24, 33, 148–51, 176, 180,
    189, 266; career, 24, 35, 129, 130,
    131, 133–34, 135, 142–43, 144,
    153; Chechnya Wars, 133–34, 136,
    137, 138, 140, 143, 190; childhood,
    16–18, 22, 33, 151, 175–76, 177,
    266, 270; CIA analysis of, 177–78;
    Clinton, B., on, 153; Crimea
    invasion, 149, 181, 244–45, 256,
    281–82; diplomatic agencies created
    by, 183; disaster responses, 168–69;
    Dougherty, V., comparisons, 33–35;
    education, 18, 33–35, 174; ideologies
    of, 125, 126, 177–78, 181–86, 194,
    208–9, 243, 261; informant-secret
    agents, views on, 176–77; intellectual
    conferences attended by, 185–89;
    on international security issues, 195;
    interpersonal descriptions, 151, 153,
    177, 189–93; kissing, 187–89, 193;
    leadership descriptions, xv, 130,
    150–51, 156–57, 173, 174, 177–79,
    182, 194–95, 230, 300; Lenin's tomb
    controversy, 125; letter and gift
    from, 249–50; media control, 130,
    230, 231, 232, 235, 237–38, 240;
    military rebuilding and preparation,
    170; motorcade routes of, 154; name
    origins, 8; NATO relations, 203–6;
    9/11 attacks, 198, 199–201, 202–3;
    personality descriptions, 131, 152,
    156, 228; political satire on, 230,
    231; presidential elections, 144, 146,
    148–49; presidential placeholder for,
    151, 261–62; presidential terms, 261;
    profanity and off-color speech, 137,
    191, 192–93; propagandist-in-chief
    for, 86; protests against, 221, 263–64,
    265; public appearances, 225, 226,
    244; public perceptions of, negative,
    135, 229, 231; public perceptions
    of, positive, 137, 153, 156–57, 172,

174, 192; public reception office of, 152–53; public relations and image, 191–92, 193, 255–56; punctuality, 150; religious practice, 152, 305; speaking voice descriptions, 158; terrorist attack responses, 35, 217–20, 221; Turner meetings with, 226–28; Ukraine invasion classification, xv, 173, 180, 283, 285, 297; Ukraine invasion justifications, 173, 184, 282, 297, 304; Ukraine invasion preparations, xii; Ukraine invasion propaganda, xiii, xiv–xv, 173, 242–43, 256, 282; Ukraine negotiation strategies, 139, 173; Ukrainian presidential candidates supported by, 276; US relations, general, 41, 152, 180–81, 195, 207–8, 236, 262–63, 268, 282, 284; US relations (G. W. Bush), 170, 198–99, 206; US relations (Trump), 171; on USSR collapse, 180; war strategies, 134; West relations, 41, 208–9, 271–72; Yeltsin relationship, 153; youth organizations supporting, 266–69
"Putin Generation, The" (university course), 269, 270, 294–96, 301–4
Putinism, 151–52, 245
Putin's Russia (Politkovskaya), 135, 215
Putin's World (Stent), 183
Pyongyang (North Korea), 250–51, 252

Al-Qaeda, 35, 198–202
Quarles, Norma, 71
Quinn-Judge, Paul, 140

racism, 46
radio broadcasting: Russian, in Lithuania, 288–89; Russian laws on, 213; in Soviet Union, 65–66, 86; as US public relations against USSR, 67. *See also* Voice of America
Radio Free Europe, 65, 67
Radio Liberty, 58, 65, 67
Rainbow Coalition, 74

Rakhlin, Anatoly Semyonnovich, 17
Rakhlin, Mikhail, 17
"Reaction to the Soviet Satellite—A Preliminary Evaluation" (White House Office of the Staff Research Group), 5–6
Red Moscow, 15
"Red Pencil Patrol" (column), 76–77
Red Square, 8, 113, 124–25, 225–26, 244, 267–68
Redstone, 5
"Remont" (Renovation) signs, 110
"Research and Development USA" (USIA exhibition), 44–46
Revolution of Dignity, 239, 244, 280–81
revolutions and rebellions: Bolshevik, 23, 26, 41–42, 125, 265, 290–91; color, 268, 276–79; Revolution of Dignity, 238, 244, 280–81; US blamed for, 268. *See also* protests
Riefenstahl, Leni, 244
R-7 (intercontinental ballistic missile), 5
Robertson, George, 204
Roldugin, Sergey, 189
Romania, xi, 205–6
Romanov, Nikolai Romanovich, 126
Roosevelt, Franklin D., 80
Rose Revolution, 268, 277
Roskomnadzor, 288
Rossiiskiy, 48
Rossotrudnichestvo, 183
RT (*formerly* Russia Today), 236–37
run bags, 119
Russia. *See* Russian Federation
Russia: The People and the Power (Kaiser), 61
Russia Day, 263
Russia—Lost in Translation (Shevtsova), 134
Russian Defense Ministry, 197, 228–29, 269, 281–82
Russian Federation: African objective, 68; cancer discussions, 145; cathedral construction, 167–68; Clinton,

H., trips to, 104; commonwealth membership, 99; Crimea annexation, 149, 181, 236, 243–45, 256, 281–82; cultural policies of, 245; cyberattacks carried out by, 256; diplomatic agencies of, 183; division within, 127; economic aid to, 100, 101, 102; government corruption protests, 221, 261, 262–64; government negligence and incompetence, 172–73, 212, 218, 220–21; holidays in, xiv, 165, 225–26, 263; housing in, 54; independence and economic hardship, 100; intellectual conferences, 185; LGBTQ policies, 256; life in, 123–24, 155–56; media wars in, 129–30, 213, 229–40; military preparation exercises, 170; nationalism and pride, 194; NATO relations, 203–6; Nicholas II and family internment debates, 125–27; 9/11 public condolences, 199–200; nuclear arms reduction, 89, 197, 198, 202–3, 227; Olympic Games in, 255–56; presidential elections, 122, 144, 146, 148–59; public education, 194; public perception of, 231; research on, 255; Soviet history, 47–48, 126, 194; Soviet lifestyle comparisons, 52; status of, 121; street renaming, 117; superstitions, 147, 167; US relations, improving, 259–60; US relations (Gorbachev–G. H. W. Bush), 96, 100, 101, 102; US relations (Putin–G. W. Bush), 152, 180–81, 195, 198–99, 200–201, 206, 207–8; US relations (Putin–Trump), 171; US relations (Yeltsin–Clinton), 102–4, 203; US relations (Yeltsin–G. H. W. Bush), 227; USSR collapse and independence of, 91; USSR collapse and nuclear arms control to, 93; as USSR successor, 95, 175; youth organizations, 266–68. *See also* Putin, Vladimir; Russo-Ukrainian War; Yeltsin, Boris

Russia House, 12, 162
Russian language: college studies in, 11–12; exchange student studies, 12–16; in Moscow CNN office, 112; as political, 21; public education classes in, 2–4, 6, 7–9, 10, 11; tour guide translating, 73
Russian Orthodox Church, 184
Russian Republic, 47
Russians, ethnic *vs.* non-ethnic, 47–48
Russian sayings, 163–64
The Russians (Smith), 61
Russian World (concept), 183–84, 208–9
Russo-Ukrainian War: Crimea annexation, 149, 181, 236, 243–45, 256, 281–82; invasion justifications, 136, 173, 184, 282, 284, 297, 304; invasion preparations, xi, xii, 242, 283; invasion propaganda, xiii, xiv–xv, 126, 173, 184, 242–43, 256, 282, 283, 284, 297, 301, 304; media coverage and control, 86, 238, 241, 242, 292; military personnel criticism of, 172; negotiation strategies, 139, 173; official classification, xv, 173, 180, 283, 285, 297; public perception of, 236, 295–96, 302–3; public perceptions and criticism consequences, 221–22; Russian war tactics, 134; US anticipation, xi, xiii–xiv, 282–83
Ryzhkov, Vladimir, 221

Salyut I, 51
"Sanitary Day," 32, 110
satire, 129, 230
saunas, 19–20
scandals, 128, 140, 274–75
Scowcrot, Brent, 90
The Second Chechen (Politkovskaya), 133
Second Chechnya Wars, 133–41, 172, 211–15
self-determination, 47
Serbia, 203, 236, 245

Sergeevna, Inna, 32
Sergeyevich, Mikhail, 85
Sergey (Russian friend), 27–29, 30–31, 38–42, 163–64
Sestanovich, Stephen, 255–56
sex, 55–56, 128, 183
sexual harassment, 89
Shadows of Forgotten Ancestors (film), 273
Shaw, Bernard, 155, 778
Shevtsova, Lilia, 134, 171, 181
shopping bags, 24, 193
Shorenstein Center on Media, Politics and Public Policy fellowship, 242
Siberia, 1, 123, 205
signs, 110
Silayev, Ivan, 85
Silina, Elizaveta, 258
Simon, Scott, 72
Simonyan, Margarita, 236–38
Sindeyeva, Natalya, 239, 241
skyscrapers, 118
Slavutich (Ukraine), 171
Slovakia, 205–6
Slovenia, 206
Smith, Hedrick, 61
smoking, 63
Smoktunovsky, Innokenty, 8
smuggling, 53
sniskhoditelnost, 188
Snyder, Alvin, 65, 67, 68, 70, 71
Soap and Perfumery Factory No. 5, 15
Sochi Winter Olympics, 238, 255–56
social media, 270, 271
soft power, 181–84
Soft Power (Nye), 182
Solzhenitsyn, Alexander, 73
SORT (Strategic Offensive Reductions Treaty), 202–3
South Korea, 250
Sovershenno Skretno (tabloid), 128
Sovietskaya Rossiya (newspaper), 230
Soviet TV, 241
Soviet Union (USSR): Afghanistan war, 200; African objective, 68; book publications, 73; capitalism *vs.* Communism debates, 43–44; car-buying system of, 53; citizen pride, 60; closed cities, 48; collapse of, 73, 81, 89–92, 93–95, 99–100, 101, 180; coups, xii, 80–88; cultural comparisons, 15; diplomatic agencies of, 183; economic descriptions, 15, 46, 56; first trip to, 14–16; health care in, 51–52; housing conditions, 54; kitsch memorabilia, 193; life in, 16, 29, 36, 37, 42, 52, 56, 86, 87, 110–11, 176, 193–94, 216; media, 46, 52, 65–66, 86, 241; "nationality," term usage, 47; national republics and ethnic groups, 47–48, 59; nuclear arms, 89, 91, 93; public perception of, 179; republic production controls, 99–100; size of, 175; social opportunities, 193; soft power of, 182; terrorism of, 126; tour guiding to, 72; US relations, 46, 50, 67, 88–89, 91–92; youth organizations, 265–66
Soviet Youth Travel Bureau, 32
Soyuz 11, 51
Space Race, 5–6, 7, 22, 51
spies, 170–71, 176–77
Sputnik I, 5, 7
Sputnik II, 5
Sputnik Travel, 56
St. Michael's Orthodox Church, 5
St. Peter and Paul Cathedral, 21, 126
St. Petersburg. *See* Leningrad
St. Petersburg State University. *See* Leningrad State University
Stalin, Josef: cathedrals removed by, 167; Communist Party purge, 176; Fifth Column concept, 221–22; philosophies of, 230; Soviet life during, 16, 29, 139–40, 194
Stamberg, Susan, 72
Stent, Angela, 102, 103, 104, 183, 269
Stephashin, Sergei, 156
Strategic Arms Reduction Treaty (START I), 89

Strategic Arms Reduction Treaty (START II), 227
Strategic Arms Reduction Treaty (START III), 227
Strategic Offensive Reductions Treaty (SORT), 202–3
Strauss, Robert, 82, 91, 120
Straw, Jack, 220
submarine disasters, 168–69, 172, 186–87, 220
suicide bombers, 199, 212, 216, 217
Suicide Squad of Islam, 212
Sullivan, John, xii, 283
superstitions, 147, 167
Swan Lake (Tchaikovsky), 241
Syria, 134, 139

Tajikistan, 95, 99, 199, 200
Talbott, Strobe, 102
Taliban, 198–202
Tanya (Russian friend), 27–29, 30–31, 38–42, 163–64
Tass, 86
Tatarstan, 45–50
Tbilisi (Georgia), 45, 299–301
tea drinking, 165
teeth, 51–52
tele-bridge television, 55–56
television journalism: camera fear and panic attacks, 70–71; demands of, 146; employment in, 68–70, 74; freelancing in, 74; live shots, 154–55; Russian independent, 129, 229–32, 238–42, 292; Russian state-controlled, 236–37. *See also* CNN (Cable News Network); Moscow CNN bureau
terrorism: in Belsan, 216–24; in Moscow, 172, 211–13, 216; 9/11, 197–202; in Russia, 35, 201–2; Russian anti-terrorism tactics against, 35, 134, 136, 137–38, 139, 140, 150–51, 173, 201–2, 213, 221; Russia–US alliance against, 200; in Soviet Union, 126, 138, 176; Syrian,

173; as Ukraine invasion justification, 126, 173, 301
"The Thaw," 73
Thomas, Clarence, 89
threshold superstitions, 147
Tiido, Harri, 206
Timakova, Natalya, 148
Time magazine, 72, 102, 140
Timur the Lame (Tamerlane), 46
Tkachenko, Maxim, 197, 198, 274
toilet paper, 23–24, 28
toilet seat wars, 20
tolerance, 245
torture, 140, 214, 216
Tostoy, Lev, 114
tour guiding, 72–73
Transparency International Georgia, 299–300
travel preparation traditions, 147
Trenin, Dmitri, 201
Triumph of the Will (film), 244
Trud (newspaper), 230
Truman, Harry S., 304
Trump, Donald, 171, 280
Tsvetayeva, Marina, 114
Tumm, Lauri, 205
Turgenev, Ivan, 12
Turkmenistan, 59, 95, 99
Turner, Ed, 75, 76, 77–78
Turner, Ted, 74, 75, 225–30, 232
Turner Broadcasting System, 74
Tuzla Air Base, 105–6
TV-Inform, 86
TV Rain (Dozhd), 238–42, 292
Tymoshenko, Yulia, 278

Ukraine: artists, 273; Bush speeches to USSR republic of, 88; Chernobyl nuclear power plant closure, 171–72; Clinton, H., trips to, 104; color revolutions in, 268, 275; commonwealth membership, 99; election fraud protests, 268, 276–79; history, 274; independence, 91, 275; NATO membership, 236;

nuclear weapons of, 273; presidential elections, 276; Russian World imposed on, 184; Soviet production controls, 99–100; status of, 273; travels to, 254; uprisings in, 238, 244, 280–82; USIA exhibition tour in, 58–59; US relations, 95, 100, 103, 275. *See also* Russo-Ukrainian War
Ukrainian Village (Chicago), 69
Union of Soviet Societies for Friendship and Cultural Relations with Foreign Countries, 183
United Nations, 75
United States: CNN references to, 75; diplomatic recognition to post-Soviet republics, 95; economic aid, 100; economic challenges, 101; nationality, word usage, 47; presidential elections, 101–2, 170; as Putin's scapegoat, 262–63, 268, 282, 284; Russian obsession with, 39–40; Russian public perception of, 236; Russian relations, improving, 259–60; Russian Ukraine invasion warnings, xi, xiii–xiv, 282–83; Russia relations, 102–4, 152, 171, 180–81, 195, 198–99, 201, 203, 206, 207–8, 227, 282, 284; Soviet relations, 88–89, 91–92; Soviet visitor tour to, 72
University of Chicago, 76
University of Michigan, 11–12, 30, 31, 162
US Agency for International Development (USAID), 104–5
US Information Agency (USIA) exhibitions: advertising, 50; attendance statistics, 46, 50, 51; CBS interviews of guides, 61; descriptions and themes, 44; guides and work descriptions, 12, 44, 45, 50, 55, 57, 58; guide skills development, 61; guide training, 46; KGB agitators/provocateurs at, 52–53, 59; purpose, 67; questions at, 48, 48 46, 51–55, 58; sites for, 49–50, 58–59; tour schedule, 45–46; travel opportunities and field trips during, 56–57, 59–60
Usov, Vladimir, 87–88
US–Soviet Cultural Agreement, 44
USSR. *See* Soviet Union
US State Department, 72, 254
Uzbekistan, 95, 99–100, 105, 200, 258

Valdai Discussion Club, 185
Valya (housekeeper), 147
Venediktov, Alexey, 208–9, 213, 233–34, 289
Verveer, Melanne, 105
Veshkin, Alexander, 171
Veshkin, Misha, 171
Veshkin, Svetlana, 171
Victory Day, 225–26
Vietnam War, 11, 12, 46
Vilnius (Lithuania), 59–60
Vinogradov, Sergei, 29
visas, xi, 48, 109, 118, 250
Vladimirovna, Irina, 97
vodka, 12, 14, 161–66
Voice of America: Donetsk citizens listening to, 58; employees of, 60–61; employment application and hiring process, 45, 60, 61; employment descriptions, 63–64, 67–68; jazz radio shows on, 66; Kazan visit and listening to, 49; office descriptions and atmosphere, 63; personnel descriptions, 64–65; purpose, 67; Russian tutors at, 63; Soviet jamming of, 65; Soviet listening statistics, 66; Soviet transmission and reception, 65
Vokhrushev, Alexander, 153
Volkov, Vladislav, 51
Voshchanov, Pavel, 142
Voznesensky, Andrei, 88
Vremya (Soviet news), 86
Vysotsky, Vladimir, 66

Waal, Thomas de, 184
"Walking Together" (youth group), 267
War and Decision (Feith), 197, 198

Warriors of Disinformation (Snyder), 65
Washington, DC, 63, 69, 78, 80
Watch Out for the Car (film), 8
Weiner, Robert, 78
West: Putin relations with, 41, 208–9, 271–72; Putin's Ukraine invasion blamed on, 282, 284; Russian relations with, 208–9, 243, 271–72, 296. *See also* United States
White House: airplane crashes at, 80; Clinton, H., former Soviet republic trips, 104–6; CNN coverage of Bush, George H. W., 78–80, 88, 107; CNN coverage of Bush–Clinton presidential election, 101–2; CNN coverage of Clinton, B., 102–3, 104–7; media and security descriptions, 79; press briefing rooms at, 79–80; public criticism of, 107; swimming pools at, 80; USSR collapse, 93–94
William F. Benton broadcast journalism fellowships, 76
Winter Palace, 23
WMAQ-TV, 68–71
Woodrow Wilson International Center for Scholars, 256
Worcester Art Museum, 44
Worldnet, 65
World Trade Center attacks, 197–202
World War II: Crimea invasion propaganda, 244; holidays celebrating victory, 165, 225; Leningrad Nazi Blockade, 19, 22–23, 35, 175, 239; Russian veterans of, 51. *See also* Nazis
Wright-Patterson Air Force Base, 259–60
Wussler, Robert, 232

xenophobia, 20

Yakemenko, Vasily, 266–67
Yakushkin, Dmitry, 136, 226
Yanayev, Gennadiy, 82
Yanukovych, Viktor, 239, 276, 278, 279–80
Yavlinsky, Grigory, 148

Yeltsin, Boris: alcohol, 164, 165; Chechnya Wars, 133, 135–36, 137, 140; coal mining issues, 123; Communist Party relationship, 122; corruption, 138, 156; coup aftermath, 86; death of, 170; Gorbachev relationship, 90, 121; health, 121, 129, 138, 142; image advisers for, 127, 142, 149; media relations, 87, 103; media relations advisers for, 127, 149; NATO relations, 127, 203; Nicholas II internment and speech, 126–27; nuclear arms treaties with US, 227; obituaries for, 121; personality descriptions, 96, 100, 119, 120, 122; political satire on, 230, 231; presidential elections, 129; press encounters with, 119–20; prime minister appointments and successors, 130, 131, 133–34; public appearances, 226; public relations issues and scandals, 128; republic independence, 91; resignation, 131, 138–39, 144; Russian economic hardships, 100; Russian White House attacks ordered by, 121–22; scandals, 128, 140; Soviet coup, 82, 83–84, 90; staff dismissals, 138; state of union addresses, 127, 130–31; terrorism responses, 221; US relations, 96, 100, 102–4; USSR collapse and presidency of, 95–96; vacations, 127–28
Yeltsin, Naina, 127, 139
Yevropeyskaya Gostinnitsa, 23–24
Young Pioneers, 265–66
youth, Russian: anti-Putin/corruption protests by, 261–65; pro-Putin centers/clubs for, 268–69; Russian organizations for, 266–68; Soviet organizations for, 265–66; studies and courses on Putin Generation, 269–72, 294–96, 301–4
Youth in Putin's Russia (Omelchenko, ed.), 270, 271
Yugoslavia, 203, 245

Yumashev, Valentin, 127, 149, 150
Yunarmiya, 269
Yurchak, Alexei, 29–30
Yushchenko, Viktor, 275–77, 278, 279–80

Zaire, 68
Zakharova, Maria, 283
"Zakrit" (Closed) signs, 110

Zaryadie (Moscow), 113
Zatlers, Valdis, 207
Zedong, Mao, 1
Zhirinovsky, Vladimir, 103, 148
Zikar dance, 139
znachki, 46, 265
Zubok, Vladislav M., 275
Zygar, Mikhail, 239
Zyuganov, Gennady, 129, 148, 158